Masculinity in the Golden Age of Swedish Cinema

Masculinity in the Golden Age of Swedish Cinema

A Cultural Analysis of 1920s Films

Tommy Gustafsson

McFarland & Company, Inc., Publishers
Jefferson, North Carolina

LIBRARY OF CONGRESS CATALOGUING-IN-PUBLICATION DATA

Gustafsson, Tommy, 1969–
Masculinity in the golden age of Swedish cinema :
a cultural analysis of 1920s films / Tommy Gustafsson.
p. cm.
Includes bibliographical references and index.

ISBN 978-0-7864-9478-1 (softcover : acid free paper) ∞
ISBN 978-1-4766-1712-1 (ebook)

1. Masculinity in motion pictures. 2. Men in motion pictures.
3. Motion pictures—Sweden—History—20th century. I. Title.
PN1995.9.M46G88 2015
791.43'65211—dc23 2014037036

BRITISH LIBRARY CATALOGUING DATA ARE AVAILABLE

On the cover: Inga (Margita Alfvén) and Gunnar (Edvin Adolphson) in the 1928 film *Jansson's Temptation* (Film AB Minerva/courtesy of the Swedish Film Institute)

Printed in the United States of America

McFarland & Company, Inc., Publishers
Box 611, Jefferson, North Carolina 28640
www.mcfarlandpub.com

Table of Contents

Preface

This book covers Swedish film culture throughout the 1920s. It is the first in-depth exploration of Swedish silent film culture that goes beyond the small number of canonized films (around 20) that repeatedly have been discussed as "art" for nearly 100 years, thus belonging to the "The Swedish Golden Age of Cinema" in domestic and international film history. The study is based on extensive research and takes all Swedish feature films produced in the 1920s into consideration; that is, both canonized and previously overlooked films (in all, 180 films). The great majority of these films have never really been studied before, and, as a result, earlier Swedish film history of the 1920s has quite drastically been modified.

The focus of the book is twofold. First, to revise the history of the films in regard to the themes and genres; and, second, to analyze the great variation of gender and ethnic/"race" relations in Swedish film culture of the 1920s. In order to achieve this, a considerable amount of source materials have been utilized, including all preserved Swedish feature-length silent films (including documentaries), fan and trade magazines, film programs, scripts of both preserved and lost films, censorship records, contemporary writing on film and film culture, government reports, autobiographies, newspaper articles, advertisements, and some 900 film reviews. This book will, hopefully, broaden the Scandinavian perspective of a large number of American, German and Russian films, included in the book, which were shown and appreciated in Sweden during the silent era.

This English edition is a revised version of my PhD dissertation in history, which was published as a book in Swedish in 2008; this work went on to become the winner of several academic awards in Sweden, including the prestigious Pro Lingua prize of the Swedish Foundation for Humanities and Social Sciences, and the Swedish Foundation for International Cooperation in Research and Higher Education. The prize consisted of a professional translation to any of the "world languages," that is, English, French, or German, and the book was eventually translated to English by American translator Karen Williams. Before the translation process commenced, the book was further revised, shortened, and internationally adapted. The new version also includes a number of previously unseen portraits and scene stills.

The book has an introduction and also a chapter that puts into context the film culture in Swedish society in the early decades of the 20th century. Thereafter, the study is organized thematically in four main chapters that have focus on subjects which have rarely been addressed in Anglo-American or Scandinavian masculinity/gender studies: (1) children and youth; (2) fatherhood and love; (3) sexuality and popularity; and (4) racial stereotypes and ethnicity.

Introduction

When brothers Auguste and Louis Lumière first demonstrated their Cinématographe in a Parisian café in December 1895, they showed, among other things, the film *L'arroseur arrosé* (*The Sprinkler Sprinkled*).[1] In the film, a man is watering flowers with a hose. A boy sneaks into the picture and steps on the hose. The man is confused, looks into the nozzle, and a comic effect is achieved when the boy removes his foot. The fact that *L'arroseur arrosé,* perhaps the first fictional film production ever, depicts an incompetent adult man and a mischief-making boy reveals something about film as a medium, about the comic preferences of the period, and about expectations concerning the behavior of men and boys. But what, exactly, can this 50-second-long film convey to us today, more than a hundred years later? Was it that the new moving pictures were not enough, but had to be structured, in this case in a humorous mini-narrative, in order to be understood and appreciated by an unaccustomed audience? That humor has not changed a great deal since the turn of the 20th century? Or could it be that boys will always be boys: mischievous, unruly and naturally impulsive? And when all is said and done, what does the easily duped man signify?

Slightly more than a century later, literary scholar Perry Nodelman carried out an experiment with his students in which he changed the gender of the storyteller perspective in some well-known texts from children's literature. The students were to read the girl characters as boys, and vice versa. The students' reaction to boys acting like boys—loudly, actively, aggressively and cheekily—was that this was normal and that they would eventually grow out of such behavior. When a girl was assigned exactly the same characteristics, however, she was regarded as admirably strong and independent, and as a model for other girls. This is hardly a revolutionary observation. But what is interesting is that when the boys were punished for being stereotypically boyish in these novels, this was accepted by the students, whereas punishing the girls for the same behavior was seen as counterproductive—as a blow to feminism.[2]

In Sweden, *L'Arroseur arrosé* was entitled *Trädgårdsmästarens Hämnd* (The Revenge of the Gardener), and the mischievous boy was punished by the gardener, who, at long last, understood what had stopped the flow of water and chased the boy down. Over a time span of a hundred years, some of the most common notions surrounding boys and men have become interwoven—namely the notions that masculinity is something natural and, thus, unchangeable, that this naturalness must be civilized, and that the civilizing is often accomplished through male violence. However, the male violence needed to check boys' behavior shows that this involves a construction. Punishment is one of many methods used to bring up boys and, ultimately, to create men.

Why is it, then, that we accept male violence and antisocial behavior in boys as something natural, whereas the same behavior in a girl is seen as deviating from the norm? The fact that boys and men are socially shaped beings should be obvious in the 21st century. Still, the idea that they are determined by nature has lived on without much revision. The notion of the unchangeable man can be found in a number of historical, cultural and political power and societal structures. These structures affirm that men have an inner naturalness, which, however, does not mean that men actually have an inner, essential core of manliness.[3] To complicate things further, notions of social gender are often associated with biological gender. As a consequence, men can claim their "natural" position in public life, or, it can also be argued, that men are violent or potential rapists "by nature." It is, therefore, of interest to make the construction visible by differentiating between social and biological gender.

From this point of view, it is not surprising that one of the many paradoxes of masculinity is already found in what is perhaps the first fictional film. It is also not surprising that film was "invented" by two men or that *L'Arroseur arrosé* has two male leading characters.[4] In view of the film industry's historical structures, and considering both general and scientific conceptions of the industry, the film medium unequivocally stands out as a male sphere.[5] But what, then, in the shadow of all this male glory, is the significance of the fooled gardener? Why is it that no one ever discusses this, perhaps, alternative masculinity?

Gender Research Focused on Masculinity

Historian Joan W. Scott considers that gender is constructed in social relations based on experienced differences between the sexes, i.e., that social gender is created in an oppositional partner relationship, and that power in the form of super- and subordination is constituted via this dichotomous relation. At the same time, Scott points out that relations between the sexes are a question of empirical research; the exact meaning of gender in different historical contexts cannot be determined in advance.[6] Much has happened in gender studies since Scott presented her theses. As I see it, however, the view that gender is created relationally has come to characterize gender studies as a whole. In gender studies, the relation between the sexes has almost exclusively been treated theoretically rather than empirically, in contrast to Scott's observation that gender can change over time and space. In other words, women and femininity have been studied in relation to an abstracting male or patriarchal norm rather than in relation to men and masculinity. This gender understanding often derives from grand, structurally inspired theories, such as that of the patriarchy, the aim being to lay bare the unequal power structures in society. However, grand theories tend to lock women and men into eternal sub- and superordination, respectively, without any prospects for change.[7] What's more, this type of gender understanding only leaves scope for studying women's positions and experiences, but is essentially impossible to apply to men. When using a concept such as patriarchy, there is a great risk that the researcher will disregard the unique element that exists in the constant, ongoing negotiation between the sexes. Thus, use of a deterministic gender theory that primarily seeks out female subordination, which is constantly reinvented in study after study, means that novel approaches to gender studies are curbed.[8]

One possible solution is to return to Scott's emphasis on the historical changeability of gender—to show, by force of example, how the unique elements of and deviations in power structures can reveal that change is possible. For this to be done, however, gender relations must be examined empirically rather than being theoretically predetermined. Gender is, by definition, a relational concept, and I think that the relational aspect can contribute to nuancing the whole of gender studies, and that, in this way, we can create greater credibility and stimulate greater public interest in the socially relevant issues addressed in gender studies. The theory of socially constructed gender, based on Scott's definition, will thus serve as the point of departure for the present study. The reason for this approach is that it offers a way of problematizing men and masculinity that has not been used in previous historical research.

Modern Ideal Masculinity

Just as women have been elucidated in gender studies, there is a need to fill the knowledge gaps concerning men's experiences and positions. The gaps here are huge, and this lack of knowledge means that many empirically unfounded generalizations are made about men and masculinity in the popular science literature—generalizations that, for want of anything better, are recycled as historical truths.[9] This is partly because masculinity research first concentrated on writing the history of male ideals, which, in contrast to the broad theoretical approach taken in research on women and femininity, served to narrow the field from its very onset.[10] In this way, a counterpart to the use of the male norm in women's studies has been sustained that goes under a number of different names—patriarchy, hegemonic masculinity, modern masculinity and true masculinity—but these essentially refer to the same thing, namely superordinate, or ideal, masculinity.[11]

It is possible to question the existence of a universally prevailing masculine ideal that affects men and masculinity in the Western world, but the unanimous picture presented in the research makes this ideal difficult to ignore. For this reason, when writing gender history, it is important to take this normative picture into consideration. Here, I will consistently refer to this ideal as *modern ideal masculinity*, following historian George L. Mosse's influential study *The Image of Man: The Creation of Modern Masculinity*. The first thing to remember when reading Mosse is that he does not describe men as they are in reality, but, rather, a stereotyped picture of ideal masculinity that men had to live up to.

Modern ideal masculinity took shape between about 1750 and 1800. This construction of masculinity was closely linked to the rise of bourgeois society in the 19th century, but it was also founded on earlier aristocratic virtues, such as honor, courage and chivalry. Bourgeois masculinity associated these ideals with a character-building morality and, in this way, distinguished itself from the older aristocracy, which had viewed the same ideals as military virtues. New ideals were also tied to this ideal, e.g., self-control, assumption of responsibility and loyalty, all of which were linked to the individual in a new way. Mosse exemplifies this by discussing the significance of the duel. Whereas the aristocracy had regarded the outcome of a duel as God's judgment, the duel now became a man's personal means to prove/defend his masculinity.[12]

Another important change was the connection between body and character emerging in the new sciences, medicine in particular, in that it was now believed that the external body mirrored the internal character, and *vice versa*. As a result, the male body came into focus in a new, previously unseen way, as the body was now a symbolic bearer of the ideals of masculine character building. The standard was thus set, but how was it to be achieved? Mosse shows how the new gymnastics became very important in strengthening the male body as well as character. Sports clubs that taught fencing, swimming, dancing, skiing, riding and contact sports sprang up like mushrooms, their goal being to create men, thereby preventing the phenomena of sedentary boys and men who were feminine in body and mind.[13]

Organized sports and the military were soon linked together, and a new element was introduced in the shaping of the male body: the idea that a real man does not fight for himself but for a higher objective—the nation. The militarization of modern ideal masculinity, and the link between masculinity and nation, had great consequences during World War I, when men, more than ever before, went to war voluntarily to prove their masculinity by fighting for this noble cause.[14]

Mosse also examines the *countertypes* of modern ideal masculinity, as he claims that a stereotype must be defined as the countertype of something else. The stereotyped countertypes primarily came to be constituted by Jews, Romanies and homosexuals. Mosse describes how these deviant groups, the Jews in particular, were used to emphasize all the positive ideals connected to ideal masculinity. This was done by associating all of the negative characteristics—disease, criminality and sexually deviant behavior—with the marginalized groups.[15] In this way, modern ideal masculinity also came to function as the norm for what was standard in society, which not only shut out the marginalized groups but also led to the exclusion of many "ordinary" men. This resulted in repeated crises for men at the individual level, but never led to a crisis for modern ideal masculinity. Despite the widespread disillusion after World War I, as well as repeated attacks from both men and women, Mosse argues that modern ideal masculinity has not changed appreciably and that the ideal has continued to serve as the norm in Western societies.[16]

Hegemonic Masculinity and the Problem of the Homosocial Thesis

During the past ten years or more, Scandinavian and Anglo-American masculinity research has, directly or indirectly, been dominated by one single grand theory: sociologist R.W. Connell's theory of *hegemonic masculinity*. The theory is actually a reaction to the one-sided emphasis, in previous research, on either the man as norm or the history of male ideals. Connell therefore poses the questions: "What is 'normative' about a norm that hardly anyone meets?" and "Are we to say the majority of men are unmasculine?"[17] To avoid the male norm, Connell presents a theory of social and dynamic gender analysis in which constructions and relations are mapped out to demonstrate the existence of several types of masculinity rather than a single normative one. Connell's proposal comprises four levels: *Hegemonic Masculinity, Complicit Masculinity, Subordinated Masculinity,* and *Marginalized Masculinity*.[18] Connell points out that, depending on mutual relationships with other men and ambient conditions, a man can move between levels or be at several levels at the same time. Thus, the theory is primarily meant to illustrate relationships between men.[19] Herein also lies the theory's great disadvantage. Applying the theory has almost exclusively led to continued talk about ideals, reformulated into hegemonic masculinity, and to nearly total concentration on men and male relationships, the consequence being that women have been left out of the investigations by definition.[20]

Connell's great predominance and the use of grand structuralist theories in gender research on women have had tangible effects on how masculinity research has been conducted. In Sweden, this has resulted in two approaches. The first approach accepts, adopts and attempts to apply theories from women's studies; this approach is taken in the minority of studies.[21]

But the majority of studies embrace the *homosocial* approach. Homosocially constructed gender means that men's social gender, or masculinity, is formed together with or in contrast to other men rather than in relation to women or femininity.[22] The homosocial approach can be traced back to the history of male ideals. In combination with the overall influence Connell's theory has had on the field, the homosocial approach has led to an accumulating spinoff effect, such that an increasing number of researchers, in Sweden and abroad, come to the conclusion that masculinity is primarily shaped and defined homosocially.[23] Thus, the thesis of the homosocially created gender is no longer a trend; it is close to becoming a historical truth.

However, the homosocial thesis can be called into question. In my view, rather than being a historical truth, the homosocial thesis is the result of researchers' choice of strongly homosocial settings. A survey of Swedish dissertations that somehow problematize masculinity also reveals the relation between choice of ambient conditions and homosociality, in that the forms of masculinity under investigation are either found in stereotypical settings, such as the military or Ling's gymnastics, or are focused on the development of bourgeois, middle-class ideals.[24]

The homosocial thesis tends to entail that neither women nor power relations between the sexes "need" to be investigated in masculinity research any longer, because super- and subordination are recognized at the very outset of the study.[25] Consequently, women are again not examined, or else they are forgotten, thus forever remaining historical victims without the initiative to, for instance, influence men or be influenced by men in a relationship. In combination with the empirical short-sightedness of women's studies and application of the male norm, this means that gender study is well on its way to being separated by increasingly watertight compartments. Joan W. Scott has used the phrase "dilemma of difference" to illustrate how analyses that focus only on one sex actually result in both the regeneration and sharpening of differences between the sexes.[26]

In a review article from 2002, Swedish historian David Tjeder holds that there has been an explosion in masculinity research, but this description is primarily applicable to Anglo-American research.[27] To be sure, research is being done in Scandinavia, but one can hardly speak of an explosion. Therefore, as a masculinity researcher, one often finds oneself in an empirical vacuum. The result is that grand, generalizing theories must often fill the empty spaces between the occasional, empirically grounded scraps—too often without adequately questioning the theory's geographical and temporal empirical foundation when the theory is transferred to a Scandinavian context. Against this background, for each individual case study, I will mainly present, discuss and apply less grand, empirically based theories. Moreover, the various categorizations of masculinity used will chiefly be derived from the study's empirical foundation.

One overall aim of the present work is to problematize the predominant picture of modern ideal masculinity as well as the persistent dichotomies found in masculinity and gender research by focusing on the complex diversity that exists. Taking as my starting point the fact that the film medium and film culture constitute a heterosocial setting, I have chosen to place the individual studies' various focal points on areas with two common denominators, namely, (1) that they have seldom been studied within gender or masculinity research, and (2) that they call for further investigations focusing on different kinds of relationships. The chosen areas are: children and youth, fatherhood and love, sexuality and popularity, as well as racial stereotypes and ethnicity.

Research on Swedish Film from the 1920s

The history of Swedish film from the 1920s is still largely unwritten. In *Svensk filmografi 2*, it is stated that "the 1920s is Swedish film's least renowned decade. It started with the culmination of what has since then been called a Golden Age and ended in the deepest of misery."[28] In the most recent survey, Swedish film historian Leif Furhammar writes, "The period of decadence of Swedish film art and the Swedish film industry during the 1920s has not stimulated a great deal of historical research."[29] The key phrases here are "golden age" and "period of decadence." The Golden Age of Swedish film occurred between 1917 and 1924. It is almost exclusively associated with three names: directors Victor Sjöström and Mauritz Stiller, and author Selma Lagerlöf. The period of decadence, on the other hand, is not associated with any names at all, but more generally with the production of artistically poor films.

The production of film during the Golden Age is usually comprised to barely 20 films, half of which were produced during the early 1920s. It is these ten films that have been the focus of Swedish and international film history dealing with the silent era. In one of the most recent, internationally oriented studies, *Nordic National Cinemas,* the authors state explicitly that they intend to start "from the basis of popular film"; however, in the chapter on Sweden, they nevertheless concentrate on about ten of the Golden Age films; only three non-canonized films from the 1920s are mentioned.[30] The fact that 180 films were produced in Sweden during the 1920s has been ignored, because the remaining films have been considered trash, thus not worthy of the researchers' attention.[31] In practice, the extremely strong canonization surrounding films of the Swedish Golden Age means that our understanding of film as culture is restricted; it also means that the films' multifaceted representations of contemporary notions of masculinity and femininity remain undetected. In this way, a complex past has been reduced to a small number of historical truths.

One of these historical truths is the one about Americanization versus national style. During the 1920s, the Swedish film industry experienced two economic crises. The first crisis, which followed in the footsteps of the postwar depression of 1921–22, resulted in reduced revenues and cinema closures—but not in any appreciable slowdown in film production. The second crisis came in 1929 when, among other things, several big but unsuccessful film company mergers knocked Swedish film production off its feet. During that year, only six films were made.[32] In his survey, however, Furhammar opts to describe the whole period as a time of crisis, thus equating the economic crises with the artistic crisis, for which he, in turn, puts the blame on Americanization: "This was apparent from the Swedish productions, which conspicuously tried to imitate American models."[33] Wishful thinking is involved here: If Swedes had continued to make their own artistic films with a national style, the crisis would never have occurred.

In film studies, "national style" is a term used to describe what was specifically Swedish about the Golden Age films. It is usually associated with characteristics such as use of nature in film narratives, a basis in literary work, photography, editing and auteurship.[34] However, concentration on the few Golden Age films has given rise to a number of myths about Swedish film from the 1920s. These myths have been reproduced over the past eighty years, which has ultimately entailed new myths about what is specifically Swedish—myths that cannot simply be reduced to the existence of a national style or the Americanization of that style. In *Film History,* for example, Bordwell and Thompson claim that "Swedish films were characterized by their dependence on northern landscapes,"[35] but use of nature in film narratives—with pictures of dangerous descents in rapids, waterfalls and high mountains—occurs only in a small number of films in relation to all Swedish films produced during the 1920s. This also applies to the Americanization of Swedish film. Without a doubt, some Swedish films were inspired by American films, but they were also inspired by German and Russian films, and a large number of European filmmakers working in Hollywood came to influence American film production.[36] It is not for nothing that the silent film is considered inherently more international than the "talkie," with all its language barriers.[37]

British film scholar Andrew Higson has criticized the concept of national film. The main reason is that it leads to disregard of the consumption stage in a film culture, a stage at which films from other countries influence how the audience sees and understands film, and even how a country produces film. He also holds that the concept of national film often leads to discussions about what a national film should look like rather than about the experiences of what it actually looked like.[38]

In addition, film studies' basic interest in the style, form and artistic quality of film often disregards the fact that film is, first and foremost, a commercial mass medium. This is not to say that the research on films from the 1920s is incorrect, but that it is incomplete and one-sided. In order to clarify the distinction between canonized and non-canonized films, I will use the terms *art film* and *mainstream film*. Essentially, this distinction is often treated as a dichotomy, where art films are considered good, commercial films are simply bad.[39] This division tends to create a number of truths about the respective contents of art film and mainstream film, particularly regarding how gender is presented. In this regard, mainstream films are often accused of containing stereotypes that maintain a predominant ideology.[40] Thereby, art film is implicitly assigned the status of something good, something that does not preserve repressive gender structures.[41] This, however, is yet another myth that is more dependent on the distinctive properties of the dichotomy, as well as on an interest in the style and form of a small number of art films, than on the findings of major empirical studies.[42]

Film, Gender and Psychoanalysis

It is uncommon for Swedish dissertations in the field of film studies to adopt a pure gender perspective in relation to the films or the film culture under study. Only about ten such dissertations have appeared since 1987. In these, either the gender perspective constitutes a minor part of the study[43] or all emphasis is put on discussing the theoretical aspects, so that theory, rather than empirical evidence, gives rise to the results.[44] One example of the latter is Tytti Soila's dissertation *Women's Faces* (*Kvinnors ansikte*) from 1991, the first (and for a long time) the only dissertation in film studies to have a pure gender perspective. Soila applies feminist film critic Laura Mulvey's psychoanalytically inspired theory presented in her essay "Visual Pleasure and Narrative Cinema."[45] Mulvey's theory came to be extremely influential, and psychoanalysis was predominant in feminist film studies far into the 1990s. The theory, however, is highly predetermining: It shows women's subordination, while at the same time locking women into a disadvantageous position—the reason being, according to the theory, that all films are structured in accordance with a patriarchal pattern of power. The woman remains forever passive.

Soila subscribes to the thesis of the dominance of the patriarchal discourse over women, but after having studied a number of Swedish melodramas from the 1930s, she discovers that deviations from the predominant discourse do occur. In a couple of films, a woman takes on the role of the protagonist. In view of this, Mulvey's theory does not make a great deal of sense.[46] Instead of rejecting the theory, Soila chooses to develop it further. In support of her reasoning, she refers to several other feminist film researchers who have run into the same problem with Mulvey's deterministic theory.[47]

Soila's investigation is thus divided into two parts. In the first part, 12 female stereotypes are identified that are submitted to the male subject's gaze.[48] In the second part, two films with Ingrid Bergman as the leading character are discussed: *Intermezzo* (1936) and *A Woman's Face* (*En kvinnas ansikte,* 1938). Soila holds that these films deviate from the patriarchal discourse because the characters played by Ingrid Bergman are allowed to occupy a hidden subject position. In other words, the main plot of the respective films are told via her, but not directly. According to Soila, this happens when deviations from the patriarchal discourse leak through the fabric of "notions, values and norms" and are manifested in the films' style, in this case *via* music and *mise-en-scène*. And because the film style is transparent, she concludes that these deviations can only occur in "high level artistic films."[49]

This is an example of how grand theories can guide conclusions, but also of confidence in the notion that what is artistic is good, as opposed to things that are commercial. However, Soila never discusses the significance of the fact that many of the films from the 1930s achieved great success with the public, especially among women. She also has no need to discuss the financial significance, because this is implicit in the dichotomy in which the commercial is bad and the artistic good—art cannot, and thereby need not, be associated with money, despite the fact that the two Ingrid Bergman films were commercial products, just like all the other films under study. Instead, on the basis of the theory, Soila conforms to a long succession of research that tends to persist in claiming that women's and men's positions have been deadlocked in the same stereotyped spots during the more than 100-year-long history of film.[50]

I believe that this is a simplistic attitude. Precisely owing to its commercial nature, film is (and has been) highly eclectic and sensitive to the great changes society has undergone during the past century. To dissolve the dichotomy between commerce and art, and to elucidate the great value of film as a historical source and go beyond the approaches typically taken in film and art studies, I will now introduce the concept *the pluralism of film*.

The Pluralism of Film

To investigate a film's narrative content, for instance, time-bound notions of gender, generation, sexuality, ethnicity and class, the researcher should, ideally, take *all* films into consideration. Thus, if researchers use feature films as a historical source, they must give up the idea that film is primarily an art form. To be sure, film *is* an art form, but it is also commercially short-lived, and both these factors must be taken into consideration. One of the factors must not be allowed to exclude the other by establishing film canons or by setting up the complex of problems in a generalized dichotomy between art and commerce, thereby recreating the enduring conception that art and money are incompatible entities.

Film is unique compared to other (audio-)visual sources in the sense that it is a super-commercial mass medium. The economic necessity of reaching as many people as possible, as well as the fact that film producers are not usually in a position to make major changes after the film has been released, is of great importance to the contents of films and how they represent human beings. This reality, which I have chosen to call "the pluralism of film," rests on three pillars that, taken together, lend considerable weight to the scholarly value of feature film as a historical source.

Feature films can be understood and criticized in the same manner as other historical documents. What is required of the researcher is a knowledge of film language, that is, elements such as framing, camera placement, lighting, editing and genre-specific conventions, which are necessary for reading the films. In addition, feature film derives much of its aesthetic value from reflecting a kinship with reality; this is where the first pillar of the pluralism of film enters the picture. A feature film is created by hundreds of people, both men and women, all of whom generate a picture, consciously or unconsciously, of the potential audience, allowing them to more easily guess as to the audience's attitudes and preferences.[51] The result of this collective heterogeneity is that a given film will reflect, in the plural, the current attitudes, values and opinions of the period during which it was produced. In other words, there is not a single, inspired director behind the creation of a film in the same way as a single author is the sole creator of a novel. The exception might seem to be art films, but these, too, contain values and attitudes. And, after all, art films are also made by more than one person. This pluralism of creation should not be underestimated.

The second pillar supporting the pluralism of film is its pursuit of representativeness. As filmmaking is and always has been expensive, films must match as closely as possible their audience's preferences if box-office revenues are to cover production costs. This has often been interpreted negatively, as if mainstream films are all alike and thus able to maintain a discriminating ideology.[52] Yet, in actual fact, the opposite is true. If mainstream film is to be distributed as efficiently as possible, and thereby recover its costs, it must "accommodate as many types of preferences as possible—you want to reach out to the right and the left, hetero- and homosexual, religious and atheist with one and the same work."[53] Thus, this pluralism compels filmmakers to closely follow several, simultaneously existing currents in society. And, as a consequence, we can claim that the feature film is inclusive by nature. It is here, then, we have the ambiguity that cultural studies ascribe to popular culture.[54]

The third pillar of the pluralism of film concerns film's mass media goals—an orientation that rubs out the boundary between the public and the private. This occurs because film uses human experience as the raw material for its production, thereby displaying the private in public. Thus, dependence on maximum distribution is not only a matter of including as many social groups as possible; it is also a question of *how* these characters are depicted in terms of their feelings, appearance, behavior, relationships, etc. Filmmakers are quite simply forced to make use of human experiences, needs and fantasies that both confirm and go beyond what is accepted in the public sphere, the reason being that film, by virtue of its photographic qualities, is so closely linked to realism.[55]

We can talk about two kinds of realism in art. According to the first kind of realism, art should deal with important social and psychological aspects of life, whereas the second maintains that art should be true-to-life.[56] In the world of film, these two kinds of realism have not always gone hand in hand. Yet, irrespective of whether a film takes place in outer space or whether it is animated, an art film or a romantic comedy, filmmakers cannot compromise the characters' human features. It is primarily in this regard that the audience can relate to certain feelings, behaviors or qualities that are found in the characters on the movie screen and that make the two-dimensional characters seem credible—and, ultimately, true-to-life. In this way, the human aspect, primarily mediated by actors, links the film and the audience together on the level of understanding. The crux of the matter is that the audience recognizes certain features or types, perhaps even to the point of feeling an alliance with certain characters, which likely entails a feeling of aversion to other characters. Given film's pursuit of pluralism, however, it is far from certain that audience members will ally themselves with, or feel an aversion to, one and the same character in a particular film. Because the audience is not a homogeneous mass, films must be pluralistically inclusive if they are to cover their high production costs and, hopefully, generate a profit. This means, in turn, that films will reflect a very complex reality in which actors serve as representations of several different notions of gender, ethnicity and class in their interrelationships.[57]

Yet, despite the inclusive nature of film, no single film or even 50 films can incorporate everything. There will always be exceptions to and deviations from the pluralism of film. However, these exceptions are interesting and deserve close attention. For example, American film presented a highly biased picture of black people far into the 20th century; and in mainstream films, homosexuals were rarely portrayed, at least not openly, until the 1980s.[58] The fact that representations of the former group had very little to do with reality and that the latter group was not represented at all may complicate arguments professing the pluralism of film. Remember, however, that film representations are made up of the ideas and prejudices that surround blacks and whites, men and women, heterosexuals and homosexuals, etc., which, in turn, are closely tied to the period in which the films were produced.[59] Attempts have been made to more or less abandon the contemporary context's ideas about sex and ethnicity in order to recreate in film the "true" history or picture of the time. These attempts have led to some interesting results, but most often to financial failures.[60]

With these exceptions in mind, the importance of the social and media context cannot be emphasized enough when films are to be used as historical sources for studying representations. It is primarily contextualization that distinguishes history from art studies. History uses a film to say something about the surrounding society, whereas art studies may draw on the context to say something about the individual work of art. Thus, exceptions to the pluralism of film—for instance the biased representation of blacks in American films—have a great deal to say about the society's attitudes toward that group. However, context isn't only important from a societal point of view, but also in correctly interpreting film contents in relation to the audio-visual literacy of a certain period.[61] Today, for example, a silent movie from the 1920s or a talkie from the 1930s may be perceived as unrealistic because the actors are heavily made up, gesticulate and grimace excessively, or speak theatrically. Yet these features are in line with the stylistic conventions of the period and were, at that time, regarded as genuine. From the point of view of film history, these stylistic changes are interesting in themselves. From a general historical standpoint, however, these constantly changing conventions are extremely important if we are to avoid misinterpreting older films. Just as stylistic conventions are constantly changing, film contents in the form of representations and ideas also change with time. Because feature films have always been short-lived commodities—owing to their pluralism and stylistic conventions, so closely linked to the period—film is an excellent source when investigating ideas and how they change over time.

Representations

In film studies, research on different kinds of representations is relatively uncommon. One reason for this can be traced back to Siegfried Kracauer's classic study *From Caligari to Hitler* from 1947. Kracauer argues that, in German film produced before 1933, it is possible to detect a German mentality that foretold Hitler's assumption of power and the submission of the German people. Although it has been severely criticized, this figure of thought is not entirely preposterous, and it is in line with the present work. What is problematic, on the other hand, are Kracauer's method and selection of material. In his search for the German mentality, Kracauer chooses to base his results on the expressionist films, German film's celebrated counterpart to films from the Swedish Golden Age. But, like the Golden Age films, the artistic expressionist films were very few in number. They were also, in Kracauer's own words, introverted and highbrow and, thus, did not become great successes with the general public. The great variety of secondary, often popular German films were simply discarded because they played to the gallery.[62]

The fact that the expressionist films suggest *one* German mentality is, in a way, symptomatic of the representation research in film studies, which tend to emphasize a small number of artistic films. But it is also symptomatic of the field in general, owing to its almost inherent teleological quest for *one* plausible explanation or truth. In other words, Kracauer's conclusions depend on the fact that all other German films were excluded—films that very likely contained a long succession of different mentalities, the existence of which would have upended his teleologically produced results. Thus, a more extensive study of a greater number of films, not least popular films that people chose to watch, should be able to more reliably capture several of the conflicting mentalities and notions circulating in a society at a given time. Studies such as these, which attempt to cover a large proportion of the films on offer at a given time, are rare. But those that have been carried out have produced completely new results that substantiate the notion of the pluralism of film.[63]

Thus, representations do not imply that films are one-way reflections of a society. Rather, they imply that the films are also interlinked with and influence society by spreading ideas, mentalities and fashion, among other things.[64] Like few other media, film has the ability to capture and, by virtue of its popularity, spread both small and large contemporary phenomena and currents.

Source Material and Outline of the Study

Here, Swedish film culture will not be discussed in terms of art. Consequently, the emphasis will only be put on style, form or directing in exceptional cases. Instead, the focus will be on the films' narrative content, actors and contemporary reception. To achieve a new interpretation of a film and avoid a traditional film analysis, film scholar Janet Staiger suggests that a historical reception study should include three levels: (1) the Text; (2) the Spectator; and (3) the Historical Context. Staiger considers that a more in-depth film interpretation can lead to the rewriting of history, in the sense that previously hidden meanings may emerge. Moreover, this method may contribute to our understanding of the way in which culture and political courses of action are interwoven and influence one another.[65]

A reception analysis aims at studying how films are received rather than what happens in the film itself. In the present study, film images constitute the primary material for investigating representations or, if one wishes, the imprints of history in the form of moving pictures. I have therefore restructured Staiger's reception analysis according to the following scheme: (1) the Film; (2) the Reception; and (3) the Historical Context.

Of the 180 feature films and feature-length documentaries produced in Sweden in the 1920s, 97 are complete, and 18 partially preserved. Of these 115 films, I have analyzed slightly more than a hundred. These analyses will be supplemented with some digressions to Swedish films produced in the 1910s and 1930s. In addition, to expand the narrow concept of national film, some 40 American, German and Russian films are also included in the discussion. In some cases, films that are essential to the various sub-studies have been lost. In an attempt to replace at least some of their contents, I have chosen to use the original screenplays, programs and censorship cards.

To anchor my interpretation of the film contents in the period in which they were produced, I have used more than 900 reviews from some 20 Swedish daily newspapers, diverse in terms of their political orientation and geographical origin. In contrast to today's newspapers, in which only the leading pages express political views, political affiliation marked the papers of the 1920s, all the way down to the film reviews. This means that differences in political interpretations, as well as consensus on different issues, appear very clearly. The film critics also displayed a remarkable distribution with regard to gender. In the 1920s, almost no film critic wrote under his or her own name; all reviews were either written under a pen name or unsigned. This was a consequence of journalistic convention as well as of film's lowly status in society, and it opened up the work to young talents—even to women. During the 1910s and 1920s, journalism was a markedly male occupation in Sweden, women making up only between 3 and 6 percent of the profession.[66] However, among the signatures that can be decoded, women constituted almost 30 percent of film critics in the 1920s.[67] Because the reviews are fairly representative of audiences of the 1920s, this relatively heterogeneous age and gender distribution among film critics entails an advantage in terms of representational.

Articles from 11 film magazines from the 1920s will constitute an additional source of contextual material. These magazines can be divided into two orientations: (1) fan magazines with a circulation as large as 200,000; and (2) trade journals for exhibition and distribution. The circulation figures for trade journals were not as large as those for fan magazines. On the other hand, trade journals were extremely sensitive to currents in Swedish society that concerned film. In that way, they provide excellent barometers for film discussions in the 1920s, discussions that are not infrequently linked to the main themes of the present study.

In this introduction, I have introduced the gender-theoretical points of departure, the research on Swedish film from the 1920s, as well as the source material of the present study. The first chapter begins with a historical background of Swedish society in the early 1900s, which is tied to the emerging consumption and entertainment culture. The discussion goes on to deal with societal attitudes toward the new film medium. Special emphasis is put on the presence of children and young people in the film culture and the reactions to this presence, based, among other things, on an audience research poll.

This is followed by four thematic studies, all consisting of an introductory specification of the context by subject matter, a discussion of previous research and theory, and, subsequently, analyses of films and the contextual material based on the theme of each chapter. Given that we are dealing with films that very few people who are alive today have seen or even heard about, I feel it is both a necessity and a service to the reader to relate the plot of many of the films that are central to the analysis. Chapter 2 deals with films in which children and young people had prominent roles, whereas Chapter 3 focuses on fatherhood and love in Swedish film from the 1920s. Chapter 4 presents a study of the actor

Gösta Ekman, based on how sexuality and popularity were discussed during the period. Chapter 5 focuses on the extensive use of racial stereotypes and ethnicity in relation to gender in Swedish films of the 1920s. In Conclusions, the conclusions of the study are presented, and refer back to the complex of problems posed in this introduction.

1

Swedish Society and Film Culture During the First Decades of the 20th Century

During the first decades of the 20th century, Swedish society underwent many changes. From a poor and agrarian country, Sweden was transformed into an industrialized nation characterized by urbanization, economic growth and political changes. The breakthrough of parliamentarianism in 1917 was followed by universal suffrage in 1921, the first referendum in 1922, the defense resolution in 1925 and the beginning of what would be a long period of Social Democratic rule in 1932. From an overall historical point of view, the development of modern Sweden appears to have been linear, without too many bumps. But this was a turbulent time in many respects. With regard to gender history, the period appears to have been rather dubious. The election turnout was low despite universal suffrage. Democracy was still a controversial concept. Political instability prevailed throughout the 1920s, with government reshuffles taking place almost every year. The labor market was periodically marked by high unemployment and unrest.

These societal changes did not only concern politics and the economy. They were tangible in many areas, primarily in the big cities where car, bicycle and streetcar traffic was becoming louder and more hectic, where construction work was going on constantly, and where a new consumption and entertainment culture was starting to flourish. Despite the new buildings under construction, people in the growing cities were increasingly cramped for space, primarily young people who had moved from the country. Many of these young people lived as "lodgers," meaning that they had access to a floor mattress that could only be used at night. They spent the rest of their work and leisure time on the town.[1]

Particularly noticeable were the children of the working class. While their parents were at work, the streets became the children's playground and sometimes their workplace. This situation disturbed the bourgeois class because it meant that children and youth were out of reach of parents and other fosterers. The visible presence of children and youth was perceived as bordering on the criminal: playing ball or marbles, shouting too loudly, fighting or just doing nothing. Such activities could lead to reprimands or arrests by the increasingly numerous—and visible—police constables. The fact that the number of police actions against children and youth was increasing caused members of established society to cry out for even more police and greater control. Crimes against public authorities increased greatly at this time, whereas the rate of ordinary crimes decreased.[2]

Due to the growing importance of the mass media as well as improved communications, the above notions did not remain in the cities, but spread and established themselves in the countryside as well.[3] The schools also came to be very influential, because it was their task to mold pupils into social beings who conformed to society's division between those doing the governing and those being governed. By means of two important reforms, one in 1919 and the other in 1927, for the first time all children would complete elementary school, which had hardly been the case previously. These reforms can be seen as yet another measure on the part of society to exercise control over children and youth.[4] In other words, the development was not without its speed bumps. This was evident in the debate on the new consumption and entertainment culture, where feature films in particular came to occupy a prominent position. Newspapers, periodicals, advertising and fashion magazines, too, began playing a more prominent role during the 1910s and 1920s. A new division of time into leisure and wage labor emerged. The consumption of various goods and services thus began to define people's identities—a role previously monopolized almost entirely by work.[5] This did not mean, however, that work and other identity-forming factors, such as religion and political activity, suddenly capitulated in the face of economic market forces.

Research has often taken an either-or view of consumption: as either something good and liberating or something bad and coercive.[6] The pessimistic view of consumers as passive victims and of popular culture as manipulative and one-sided can be attributed to the Frankfurt School, which emerged during the interwar period in parallel with the emergence of the modern consumption society.[7] The Birmingham School, or Cultural Studies, arose in the 1960s as a reaction to the elitism of the Frankfurt School. It had a much more positive outlook on both the consumer and popular culture. Both schools' views on consumption and popular culture were highly evaluative in one direction or the other, the dichotomy resembling that between art and commerce.

American historian Peter N. Stearns has claimed that such dichotomies were discussed more and more forcibly around the turn of the century, circa 1900, the reason being that the new mass consumption came increasingly to include everyone in society. For this reason, Stearns prefers not to interpret the development as black or white, but as a "fascinating juggling act" in which individuals who both favored and disfavored the effects of consumption did not necessarily abandon older values or completely embrace new ones. Consumption was governed by social structures, while at the same time stirring up and making a mess of these structures.[8] This means that the researcher must have some insight into "the fundamental ambivalence of the modern." Ambivalence arises because modernization is unstoppable. But attempts to check this process—often on a cultural symbolic level—cause it to find new paths, for example on the commercial economic plane.[9] It should be pointed out that Sweden lagged behind Britain and the U.S. by at least 20 years, and that the breakthrough of the consumption culture in Sweden took place during the interwar period.[10]

Based on the source material I have examined, it becomes clear that the appearance of mass consumption during these decades resulted in open opposition between the traditional and the modern, the useful and the useless, as well as the old and the young. Consumption was regarded alternately as good and bad—and cutting through all of this like a main thread were different attitudes toward gender. This was not, however, a question of clinical distinctions. The dividing lines were more diffuse—both older and more recent influences could coexist in one and the same individual or organization. To lay bare this complex web, I will constantly attend to the economic aspects and the way in which they influenced the construction of gender, generation and ethnicity within and outside film production. In this way, I hope to show that consumption had a positive as well as negative effect, but primarily that it created, in a relatively short time period, major changes in people's outlook on the sexes.

The commercial feature film came under fire as society's enemy number one in the debate on the new consumption and entertainment culture. This confirmed its central role in the play for interpretative space when it came to defining new gender codings for men and women, children and adolescents as well as the working and middle class. However, the debate on the early film culture was largely centered around children and youth. In presenting the context, children and youth will thus function as a prism. But the discussion should be regarded as symptomatic and as the foundation of the work as a whole.

Film's Bad Reputation and Censorship

In the summer of 1896, the Cinematographe came to Sweden, more specifically to the Malmö Industry and Handicraft Fair. Originally, film was a scientific invention. The noise and steam coming from the device showing the film in the darkened room was just as great an experience for the audience as the moving pictures themselves. Film historian Tom Gunning has named the period "the cinema of attraction" to point out that the narrative aspect so closely associated with today's film hardly existed before 1905.[11]

Around 1905, an extensive structural transformation began that was to change film from an amusement park attraction to a large-scale industry. Permanent locations were established, first in the major industrial cities. Within a few years, however, one could find one or two Cinématographes, even in smaller towns. Permanent premises required a constant influx of new films, as the audience remained the same. This resulted in the professionalization and commercialization of film production and distribution. In the long run, it also led to a change in the length and content of films. Films kept getting longer and began to tell stories.[12] The explosive development of film troubled established society. What was actually being shown, and what was really going on in those rooms where children and adults, men and women, sat side by side in the dark?[13] In Sweden, where temperance organizations and free church congregations had leased out their premises to itinerant film demonstrators, the Swedish Church now dissociated itself from "the cinema nuisance." The first appeals against children's filmgoing had come already, in 1904.[14]

During the early years, then, film transitioned from being a scientific curiosity, relatively expensive to watch, to a cheap pleasure for the masses. After 1905, the idea that only the working class frequented the cinemas grew, and that on such premises they were being exposed to all sorts of cheapness that would break down their moral fiber. To be sure, many working-class people did go to the movies. In Sweden, however, not a single study of the social stratification at the time has been carried out. Research has simply assumed that the audience came from the working class, leaving it at that. However, studies from the U.S., Britain and Russia have shown that people from all social classes went to the cinema regularly.[15]

The earlier attacks on film must be seen in a wider perspective. In the established social stratum in Sweden, there was strong opinion against the entire emerging entertainment and consumption culture. That culture, in turn, was regarded as one large and ill-boding symptom of the major social changes taking place. This was particularly because the new life of pleasure enticed people away from the home as never before, often to attractions that transcended class.

Dances, restaurants, cafés and cinemas came under fire. Sweden was shaken by several outbreaks of downright moral panic that ended, among other things, in book burnings in several big cities. So-called dime novels were burned in order to, as the saying went, protect children and youth.[16] But whereas attacks on cheap literature were stopped by the principle of freedom of the press, the new film medium did not have a chance.

In February 1908, Marie Louise Gagner, an elementary-school teacher in Stockholm, gave a speech entitled "Children and Cinema Shows." It was an important speech because it summarized for the first time a number of notions about film and its connection to children and youth, notions that lived on into the 1920s and even longer. The speech was a frontal attack against film and its proliferation through the establishment of new cinemas. Gagner was convinced that film was detrimental to people's taste, and that filmgoers were different from people who typically visited lecture halls and libraries. She was particularly concerned about the fact that children visited the cinemas by the thousands: "It is not just a few boys and girls who have a passion for moviegoing. They would rather go without candy and the like than without the cinema. Many, many of our elementary-school children go to the cinema at least once a week."[17]

In the speech, a distinction was made between "good" and "ugly and unpleasant" features. The good features consisted of nature scenes and films about industry, sports and military films—"these features are particularly suitable for boys"—as well as films presenting news. The bad features were films containing murder, suicide and robbery, films with obscene images, and, finally, films with comic features, most of which "are downright idiotic and coarse." The latter features were in the clear majority according to the "eighty or so cinema programs" Gagner quoted frequently to support her attack. On the other hand, she had some difficulty explaining the popularity of these films. When Gagner asked a little girl why she wanted to see such ghastliness, the girl replied: "Well, Miss, it's worse at first, when you get there. Then your whole body trembles and you think: I wonder what horrors I'll get to see. It's just like when you're about to go to the dentist." Gagner continued:

> To the audience's shame, concerning its taste, it should be said that it is precisely those cinemas that make a display of the most revolting criminal cases and trashy novels that have the largest audiences. Someone uninitiated in the matter might wonder how the pictures for these features are obtained.
>
> Well, the major filmmakers abroad have a whole staff of actors and actresses at their disposal who are photographed while they perform the most dramatic parts of the novel in question. All these scenes are *constructed* in this manner. And I promise that they taste of construction.[18]

Apart from the girl's expectations, a couple of enduring ideas come to light here. First, we have the idea that the filth comes from abroad, where an entire staff of people stand at the ready to inundate Sweden with all kinds of unpleasant pictures just to make a profit. Second, there is the notion that films are constructions and that something unnatural cannot be good.

It is evident that Gagner had not seen the films she was discussing, which is a typical feature of the occurrence of moral panic.[19] Her entire argumentation is based on the cinema programs and the lines of children she had seen standing outside the movie houses. However, because the cinema programs were the equivalent of advertising, in which "the sensational" tends to be exaggerated, the picture she described was exaggerated and false. Nevertheless, Gagner's speech resulted in the formation of a committee, whose report formed the basis of the government bill that, in turn, led to the parliamentary resolution to establish a state board of film censorship in 1911.[20] Gagner was subsequently appointed one of the first three censors on this board—the Swedish Board of Censorship.

The guiding paragraph of the cinema ordinance stated that a censor was not to approve films that could

> be in conflict with general statutes or proper morals, or otherwise have a brutalizing or inflammatory effect, or act to confuse concepts of justice. Thus, pictures portraying horror scenes, suicide or serious offenses in such a way or in such a context as to bring about such effects shall not be approved.
>
> For performances to which children below fifteen years of age are admitted, pictures that are liable to harmfully upset children's imagination or otherwise have an injurious effect on their mental development or health shall not be approved.[21]

To grade the previewed films, the censors used cards with three different color markings. White represented a total ban; yellow was used for films approved for adults only; and red was used for films appropriate for general audiences. The dividing line between yellow and red films was set at 15 years of age. From the outset, the censors worked hard to clean up the cinema quagmire. Between 1911 and 1922, over 1500 films were totally prohibited. This number was then stabilized at, on average, 53 banned films a year during the period 1923–30. In addition, many films were cut or censored prior to their premières. Of the films produced in Sweden, nine were totally prohibited in the 1910s, whereas not a single film was banned during the 1920s.[22] A total ban meant economic disaster for the production company. Thus, the fact that no film was prohibited in the 1920s clearly indicates that the Swedish film industry quickly adapted to the new censorship norms. Moreover, the Swedish film industry did not regard censorship as something negative. The fact that the censors had assumed responsibility for what movies could be shown helped to wipe clean some of the dirt from the industry's tarnished reputation.[23]

Yet, despite censorship, there was no decrease in the criticism of film or in the belief that movies could cause people to commit material as well as moral offenses.[24] In the shadow of the war and under the pressure of poorly planned rationing, there was a tendency toward rising juvenile delinquency in the years 1917–18. The blame was offhandedly put on film rather than on the period of crisis, overcrowding or unemployment.[25] The fact that the minimal increase in crime disappeared immediately after the war played a less important role for moralists—frequently in close collaboration with medical expertise—who continued to attack film for causing the "laxity" afflicting society. In 1922, a certain Professor Lange wrote the following regarding the mental dangers of film:

> When a child runs to the cinema once, twice or three times a week, he or she becomes spiritually ruined simply because of the way film is rendered, regardless of its contents. The theater may be ever so respectable, showing ever so well-censored programs, but merely becoming accustomed to these jumpy, jerky and fluttering pictures on a gleaming surface slowly but surely breaks down people's intellectual and, ultimately, moral self-control.[26]

The argument that film blunted the intellect was recurrent and concerned both children and adults.[27] This notion comprised a line of reasoning that identified children, youth and the uneducated as incapable of independent thought. However, if children did go to the movies so often, then they must have been among the most experienced filmgoers, implying that they had learned to watch films and were thus more knowledgeable about films than the moralists were.[28]

According to Swedish historian Henrik Berggren, there were two distinctive views on youth at the time: *the discipline model* and *the optimism of evolution*. The discipline model implied that young people should be introduced to adulthood through discipline. The optimistic outlook on development, on the other hand, implied great confidence in the younger generation, as they were to reform an old and tired society. According to Berggren, the discipline model was the predominant one. This seems to be confirmed by established society's views on film and youth.[29] The mass media, however, helped to corroborate the notion that children and youth, as well as workers and women, would imitate what they saw in the movies—which, ultimately, was thought to have consequences not only for the individual, but also for society as a whole.[30]

To counteract this social distrust, film producers in the U.S. and Europe, beginning with the French company Le Film d'Art in 1908, began making more "artistic" films, based on well-known novels and stage plays. Stage actors, writers and theater directors were also engaged to increase the prestige of films. The building of magnificent movie theaters began. The same development took place in Sweden during the 1910s. This has often been considered a way to win the respect of the middle class, but it was primarily a question of money. The film industry wished to legitimize its existence. At the same time, it wanted to attract an audience with greater spending power without losing the mass ticket buying of the working-class audience.[31]

It is not difficult to see the attempts made to steer developments onto the "right" track as desperate efforts to stem the "perilous" march of events. However, the moralists overshot their goal, as the overall trends in society were beyond their control. They tried to treat the symptoms by designating assailable scapegoats, such as the new film culture.[32]

Children at the Movies?

One relevant question in this context is whether children and youth actually went to the cinema to the extent claimed. According to the moralists, it was virtually only children who were flocking around the movies theaters, where they were clearly visible to passers-by.[33] But this claim was denied emphatically by the cinema owners who, during the worst onslaught, had every reason to maintain that the number of children at the movies was exceedingly small.[34] Between 1911 and 1920, however, the number of visits to the cinema increased greatly, from about 12 million to more than 40 million.[35] These high figures provide a sort of guarantee that at least working- and middle-class children, youth and adults went to the cinema fairly regularly.

What kind of movies did children and youth like to see? It is hard to give a definite answer to this question, because the first major investigation was not conducted until 1945.[36] If we wish to look at genres, however, it is possible to reference a minor report published in connection with the overall campaign against film. In addition, owing to the Swedish Motion Picture Exhibitors' Association's application for a change in the 1911 cinema ordinance, the Stockholm Elementary School Board carried out a major investigation of schoolchildren's filmgoing in 1929. The cinema owners requested a change in Paragraph 3, which prohibited children under 15 years of age from going to the movies after eight o'clock in the evening. The reason for the change was that the films were now so long they continued until after eight.[37]

In the earliest investigation, conducted in 1918, 550 children at Adolf Fredrik's Elementary School in Stockholm were asked how often they went to the movies, what they preferred to see and which actors had caught their attention. Based on their responses, it seemed that a majority of the children went to the cinema once a week, Sunday being the main movie day. There was no difference between boys and girls in the frequency of visits. On the other hand, boys could see a movie by themselves, whereas girls always "wanted" company, be it that of friends, siblings or parents.[38]

The fact that girls always wanted company was not called into question. In this respect, however, a clear gender distinction is found with regard to children and youth. Boys were allowed to go into town on their own, though the same did not apply to girls. In this respect, a connection could be made to the private and the public spheres and their separation of the sexes. Reversing this line of thought, however, it can be maintained that girls were allowed to go to the cinema already in 1918, albeit in the company of others. This was also in focus during the 1920s, when the new, modern young woman became increasingly visible out on the streets and in public entertainment establishments.

How, then, did children pay for their movie tickets? To the moralists, the answer was obvious: they stole.[39] However, the investigation showed that parents paid for the tickets, either as compensation for completing a task or just because "Mom wants to get rid of us for a while."[40] The notion that parents paid for cinema tickets to get rid of the kids is recurrent in the surveyed material. It was probably a common phenomenon related to people's overcrowded living conditions. In most cases, this is elucidated through moralists' strong condemnation of the (implicitly working-class) parents who sent their children to the movies.[41] Several factors are involved here. If the cinema was to function as a babysitter, there had to be one nearby. This requirement was fulfilled by the local cinemas. Another aspect is that the great majority actually accepted the cinema as a normal ingredient in the townscape.

But what kind of movies did the children watch? Were there any differences between the sexes?

Genres	*Boys* (290)	*Girls* (260)
Drama	150	180
Detective/Adventure	88	22
Comedy	64	51
Nature pictures	42	38
War pictures	16	13

Table 1. The figures are based on the study "Hur barn gå på bio" ("How Children Go to the Cinema") in *Filmbladet* 1918:6. The children were asked to state the titles of films (often more than one) they had seen. These were then counted and grouped by genre.

Two main differences can be observed here. Boys saw detective or adventure films four times more often than girls did. The girls were in the lead when it comes to dramas, though the latter difference is not as great as the former. Otherwise, the figures are relatively equal. Nevertheless, for both boys and girls, the high figures for feature films should be noted in relation to the lower figures for the "good features" found among the documentary, nature and war pictures.

The Stockholm Elementary School Board's 1929 report on schoolchildren's moviegoing was sophisticated. It was carried out in several stages and included all children in Stockholm in grades 3 to 8. First, a list was compiled containing all films that had been shown in Stockholm's movie theaters during the 12-day-long study period. The list, which separated the red from the yellow films, was used to verify the children's responses. Each individual homeroom teacher was then asked to obtain information from all the children on how many times they had gone to the cinema and which films they had seen. This was done to calculate how frequently children went to the movies after eight o'clock in the evening prior to the possible law reform, as well as to discover which adult films the children had seen. Subsequently, the headmaster summarized the results for each school. On the basis of these results, a memo was put together that would form the basis for the Stockholm Elementary School Board's answer to the proposal circulated for consideration.[42]

Grades	*Number of children in the various grades*	*Total number of cinema visits*	*Average number of visits per child within the 12-day period*	*Total number of visits to adult films*	*Visits to adult films in relation to all visits to the cinema (percent)*
Both sexes, grades 3–4	9,236	7,497	0.81	209	2.8
Boys, grades 5–8	5,990	6,761	1.13	724	10.7
Girls, grades 5–8	6,137	4,536	0.74	584	12.9
Total	21,363	18,794	0.88	1,497	8

Table 2. The figures represent the sum of the headmasters' compilations for the respective schools. All of Stockholm's schoolchildren in grades 3–8 were asked how often they had gone to the cinema during the period 20–31 October 1929. The Stockholm City Archives (SSA), Archives of the Stockholm Elementary School Board (SFA), Documents on schoolchildren's filmgoing (Handlingar angående elevers biografbesök) 1929, SE/SSA/0569/F II c, Volume 2.

As we see in Table 2, children in grades 3–8 went to the cinema quite frequently, and there was a weak increase in the number of visits as a function of age. Converted into a seven-day period, children below 15 years of age went to the cinema 0.5 times a week, or twice a month. Judging from the headmasters' summaries of the different schools, there were no substantial differences in the moviegoing rate between the schools in fashionable areas, such as Östermalm, and those in less reputable areas, like Södermalm.[43] The table also shows that boys went to the cinema more than girls did, but that, proportionally speaking, girls saw adult films more often than did same-age boys. The school board's memo also contains a list of the 38 most-visited adult films. At the top of the list are 99 visits to the romantic film *Wild Orchids* (1929) with Greta Garbo, closely followed by the adventure film *The Triumph of the Scarlet Pimpernel* (1928), with 91 visits.[44]

The school board's answer to the proposal for a possible law reform was irresolute. They considered that if the reform were to be carried out, in a *fait accompli* situation, the eight o'clock limit could possibly be extended to nine. The main reasons for the board's apprehension were that the children had to get up and go to school early the next day, and that "going home alone at nine, perhaps eleven o'clock at night must be considered to involve certain risks for children" because, at that late hour, they are more likely "to fall into bad company."[45] The report showed, however, that such misgivings were exaggerated, as only 1.6 percent of all visits to the cinema took place after nine o'clock in the evening.[46]

The same week the report was disclosed, *Aftonbladet* opted to fan the fire with the banner headline, "Schoolchildren see eight movies in twelve days," in an attempt to create a sensation.[47] As a matter of fact, only two of the approximately 21,000 children involved in the study had gone to the movies eight times during the 12-day period. And those two children were not movie crazy, either. A homeroom teacher of one of the two children who had gone to the cinema eight times offered the following explanation: "One boy, whose brother is a projectionist at the movie theater Rekord on Götgatan, takes the tram there almost every day. He attends the seven o'clock performance on weekdays and the afternoon performance on Saturdays."[48] It would certainly not be too bold to guess that the big brother was looking after the lad while their parents were at work.

Asserting that the moralists' fierce attacks on film went uncontested would be a serious over-simplification. The film industry regularly challenged attacks from scientific or religious sources by having the film magazines publish opposing opinions from representatives of the same groups.[49] Even the former head of the censorship board, Gustaf Borg, came to be the driving force behind the use of film for educational purposes in the schools. As this legitimized film as a whole, it was immediately snapped up by the film industry and given space in its magazines.[50] The production company Svensk Filmindustri (SF) started an educational-film department, with Borg as director. The first issue of *Tidskrift för Svensk Skolfilm och Bildningsfilm* (*Journal of Swedish School and Educational Film*), edited by Borg, appeared in 1924. Late in 1923, the school cinema program was shown to be a success, with one million children attending.[51]

All in all, this shows that film was a complex societal phenomenon and that it is impossible to divide representatives of the different camps—scientific, religious or political—into those who were for or against film, because opinions literally cut across the camps. On the other hand, the advancement of the documentary genre does provide an example of the increasing rift between a "higher" and a "lower" culture during this period.[52] In 1923–24, the attacks against film as a corrupter of children and a cause of juvenile delinquency declined. Instead, moralists transitioned to criticizing young people's increasingly visible consumption, which was thought to be influenced by films and film stars.

The Modern Young Woman

Two of the most visible—and, looking back on the period, characteristic—phenomena of the 1920s were the short skirt and shingle-haircut fashions. Short skirts caught on in the mid–1910s, whereas the shingle haircut did not appear for another ten years. These fashions were coded as feminine, but nevertheless had a great deal to do with young men. Swedish film scholar Mats Björkin holds that the short skirts were an expression of a more profound change in mentality, to which the film industry was forced to relate. This entailed trying to strike a balance, because the audience's and society's preferences did not always coincide.[53] In *Becoming Modern*, Birgitte Søland studies young Danish women's self-reconstruction as modern during the 1910s and 1920s, as well as the great anxiety this provoked. According to contemporary analysts, it was the war that changed everything, renewing both masculinity and femininity. Using a somewhat longer time perspective, however, Søland is able to show that the changes had already been set in motion prior to the war, which served only to accelerate them. The same was true of urbanization and industrialization; they expedited but did not cause the change. Rejection of the war as a direct cause builds on the fact that Denmark, like Sweden, was neutral during World War I. Another reason is that, even though urbanization and industrialization were certainly gaining ground in the Scandinavian countries, these processes were not as strong as in Germany, Great Britain, France and the U.S., i.e., countries that have usually been the basis for studies of changed sex roles during the interwar period, and for which the war has been emphasized as the main cause of change.

Instead, Søland points to the commercialized mass culture as providing the basis for the new ideas about modern femininity and their spread.[54] Film, given its dominant position, came primarily to influence its environment with regard to clothes fashion as well as a lifestyle that idealized movement and physical energy.[55] Søland describes a clear connection between the influences of popular film and the way in which young Danish women assimilated the new lifestyle, which was a stark contrast to the sedentary, bourgeois, Victorian ideal for women.[56]

The modern ideal—involving movement, energy and insistence on participating in public amusements—led to conflicts that the young women solved by undermining older, more traditional values. In this way, they also took a step away from the private and into the public sphere.[57] Like in Sweden, young Danish women left school at the age of 13 to 14 and usually worked until they married. Unlike their brothers, they often had to help with household work. As a consequence of industrialization, however, a clearer division into leisure and working time developed. During the war, the male-coded breadwinner salary made itself felt, thanks to various temporary cost-of-living allowances. Because young women had begun to earn their own money, they thought—inspired by the men in the family—that they had a right to their own spare time. "Going out" (walking, window-shopping, skating, swimming, or visiting a cinema, café or a free Sunday concert in the park, etc.) became a new popular activity.[58]

There was a risk, however, that young women out on their own would be mistaken for prostitutes. The tactic used to avoid such a risk was for several women to go out together. But there was also considerable uncertainty as to the boundaries between good and bad. Neither parents nor teachers, clergymen nor advice columnists could provide any clear answers. For this reason, young women were often forced to make their own decisions, and thus to set up their own limits for what was and was not allowed. It was not really *what* they did that determined how they were judged as much as with *whom*, *where* and primarily at what *time* of night they did it. By maintaining the distinction between good and bad girls, and by being careful to maintain that they were good girls who just wanted to have fun, they were able to resist all the criticism against young women's entrance into public life.[59]

According to Søland, however, setting up new boundaries led to a conflict with young men, who asked themselves how this new woman was to be treated: like a man or like a woman? The women thought the young men were impudent and lacking in gentlemanly manners. The men, in turn, asked themselves why they should be gentlemanly toward women who were supposed to be their buddies. Why should men open doors for women and escort them home if men and women were now equals?

On the one hand, women regarded men's traditional, restrained conduct as a kind of sexual safety valve, and when men didn't want to continue behaving in that way, a conflict arose. On the other hand, gentlemanly behavior was associated with power and control of women, who were expected to return the favor with submissiveness. But the young women did, in fact, pay their own way, which could be perceived as a threat. The flip-side of the conflict—which has survived to the present time—was that women came to be perceived as sexually provocative in their fashionable short skirts. Men's "uncontrollable" sexuality became a threat and, thus, the notion was created that women who dared to appear in public had only themselves to blame. As Søland sees it, this opposition was reproduced as a misogynist gender conflict in the popular culture. I will return to that conflict as well.[60]

Youth Culture?

The fact that young women had stepped out into public life and were exploiting the growing entertainment culture meant that young men also took the same step. In 1959, Mark Abrams published a pioneering work on teenage culture that, almost mythologically, positioned the emergence of a completely new youth culture and its material prerequisites in the 1950s. However, because these prerequisites already existed during the interwar period, the appearance of a new youth culture should instead be tied to that transformative period.[61]

The supply of entertainment in the 1920s would not have grown had there not existed certain financial and material prerequisites, which can be summarized using four factors: work, money, overcrowded homes and evening leisure time. Most young people who left school at the age of 14 or 15 began to work. Young women were engaged in paid work more between the ages of 14 and 25 than during any other period in life. As mentioned above, most young people continued to live at home owing to the serious housing shortage. However, they did not contribute all their income to the household, but paid only for room and board. Thus, they had money to spend on leisure time amusements. There is evidence to suggest that men and women had about the same amount of money to spend.[62]

To be sure, young people were not alone in spending money on pleasures, but youth of both sexes (and their money) came to have an increasing influence on the supply of films and, to some extent, on the films' orientation. This becomes clear if we look at the constantly increasing number of advertisements in Swedish fan magazines during the 1920s. The advertisers paid for commercials in forums through which an expected clientele could be reached. Thus, advertisements give us some indication of which groups read the magazines and went to the movies. A number of products targeting young people were advertised: dance halls featuring jazz music; engagement rings; face cream to fight blackheads; film schools; and whitening toothpaste.[63]

One reaction to young people's increasingly visible consumption were the grievances advanced by the moralists. Film was not the only scapegoat here: there was also the odious "negro jazz" from the U.S. But film was often denounced as the evil tool that spread all this wretchedness. The fact that young people were inspired to take on such innocent styles as the short haircut à la Gloria Swanson, to sew their own clothes to keep up with recent fashions, perhaps to buy a hat, or hold a cigarette like Douglas Fairbanks did result in furious denunciations from adult moralists. The whole development was regarded as objectionable because it showed clear indications of an undermining of the home as an institution and, in the long run, the fall of traditional society. The moralists would rather have seen young people's money being saved for a future normative marriage that would consolidate the conservative order. However, youth wanted something different, which caused a conflict between the generations. In this context, censorship was highly inefficient in the wake of rampaging consumption.[64]

This phenomenon, in all its complexity, can be illustrated by an example from the period: the trial against and commotion surrounding Swedish actor Einar Hanson in the fall of 1923. Hanson was charged with having caused the death of a female passenger in an automobile accident. Naturally, the involvement of a well-known actor in a car accident resulted in publicity. However, the direct cause of the commotion was that *Filmjournalen* used Hanson as a cover boy the same week as the trial began. This prompted Erik Lindorm from the newspaper *Social-Demokraten* to write an angry article in which he expressed his rancor over Hanson and the movie-star culture, like that in the U.S., that had made its way to Sweden. At the outset of the legal proceedings, the Christian daily *Svenska Morgonbladet* launched a downright crusade against Hanson, film, the unsound celebrity cult and the young people who cherished it. The scene in which Hanson was led into the courtroom was described as follows:

> A silent murmur is heard from the crowd and, as if obeying an order, all the girls turn around. Now a veritable cult ceremony begins, devoted to the new god of the time. With eyes glowing of sensuality and excitement, they devour their idol. Their cheeks flush, their lips form small trembling smiles, their hands rush through their hair (is it in place?). With giggles and quiet laughs, which reveal their immeasurable joy, the girls bring their incense-offering to "the divine one."
>
> It is disgusting, it is filthy. And it does not make matters better that the same spectacle would have been enacted in any town where the trial had taken place.
>
> It has been said that the boxer and the screen actor are today's gods. What happened on Tuesday in the court house in Strängnäs provides evidence for that statement. Others say that the youth of today are on their way toward complete demoralization. The girls in Strängnäs demonstrated that there is good reason for this statement as well.[65]

Through the description of youth as completely demoralized, the function of film as a tool of evil becomes explicit. However, reports of this kind caused many other daily newspapers to react. On the one hand, this demonstrates film's association with the emergence of a new mentality comprising the star cult and consumption; on the other, it reveals the schism between traditional and modern values. *Svenska Morgonbladet*'s reaction against the new "idols," *Social-Demokraten*'s attack on Einar Hanson, and other newspapers' counter-responses illustrate the "fascinating juggling act" referred to by Peter N. Stearns in connection with the great societal changes that took place at the beginning of the 20th century. This came to light in particular in the bewildered conclusion of *Filmbladet*'s article on all the commotion: "The anger of the Saints' Paper [*Filmbladet*'s sarcastic renaming of *Svenska Morgonbladet*] is understandable. As we know, they have long considered the cinema the devil's deception. But what about *Social-Demokraten?* Its staff's unreasonable rage at the main diversion of the masses seems more mysterious and less justified."[66]

However, workers were not the only social group going to the movies. The film magazines contained advertisements for jewelry, fur coats, cars and grand pianos—items intended for the upper middle and the upper classes—again suggesting that the cinemas were visited by everyone.[67] But the working class made up the overwhelming majority of the population, and thus dominated cinema box offices. The fact that working-class youth spent time and money on pleasures instead of education and personal improvement gave rise to left-wing criticism against film and youth similar to that leveled by the church.[68] It is no wonder, then, that *Social-Demokraten* took the opportunity to aim a blow at the cinema nuisance. It is thought-provoking, however—as well as a very good example of the equivocal logic of consumption—that the same newspaper had a standing advertisement in *Filmnyheter* that read: "Moviegoers! Read the reviews in Social-Demokraten!"[69] They knew, of course, that many work-

Einar Hanson on the cover of *Filmjournalen* the same week he was involved in a car crash that killed a young woman (*Filmjournalen* No. 37, 1923).

ers went to the cinema. In addition, *Social-Demokraten* advertised regularly in *Filmbladet* and *Biografägaren*, claiming that their paper was the best advertising medium for cinema owners, the reason being that everybody knew it was read by the working class; in other words, by the majority of people at the ticket counters.[70] On the whole, movie advertisements provided the most important of the daily newspapers' advertising revenues during the 1920s.

Advertisement for jewels and pearls in the fan film magazine *Filmnyheter*, something which indicates that the middle and upper-middle classes also went to the movies during the 1920s (*Filmnyheter* No. 39, 1922).

The Increased Body Awareness of Both Sexes

The slim body ideal, and thus the tyranny of dieting, also appeared at this time, as it became important to look good in clothes. As a downside of the greater media influence, Søland claims that femininity came to be stereotyped. Health, activity, an energetic body and a charismatic personality became the norm for what a woman should be like. Film played an important role in creating the new modern female ideal and its associated body awareness.[71] This is evident at an early stage in the film magazines' articles on fashion as well as in features on dieting, where film stars describe how they keep in shape through a regimen of strict diet and exercise.[72]

Yet the increased body awareness that followed in the footsteps of clothes fashion also included men. This has seldom been considered, however, a major reason being that mass consumption was subjected to extensive moral criticism at an early stage, and that this criticism was specifically aimed at women. Mass consumption was thus coded as a weakness, as something feminine, whereas thriftiness demonstrated strength, i.e., masculinity.[73] This gender dichotomy has proved to be extremely persistent, even though there have been many historical examples of men with an interest in clothes and fashion; for instance, the 18th-century dandy.[74]

The notion thus implies that men cannot be interested in fashion, clothes or the body, and that men passed unaffected through the period that, in Søland's view, was so revolutionary for young women. Plainly stated: This notion is false. The fact is that, up until 1945, Swedish men spent more money on clothes than Swedish women did.[75]

Young men (and men in general) were influenced to the same extent as young modern women were when Sweden transitioned from a production-based to a consumer-oriented society. This does not mean that men and women were affected in exactly the same way. But there is no question that a change took place. I doubt, however, that this should be interpreted as some kind of crisis for men and masculinity, though several researchers have come to such a conclusion.[76]

Advertisements aimed specifically at men increased with each year during the 1920s. Here an advertisement for soap claimed that any man could find success with women if he is suitably clean (*Filmjournalen* No. 17–18, 1929).

In the film magazines' fashion and dieting stories, but not in their advertising, there was a preponderance of women as intended readers, but there was also considerable talk about men's bodies and their interest in fashion—talk that increased from year to year.[77] One example is an article in which one of the greatest film stars of the 1920s, Douglas Fairbanks, describes his rigorous slimming program, stressing "that a man who allows himself to get fat lacks character."[78] As a

The American actor George O'Brien, stark naked, in a typical ideal pose inspired from ancient Greece (*Filmjournalen* No. 11, 1927).

kind of proof, the film magazines contained many photographs of Fairbanks, often stripped to the waist and with flexed muscles.[79] But Fairbanks is not the only undressed male film star figuring in the magazines.[80] The clear trend in the Swedish fan magazines is that, during this ten-year period, many photographs changed from being of appropriately dressed to more undressed and even completely nude people, both men and women.[81] In this regard, we see a great discrepancy between magazines and films, the latter being rigorously controlled (by Swedish state and American moral censorship). In films, nakedness—particularly female nakedness—occurred extremely infrequently during the 1920s. The difference was due to the fact that the magazines were not subject to pre-censorship. This allowed some scope for exploiting the "sensational" in relation to the film industry, its stars and their nudity, which could then be linked to the films themselves.

The lavish magazine *Våra nöjen* was first published in 1925. Intended for a somewhat older, pleasure-seeking metropolitan youth, it featured stories on film, sports, dance, music, fashion, literature, radio, theater and art. In the magazine's policy statement, we can read the following: "*Våra nöjen* wishes to share with its readers of both sexes not only the whims of ladies' fashion but also the more or less peculiar contrivances of men's fashion."[82] Thus, this increased body awareness—commercially mediated through film, advertising and other mass media—greatly affected men as well. We can talk about a stereotyped picture of masculinity. However, whereas Søland holds that a stereotyped picture of femininity became the norm, I am more inclined to discuss male stereotypes in the plural—and this pluralism should also apply to women.

2

An Enemy of Civilization
Children and Youth

> Swedish youth of today do not have the boorishness and diffidence that characterized the older generation when they were young. The youth of today are frank and secure. Film has perhaps contributed to this decided progress to some extent. Swedish youth of today know considerably more than young people did in, say, the year 1900.[1]

The last shivering autumn months of the 1920s were passing when the editor of *Biografägaren* (*The Cinema Owner*) confidently stated that Swedish youth were more advanced now than before and that film had probably contributed to this. The difference from the constant apologies heard only ten years earlier is remarkable. Something had happened to children and their relationship to film.

That same year, Gunnar Bjurman, head of the Swedish Board of Censorship, debated with a cinema owner about the lack of children's films in the cinemas. Bjurman felt that red films were not the same as children's films, and that it was not the fault of the censorship board "that far too few films are produced for a child audience." In the U.S., there was an economic basis for making children's films, but most of those films were not "suitable for children, according to any Swedish assessment with a sense of responsibility."[2]

In his reply, the cinema owner maintained on the basis of daily observations that children below 15 years of age were far ahead of the censor, and that the red films that were let through, cut or uncut, were substandard because "children, too, require a story in a film." He also thought that society was developing at a furious pace and that "with only minimal powers of observation, one must understand that children, too, are part of this tremendous progress." The cinema owner therefore demanded that the censors should have more confidence in children's ability to assimilate films. As an example, he mentioned a scene from Charlie Chaplin's *The Kid* (1921), in which the little boy (Jackie Coogan) breaks window panes to provide more work for his foster father, a glazier (Chaplin). "As an *isolated scene*, it was reprehensible, *but the overall impression redeemed the more or less illegal acts carried out in the films.*" Finally, he likened Prince Guatama to children, believing that Guatama, who was to be protected from all evil, would not have become Buddha had he not slipped out to see all the misery in the world.[3]

The representatives of the cinema owners thus took an optimistic view of children's development, according to which children could assimilate films and make their own decisions. In this way, film would function as a kind of preschool of reality in which good and bad exist side by side. By watching films, children could learn, through training, to recognize the difference between good and bad. However, this provocative line of thought was not to be paraded around at the beginning of the 1920s, a period in which the discipline model overshadowed the optimistic outlook on development.

Not one single film intended exclusively for children was produced in Sweden during the whole of the 1920s. Instead, the red films could be characterized as family films. In some of the films that were made, however, children of both sexes had principal or prominent roles. What is interesting, and at first somewhat surprising considering the period's moralistic attitude towards children, is that the children's roles, almost without exception, portrayed young rascals and rogues who defied authority. Why were children given such roles? And why were most of these films so successful among both adults and young people?

Boys, Masculinity and Douglas Fairbanks

Linguist Sally Robinson discusses a thought-provoking paradox connected to modern ideal masculinity. According to her, male self-control, as manifested through character-bound "silence," may not mark powerful masculinity at all. Instead, it may be a symptom of weakness and nervous strain—coded as hysterical feminine characteristics—and, thus, a sign of male emotional blockage. Robinson regards this silence as detrimental to the male body/mind. By drawing attention to two competing truths that have structured male experience during most of the 20th century, she wishes to reveal the origins of this blockage.

The paradox between the two truths is that normative masculinity, based on control, iron will and restraint, constituted the foundation of civilization, white supremacy and power. By means of this idealized silence, the upper and middle classes could hold on to their power. However, the upper and middle classes began to worry about their own, less physical masculinity as the economy turned towards consumption, and as the working classes (immigrants and Afro-

Americans in the U.S.) became increasingly visible through their embodiment of a more physical, primitive masculinity. Accordingly, the middle classes came to long for a more primitive masculinity, whereas the working classes adopted the civilized, silent one. The paradox is that the two competing truths of what represents "real" masculinity became, and still remain, quite unclear.[4]

In four thematic case studies, film and gender scholar Gaylyn Studlar has studied how masculinity was represented on the silver screen in the 1920s. She does this by analyzing America's greatest male silent movie stars—Douglas Fairbanks, John Barrymore, Rudolph Valentino and Lon Chaney. The book title, *This Mad Masquerade*, alludes to the fact that the roles played by these four stars were adapted to deal with and correspond to the period's changed gender relations and social expectations; but it also alludes to what Studlar refers to as *transformative masculinity*. She uses the films of the four stars as a mirror of society; she does not see in these very popular movies a fixed ideal masculinity cast in one and the same mold, rather she sees the masculinity of the 1920s as an ongoing and changeable process—a negotiable construction.[5]

In the U.S. of the 1920s, there was considerable concern about the new consumption-based feminized masculinity. As regards the paradox of the two competing truths, it was probably expressed most clearly in the films of Fairbanks and Valentino, the difference being that Fairbanks was primarily thought to appeal to boys and men, whereas the films of Valentino were regarded as a direct concession to the female audience.[6] However, this division by sex is far too simple to be compatible with the pluralistic reality of film. Naturally, women went to watch Fairbanks's films, and men went to watch Valentino's. But if we look at the study of children's film habits referred to previously, we find a great difference in that four times as many boys preferred adventure movies—and Fairbanks was the greatest adventure movie star of them all.

Fairbanks's masculinity was strongly linked to body and muscles, a fact made evident by the recurrent dieting and exercise features in the film magazines. Fairbanks's masculinity was athletic, but it was also childish. In his films from the 1910s, he continually played a middle-class tenderfoot from the urbanized eastern U.S., who, through various adventures, got to run, jump, hit and smile his way to a more virile and powerful masculinity, without ever losing his gentlemanly manners. In this way, Fairbanks came to combine Robinson's two truths in one and the same idealized and, as it happened, highly popular masculinity. Childishness was part of this actor's youthful personality, which had not lost an ounce of its instinctive boyish eagerness and desire to explore. He was a man who, through his physique and personality, became every boy's wishful dream and the model adult men used when they looked back at their idealized childhood.[7]

Contemporary commentators linked the new consumption to increasing civilization and bureaucratization, which were said to lead to a more feminine America in general, and to the feminization of masculinity in particular. Another cause of overcivilization was thought to be women's assumption of greater and more visible responsibility for bringing up the children, while the men were, at least in theory, at work all day long. Given only feminine models, the children—primarily the boys—became soft, irresolute and feminine.[8]

To remedy this "crisis," an abundance of publications appeared putting forward theories of character formation. The contents of these publications were largely based on nostalgic retrospection on the "wilder, more primitive time" that had preceded the consumer society. This was also linked to boys' more natural and primitive instincts, which were now to be encouraged instead of civilized. Among the best-known reformers were ex-president Theodore Roosevelt, Robert Baden-Powell and, of course, Fairbanks. For some time, a veritable "boy cult" sprang up, in the wake of which a number of boys' clubs were formed. These clubs were to restore boys' dawning masculinity; the best known is probably the Boy Scouts of America.[9]

In this context, people's great faith in the direct developmental link between boy and adult man was clearly expressed. But while the reformers attempted to construct the men of the future, they emphasized just as forcibly, or even more so, the idea that boys have an inner primitive and natural core that must be allowed to develop. The reasoning is not unlike that which Swedish moralists pursued with alarm when they tried to demonstrate the unwholesome link between crime in popular culture and children, as well as the possible consequences of this connection in adulthood. However, the crucial difference was that the Swedish moralists sought to discipline the inner core.

This "boy cult" existed in Sweden, too. A number of boys' clubs were started, not least the Swedish Scout Association, which was founded in 1912 with a culture-critical and antimodern program intended to save Swedish youth and make real men out of boys.[10]

Ethnologist Bo Nilsson has studied how masculinity was created rhetorically during the first decades of the Swedish Scout movement. According to his studies, a great gender uncertainty arose in connection with structural changes in society at the beginning of the 1900s; and this uncertainty gave rise to a need to publicly discuss the meaning of both femininity and masculinity. Nilsson considers the Scout movement and its rhetoric to be a symptom of this gender uncertainty.

A Boy Scout was expected to be independent, proud, strong, conscientious, diligent, humble, obedient, helpful and courteous. He was expected, in particular, to bear in mind his duty to God and Country, and to willingly obey his parents, teachers and superiors. However, if a boy was to become or do all this, his "natural" instincts would first have to be given free scope through games and physical activity, intended to strengthen his body and, thus, shape his inherent, markedly male character. Or, as one of the leaders of the Scout movement put it: "It is a bad sign when boys are too nice and well-behaved during puberty. Such behavior may suggest some kind of infantilism."[11] Another example of this current of thought is Emil Norlander's highly esteemed, best-selling novel from 1901, *Andersson's Kalle*. The main character of this novel personifies the ideal of the instinctively mischievous boy.[12]

Worth considering here is the observation that both the Scouts and *Andersson's Kalle* appeared before the war. This, and the fact that consumption did not fully catch on in Sweden until the interwar period, would seem to indicate that thoughts about the overcivilized boy/man were in circulation on an international level.

As the 1920s drew on, Fairbanks began to appear in increasingly large-scale productions. This meant that only one Fairbanks movie was released each year. Naturally, the result was great expectations among his fans, as shown by the enormous attention paid to the premières of his films all over the world. Another interesting aspect is that Fairbanks's leading characters continued to be sons trying to prove their masculinity to their fathers through character-building, athletic escapades. However, the plots were transferred from modern times to the past. Studlar interprets the ideal-typical boy-man's shift to historical costume films as a retreat, where traditional male values were left alone at a time when new demands were being made on masculinity. Among other things, this was made evident by the fact that the childish man was no longer considered capable of coping with the new modern femininity.[13]

One example is *The Black Pirate* (1926), in which Fairbanks played the nobleman Michel, the only survivor of a pirate attack in which his father was murdered. Washed ashore on a desert island, he swears that he will avenge his fathers death. Then the adventure starts. Michel begins by defeating the pirate captain in an honest sword duel; then he captures a merchant ship single-handedly. Through these physical feats, he becomes the bloodthirsty pirates' new captain. Onboard the merchant ship, there is also a princess (Billie Dove). Michel takes a fancy to her and has to protect her constantly from the pirates' primitive lusts. He also uses his cunning to prevent the pirates from completely massacring the crew of the merchant ship. This all develops into an interplay between bourgeois, controlled masculinity and the more powerfully muscular masculinity. In the end, the weak are protected and evil is defeated. Having taken his revenge, and having proved his physical masculinity, Michel receives his reward in the form of the princess, whom he has not yet approached. Thus, his controlled masculinity is established before we see the obligatory, chaste final kiss.

The film gave the audience a good dose of "the princess and half the kingdom." Thus, it was a fine example of a male nostalgia trip in which adventure and guileless chivalry could be given full expression in the absence of real-life pressures. But this is not to say that the Fairbanks ideal, even when fictitiously moved to the past, did not have a great impact on the thinking about boys' masculinity during the 1920s. The editor of *Filmbladet*, Karl Lundegård, expressed this clearly after having seen *The Mark of Zorro* (1920):

> Because for us blasé and overworked poor humans, Doug has meant—at least in his best films—speed and dash, energy, and the courage to face life. We have learned from Doug never to lose our temper, never to lose heart. There has been an air of fairy tale and adventure about Doug. In his presence, one has forgotten about life's dullness and sullenness. Fresh, strong winds have blown from the screen over the rows of seats. I am sure that, for thousands of young boys, Doug's agile jumps and leaps over small and large buildings have been an exciting example. Lively games have ensued among the boys after watching Doug at the cinema. And we Swedes and our Swedish youth are particularly behind the times when it comes to physical culture. For example, what do our university students do to keep their bodies young and fit? Absolutely nothing! If you visit a university or high school in England or America, the first thing you are shown are trophies from sporting events.[14]

This reasoning is identical to that of the boy reformers. And, at a general level, a similar line of thought would come to influence how boys were portrayed in Swedish films from the 1920s. This was not, however, a matter of simply copying from the U.S. and transferring to Sweden, but of a complex aggregate of factors. The discipline model, an optimistic outlook on development and the two truths of masculinity fought for public space both inside and outside the world of film. And in the middle of all this, the period's complicated attitudes towards children, youth and consumption were making a muddle of traditional social structures as well as views on the sexes.

Rascals

Andersson's Kalle—The First One on the Field

> When today's children have grown up and, in their turn, mean to impress on their children by telling them what exemplary children they were, all that those kids will have to do to catch them out is to consult the film archives.[15]

The first in a series of films about young rascals produced in Sweden in the 1920s was the now-lost *Andersson's Kalle* (*Anderssonskans Kalle* 1922), directed by debutant Sigurd Wallén and written by Emil Norlander, the author of the original novel. Like the novel, the film is built around a number of loosely connected pranks perpetrated by Kalle to take revenge on the neighborhood's gossiping old women. In their turn, the gossipmongers give Kalle a good thrashing when they get hold of him. The story is told through these old women—how they have been the victims of Kalle's revenge, or how they have given him such a whipping that he "couldn't sit for three weeks." The themes of the novel are somewhat misogynous, and the feminized husbands have nothing on their gossiping wives. Only Kalle, who keeps his "natural" behavior intact, can stand up to them.[16]

A new company, Bewefilm, was set up to make the film. The whole enterprise was risky, with a new director and unknown actors, given that most new film companies went bankrupt after one film. In addition, a good deal of resistance on the part of the moralists was to be expected, as Kalle did not behave like an ideal boy should.[17] On the other hand, the novel had been a success ever since it appeared 21 years earlier. Also, when deciding to make the film, the filmmakers were probably influence by the success of American child film stars Jackie Coogan and Wesley Barry, who made their entrance at the beginning of the 1920s.[18] In other words, the filming of *Andersson's Kalle* was done at an opportune time. To appease the prevailing morals, censorship norms and film conventions, however, the filmmakers had to revise the original story.

There are two main differences between the novel and the screenplay, and both have previously been attributed to film conventions. This is, however, not quite correct.[19] Instead, it was a combination of film conventions and censorship that redirected the film away from its somewhat anarchical path, that of "natural" boyish behavior toward middle-class, controlled security.

The original Swedish rascal and Sweden's first child film star, Gösta Alexandersson, as Andersson's Kalle (*Anderssonskans Kalle* [1922]/B Wahlströms förlag/courtesy Swedish Film Institute).

At the opening of the film, Kalle knocks down a sweet little girl, Ann-Mari Graham, whom he falls in love with and admires at a distance—between pranks. In the final film version, he even saves her from drowning. As a reward, he gets to move in with the rather well-to-do Graham family, who intend to take care of him and bring him up to be a capable boy. These two conventions, love and the happy ending, became almost obligatory during the 1910s, when film was developing its narrative style. The chaste love story is not part of the novel; Norlander added it to the screenplay, probably as a kind of glue to hold the loosely connected pranks together. Also, the original screenplay included neither Kalle's rescuing of Ann-Mari nor the Graham's "rescuing" of Kalle. Instead, the film would have ended with Kalle carving his and Ann-Mari's names on a tree, still without really having made any contact with her and, thus, with his "natural freedom" intact.[20]

The reason the film ended as it did was that the censor demanded deletion of a scene in which Kalle acquires by trade a stick of dynamite.[21] The result was that reel 3 had to be cut out in its entirety. Originally, this was the part of the novel in which Kalle plays Spanish-American War by taking Mrs. Boberg prisoner in the washhouse and tying her to a chair with the stick of dynamite under it. The reel was cut because all the excitement of the mischief would have been lost had the audience known from the beginning that it was just an ordinary spool, not a stick of dynamite, that Kalle had received in the trade. So that the film wouldn't be too short, an entirely new act—reel 6—was added. In this act, Kalle rescues Ann-Mari from drowning and gets to live with the wealthy Graham family.[22] In this way, the censor managed to maneuver Kalle toward the "right" masculinity, i.e., the controlled, middle-class variant.

However, it was another scene entirely that caused the moralists to lash out and cry for a ban on the film. In reel 5 (originally no. 4), Kalle is supposed to help Mrs. Boberg move. In the process, a mirror, a basket filled with china, a lamp, a rocking-chair, a hatbox and a plaster statuette are broken, among other things. Kalle's mistake is that he unintentionally places the items on the horse-drawn furniture cart in such a way that it is actually the movers who break them. Kalle acts without thinking; in other words, with boyish impulsiveness. When everything is loaded, he happens to startle the horses, causing the rest of the household goods to fly every which way. This is followed by the intertitle: "It's remarkable how much a boy can accomplish. What had taken Mrs. Boberg thirty years to acquire, Kalle turned to rubble in twenty minutes."[23]

The scene was subject to indignant comments in almost every newspaper review; in a couple of them, even the censor was blamed.[24] One left-wing paper writes: "The film is for a general audience, but should not be, because it includes the anti-social and, educationally speaking, destructive story of Mrs. Boberg's moving."[25] In other newspapers, the scene was variously characterized as "crude and unsavory."[26] The criticism spilled over onto the debate pages, where moralists took the opportunity to point out the connection between film and society's depraved youth. A mechanical engineer, Anders Rosberg, wondered: "Imagine what an example this sets for young adolescents to hear their fathers and mothers and other adults laughing loudly and approvingly at this extreme coarseness in the company of children. It is hard to imagine them laughing later, when their own kids follow this example, one recommended by the 'film censors' and their own parents."[27]

On account of this, the newspaper *Svenska Dagbladet* asked a number of experts for their opinions on the matter. Chief elementary-school inspector Karl Nordlund felt that *Andersson's Kalle* was "so grotesque and exaggerated that it can hardly be viewed as an example a young audience would consider worth following." However, Swedish Scout leader, Major Ebbe Lieberath, defended the film: "Whoever is disturbed by this film [...], firstly, does not understand boys and, secondly, has no sense of humor. The film is completely harmless."[28]

Otherwise, the film got good reviews and, despite (or, perhaps, because of) the moralist attacks, *Andersson's Kalle* became a gigantic financial success, recovering its expenses 14 times over. This makes the comedy one of the most financially successful in Swedish film history.[29]

Kalle was played by Gösta Alexandersson, a working-class kid just over ten years of age, who, for the next few years to come, would be Sweden's first real child star. We have seen how both the novel and the film portrayed this character as an impulsive, natural and still-unspoiled boy. But we have also seen how Kalle came to be hemmed in by and pushed toward controlled, middle-class masculinity. Yet what were people's actual ideas about boys and masculinity at the time?

In his memoirs, Sigurd Wallén has related how he, almost mythically, found his juvenile star at an audition:

> He was just standing there, looking at them to find the best representative of the guild of young rascals, when a thin little young man came marching into the room. The child had a plucky and impertinent expression as he looked calmly around the room. As all the seats were occupied, he walked straight ahead and sat down quite plainly in the "boss's" big director's chair.—Aha, I thought, this must be my "Andersson's Kalle."[30]

Once again, the spontaneous character of the rascal is held up as something good. It is contrasted to the obedient and well-bred behavior of the remaining 20 boys, all of whom had gone through several auditions and been singled out from a thousand applicants.[31] The reviews also used words such as "fresh"[32] and "natural"[33] to describe Kalle/Gösta Alexandersson. Not one reviewer had anything bad to say about the freshness of the boy's behavior except, of course, in connection with the moving of Mrs. Boberg.

The screenplay also contains some highly interesting connections showing that the film medium had become a great source of inspiration for the fresh and "natural" boyhood ideal—a phenomenon not exhibited by the novel, for obvious reasons. The opening of the screenplay states: "The boys chase Kalle, who jumps over carts, barrels, slides down handrails, etc., finally he climbs up on a roof, runs across the roof." Here Wallén, the director, has added in pencil: "Kalle poses as Chaplin, then switches to Douglas Fairbanks." And then in parentheses: "(He had many ideals ... Chaplin was one.)" In addition, Norlander mentions several times in the screenplay that Kalle has been inspired by something he saw at the cinema.[34]

Another striking thing is that not a single review comments on the scenes in the novel or the film in which Kalle gets licked by the gossiping women. The film contains a scene in which five of the women take turns whipping Kalle with a carpet beater so hard that he can't sit for three weeks.[35] Today, this scene would quite simply be called child abuse and never be presented as a comical feature. Slapstick comedies were also extremely popular at the time. Most popular of all was Charlie Chaplin, whom the Swedish moralists had long considered the most abominable of all movie stars.[36] In this connection, beating up children was not regarded as odd in the slightest, particularly when it was a matter of checking boys' "naturalness."

The above-mentioned Karl Nordlund asked a boy who had watched *Andersson's Kalle* if he thought the film was immoral. The boy answered: "No, because the boy got such a licking."[37] Norlander, too, defended his creation, saying: "He must get a thrashing and he does, all according to an excellent rule: Even if he *hasn't* played a prank, he *will* play one or more."[38] Boys' "natural" behavior was, thus, a sign of good health, but this kind of naturalness could use a bit of control, thereby a constructive beating. However, it was not considered equally beneficial when naturalness was affected or damaged by something less "natural" than a carpet beater.

Boyish Masculinity vs. Consumption

Andersson's Kalle was preceded by a publicity campaign that was unusually extensive for Swedish film, and that featured, among other things, full-page advertisements in the film magazines.[39] This was not a new phenomenon. American film agencies had used the same strategy for several years. The novelty was that boys and girls were increasingly being highlighted in advertising and news stories as the films' great stars. There were even reportages from the children's homes.[40] When Bewefilm used this strategy, the result was great success at the box office. Naturally, this meant continuation and development of the strategy, not only in connection with the sequel *New Pranks by Andersson's Kalle* (*Anderssonskans Kalle på nya upptåg*, 1923), but in the film branch as a whole. In this way, children and their gender came to be commercialized.

In *Pricing the Priceless Child*, Viviana Zelizer presents a thought-provoking discussion of children and their (in the eyes of Western society) problematic connection to economy and money. In her opinion, children had been transformed from being economically valuable, owing to 19th-century child labor, to being increasingly economically worthless during the 20th century. At the same time, their emotional value had increased, only to reach as yet undreamed-of heights. From this ensued a conflict between proponents and opponents of child labor. The proponents pointed out the economic and moral benefits of a child working instead of being idle; work built character. The opponents, on the other hand, wished to protect children from all things commercial, as these could be detrimental to their souls. To the opponents, children had become sacred. After a long, complicated and very heated process, the opponents of child labor finally came out as winners in the 1930s and 1940s. This was, however, only a half victory, because these economically worthless but emotionally invaluable children now lived in the consumption society that had emerged during the long-standing conflict, and the very development of this society had contributed to the vehemence of the conflict. In a consumption society, economy and money play a more direct role in everyday life than they do in a production-based society. This transition gave rise to, among other things, a rather complex situation in which parents gave money or presents to their emotionally invaluable children to show them their love.[41]

We have already learned from all the tirades that children had achieved a degree of sanctity and thus needed to be protected from popular consumption. However, the explicit mix-up of economic interests and children made in the Swedish film industry served to fan the flames, which is evident if we look at the contemporary discussion on "natural" boyish masculinity.

Already in connection with *Andersson's Kalle*, some newspapers complained about the "roaring publicity"[42] that had preceded the film; they also complained that the young Alexandersson's "natural assets" had been partly ruined by all the praise and advance publicity.[43] For the sequel, Gösta Alexandersson was used for publicity purposes in a direct manner; in the Stockholm cinema Olympia, he entered the stage before each performance, greeting the audience with a "hello." In addition, both he and nine-year-old Aino Schärlund-Gille, who played opposite him, appeared frequently in film magazines and daily newspapers before the opening performance. This caused Wolodja (a pseudonym) to write a lengthy contribution attacking the celebrity cult of children, claiming that "this foolish vulgarity" was detrimental not only to the portrayed children, but also to the children watching the films: "I have seen girls' as well as boys' rooms decorated entirely with film portraits, revealing that all their money has been spent on 'flicks.'" This applied not only to children from poor homes, but also to children from well-to-do and respected families. Children should not believe that they were stars, and they should not waste their money on an unattainable, false dream.[44]

In *New Pranks by Andersson's Kalle*, we can see how the main character and the plot were influenced by the criticism. If Kalle's antisocial behavior in the first film was accepted and even applauded as a kind of natural counterweight to society's increasing feminization, then the adaptation depicted in the sequel was problematic given its direct connection to masculinity and consumption.

In the sequel, there is less mischief—mainly what is left over from the novel, though there are a few newly invented pranks in connection with Kalle's sojourn in the upper class. Recall that, at the end of the first film, Kalle was "rescued" by the Graham family. The first half of the sequel shows the problems he has adjusting to his new environment, with all its nice clothes, manners and school attendance. One of Kalle's few real acts of mischief (that is to say pranks not owing to his want of practice) takes place when he—with intertextual reference to *L'arroseur arrosé*—steps on a water hose, leading to the same, comical outcome. On the other hand, what is given room, to some degree replacing the pranks, is the emergence of another side of Kalle's character. For example, when he happens upon some boys pillaging a bird's nest, he gets into a wild fight defending the nestlings. Shortly afterwards, he discovers his mother is ill—the same mother who, in the first film, became "giddy with joy" over the one-hundred-krona note she received for giving up Kalle.[45] He leaves the Graham family immediately to take care of her. Back home, he roots up his old rags and begins cleaning and washing the dishes. "Mama, I don't belong in that nice house. I only caused trouble there anyway. I'll stay home now and care for you," he tells his mother, who weeps with joy. This change in Kalle is explained in an intertitle: "Andersson's Kalle is not quite the same as before. The 'civilization' of the Grahams had not failed to leave its mark on him; he had acquired new interests, which he had never before cultivated." These interests include his beginning to read books and to mend galoshes to earn money for the household. Now and then, this is interrupted by the occasional act of mischief, but essentially, Kalle has been transformed into a conscientious boy with clear connotations to middle-class, controlled masculinity.[46]

By and large, *New Pranks by Andersson's Kalle* was less favorably received than the first film. Moreover, it was not nearly as successful with audiences. Could this be because the film played down and adapted boyish masculinity? Judging from comments in the newspapers, the problematic union between "natural," impulsive boyishness and a controlled masculinity of firmer character becomes clear enough. The sequel was thought to "have such an arranged and affected tone that it misses its purpose altogether—to be funny. To the same extent that the previous 'Kalle movie,' despite a certain crudity and exaggeration, was fresh and bubbled over with cheerful boyish spirits, the sequel is mediocre and empty."[47] On the other hand, a couple of reviewers expressed their appreciation of the fact that the second film was not as crude as the first one.[48] Also, many had positive views about Kalle's new ambitious character and "compassion for his 'mom.'"[49] In the well-chosen words of *Stockholms Dagblad*, Kalle had become "moderately roguish."[50]

Even a class perspective was apparent among the reviews. A critic for the right-wing newspaper *Aftonbladet* wrote: "At the beginning of the film, Kalle has been thrown into a setting he does not fit into for natural reasons and owing to innate habits."[51] This is interesting, because the detour into "high society" made in *New Pranks by Andersson's Kalle* was one of just two such examples from the rascal films made in the 1920s. All the other films were enacted in and all the main characters came from the working class. Couldn't filmmakers or society at large even imagine this "natural" behavior in middle-class boys—boys who, according to the rhetoric of the boy reformers, really needed to be more masculine? As shown by Wolodja's horrified outcry about the poster-covered walls in well-to-do boys' and girls' rooms, middle-class children at least watched the films and idolized Kalle or Fairbanks just as much as the working-class children did.

Pirates of Lake Mälaren—*A Class Perspective on Boyish Masculinity*

A couple of months after *New Pranks by Andersson's Kalle*, the next film based on a book for boys had its première. This time, the film was *Pirates of Lake Mälaren* (*Mälarpirater*, 1923), based on a novel by Sigfrid Siwertz. The screen adaptation, an expensive and large-scale production, was made by Svensk Filmindustri (SF), Sweden's leading production company. The fact that an established company with great resources was behind the production was evident from the large-scale advertising campaign that preceded *Pirates of Lake Mälaren*. The campaign included a publicity stunt in which Gustaf Molander, the director, was said to be looking for "dashing youngsters" of both sexes for the shooting. Ads were put in all major daily newspapers and film magazines, and on the 15th of April, 400 "film applicants" gathered in Röda Kvarn in Stockholm for an audition. This was obviously more a stunt than a serious audition, because Molander selected only a few extras out of the four hundred young people. All important roles were instead given to actors with previous experience. Nevertheless, the gimmick was a success because it was surrounded by so much publicity.[52]

The filmed version of *Pirates of Lake Mälaren* differed considerably from Siwertz's popular original from 1911. The reason was that Molander and SF wanted the film to be for general audiences. They adapted the novel very freely, simply removing any sensational features, such as murder or alcohol consumption, without ceremony. Really, only the basic framework of the original story was used in the film: Three boys—orphaned brothers Georg and Erik and chimney-sweeper's son Fabian—run away from home and their mean, indifferent parents. For a whole summer, they drift around as "pirates" in a boat on Lake Mälaren. In the novel, the boat is stolen, whereas in the film, it is found adrift after a storm. As a kind of compensation, the obligatory love story was added to provide a framework for the boys' adventure in the film. There was no trace of this in the original.[53]

The novel contains a toned-down class perspective that found its way into the film. In the film, however, this perspective was accentuated to the point of becoming a clear conflict, which is relevant to our discussion of the two competing truths about masculinity. Siwertz's toned-down class perspective in the novel favors adulation of the more homogeneous, "classless" ideal boyish masculinity that was typical of the period, as exemplified by the Boy Scouts. Twelve years later, the film version literally visualized the difference between controlled, middle-class masculinity and a freer, more "natural" masculinity.

Fabian, the chimney-sweeper's son (Tom Walter), is introduced as "the terror of the town." When we first see him, he is sitting in a tree, playing a prank by lowering a frightened kitten down on a string so it will set its claws in the toupee of a man standing below. In addition, Fabian's obscure background is deliberately emphasized by fitting him with dark, bushy and uncombed hair as well as worn-out clothes. In contrast, the orphaned brothers Georg and Erik (Einar Hanson and Albert Christiernsson, respectively) are presented as well-groomed, well-behaved boys dressed in suits. Their deceased father was an author. On the first day of their summer holiday, we learn that the father's brains had passed on to Georg, who receives top grades at school.

Georg and Erik live with their uncle, the mayor of Granhälla, and his wife. The mayor has a problem with alcohol and card-playing. Neither he nor his wife is overjoyed about taking care of the boys. Like in a work of Dickens,' the brothers have to chop wood and go without food until, one day, the mayor's wife insults their dead father. This is the reason Georg and Erik run away from home, with Fabian.

The actual conflict begins when the boys find the boat, the *Vindrosen*. The lazy Fabian immediately takes command. Sitting down and smoking a cigar, he bosses the others about, making them serve him for three stormy days. Onboard the boat, they find a shotgun and canned food. They eat the food despite some hesitation on Georg's part; it is not, after all, their food. When the storm calms down, they get hold of a newspaper. Here they discover that they have been officially declared dead by drowning. Fabian suggests they take advantage of their freedom, and let their parents sit at home and mourn as a punishment. With great enthusiasm, the boys agree to carry out this plan.

Subsequently, a couple scenes follow in which Fabian is portrayed as a careless fellow whose clothes become more and more ragged. Georg, on the other hand, is depicted as well-behaved; he wears clean, untorn clothes. They quarrel about who should sit at the rudder. As they go ashore one day, the conflict turns into a fierce fight, cowardly started by Fabian but finally won by Georg. While Fabian sits crying at the water's edge, an intertitle reads: "And from that day on, he was just a low and wretched implement, a fawning Caliban." Controlled masculinity thus wins by a knockout.

A bit later, Fabian steals a chicken. When he is discovered by the Count of Tollerö, he begins lying, while the two nice brothers stand beside him, ashamed. In the novel, however, Georg felt great admiration for Fabian's lies.[54] The Count takes a good look at Fabian and says, in a way characteristic of the period: "You do have a pleasant physiognomy!" This racially stereotyped way of reasoning becomes even more evident when the Count locks the three boys up in the castle's cellar. This is visualized through Fabian alternately crying and fiercely attacking the locked door, while Georg sits quietly, waiting to see what will happen. When Fabian has calmed down, he starts making ugly faces. Through the use of dissolves, his head is toned over into a chimpanzee head, a very immediate metaphor of his uncontrolled brutishness.

Finally, the boys manage to escape from the castle, chased by dogs. When Fabian and Erik reach the boat, they find that Georg has fallen behind. Fabian doesn't care, and forces Erik to come along, leaving Georg on land. Owing to a previous complication, the Count's daughter Rose is already on the boat. Fabian takes advantage of the situation by kidnapping her and sending a blackmail letter demanding 1000 crowns, signed "An enemie of sivilizashon." While the Count is conferring with the boys' parents—who quarrel among

The three young pirates on board the yacht *Vindrosen*. From the left: George (Einar Hanson), Erik (Albert Christiernsson), and Fabian (Tom Walter) (*Filmnyheter* No. 33, 1923).

each other about whose boy has got the others into this mischief—Fabian dreams about "the wide expanses of the oceans" and "the promised lands of the Wild West." Finally, Fabian decides to go to America, abandoning the boat and leaving Erik and Rose locked up in the storage locker. As luck would have it, Georg arrives—on a white horse—and saves both of them.

With Fabian out of the picture, Georg and Erik decide to accept their punishment. In the meantime, however, Rose manages to persuade her father, the Count, to take care of the brothers instead. Upon finding this out, the boys' foster parents are overjoyed. The film then jumps ahead one year to a fancy-dress ball arranged on the occasion of Georg's high school graduation. In the crowd we find Erik, dressed up as a pirate, à la Fairbanks, and attracting the attention of girls his age by relating tall tales of last summer's manly adventure. Outside, on the doorsteps, Georg and Rose are united in the film's final kiss.

In contrast to the hearty working-class kid Kalle, Fabian in *Pirates of Lake Mälaren* actually becomes an enemy of civilization, despite the fact that both personify the same "natural," impulsive and ideal boyish masculinity. This outcome is tied to the fact that the middle-class sons Georg and Erik come into the picture as rivals. Thus, Fabian's fresh boyishness is transformed into a distorted countertype that emphasizes the manly virtues of the controlled middle class. From this point of view, we can say that the impulsive boyish masculinity applauded in Siwetz's novel from 1911 was about to be run over by "civilized" masculinity. At the same time, however, we can also observe that Georg did not become a man until he used violence to thrash Fabian; thus, even Georg's self-controlled, middle-class masculinity was transformed into a harder and more "natural" masculinity. The question is, however, whether being an enemy of civilization was a good thing—as a way to counteract the increased feminization of society—or whether it was bad to be an enemy of civilization, meaning that one was in favor of increased civilization, consumption and a more feminine masculinity. There is no doubt that *Pirates of Lake Mälaren* presents the latter alternative; and at first sight, the reviewers seemed to agree.

Pirates of Lake Mälaren received gushing reviews, proclaiming the film "a masterpiece of Swedish film art"[55] and "a Swedish film for Swedish boys."[56] Note that, in the 1910s and 1920s, calling something "Swedish" essentially meant handing out the very highest mark of distinction. Moreover, many reviewers breathed a sigh of relief over Molander's tempering of the "less agreeable elements" of Siwertz's novel.[57] On the other hand, many others thought that the original was a "splendid book for boys"[58] just as it was. But it becomes even more interesting when we look in greater detail at how the reviewers discussed the hero, Georg, and the rascal, Fabian. In view of the plot of *Pirates of Lake Mälaren*, and of the unanimously favorable reviews, Georg (Einar Hansson) should get first prize. But as a matter of fact, Fabian (Tom Walter) wins by a landslide:

> To be sure, of the three he is the rascal; he lets himself go whole-heartedly into his role, rolling his eyes, cursing, bossing about, bullying the others as well as doing various nasty and unsporting things. But despite all that, he has a certain rough sense of humor and a dash that makes one wish the director had added at least a suggestion that the young man would eventually develop and improve himself a bit. However, he puts on a good performance [...] and is extremely well trained gymnastically, agile and quick.[59]

Here, the physical link to impulsive boyish masculinity, à la Fairbanks, is made explicit. As a comparison to the softer, middle-class masculinity, the same critic described George as "lively, genial and, above all, handsome, of course," adding that he had a little too much of theater in him.[60] In other words, the conception of how a boy should be—spontaneous, impulsive, spirited and natural—applied better to Fabian than to Georg.

One circumstance that probably contributed to the negative attitude toward Einar Hanson was the considerable media exposure he received for *Pirates of Lake Mälaren* and *The Blizzard* (*Gunnar Hedes Saga*, 1923), as well as the great commotion surrounding the trail following his car accident that same year. Thus, his soft masculinity was already associated with consumption and the "unsound" celebrity cult. This is an example of a new connecting link, a kind of intertextuality, that was created between the real people and the characters they played; this phenomenon arose when mass media coverage increased at the beginning of the 20th century.

Alternative Boys and Girl Rascals

The impulsive rascal also appears in minor roles in *The Queen of Pellagonia* (*Drottningen av Pellagonien*, 1927) and *Jansson's Temptation* (*Janssons Frestelse*, 1928). However, children's participation in Swedish films of the 1920s was a relatively unusual phenomenon. Disregarding films in which children of both sexes only had a decorative function, it is difficult to find alternatives to the rascals in the predominant "little rascal" film genre.

One example of a somewhat more important, alternative role is that of Putte (Lauritz Falk) in *The Norrtull Gang* (*Norrtullsligan*, 1923). In this film, Putte is a clean and orderly, rather quiet boy. He is a well-mannered child in a grown-up world. The primary function of the character is to be mistaken for an illegitimate child. Another film with children in important roles that is worth mentioning is *The Children of Fortune (Lyckobarnen*, 1926). This film is about five orphaned children who go out into the world to avoid ending up in the workhouse. Unfortunately, the film has been lost, as have both the screenplay and the program sheet.

The most interesting alternative to the predominant boyish masculinity is instead to be found in two other films: *A Little Rascal* (*En rackarunge*, 1923) and *Boman at the Exhibition* (*Boman på utställningen*, 1923), the essential difference being that, in these films, the leading roles are played by girls.

A Little Rascal is based on a novel from 1919. The orphan heroine Ann-Mari (Elsa Wallin) is placed in a vicarage in Småland where she is to spend the summer. As an inveterate big-city kid, she has a hard time adapting to life in the country. Ann-Mari's mischief is of the impulsive kind: she laughs in church, eavesdrops, drives a log in a slip, scares the housekeeper with rats, and runs down or cycles over Silverclou, the vicar, on numerous occasions. During the early reels, we see a great difference in how she is treated in comparison to the boy rascals. Each time Ann-Mari is to be punished, the scene ends and the penalty is imposed outside the picture, so to speak. Later on in the movie, she is told off for soiling her clothes in a water fight. As a punishment she is sent to her room, where she is supposed to read the Acts of the Apostles. Once in her room, however, Ann-Mari secretly reads love and adventure stories, with titles such as "Queen of the Parachute. Mistress of the Air" ("Fallskärmens Drottning, Luftens Härskarinna"), which inspire a jump from the roof and a passage through the air with an umbrella.

Ann-Mari tells the other children in the yard what to do. She initiates all the mischief. One example is her excursion to the Värnamo fair, when she entices a younger boy, Rudel, to follow her. Ann-Mari's impulsiveness is at least as intense, or hearty, as that of the boy rascals; it is even physical. On the way back from Värnamo, Ann-Mari and Rudel get a lift with a drunken farmhand who has been cheated into buying a blind mare. When he realizes this, he begins to whip the horse recklessly. Both Ann-Mari and Rudel fly at the farmhand to stop the ill-treatment. Rudel holds his legs while Ann-Mari beats him until he calms down and apologizes.

There are, however, distinguishing gender codings. Whereas Andersson's Kalle pretends to be Douglas Fairbanks or Charlie Chaplin, a wedding is staged at which Ann-Mari and Rudel get married. In *A Little Rascal*, even the unruly Ann-Mari is pushed toward the morally correct path after she meets Josef, a murderer who beat his uncle to death because of the latter's cruelty to his hunchbacked daughter. Now, however, Josef has atoned for his crime. In the village, no one is willing to acknowledge Josef, and because of this he plans to go to America. Ann-Mari becomes Josef's friend, which results in a row at the vicarage. Ann-Mari then willfully decides to give her confirmation money to Josef. She makes a fiery defense speech before the dumbfounded residents at the vicarage. The film ends with Josef being able to leave. When he says farewell, Ann-Mari does everything she can not to burst into tears—"she tried to behave like a man"—but then she cries anyway.

A female rascal is no more meek and mild than the boy rascals. There are clear similarities between these portrayals, the common denominator being the positive enterprising spirit thought to characterize the optimistic outlook on development held by children and youth of both sexes in the 1920s. However, *A Little Rascal* gave rise to very mixed reactions. In half of the reviews, Ann-Mari was thought to have the "sparkling temperament of a boy rascal."[61] The other half complained that "her various tricks seem to be carefully prepared and crafty"[62]—in other words, not as natural and impulsive as boys' pranks were thought to be.

Boman at the Exhibition was not, strictly speaking, a rascal film. Rather, it was a feature made to display and take advantage of the Jubilee Exhibition in Gothenburg that took place in 1923. The film was directed by Karin Swanström, the first woman to helm a forma Swedish feature. However, *Boman at the Exhibition* did contain elements of a rascal film through Brita (six-year-old Ann-Marie Kjellgren), who is a lodger in a tailor's house. The tailor's wife treats Brita and her faint-hearted husband very badly; she even beats them. Brita's only friends are the dog Napoleon and a perpetual student, Boman, who has a drinking problem. One day, Brita happens to find out that the tailor and his wife are not her real parents. It turns out that she is an illegitimate child who had been given up because her poor mother had not been accepted by her father's wealthy mother. Brita's real mother had gone to America, and her father—who had broken with his mother—had followed her. Now, however, their ship is to return to Sweden. Brita asks Boman for help. Together, they go to Gothenburg to find her parents.

Here, too, the youthful enterprising spirit becomes visible through the young Brita, who plays a number of pranks. Among other things, she pricks the tailor's mean wife with a needle and takes—with Boman's help, to be sure—the initiative to run away from home. At the Jubilee Exhibition in Gothenburg, Brita becomes separated from Boman, but immediately makes friends with a shoeshine boy. Together, they explore "The Children's Paradise," which was an actual part of the exhibition and which featured swings and roller coasters. The money for these pleasures comes from the shoeshine work. The two children realize that they get even bigger tips when they smear their faces with shoe polish to look like "darkies."

Next to Boman, Brita is the most important character in *Boman at the Exhibition*. However, this was not reflected in the reviews. Even though she received an A+ in *Svenska Dagbladet*,[63] most reviews mentioned her only in passing or not at all.[64] What is the reason for this silence? Is it linked to gender? At first glance, the answer is no. However, in an interview with Ann-Marie Kjellgren, an ironic angle emerges that first makes fun of her young age, and then ridicules her contribution to the film.[65] In my view, however, this has more to do with age than with gender. This, in combination with the silence of the reviews, indicates that there existed an age limit below which children's work or position in the public was not acceptable. This is in accordance with the problematic connection between children and money discussed by Viviana Zelizer. Film historian and former child star Diana Serra Cary (Baby Peggy) also holds that, at the time, there was great resistance to child stars making money. There were two reasons for this: the phenomenon challenged the sanctity of childhood, and there were strong suspicions about parents of child stars who lived off their children's work.[66] In Sweden, the wages for children in film were negligible, but the moral principle was the same.

The young girl rascal Brita (Ann-Marie Kjellgren) and the dog Napoleon in *Boman at the Exhibition* (*Filmnyheter* No. 36, 1923).

Even if film representations of male and female rascals were relatively equal, the considerable difference in frequency should be emphasized. The presence of boy rascals gives rise to a genre in which girl rascals merely constitute an exception. The small number of girls' roles was also explained in terms of the "natural" fact that girls lack "the at once courageous, chivalrous and callow fumbling qualities of a boy" and are, for that reason, unsuitable for rascal films.[67]

The last rascal film of the decade, *Ville Andeson's Adventures* (*Ville Andesons äventyr*, 1929), contained all the usual ingredients. Ville Andeson (Sune Holmqvist) is a working-class kid with peering eyes and his cap turned back to front. He plays soccer in the streets, tars gossipmongers to the pavement and gets a great deal of thrashing. In the film, Ville comforts his mother when his working-class father drinks away all the money. The only real novelty is when the Andeson family goes on an amusing camping trip, a plot element that, for a change, ridicules big-city dwellers in a setting unnatural to them—the Swedish countryside.

In the reviews, Ville's behavior was, as usual, commented on as being somewhat "hearty."[68] However, all of the fierce and divided reactions were absent. Instead, *Ville Andeson's Adventures* was pointed out as a film intended specifically for children.[69] This, too, deviates from the great adult interest in rascals and boyish masculinity observed just a few years earlier. At the end of the 1920s, what used to be a controversial mixture of moral attacks and adult mens' nostalgic reflections on the past seems only to consist of a nostalgic longing for a mystified and "natural" childhood: "Because [the rascals] take us back to the time when we were young, before we had become men of the state. [...] But we always have something on our conscience—something deserving of punishment and reprehensible, but which we now look back on with quite a bit of sympathy and not just a little sadness."[70]

There is no doubt that ideal boyish masculinity was affected by the mechanisms of consumption. Some saw it as corrupting, whereas, in the opinion of others, it was an improvement that created more enterprising young people. The fact that wilder and, in some cases, antisocial behavior was accepted from boys is thus linked to the idea that the civilization of society is unwholesome. In other words, the more controlled, middle-class masculinity, which has been taken as the predominant form of masculinity in earlier research, was being subjected to severe competition.

The Complicated Road from Boy to Young Man

Students

"Does she admire only film stars?"

"Of course not [...] but film *stimulates an interest in purely superficial phenomena!* If film did not exist, there would be no shingle haircuts or short skirts or this bloody jazz from morning to night! [...] You certainly cannot deny that almost all films are set in luxurious places [...]!

"Clearly, film may play a small role in what you call a craving for luxury, but it is a very small part [...] And there is *one thing* that our young jazz girls can learn from the film stars: the art of moving in a stylish and balanced way. And the jazz boys, too, can learn from Valentino *et consortes* for that matter!"[71]

In the 1920s, male youth in films was almost always synonymous with a student. If a young man played a leading role in a movie he was, with only a few exceptions, either a university student or else he had newly graduated (or failed to graduate) from high school. In contrast to portrayals of boys, which were almost exclusively set in a working-class environment, young men were depicted in a middle-class or upper-class context. Why was this the case? Could it be that bouncy boyish masculinity, which was seen as a sign of good health in boys, was not considered a proper ideal for young men about to shoulder the heavy responsibility for the country's future—a responsibility for which self-restraint and control were the bywords and in which there was no more room for impulsive passion?

In connection with the première of *Carolina Rediviva* (1920), a drama portraying the student environment around Uppsala University, a couple of articles about Swedish university students were published in the film magazines. In the first article, Swedish and foreign students were compared. According to the writer, the "perpetual student" is a typically Swedish phenomenon—and being Swedish, it was turned into something good: an "educational foundation lacking in more specialized students who are hurrying after a fast career."[72] In the second article, too, the rush and tear of the modern student was discussed as something new. On account of the "erotic adventures" in *Carolina Rediviva*, the writer also brought up another novelty that had invaded the university: "Her Majesty, the Woman." Female university students could be divided into two groups: "Those who just study and those who study as well as flirt." Here, reference was made to a Swedish female writer who had stated recently that "the Swedish man is a piece of ice when it comes to eroticism; he is not interested in the woman, he only cares about Swedish arrack punch." However, the writer asserted that this might possibly be true of "some circles in our country, particularly in small towns and in the countryside," but that it was not true of university students at the time. The writer had had the opportunity to observe that male and female students met as well as flirted frequently, albeit under controlled conditions.[73]

There is no doubt that the modern frenzy was seen as a problem for those elderly gentlemen who nostalgically compared it to their own time at the university. Women's admittance to the universities, however, was seen as something positive, even if it was associated with "eroticism." The question is whether the perceived rush could be characterized as a youth problem? Was the entrance of these young women into public life seen as a problem for young masculinity?

The Careless Young Man

The Gyurkovics Family (*Gyurkovicsarna*, 1920) provides the decade's first example of a young male student. The film is based on a popular novel by Hungarian author Ferenc Herczeg. It is a comedy about the Gyurkovics family and their 12 children. Most of all, it circles around the eldest son, Géza (Gösta

Ekman). The first time we meet him, he is studying for his examination along with his brother. The brother reads aloud while Géza sits, poised to write down the answers on his new white spats. However, he changes his mind, throws the pen away, saying: "No, damn it, I won't smudge such nice spats. If I don't pass, I'll just put a bullet through my head." At the same time, his father receives an expensive bill for the spats, and angrily announces that the money will be deducted from Géza's monthly allowance. Protesting against this unparalleled injustice, Géza takes to his bed, absolutely refusing to take the examination. Finally, however, he is pulled out of bed and dressed forcibly by two of the headmaster's assistants, who then drag him to a waiting carriage. Trapped, he sticks his tongue out at them in childish defiance.

Géza is not representative of controlled, middle-class masculinity, but rather a typical example of a somewhat more adult version of impulsive boyish masculinity. He behaves like a spoiled child who is more interested in expensive, fashionable clothes than in assuming responsibility. To solve this problem, Géza is enrolled in the military, where, according to tradition, boys become men.[74] In this case, the military are the Mounted Hussars, which, at that time, had the showiest of uniforms, well suited to a fashion-conscious dandy like Géza. Among other things, there is a scene in which Géza stands in front of a mirror, admiring his uniform. In his imagination, he is quickly elevated to higher ranks, and the mirror image shows uniforms of increasing garishness.

In the military, he continues along the same lines, playing regular pranks. He falls in love with the daughter of a choleric colonel, runs away with the general's wife, gets involved in reckless adventures meant to impress, challenges people to duels, and during all this, is constantly threatening to shoot himself if he doesn't get his way. Géza is simply incorrigible; in contrast to the general tendency in the rascal films, in which boyish masculinity is channeled toward a more controlled masculinity, this film follows through with the theme: Géza never grows up. The film ends with the brother, not Géza, marrying the colonel's daughter. When the camera finds Géza among the guests, he is standing there with a mischievous smile, thinking: "She is pretty, but if I had been forced to marry her, I would have put a bullet through my head."

The Gyurkovics Family was a great success with audiences. In the reviews, Géza/Gösta Ekman was described in the same terms of approbation used to refer to impulsive boyish masculinity: "fresh"[75] and "natural."[76] Thus, we have here an example of the careless young man with a very clear connection to idealized boyish masculinity. What made *The Gyurkovics Family* stand out was that Géza's childish masculinity was carried through so consistently.

Two films, *Thomas Graal's Ward* (*Thomas Graals Myndling*, 1922) and *Kalle Utter* (1925), returned to the theme of the young male student who does

The careless young man, Géza (Gösta Ekman), looks rather coquettishly at his reflection in *The Gyurkovics Family* (*Filmjournalen* No. 10, 1920).

everything except study, instead indulging in money-consuming pleasures. In both films, the energetic students are brought back to the fold, pass their examinations and, ultimately, settle down. Here, too, we find a similarity to the rascal films, with the possible exception of *A Little Rascal*, given that heterosexual normative marriage was at least hinted at the end of the films. The little rascals were, of course, too young to get married.

Thomas Graal's Ward begins with the aging Graal—who was the main character in two films typically considered to belong to the Swedish Golden Age, *Thomas Graal's Best Film* (*Thomas Graals bästa film*, 1917) and *Thomas Graal's Best Child* (*Thomas Graals bästa barn*, 1918)—nostalgically reflecting on his youth. Then we get to see his ward, Paul (Einar Axelsson), playing soccer, sculling and having a good time with his male friends. One day, Paul becomes "sick with love" when he meets Babette, a poor girl who dreams about nice clothes and film stars. Shortly afterwards, Paul passes his examination—"fantastic things do occur on occasion"—and, as a reward, he gets to borrow Graal's yacht. Paul and his friends immediately conspire to use the spectacular yacht to attract a beautiful and rich heiress who can support Paul. They sail to the Bjerre seaside resort, where Babette is also to be found. Both Paul and Babette lie about their respective wealthy backgrounds. This goes on for a few days until they part. When Graal hears the story of Babette, however, he realizes that her father is an old friend from his student days. The film ends with him bringing the two young people together. Moreover, he makes Paul his sole heir.

The film was considered very entertaining, presenting a realistic interpretation of student life that was "as genuinely Swedish" as it could be.[77] And Paul was both "dashing"[78] and "natural,"[79] but perhaps not to the same degree as Géza and various other rascals. It is evident that the films as well as the critics—of both sexes—regarded the male students' merry-making as quite normal. But was this actually the case? In literature advising young men on rules of conduct and etiquette, the authors constantly returned to three phenomena: passion, youth and character. Passion and character were thought to be connected in the sense that they were found inside the man. At the same time, they were each other's opposites, because passion had to be suppressed by one's strong character, which was created only through hard work; a strong character could only be achieved by controlling a man's baser elements—his passions. The picture became even more complicated when the concept of youth was brought into the discussion. The reason was that adolescence was the period when passions were strongest; it was also regarded as a transitional period during which the future man was to be molded. In the literature, then, the young man was faced with a choice between virtue and sin; if he made the wrong choice, he went straight downhill. In this way, character became the guiding male ideal.[80]

However, David Tjeder contrasts the ideal character to what real men have chosen to recall in their memoirs. He shows that moral abstinence in relation to passions was an ideal only found in the advice literature. In reality, men considered that drinking, gambling and having sex were highly masculine occupations, particularly during youth. Being masculine was instead a matter of making merry and managing one's studies at the same time.[81]

Here we find an explanation for the cult of boys and for the fact that idealized boyish masculinity was "naturally" transferred to the young man—which also explains the nostalgic popularity of the careless student. This view, however, came to be both influenced by and intermixed with the emerging consumption and entertainment culture. Whereas a man's character had previously been determined by hard work, during the 1920s it came to be equally marked by masculine fashion and consumption. In the films, this is evident with the addition of pleasures and consumption to the youthful passions. The film magazines discussed "male coquetry" and the fact that films equip men as well as women with new weapons in the form of stylish clothes and other consumer commodities, such as cars.[82]

A Modern Addition—The Young Count Wins the Girl and the Prize

The Young Count Wins the Girl and the Prize (*Unga greven tar flickan och priset,* 1924)—with Gösta Ekman playing the young count, Hans Lewenstierna—should actually be counted as one of the "careless fellow" films, but it also illustrates the conflict between the traditional and modern in a consumption society. This was also Sweden's first "car film," an action-film genre originating in the U.S., where the car and other modern technology were exhibited as an attraction and integrated into the plot.

The Young Count Wins the Girl and the Prize is set in an upper-class environment, something that the critic at *The Social-Democrat* could not refrain from pointing out when the film was shown: "Modern seaside resort life, playing golf, driving cars and other upper-class sports."[83] Gösta Ekman's portrayal of Count Hans is not totally unlike his portrayal of Géza in *The Gyurkovics Family.* Here, he plays the same mischief-maker, with a mania for stylish clothes and, above all, cars. This does not meet with the approval of his uncle, the Count of Stensiöö, who breeds horses and refers to cars as "bloody upstart mechanics." To irritate his uncle, Hans comes rolling in to breakfast one day on a pedal car. When he announces that he has signed up for a motor race, his uncle has the servants take Hans's car away, locking it up in a barn.

In Stockholm, we have the Countess Behrencrona, who lives with her equally car-crazy daughter Sonja (Anita Dorr). Sonja, too, has registered for the motor race. However, Countess Behrencrona wants Sonja to drive her to the town of Falsterbo, in the southern province of Skåne, the reason being that the Crown Prince and Princess are expected to be there. Sonja has no choice but to obey. After all, "Young ladies should be trained for marriage, not for car races!"

In Falsterbo, Hans and Sonja get to know each other and discover their common interest. Despite the resistance of their elders, they decide to take her car to the race in Stockholm. Then the film takes us on a wild journey through Sweden, north to Stockholm. The young people's escape is soon discovered by the Count and the Countess. They join forces, and with the help of the police and other contacts, they try to stop the two youngsters' journey. This constitutes the film's element of excitement, in combination with the attraction of the quickly passing views of the Swedish landscape. In Stockholm, the young couple win the race. However, just after passing the finish line, Hans has to steer the car away from a small child, and it overturns. But all ends well, and because Hans loses his driver's license following their mad drive through Sweden, he is even able to reconcile things with his uncle. The film ends with Hans and Sonja riding away on horseback rather than being propelled by horsepower.

In *The Young Count Wins the Girl and the Prize*, the filmmakers utilized the car and humor to create a conflict between old and new. Virtually every critic took the opportunity to point out the connection between the U.S. and modernity, adding that this was something new for Sweden. With regard to the pace of the film, some reviewers thought it was too fast,[84] whereas others found it to be too slow in comparison with American car films.[85] From a gender perspective, however, the lines of thought concerning Hans/Gosta Ekman and how they had changed since *The Gyurkovics Family* are more interesting. In *The Young Count Wins the Girl and the Prize*, he was still described as having "a boyish freshness and charm,"[86] but the implication of these words no longer has the same positive ring. "It would certainly have been more appropriate to give the task to a more masculine actor. It is at times difficult to distinguish Ekman's face from that of his female co-star—sometimes she is almost more masculine than he is."[87] Was this change perhaps related to the fact that Ekman had become feminized because in the film he "sometimes introduced new fashions for men,"[88] as one critic put it?

In comparison, Sonja/Anita Dorrs was mentioned only in terms of being "pretty, nothing more was needed." One appreciative reviewer went so far as to call her "a splendid female representative of the Swedish race."[89] This is a bit surprising considering that Anita Dorr's role was just as important as Gösta Ekman's. The role of Sonja was remarkably gender equal for its time, and she and Hans drove the car the exact same number of times over the course of the film. Are these two observations possibly linked to the retreat of the ideal-typical boy-man that Gaylyn Studlar points out in connection with the notion that the childish man was no longer considered capable of handling the new, modern femininity?[90]

The Orderly Student

In the same year *The Young Count Wins the Girl and the Prize* appeared, the country's high school students could choose "cinema and theater" as a topic for the national essay examination. When the essays became public, *Filmbladet* surveyed the material to try to understand the feelings and impressions that "the two culture factors gave rise to among the rising generation." A number of interesting opinions came to light, among other things that the cheaper prices at the cinemas were putting the live theaters out of business. Moreover, many of the essay writers praised "the great realism of film and its capacity to reflect real life without any flavor of the artificial." Another interesting observation is that the majority of students who chose to write about the cinema came from private schools.[91]

If the attitudes toward the careless young male student were ambivalent, then the same can be said of the orderly male student and his modern ideas. This ambivalence became evident in three films: two dramas and one adventure-comedy, with a direct connection to the contemporary consumption society. In *The Blizzard*, *The Counts at Svansta* (*Grevarna på Svansta*, 1924) and *His Royal Highness Does the Shingle* (*Hans kunglig höghet shinglar*, 1928), a young male student returns home from the university with his degree only to encounter different kinds of resistance when he tries to put his ideas into action.

In *The Blizzard*, Einar Hanson plays the leading character, Gunnar. The background of the film is that Gunnar's grandfather had been an itinerant fiddler before becoming rich when he moved a large reindeer herd south. With that money, he bought Munkhyttan, the large family estate. Gunnar admires his grandfather, and he too begins playing the violin. But his parents disapprove. They send their son to a technical university to be trained as a mining engineer. When he returns home, however, he continues his violin playing. A heated scene ensues in which Gunnar's mother breaks the violin. Gunnar then leaves the estate with a strolling company, earning his living as a violinist. Time passes; Gunnar now intends to save the insolvent Munkhyttan with the money he earned playing the violin. But one day he hears that it is still possible to earn easy money by moving reindeer herds south. He buys a herd with his savings, but a blizzard scatters the reindeer. Gunnar is severely injured. When he is brought back to Munkhyttan, he has lost his memory. The situation looks bleak until his sweetheart from the strolling company returns one day. Gunnar's regains his memory when she plays her violin. It also turns out that a few stones Gunnar found lead to a large copper deposit on lands belonging to Munkhyttan.

The story is complex. Here, the resistance comes from Gunnar's parents, who want him to be more modern, whereas he wants to follow in his grandfather's footsteps and pull off a traditional masculine deed in order to make some easy money. However, he is unable to carry out this feat and, what's more, he loses his mental edge. In other words, he doesn't measure up to the manly courage of the past and must content himself with falling back on his modern mining engineering degree, which is tied to controlled, middle-class masculinity.

The Counts at Svansta is, in many ways, similar to *The Blizzard*. Here, too, a young male student, Per (Hugo Björne), returns home to an estate upon completing his studies. This time, he gets into a conflict with his father, becomes mentally weak, but is ultimately saved by love. The difference is that, in this film, the conflict between old and young, traditional and modern, is depicted in an explicit manner. Per's father, the Count at Svansta, has conservative views—to say the least—on democracy and university studies. We, as well as Per, learn from the Count that democracy is just a modern contrivance that will soon fade.

And as regards reading books, this is a useless habit that Per must break himself of; he must begin working on the estate instead. However, Per, who has come home with a wagonload of books, opposes his father's wish. The conflict takes on still another dimension because Per has been in love, from childhood, with Elina (Magda Holm), a *tattare* child who grew up in the estate steward's home. But Per's father is against this love story, and one day he even attacks Elina, who falls into a rapids and disappears with the stream. Per witnesses the event. A fierce fight breaks out between father and son. The upshot is that both fall into the rapids and later fall ill. Per recovers, but when he discovers that his father has died, he becomes mentally deranged, barricades himself in his room, neglecting his appearance, clothes and everything. As a consequence, the estate falls into decay. Meanwhile, Elina has returned to the *tattare* camp in the woods, where she finds out that she is not a *tattare* at all, but Swedish. She returns to Svansta, and Per gets well immediately.

Both films portray the conflict between the traditional and modern as a conflict between old and young, with clear elements of an antimodernity that is primarily directed at the young men. It is also not difficult to see the symbolic significance of the family estate as a preserver of traditional society. In accordance with Mats Björkin's observation, both Gunnar Hede and Per have become feminized in the sense that they are not as tough as the imaginary construction of the supermen of times gone by.[92] They also represent the optimistic outlook on development to which Henrik Berggren calls attention. However, being impulsive boyish men, neither of them manages to handle "freedom"—they go mad. Doubtfulness concerning the masculinity of these characters was also shown by the reviewers. In *Svenska Dagbladet,* for example, Gunnar/Einar Hanson was described as "soft" and "sensitive." The reviewer could not hide his disappointment over the fact that Lars Hanson, a real man, did not get to play the role as originally planned.[93] Per/Hugo Björne was also described as "sensitive."[94]

The third student to return home is Nickolo (Enrique Rivero) in *His Royal Highness Does the Shingle.* This is a light adventure-comedy, one in a series of films made by the Isepa Company. These films constituted a collaboration between Sweden and Germany. They aspired to be in keeping with the times and modern enough to compete with American films.[95] This, and the fact that a few years had passed, is evident, as the friction between, in this case, grandfather and grandson is not portrayed quite as seriously as in the previous films. Rather, the grandson's enterprising spirit and modern ideas are met with resignation instead of open conflict. As a matter of fact, Nickolo returns home as a newly fledged Master of Arts in hairdressing, with expert knowledge of the shingle haircut. When the grandfather, who himself is a barber, hears about this he exclaims: "Do you think I let you study in Uppsala to become a barber!" The young Nickolo assures him with a smile that he only wants to be useful to and help him. He puts an advertising board in the show window that reads: "Shingle haircut done by newly arrived expert." It doesn't take long until the town's young girls are flocking around the hair salon and around the young, handsome Nickolo to get a haircut. When the grandfather sees the braids fall, he shakes his head with resignation. He sees a bottle of hair restorer for women on which it is written that, throughout time, women have had long hair and that this is the height of femininity. Here, however, is where the conflict between the traditional and the modern stops—with the young enterprising spirit coming out the winner.

The Relation to the Young Modern Woman

In *His Royal Highness Does the Shingle*, Brita Appelgren plays the role of the young, shingle-cut heroine Astrid; she got a shingle haircut in spite of her mother's fierce resistance. In the relationship between her and Nickolo, which ends in marriage, Astrid is also the winner, as Nickolo/Enrique Rivero is unquestionably the film's beheld object.

The modern woman appeared in several films, for example, in the abovementioned *The Norrtull Gang* and *The Lady Incendiary* (*Mordbrännerskan*, 1926). Here, however, I will focus on two other films, *A Housemaid Among Housemaids* (*En piga bland pigor*, 1924) and *The Girl in Tails* (*Flickan i frack*, 1926), in which male youth encounters modern femininity.

As shown in Birgitte Søland's study, young women found great inspiration in films, expressing their modern identity through consumption, as is evident from, among other things, the shingle haircut and short skirts. Short skirts had already begun getting shorter in the mid–1910s, but this did not prevent the debate on women's morality from flaring up on occasion. In a speech made in the fall of 1926, Swedish archbishop Nathan Söderblom attacked women's clothes and the loose morals they brought with them. A few days later, *Dagens Nyheter* published an article in which a male vicar, a male director-general, a male professor, and feminist author Frida Stéenhoff defended short skirts. The men's argument was: "I didn't know there were so many beautiful legs," whereas Stéenhoff wondered why only women should be moral.[96] Short hair caught on in Sweden around 1924–25. In an article in *Våra nöjen*, this new fashion was very distinctly connected to a modern feminine identity: "A little girl with long braids—she would only seem lost in the threatening environment of the capital, and I would like to see the Stockholm charmer who wants to court and seduce her in public and fashionable places."[97]

At about the same time, the difference between the young woman in films and the young woman in reality was a topic of discussion. According to the writer, women in films were already behind the times—they were much too good and innocent—whereas real young women "of the short-cropped, cigarette-smoking type are everywhere. [...] *She*, the modern one, is worldly-wise, she will appall you with her knowledge of life, no veiled insinuations does she utter, she brings delicate subjects up for discussion, doing so in terms so explicit they will freeze you."[98]

In *A Housemaid Among Housemaids*, Magda Holm plays Alice, a modern young woman who sleeps late, does gymnastics when she wakes up, and then goes and does the shimmy in expensive clothes. Her fiancé, Sven (Carlo Keil-Möller), disapproves of her lifestyle. They quarrel at the beginning of the film because he has had to wait for Alice to get up; and not long afterwards, he discovers her dancing the Slowfox with a Southern European dancing teacher in the restaurant Jazzil, where she is a regular customer. Raging with jealousy, he leaves the restaurant. The next time they meet, he presents her with an ultimatum: "Now you have to choose—either your sloppy, idiotic jazz lifestyle or me, not both!" He says, moreover, that "the simplest housemaid is worth more than you and those creeps put together." This is more than Alice can take; she breaks the engagement and throws her ring across the room. She regrets this, however, and as revealed by the film's title, she decides to take a job as a housemaid in the country to show her fiancé that she can manage it. What follows is a comical comparison between town and countryside, in which the countryside is mocked and the people living there are portrayed as complete idiots. But Alice adapts and learns to get up early in the morning to do the washing and take care of the animals. Finally, she makes friends with the people living on the farm. Meanwhile, Sven has also changed his mind. While looking for Alice at Jazzil, he meets the dancing teacher, whom he gives a good spanking. When Sven finds his way to the farm, it is his turn to be scared by the bull, while Alice stands alongside laughing, just as the farmers had laughed at her when she encountered the bull for the first time. At the end, while they sit on a wooded hillside, Alice asks Sven: "Are you satisfied with your little housemaid now?"—which he is, of course. Final kiss.

A Housemaid Among Housemaids received mixed reviews as a "light summer film." Many were upset over the negative representation of the countryside.[99] Somewhat surprisingly, however, the film became a success with the public, exceeding all expectations. This was probably because it tied into the then-current topic of the young modern woman. To be sure, the film ends with a restored gender order, given that Alice is transformed into a "real" woman. It was the strong woman's role, however, that remained on the reviewers' minds when they put their impressions in writing. Alice/Magda Holm was a woman "with guts."[100] She had realized the necessity of physical culture, exercise and carriage.

Alice's fiancé, Sven/Carlo Keil-Möller, on the other hand, was treated in a manner more in line with his outward appearance and well-pressed clothes.[101] We can see here how consumption "makes" the man, and this was not regarded as something positive: "Apart from his good looks he has yet another serious shortcoming: He will never become, as the Americans do, a gentleman with nice clothes on; he will always remain nice clothes with a gentleman in them."[102] Sven is, in other words, not a "real" man, even though the traditional gender hierarchy has been restored; and this is due precisely to his consumption, which weakens the "natural" masculine superordination. In all likelihood, this deviation was not intentional, particularly if we consider the fact that Keil-Möller himself wrote the screenplay for the film.

Two years later, *The Girl in Tails* appeared, again with Magda Holm as the main character: the young student Katja. The film was based on Hjalmar Bergman's then-topical novel of the same title, from 1925. Bergman also wrote the screenplay, the plot of which centers on a small-town scandal caused by Katja when she attends a student ball wearing tails, a garment coded as masculine.

In the film, which is set in a university environment, fashion, clothes and money constitute an important driving force. Katja, a good student, is helping a weaker student, Ludwig (Einar Axelsson). When she, on one occasion, complains about his mental inertia, he replies by criticizing her old-fashioned clothes. We then find out that the family's clothing account is spent on outfitting Katja's snobby brother, Curry. When Katja asks her father for 500 crowns for a new dress, he refuses point-blank, despite the fact that Curry just got a new tail coat. It is this tail coat that is significant in the film's central scene, where Katja simply borrows it from her brother and, in protest, arrives at the ball, dressed in tails. Once at the ball, she is treated with coldness and contempt. Ludwig tries to save the day by dancing her out of the ballroom. Out on the steps, however, they come across the old university president, who offers her his arm and the moral encouragement to go back inside. Once inside, she demonstratively drinks brandy, smokes a cigar and

"Snälla gossar dricka aldrig punsch!"

A cinematic example of a female cross-dresser. Katja (Magda Holm) jauntily smokes a cigar in *The Girls in Tails* while being approached by a male admirer (*Våra Nöjen* No. 37, 1926).

asks the other young women to dance—in other words, she not only wears men's clothes, she also does her best to act like a man.

Still at home, her brother discovers that his tail coat is gone. He tells his father, who goes to the ball and forces Katja to go home with him. Back home, Katja's father calls her a "hussy!" and she dissolves, literally, before his eyes. What happens next is that Katja takes refuge from the scandal in Ludwig's entailed estate, which is inhabited by a collective of learned women's libbers. There the couple gets into an argument, but in the end they get engaged.

Based on a speech Nathan Söderblom made around the time of the film, it is clear the film was as in line with current trends as it could have been. This is even evident if we compare the film reviews with the defense article published in *Dagens Nyheter.* In fact, most reviewers pointed out that the sensation of a woman in men's clothes did not really seem sensational at all.[103] One critic even wrote that Katja/Magda Holm was more gorgeous in a tail coat than not in one.[104] Otherwise, the words most commonly used to describe her character were the usual "cheerful"[105] and "dashing."[106] The young fashion-conscious men in the film, Ludwig/Einar Axelsson and brother Curry/Erik Zetterström, were, unfortunately, mentioned only in passing.

The misogynistic conflict that Søland claims was present in the contemporary popular culture is not observed at all in the film material. Instead, the above examples indicate the continued presence of a male self-confidence based on the "natural order" of the relationship between the sexes.[107] Occasionally, however, we see the glimmer of a feeling that contemporary society did not believe this new consumption-oriented young man would be able to deal with the enterprising young female spirit. More evident is the emergence of a generational conflict with clear ties to consumption that occurred both within and between the sexes. As we have seen in the various examples, it is nevertheless impossible to establish any exact lines, because opinions cut across all strata and could shift over brief periods of time.

Becoming an Adult

I have previously discussed the pluralism of film, and that it was primarily this pluralism that stood in the way of what we would today call "youth films." None of the films surveyed here can rightly be referred to as youth films. Nonetheless, young people of both sexes have a prominent place in them. In all of the films, adults of both sexes are also found. In an article in *Filmnyheter*, the presence of elderly actors in American-versus-Swedish films was discussed. The writer felt that Swedish films were more realistic because adults were still given about as much space as younger people. In addition, all "the older people are far from being saints or jovial or pleasant." The writer thought that, in American films, older people merely constituted the "idyllic" element.[108] This is, of course, an exaggeration. According to film scholar Heather Addison, early Hollywood films did play a role in creating a youth cult, but she also shows that the average age of the actors increased during the 1920s.[109]

In 1927, a film with the appropriate title *Youth* (*Ungdom*) was released. This film caused the critics to exclaim, "The young people have won."[110] However, this youthful victory was on a symbolic level in the opposition between old age and youth.

The film's youthful element consists of a marginally successful artists' collective of two young men and a young woman; Pontus (Gunnar Unger) and Lisa (Brita Appelgren) are a couple. The two men are artists, whereas Lisa is a dancer and a model who also does the housekeeping. Because they have no money, the two lovers are constantly quarreling. One day Pontus asks how he is supposed to work as an artist when he is "encumbered by a girl." Lisa, an independent young woman, then leaves Pontus, and applies for a job as a companion to a well-to-do elderly couple. She gets the job after performing a dance for the lady of the house, a performance that the unfaithful elderly husband Aron (Ivan Hedqvist) happens to see and that makes him fall immediately in love with the much younger Lisa.

In the meantime, lacking any artistic success, Pontus and his friend have begun working as motorboat painters. After a heroic deed—in which he saves a man from drowning—Pontus, too, is hired by Aron to paint the fences surrounding the shipowner's villa. There he runs into Lisa, who ignores him because she is flattered by Aron's courting. But Pontus endures, showing that he can manage a real job and help with the dishes. Eventually, Lisa, though not Aron, realizes that their relationship is untenable owing to the age difference. She returns to Pontus, they talk things over and decide to try anew. Youth and love have thereby conquered old age and money.

The film is a song of praise to the phenomenon of unspoiled youth. When Lisa chooses a poor but pure love, she also symbolically chooses to give up consumption and luxury. The fact that this choice was seen as a sort of ideal runs like a main thread through the reviews.[111] Interestingly enough, all the credit goes to Lisa—a young modern woman, but without the luxurious manners of consumption—who can thus be called an "unaffected representative of young girlish romanticism of a genuinely Nordic kind."[112] On the other hand, Pontus/Gunnar Unger was mostly seen as a disappointment, because he lacked "life and speed."[113] The film nevertheless has a down-to-earth and realistic perspective on a concrete problem of youth, with the young couple fighting over their lack of money—a common cause of divorce at the time.[114]

In *The Students at Tröstehult* (*Studenterna på Tröstehult*, 1924), the theme of the problem-filled transition from adolescence to adulthood is raised, this time from a more purely male point of view. At the beginning of the film, Karl Oscar (Nils Ekstam) is playing "mother and father" with the poor farm girl Ann-Marie. His father, the harsh Baron Brusenhielm, does not approve of this. Time passes, and the next time we see Karl Oskar, he is studying ecclesiastical history with Tobias (Edvard Persson), perpetual student and private tutor. But in reality, Karls Oskar is reading "The Diary of a Seducer" while gazing longingly at Ann-Marie through the window. Even the poor Tobias is interested in Ann-Marie, who is undecided concerning the two young men.

Karl Oskar passes his examination. He celebrates a very wet and jaunty night with Tobias and two other friends, one a student of theology and the other of Latin. They are then driven to Tröstehult, where they continue their celebration. The theologian vomits and falls into a milk barrel, while the Latin student flirts with Karl Oskar's sister—who, in one scene, asks Tobias for advice about love. Tobias also has a serious talk with Karl Oskar when he realizes that Ann-Marie is going to choose a rich future baron over a poor private tutor. Before parting, the four friends decide to meet again in ten years.

In the second half of the film, it turns out that the theologian has become a parson and a teetotaler. The Latin student has become an officer and is married to Karl Oskar's sister. Karl Oscar has inherited the title of baron and is married to Ann-Marie. They have a son. On the surface, the three gentlemen have managed the transformation from irresponsible boyish masculinity to a controlled, middle-class masculinity more in keeping with the ideals of the time. The only one who has failed is Tobias, who is now single—a shyster and journalist at a local newspaper. Below the surface, however, these men do not display any happiness over their "success" in life. Karl Oskar is unfaithful, and in line with the motto, "Like father, like son," he is also highly annoyed when his son plays with the servants' daughter.

When Tobias arrives at the reunion, he is at first refused admittance owing to his shabby appearance. Once inside the middle-class idyll, however, he serves as the pessimistic teller of truths who, among other things, advises the officer, "Watch out for the war, my man, you might easily get shot." He observes Karl Oskar's unfaithfulness and sees how unhappy Ann-Marie has become. After a confidential farewell talk between Tobias and Ann-Marie, she asks Tobias how things could have gone so wrong. He answers that "some trees grow crooked," then leaves Tröstehult. While Tobias is on his way, the film cuts effectively between him and happy pictures of midsummer celebrations, with people dancing around the Maypole.

The Students at Tröstehult raises and problematizes the transition from adolescence to adulthood in a way that, at the time, was unusually straightforward—first from a comical point of view, then more seriously, questioning the ideal position of controlled, middle-class masculinity. The emotional value of idealized youth thus acquires a wider significance than the purely nostalgic; it functions as a criticism of both society and ideal masculinity. The film's success was also reflected in the reviews, in which Tobias/Edvard Persson—a failure from the point of view of ideal masculinity—was praised for being "excellent"[115] and "the best",[116] whereas the representative of controlled, middle-class masculinity, Karl Oskar/Nils Ekstam, was simply "boring."[117]

3

Men with Emotions
Fatherhood and Love

> This happened, for instance, at a performance at Röda Kvarn in Stockholm during the first week of February 1921. The film *Go and Get It* (1921) so upset one middle-aged gentleman's nerves that he had to leave during the third act. His lady companion, who was reluctant to miss the end, tried for a long while to persuade him to stay, but in vain, "*He* really couldn't stand it." The example can be duplicated. It is remarkable that it was the man, not the woman, who experienced the nervous shock. One might think that the roles should have been the reverse. But times change, and we change with them![1]

This observation, made by Uppsala academic G. Halfdan Liander, depicts a man and a woman who do not react in accordance with a seemingly given gender pattern. Liander pointed out that the roles should have been reversed and denounced this adult man as unmanly because he could not sit through *Go and Get It.* This idea is in accordance with the picture of modern ideal masculinity found in the motto: Real men should not show their feelings. However, this notion does not mean they are emotionless. As for tears, Swedish gender historian Claes Ekenstam has shown that male and female manifestations of emotion are historically and culturally conditioned. Expressions of emotion cannot simply be derived from an essential core that separates men and women from one another.[2]

Emotions have received little attention in masculinity and gender research. This shortcoming can be explained by the fact that the power aspect that is part of gender analyses complicates the study of emotions. For example, it is difficult to place a man with emotions in a power structure because he will then, by definition, be coded as weak.

For this reason, bell hooks has criticized gender research, claiming that "feminist theory has offered us brilliant critiques of patriarchy and very few insightful ideas about alternative masculinity." According to hooks, the patriarchy oppresses not only women but also men, in the sense that men are not given any room to express emotions other than anger. She holds, therefore, that additional gender studies specifically focused on men are needed, not least in order to offer alternatives to the emotionally repressed, patriarchal masculinity.[3]

Feminist critics usually identify this emotionally repressed masculinity, which is equivalent to modern ideal masculinity, as harmful and as the cause of the masculine violence that affects women, children, and other men as well. The repression of emotions and the inability to love are traits boys learn at an early age. It is primarily from parents that boys learn how a so-called real man should behave.[4] hooks is extremely critical of the mass media's considerable influence in conveying this picture, particularly through film and television. At the same time, however, she points out that the mass media can function as a powerful tool for teaching alternatives.[5]

The notion that the media convey a biased picture of masculinity can be traced back to Laura Mulvey, and, further, to the theses of the Frankfurt School, which state that the mass media function through a one-way communication that serves to indoctrinate the masses.[6] In her study of fatherhood in Hollywood movies, film scholar Stella Bruzzi takes a critical stance on Mulvey's influence over feminist film research. According to Bruzzi, the lack of film studies that include fathers, as well as men with emotions, can be directly derived from Mulvey's psychoanalytically oriented theory, the reason being that this theory focuses entirely on analyzing phallocentrism, oppressive male gazes and sexualized female bodies. When the theory has subsequently been applied to men, the results have been studies dealing almost exclusively with muscular bodies, sex and violence—and almost never with fatherhood or other expressions of soft masculinity.[7] As a consequence of this gender-theoretical preconception, the barriers between the sexes are recreated and maintained. Exceptions, such as hysterical or effeminate masculinity, thus, tend to be discussed based on the notion that deviant behaviors constitute anomalies in the world of film.[8]

However, some backlashes have occurred of late. The explicit purpose of the anthology *Boys Don't Cry?* is to resist the traditional picture of masculinity. The editors discuss the truism that men develop complete control over their emotions by practicing emotional self-isolation. They consider it important to discuss the possibility of achieving change by exposing men's emotions to show that men have actually made use of emotions throughout history, but also because such a demonstration, per se, may help tear down conventional thinking about emotions and their gender coding.[9]

Historical research on fatherhood is sparse, too, particularly in Scandinavia. As a consequence, the notion of historical fatherhood primarily comes from Anglo-American research, which has focused on the father as absent, owing to industrialization, or on referring to the father as effeminate, as a result of the upgrading of motherhood.[10] This reasoning is based on the theory of the two spheres—according to which, as a consequence of social changes, men were at work while women stayed at home with the children—which has continued to permeate gender analyses at the theoretical level. For example, John Tosh considers that the transition to absent fatherhood can be dated to the end of the 19th century, and that men's flight from home can be explained by their unwillingness to be feminized.[11] In the social scientific, primarily sociological, research, this has often been put forward as an opposition between *cash* and *care*, meaning that the breadwinner and care-giving father roles are mutually exclusive.[12]

Historians Jørgen Lorentzen and Tomas Berglund have questioned how the theory came to be used to gender code parenthood.[13] One reason is that there is a temporal shift in the effects of industrialization in Scandinavia. Moreover, recent masculinity-historical research has emphasized marriage and fatherhood as possibly the most important criteria for being regarded as a complete man.[14] Berglund thus maintains that the depictions of absent and effeminate fathers are historically unfounded. In his thesis on Swedish fatherhood in the 19th century, Berglund shows that fatherhood was neither marginalized nor feminized, and that the ideal of soft fatherhood has a long history characterized by continuity. A father who stayed at home and was affectionate with his child did not lose masculinity; in fact, it was just the opposite.[15]

The Melodramatic Format

In this chapter, the focus will be on various representations of fatherhood and love in films, the reason being that the source material is teeming with father characters and love stories. The core of the analysis is the melodramatic and sloppy sentimentality of which the film culture has often been accused, and that is still regarded as negative. But before beginning the analyses, a discussion of the melodramatic format is in order.

The popular film melodrama is based on a long tradition originating from the stage melodrama, the form of theater most highly in demand during the 19th century. The word *melodrama* derives from the Greek *melos* (song) and *drama* (play). As discussed by Swedish film scholar Ann-Kristin Wallengren, silent pictures were always accompanied by music.[16]

Apart from its musical aspect, the melodrama has been characterized as subversive, as an expression of bourgeois realism, as a popular entertainment and, perhaps above all, as a markedly female genre—both in terms of the subjects treated and the audience—which provides a partial explanation for its low social status.[17] The assumption that the film melodrama was a specifically female genre, however, may be called into question in view of, among other things, the pluralism of film. As Rick Altman has pointed out, the designation "woman's film" had never been associated with the film melodrama prior to 1970. The melodrama was then renegotiated when feminist film scholars wished to rehabilitate female activities in films, moving them from family melodramas to a women's genre.[18] Ben Singer has also shown that the early film melodrama contained love and excessive emotions, but that the central building blocks were action, adventure and sensation, i.e., male-coded activities that were often centered around a heroine.[19]

Gender coding has meant that the film melodrama has almost exclusively been studied from a feminist perspective, focusing on female identity and "female" activities. Theory-driven studies also emphasize that the melodrama is in "the service of the bourgeois-patriarchal ideology" but that, owing to its subversive character and realism, it may, in exceptional cases, portray gender oppositions and ideological criticism. Thus, the hard patriarchal surface may conceal an alternative narrative that, according to the studies, can only appear as cracks in the patriarchal façade.[20]

This represents a pessimistic attitude that grossly underestimates the historical qualities and possibilities of the melodrama. It is an attitude that cements the gender dichotomy on the basis of predetermined patterns of power. But what, then, does the melodrama signify, and what happens if men and relationships come into focus as well?

According to film scholar Tom Lutz, the dramatic moment that triggers tears in the film melodrama always coincides with the fulfillment of a role on the part of the male and the female characters. Which role this is not determined in advance, however. Lutz emphasizes that, to widen our understanding of the melodrama, the discussion should concern which role is *actually* fulfilled. By taking the subversive element as his starting point, he criticizes the disparaging view of the melodrama as an upholder of a patriarchal order, because the subversive also contains a male—and, thus, not exclusively a female—criticism of the patriarchy. Lutz claims that the charm of the film melodrama lies in its realism and in the fact that fathers, mothers and children are not only fictitious roles, but also social roles that real people may manage or fail to fulfill.[21] Thus, perhaps in contrast to other genres, the film melodrama is more dependent on an emotional realism that allows the audience to relate to everyday relations, such as love, fatherhood or motherhood.[22]

Lutz brings up the subgenre male melodrama, wherein the "natural" male right of priority is problematized and criticized in films such as *Stella Dallas* (1925) and *The Champ* (1931). In these films, the male heroes are normative but at the same time unique individuals who invent or suggest new norms when the old ones tumble. The status quo that they seem to embrace is, thus, always more about a discussion of what the status quo should consist of than about the maintenance of a patriarchal structure. Acknowledgment of a social destiny and a strong wish to change this destiny constitute the core of the film melodrama as well as, ultimately, the explanation for the tears or laughs that ensue, depending on the upshot of the story.[23] One Swedish example is the above-mentioned *The Gyurkovics Family*, in which Gösta Ekman's character Géza, at the end of the film, regards having avoided marriage as a victory, thus opposing the patriarchal order.

One factor that further complicates the notion of the melodrama as patriarchal is the substantial influence on the representation of masculinity exerted by the female audience, both the actual, paying audience and the audience imagined by the film producers. In a study of the actor John Barrymore, Gaylyn Studlar shows that the "patriarchal" structure of film melodrama was on quite shaky ground during the 1910s and 1920s. This was particularly the consequence of the emphasis on a more sensitive masculine ideal—one that was created by women or for the benefit of women. In contrast to the robust Douglas Fairbanks, Barrymore gave shape to "one that promises that he will become the ideal lover who combines heterosexual satisfaction with an ability to nurture the heroine in a feminine, even maternal way. Thus, it is the hero's emotional transformation that satisfies the central fantasy of a utopian reconciliation between masculinity and femininity."[24]

Sally Robinson asks, in her turn, whether the fact that men are not allowed to show emotions has become a necessary part of the concept of blocked masculinity in the men's liberation movement since the 1970s. She wonders why this blocking is seen as unhealthy for men and why it is only a matter of anger, never of blocking love or fear. In addition, she suggests that the answer should be sought in a continuous shifting between emotion and sexuality: "For, isn't it the case that the ideology of emotional thrift and spending, blockage and release, runs parallel to an ideology of sexual thrift and spending, blockage and release?"[25] In other words, there is a risk that talk about men's emotional liberation will shift over to men's sexuality, which, in a feminist reading, would only re-legitimize male privilege.

Film is largely defined in terms of its emotional building blocks.[26] Thus, through the pluralism of film, where the private is shown publicly, we have a chance to nuance the picture of what was regarded as acceptable or unacceptable in relation to masculinity and emotions, but without losing the power aspect along the way.

Fatherhood

The Asexual Father as the Norm and Exceptions to This Norm

Father characters are found in practically every film. The films discussed here, therefore, constitute a sample based on the predominant trends. Although the majority of Swedish films from the 1920s contain one or more father characters, fatherhood itself very seldom constitutes the films' narrative core. In other words, the father characters are not primarily present as fathers but as men who happen to be fathers. The observation that the father is very seldom the film's hero has been made by Stella Bruzzi. Bruzzi also makes the general observation that father figures are always constructed as non-erotic in the sense that they are not defined in relation to their bodies or their sexuality. To be a good father on the screen, one must suppress one's desires.[27]

This ideal of father figures' lack of sexuality can be derived from the Christian religion. The continence ideal—formulated around the turn of century, circa 1900, as a zero-sum game of energies, and according to which each man only has so much energy to expend—stems from the idea that men and women should devote themselves to the spiritual rather than the physical. This is exemplified by the early Church's disparaging view of the family, and by Pope Gregory VII's dictate of celibacy of the synod in Rome in 1074. This, in turn, created a paradox, which implied that if men wanted to emulate God, they had to produce children, after which they had to refrain from sex and be free of desire. However, this paradox was partly resolved through the Reformation and Martin Luther's upgrading of the family. At the same time, it has been claimed that this marked the beginning of the feminization of parenthood, as motherhood gradually became part of "true" femininity.[28]

According to this line of reasoning, a father is feminized more or less automatically by virtue of his parenthood. Yet, as shown by Tomas Berglund, no negative "feminization" of fatherhood or masculinity took place during the 19th century.[29] What we are actually dealing with here is a de-sexualization of masculinity via fatherhood—which is not the same as a feminization. In Swedish films from the 1920s, paralleling Bruzzi's observation of Hollywood's offerings, fathers were largely represented as entirely lacking in sexuality.

In connection with the Swedish première of the American film *Why Men Leave Home* (1924), an article discussing the typical husband was published. In the article, we learn that the leading actor, Lewis Stone, had "become a representative of the American husband at his best. He is amiable, good, considerate, masculine. But—he is a husband, not a lover." According to the article, lack of attention is the cause of the many divorces taking place. Prior to marriage, men are agreeable and charming gentlemen, but they "are transformed afterwards, they allot housekeeping money as if it were charity, they kiss as if it were a duty. And the latter is probably the most serious error!"[30] The marital rut was thus held up as a reason why married men cannot be lovers—at least not to their wives, which may provide a realistic, partial explanation for the many asexual fathers seen in films.

However, there are some striking exceptions to the rule of the asexual father in Swedish films from the 1920s. In *Sin* (*Synd*, 1928), Lars Hanson plays the poor writer Maurice who lives with his wife and child, Marion, in Paris. The film opens with a number of scenes showing that Maurice loves his wife and Marion, but that, owing to his lack of self-confidence, he is not always able to show it. He tries to write, but is disturbed by Marion's loud playing. He begins to scold her but changes his mind, showing sentimentality in his eyes when he finds a toy on the sofa. A while later he plays with Marion, letting her ride on his back. However, his relationship with his wife is strained owing to their financial situation. "Why don't you leave me?" Maurice asks during a fight. His plays are not selling and his wife is supporting the family, mending napkins.

Some time later, one of Maurice's plays is accepted. It becomes a hit, with a dark-haired *femme fatale*, Henriette (Gina Manès), in the leading role. While working on the play, Henriette has shown an interest in Maurice. Carried away by the play's success, tired of his impoverished family life, but above all enchanted with the vision of Henriette, Maurice accompanies her after the première. They end up in a closed restaurant, which becomes the site of the most passionate petting scene ever witnessed in Swedish films from the 1920s. There can be no doubt that they are on their way to beginning a sexual relationship, when suddenly Maurice backs away and walks up to the open window. Henriette angrily asserts that "it's the child who is tying you down!" and gets ready to leave the restaurant. Maurice hesitates, but then states that it would have been better if the child had never been born.

This is followed by a melodramatic final act in which Maurice and Henriette are accused of child-murder when Marion appears to have vanished without a trace. Under police interrogation, the two make accusations about each other. When Marion is found—she had simply gotten lost—Maurice leaves Henriette and returns home. His wife is doubtful at first, but gives in when she sees Maurice looking regretfully at the sleeping child.

Another example of the sexually desirous father is Anders de Wahl's role as the miller Jacob in *The Windmill* (*Kvarnen*, 1921). At the outset, Jacob exhibits a more direct love relation to his ailing wife and his son. But his wife passes away early on, and during the rest of the film, Jacob is at times completely obsessed with the hot-blooded *tattare* girl Lise, while showing a quieter interest in the maidenly Anna.

We can first establish that not a single reviewer referred to Maurice or Jacob as fathers. Bengt Idestam-Almqvist came closest. Apart from praising Lars Hanson's moderated acting style, he mentioned the "deep love of children, wife, home." The reviewer asserted that Maurice had not committed any sin at all, and that the film's title was, thus, erroneous. According to him, it is the intoxication of it all, here a "natural" masculine excuse, that drives the "helpless" Maurice into the arms of "the experienced actress-vampire."[31] The paper *Folkets Dagblad Politiken* was of the opinion that the plot of *Sin* was slightly old-fashioned, particularly with reference to its melodramatic ending: "There is no doubt that marital conflicts of that kind still occur, but they are usually resolved without excessively violent showdowns between the parties." However, according to the reviewer, because the setting is "French" in the sense of it dripping with emotions "perhaps one has to give in."[32]

Jacob, on the other hand, was said to "fawn on one woman and then the another",[33] the consequence being that de Wahl does not "really move [...] the spectator until the very last scenes"[34] when Jacob finally rejects the *tattare* girl Lise by brutally killing her. In short, when sexuality and masculine passion come into the picture, fatherhood seems to move out—and this occurs despite the strong initial portrayals of Maurice and Jacob as good fathers who care for their families. Thus, given the norm of the asexual father, a father who is torn between two women stands out as irresolute, irrational and weak.

Humor and Class— The Incompetent but Good Father

Disarming humor occurs quite often in Swedish films from the 1920s. Half of the 180 films produced can be described as some form of comedy. In Bruzzi's view, infantilization and clownery are recurring characteristics in portrayals of the good father. Sociological studies have shown that, in the first half of the 20th century, American popular culture abounded with incompetent father types, whereas mothers were rarely portrayed in this way.[35] Based on a study of comic strips published between 1920 and 1970, sociologists Randal Day and Wade Mackay have put forward the hypothesis that the incompetent father figure appeared more often when male supremacy was stronger. Day and Mackay characterize the 1920s as a period during which the gender hierarchy was strong.[36]

Based on my general overview of Swedish film from the 1920s, I am not able to confirm the latter hypothesis. The incompetent and humorous father figure certainly occurs, but quantitatively speaking, he does not stand out in comparison with father characters represented as being more serious. I am also not prepared to claim that the clownish father always represents a good father, although this does occur. An outstanding example of this is the comedy *The Hatter's Ball* (*Hattmakarens bal,* 1928)—one of the few films from the 1920s in which fatherhood is the focus.

The rich hatter Cederström (Edvard Persson) has two daughters of marriageable age. He has decided high-handedly that his elder daughter is to marry an estate owner (in whom the younger daughter is interested) despite the fact that she loves a poet. Back home from Lund University, the poet accuses Cederström of being tight with money because he does not reciprocate all the times the daughters have been taken to the ball. Cederström takes offense and decides to arrange a fantastic ball at which he will announce Marianne's engagement to the estate owner. This triggers a chain of comic complications in connection with which the incompetent father can be ridiculed. The derision is created particularly in a number of scenes in which Cederström good-naturedly makes a fool of himself when he is drunk. Among other things, he sets his watch after a barometer believing it is a clock, and he searches for a lost key under a streetlamp on a dark street, justifying himself by saying: "Don't you understand that it's easier to search here where it's light."

At an early stage, however, the superficially tyrannical Cederström is established as the good father. One of the daughters asks for 50 crowns for a dress, but instead she gives the money to one of Cederström's poor tenants. When the tenant pays with the banknote, which is folded in a special way, the father immediately recognizes it and displays an obvious pride in his daughter's conduct. Soon thereafter, when Cederström's wife asks for 100 crowns for a new coat for the other daughter, Cederström gives her 200 crowns, because he doesn't want her going around in rags. The comic element is thus created in the friction between the self-image of fatherhood—He is the boss—and Cederström's behavior, which reveals that it is his modern daughters who are actually in control. In the end, the daughters also have their way when it comes to choice of husbands, and Cederström, too, is satisfied, because his daughters' happiness is his own.

The Hatter's Ball was considered rather amusing, but the reviews contain no direct comments on the fatherhood that was held up to ridicule. On the other hand, the reviewers felt the film contained too much "unnecessary custard-pie comedy,"[37] a paraphrasing of degraded slapstick humor. This, in turn, can be linked to the fact that it was only Edward Persson's father figure that was ridiculed—a practice that was by no means taboo, but that gave rise to bitter remarks such as: "The film has a lot in common with the hatter's newly invented combination of cylinder and suitcase, in which he has provided room for hair-, tooth- and nailbrush and other instruments of torture, but forgotten to reserve room for the head."[38]

Carolina Rediviva met with quite the opposite reaction. In this film, a whole collective of men assume the role of the incompetent father—for a while. A single woman leaves her newborn child on the doorstep of a house she believes belongs to a rich family. The building turns out to be a fraternity house. Upon returning home after having celebrated the eve of May Day, the tipsy male students find the child. They wonder what to do until one of them shouts out that they must adopt the child. They bring the child inside and place her on a table, using several thick books as a pillow. After consulting another book, they give a cheer and christen the child Carolina Rediviva. After this promising beginning, however, they at once hand the child over to the fraternity's housekeeper, their fatherly responsibility being limited to collecting money for the child while continuing to drink and rejoice. In the reviews, this scene is referred to as "the sweet element."[39] Thus, the obviously fantastic parts of the film neutralized the ridiculing of the presumptive fathers in *Carolina Rediviva*. This did not occur in the case of the hatter Cederström's father figure, which was more typical of the period, despite the comical depiction.

In the rascal film *Ville Andeson's Adventures*, we find a class perspective on the humorously represented and incompetent father. The film is enacted in the Södermalm area in Stockholm, a characteristic working-class setting up until the 1960s. Ville's father, Andeson (Carl Hagman), is portrayed in a way occasionally seen in the representation of working-class men in Swedish films from the 1920s—as a habitual drunkard and rake. The effect of alcohol turns Andeson into a weak man, as it did Cederström in *The Hatter's Ball*, but it does not make him a good father. Throughout the film, Andeson beats his son, drinks up the housekeeping money and quarrels with his wife—and all this is presented in a comical veil.

Although this can hardly be regarded as an ideal picture of fatherhood, the variety actor Calle Hagman was applauded for his role.[40] However, Nils Edgren, writing in the paper *Social-Demokraten*, was disapproving:

> When a film director tries to make his audience laugh by showing how people tumble or get kicked in the pants, how old hags speak a backyard Stockholm dialect or how clumsy men handle alcohol, it is called slapstick. This means more or less that the audience and the critics are expected to come without any pretensions whatsoever.[41]

A serious counterpart of Andeson is to be found in the working-class father and bricklayer Brand (Eugen Nilsson) in *Laughter and Tears* (*Löjen och tårar*, 1924). This film is essentially a melodramatic story of burglary and love involving Brand's daughter, but a great deal of room is left for a serious depiction of the

Three working-class fathers, on vacation and happy to get drunk, in *Ville Andeson's Adventures*. From left to right: Henrixon (Eric Gustafson), Lövberg (Gustaf Lövås), and Andeson (Carl Hagman) (*Ville Andesons äventyr* [1929]/Filmfred/courtesy Swedish Film Institute).

working class. Brand is portrayed as a hard-working man whose wife is seriously ill. On their daughter's birthday, they give her an organ as a present—because her "father has quit drinking." Thereafter, however, the ill fortunes begin to accumulate. A strike breaks out at the construction site, and as it drags on, destitution seeps into the working-class home. The organ has to be sold. In order to support his family, and after much persuasion from his employer, Brand agrees to be a strikebreaker. He is immediately frozen out by his fellow workers. In order to endure the disgrace, he starts going to the tavern again. Following the conflict, all of the strikebreakers, including Brand, are laid off. This causes Brand to drink even more. Meanwhile, his wife dies and his daughter is falsely accused of theft. The accusation is strengthened when the judicial authorities refer to the daughter's genetic links to her father, who has now gone under completely. At the trial, however, Brand stands up for his daughter, and the film ends with him getting a new job.

Laughter and Tears was given a proper dressing-down by the reviewers, who called it "an in every way infinitely unimportant film creation that leaves the spectator completely indifferent."[42] The only actor given praise was Eugen Nilsson as the "sometimes conscientious, sometimes carousing old bricklayer.[43]

But the strongly conservative *Aftonbladet* ended its review by saying: "In Södermalm, 'Laughter and Tears' will probably be given the red-carpet treatment."[44] This class perspective was reflected in the Communist paper *Folkets Dagblad Politiken*, whose reviewer was alone in praising the film: "One can recommend with a clear conscience that workers go and see the film. Employers' usual tactics against workers, even against the poor wretches who sell their honor for a mess of pottage—the strikebreakers, are illustrated extraordinarily well."[45] Here we see the emergence of a Catch-22, at least from a leftist point of view, concerning the consumer society's hyper-masculine breadwinner role. Brand becomes a strikebreaker to support his family, but at the same time he loses his honor—and, thus, his masculinity.[46]

Humor and the good father role are not always compatible. Part of the reason is that the humor, particularly the often-reproached slapstick, with its connection to so-called low culture, undermined the putative authoritarian father figure in the wrong way. The humorous effect of alcohol was also linked to class, such that upper- and middle-class fathers became somewhat weaker men, but much better fathers, if they were allowed to have a drink. Alcohol had a more destructive effect on working-class fathers. This is in contrast to the Swedish "pilsner films" from the 1930s (comedies including considerable beer drinking in working-class settings), where drinking humor was used as it was in upper-class settings in films from the 1920s.[47]

Monumental Fatherhood as a Good or Bad Model

As a consequence of its inherent conservatism, monumental fatherhood—primarily embodied by brute force or wealth, occasionally even by intelligence—tends to bring out conflict with others in the environment. This traditional father has been discernible in, e.g., *The Students at Tröstehult*, *The Counts at Svansta* and *The Girl in Tails*, but he also appears in *Björn Mörk* (1924), where, like in the other films, tradition confronts modernity. Thus, the son or daughter wishes to study, choose a wife or husband irrespective of class, or achieve more freedom by breaking with traditional patterns in other ways. In these films, the father character is opposed to change—the result often being that the father is written off early in the story, simply by dying.

The monumental father figure appears frequently in my empirical material. This means that, thanks to the pluralism of film, there is a good deal of variation. Thus, in films where the character is not written off at an early stage, it is possible to distinguish between the monumental father as a good or a bad model.

Intellectual father figures were exceptions, but they did occur in films such as *Johan Ulfstjerna* (1923) and *Pirates of Lake Mälaren*. Represented as intellectual liberals, the father characters (Ivan Hedqvist and Nils Arehn, respectively) end up in conflicts with the younger generation, owing to their initial difficulty in coming to grips with youthful eagerness. But thanks to their ability to act physically, these monumental father figures are transformed into heroes and good models—and they were applauded by the reviewers accordingly.[48]

Another good model appeared in *The Strongest* (*Den starkaste*, 1929), in which Skipper Larsen (Hjalmar Peters) waddles around like a stout fur seal with a pipe in his mouth, as if taken directly from *The Old Man and the Sea*. In this case, it is not a matter of intellect, but of masculine brute force, in the sense that the strongest always wins. One might assume that this father figure, who is high up on the food chain, would appear frequently in Swedish films from the 1920s, but, in fact, he constitutes a good model only in exceptional cases.

Strong, tough and masculine: three adjectives to describe this advertisement for *The Strongest*, which had been inspired by Soviet film and propaganda art (*Filmjournalen* No. 17–18, 1929).

The Strongest was stylistically inspired by the Soviet film wave that swept across the world in the second half of the 1920s. This fact was observed by several reviewers and was also apparent in film advertisements, in which, among other things, a stylized clenched fist was used in Soviet propaganda style to symbolize masculine power.[49] The film was set and shot in the Arctic Ocean, more exactly in the ice-covered waters surrounding Bear Island and Spitsbergen, to which the film team had traveled for a three-month-long hunting and filming expedition. The idea was to finance the film through bear and seal hunting and to share the revenues equally with the shipping company that provided the two vessels. In the end, the film workers only managed to shoot five polar bears and six hundred seals (usually ten times as many were killed), but the "grandiose" framework helped to evoke a robust macho aura around the film and its male actors.[50]

Skipper Larsen is the absolute boss on his ship, which has the telling name *Viking*. Because of the long hunting expeditions, he can only spend short periods at home, where his wife and his very affectionate daughter, Ingeborg (Gun Holmqvist), are waiting. At the beginning of the film, it is suggested that Skipper Larsen is just about to leave the rudder to his second-in-command, Ole (Anders Henrikson). The father would thus like Ole to marry Ingeborg, a prospect she clearly does not relish. During one of Skipper Larsen's long periods of absence, a new farmhand is hired, Gustaf (Bengt Djurberg), in whom Ingeborg takes an interest. When the father returns after several months at sea, his exhilarated daughter rushes to meet him, but the emotional reunion only amounts to the father taking his daughter's hand with a slight twitch of the corner of his mouth, the latter passing for a smile. The reaction is stronger when Skipper Larsen meets Gustaf—"Watch it, boy!"—who is immediately turned out when Ingeborg says she wants to marry him.

But, as it turns out, Gustaf is both a sailor and a good marksman. He gets a job on the competing hunting ship *Maud*, which is skippered by another patriarch, Olsen (Civert Braekmo). The two ships and their entirely male crews meet out on the ice, guns in hand, where they compete over killing seals—constantly cheered on by the two patriarchs.

One day Gustaf and his hunting group are caught in fog out on the ice. They lose their way, and Gustaf, the only survivor, is saved by the crew of the *Viking*. Seeing the unconscious body, Skipper Larsen cries: "But it's the farmhand!" Later, when Gustaf has recovered, Larsen feels the time has come for him to make himself useful. But Gustaf does not want to drudge like an ordinary seaman. He asks to be made a marksman—the most prestigious duty on board. The only problem is that Ole is the first shot on the *Viking*. Therefore, a contest is arranged between the two, under the supervision of Skipper Larsen—a contest in which they are implicitly competing for Ingeborg as well. Gustaf wins the contest. Later, he also saves Ole's life during a polar bear hunt.

Back home, the father offers Gustaf, who now has Ingeborg by his side, the job as marksman. But Gustaf declines. Larsen is indignant and walks away, slamming the door behind him. The daughter looks anxiously at Gustaf, who gets angry and throws his cap on the floor. When he later offers some words of comfort to the girl, the door opens again. It is Skipper Larsen, who looks angrily at Gustaf, offering him "both the boat and the girl, so you won't sail for a rogue like Olsen." Then he slams the door again. The door is opened once more, and

Skipper Larsen comes into the room, stretching out his hand to Gustaf. Finally, the daughter gets a big bear hug, too.

Skipper Larsen's sullen and abrupt manners, his bottled-up emotions—which hardly sufficed for a smile for his beloved daughter—greatly impressed the (mostly male) reviewers, who said they were pleased with the absence of the "almost obligatory flow of sentimentality."[51] With regard to the film's masculinity factor, the indicator hit the ceiling. Here, "all the theater dust"[52] had been blown away from the actors:

> There are some strong, harsh, male strokes in this new Swedish film. The sugary, the sentimental is all but banned from the manuscript. We are dealing with people who fight for their livelihood under difficult circumstances, men who have to wrestle with the forces of nature in the majestic but desolate and hazardous regions of the Arctic Ocean. "The Strongest" is above all a film about men and their struggles.[53]

However, the choir of praise was disturbed by a couple of dissonant voices, who "wonder why the film did not end when the Skipper slammed the door the second time,"[54] that is, before Larsen took Gustaf's hand and hugged his daughter. Such objections show that the slightest release of emotions could be perceived as a failure to uphold modern ideal masculinity. There is no doubt that Skipper Larsen, despite his callousness, stood out as a good fatherly model.

In Hollywood movies, the archetypal conflict between the powerful father and the willful son often took place in Westerns in which majestic American nature environments served as the dramatic backdrop. Bruzzi holds, however, that the traditional father stopped functioning as a good example toward the beginning of the 1950s, when "the law of the father"—based on brute force, conservatism and violence—was replaced by "the law of the son," which was, rather, founded on common sense, negotiation and change.[55]

This crisis was already a fact in Swedish films from the 1920s, which is apparent in a number of portrayals of rural life in which the monumental father, despite his strong connection with nature and physical strength, nonetheless appears to be a poor model of both fatherhood and masculinity. In these films, the father characters were monumental in the true sense of the word. Their arbitrary behavior, however, is not held up as what is best for the town or the family, but is instead framed as harmful. In *Karin Ingmarsdotter* (1920), the mean and boozing stepfather Eljas (Nils Lundell) has the opposite affect on his son. In *The People of Närke* (*Närkingarna*, 1923) and *The People of Värmland* (*Värmlänningarna*, 1921), the sons' misalliances create conflicts. In both cases, the father characters (played by Gustaf Ranft and Hugo Björne, respectively) have to yield to this modern phenomenon—but not until they have caused great discord within both the family and the town. In *The King of Boda* (*Bodakungen*,

1920), the powerful he-man, the King of Boda (Egil Eide), is introduced with a whip in hand. He bosses his servants about, using violence and humiliation. The only person with the power to restrain the destructive and violent behavior of this single father is his daughter, Eli (Winifred Westover). It is shown in a number of scenes how the King of Boda makes life miserable for everyone around him by abusing people and wielding his financial power. Among other things, he pays the promissory notes of an old enemy, Mårten (August Palme), for the purpose of evicting him from his farm. After the eviction, Mårten returns to burn the farm down, locking himself inside it. The King of Boda sees the fire, hurries there with his henchmen and pulls out the dazed old man. Then, in cold blood, he whips Mårten to death—a deed his daughter witnesses from a distance. She approaches her father as he is wiping the blood off the whip. When the King of Boda sees his daughter's gaze, he understands that he has lost her love. The King of Boda is cast out of the social community and, after a period of uncontrollable drinking, his daughter states: "Our name is a disgrace" and "I don't want to see you ever again, Father—until you have been punished by God."

The King of Boda sets out on a journey of penance as a beggar, neglecting his property and letting his beard grow. Interestingly enough, he earns his living wandering from one farm to another telling stories to children, whom he hugs tenderly. As a very old man, he finally returns home. Upon seeing the forgiveness in his daughter's eyes, he collapses and dies.

The common element of the father characters in these films is the focus on their weakness. In the newspapers, Nils Lundell's "boozing life"[56] was mentioned, and Hugo Björne was mostly referred to as "weak and timid."[57] As for Egil Eide's King of Boda, "hard-hearted to the point of cruelty,"[58] a problem arose when his overbearing and brutal natural force was finally curbed. The reviewers were of the same mind, stating that, for this reason, the second half of the film was mediocre compared to the first half. The female critic Tora Garm explained why this was the case, using a comparison between the King of Boda and Mårten:

> Both are interesting types, but only one of them—the weak Mårten—comes up to the standards of reality through to the end. Egil Eide as Sören King of Boda does the best he can with the task laid before him. He is strong and ruthless in all his glory as long as he may, but then he turns as mild and white as Father Christmas after an idyllic pilgrimage and is called "Nameless the Mild." Understandably, this may be a bit too sweet for a sentimental Swedish audience. If the narrative had been allowed to continue along the realistic track it started on, and if the outcome had been more natural, the film would certainly have gained a lot.[59]

In brief, the transformation of the "naturally" masculine King of Boda was not perceived as realistic. Despite, or perhaps thanks to, the fact that the fathers, figuratively and literally, derive their strength from nature, they appear weak in the face of change. Most of these portrayals of rural life were produced early on, i.e., in connection with the Golden Age, 1917–1924. Later on they thinned out, only to return in a romanticized form in the 1930s, 1940s and 1950s as a nostalgic reaction to the effects of modernization, particularly urbanization.[60] During the Golden Age, however, the films served as a showcase for Swedish nature, which, on a metaphorical plane, included displaying the Swedish masculine primordial force to the world.[61] For this reason, the transformation of the King of Boda into a gentle Father Christmas was problematic during the early 1920s.

This is noticeable in *The Poetry of Ådalen* (*Ådalens poesi*, 1928) as well, a relatively late portrayal of rural life, both regarding the concept itself, but also regarding how masculinity and fatherhood are treated. Reviewer Bengt Idestam-Almqvist felt that "one seems to be in a museum of antiques" and that the history may "well work in a short story from the 1800s, but it is not suitable as the subject of a film in 1928."[62] What makes the film old-fashioned is precisely its use of nature—in the form of wild fights with bears, shooting the rapids and log-driving—all to present a rough Swedish masculinity.[63]

The images of fatherhood in Swedish films from the 1920s are complex. In his summary of fatherhood during the 19th century, Tomas Berglund stresses that a "good father must be wise and sensible in guiding the children" and that he "is expected to act firmly," with "his own conduct serving as an example."[64] Yet this ideal picture contrasts sharply with the way in which fathers were given shape in films from the 1920s. This discordance is mainly due to the fact that Berglund's study only deals with the ideal picture of fatherhood, whereas a film is necessarily driven by some form of narrative conflict. In the chapter on children and youth, a generational conflict emerges in which the young are presented as the protagonists, whereas adults, particularly fathers, are most often portrayed as antagonists. It has also been said of Swedish films from the 1920s that a striking number of them were "about homes and households that in a very concrete sense find themselves in a state of change, transformation and disintegration."[65]

Love

If fatherhood was very rarely discussed as such, the same cannot be said about love. In 1920, the editor of *Filmnyheter* maintained: "It can well be said that ninety-nine percent of all films are about love. [...] The audience wants to see happy people no matter how unsuccessful their own marriage may be. [...] Everyone can [...] relate to it to some degree."[66]

In the film magazines, no topics were discussed more than love, marriage and various ideal romantic types of masculinity and femininity.[67] And although the figure 99 percent is somewhat exaggerated, it is not far from the truth, because during the 1920s a love story was almost obligatory in Swedish and imported feature films. The love theme and the happy ending were often considered trivializing elements as well—a condescending attitude that has hardly changed over the years and that can be explained in terms of the gender coding of melodrama. At the same time, these elements constituted the substance of the melodramatic format, because, as the editor of *Filmnyheter* pointed out, everybody could relate to them in some way. This includes men—those on the screen and those in the audience. This indisputable fact has often been neglected despite, or perhaps because of, the fact that it complicates the one-sided gender coding of the melodrama. To this we can add the not insignificant fact that several of the greatest Swedish hits of the 1920s can be found in this category.

Thomas Meighan was one of the most popular romantic characters in American films during the silent era. His film persona comprised a number of brutal features. An interview about women and love reveals that he "appreciates the modern woman precisely as she is," but also that his "philosophy of the rationality of a certain male hardness in relation to women is entirely based on the experience I have gained as a professional lover, so to speak." We also learn that "the man who is equipped with a bit of male brutality always wins when competing with less masculine rivals." In this context, brutality is to be understood as honesty—as a "natural" male trait that no woman can resist. Women's only weapon against this honesty was humor, because "no man can get anywhere with a woman who laughs at him."[68]

It can be noted that Meighan's type of masculinity did not have any Swedish counterpart, even at a time when Swedish film was accused of having been Americanized. This does not mean, however, that the brutal character was not popular and did not continue to be popular in Sweden. Among several others, Clark Gable cultivated this brutal/honest image so successfully that he developed into the world's most popular romantic idol in the 1930s.[69] One can interpret the absence of the brutal lover in Swedish films from the 1920s as Swedish lovers being "less masculine," to use Meighan's words. But it can also be seen in the cautious dissociation that is glimpsed at the end of the interview, when the Swedish writer hopes that "our esteemed female readers have a sense of humor and understand how to correctly appreciate Mr. Thomas Meighan's, in our opinion, very sensible but not very polite [...] philosophy of women and love."[70]

At the other end of the spectrum was the handsome charmer who looked up to women, something expressed by Mexican-American Ramón Navarro in an interview: "I admire most of all a woman who can take care of herself, who is something *in her own right*, not only through a man." But this kind of yielding respect does not imply a lack of masculine power, as women were placed on a pedestal, especially in the home, where "women are men's enemies, for they are the enemies of work, and work, it is men's life, whereas women and love are only men's dream of life."[71]

In a third interview, Constance Talmadge spoke of men and love:

> People say that we, women, couldn't live if we weren't allowed to go around "believing" things, and therefore we always believe so much and think so much about men. What I go around "believing" is that every man is "crammed" with love from 15 to 50 years of age. [...] Between these age limits, men love many women [...] sometimes as many as ten a year, but sometimes only one during that same period of time. [...] By this I don't mean to say that I wish men didn't love us. Far from it! Whether he betrays you or remains faithful to you all your life, in both cases you've had an experience that you wouldn't want to miss. But the fact remains: most men admire actresses—but aren't all women actresses more or less?[72]

In referring to actresses, Talmadge means that men easily fall in love with what is on the surface, but that they soon become tired of it and move on when everyday life makes itself felt. Here we see once again how men's sexuality is described as natural, as something to which women must adapt. Sally Robinson, too, stresses that sexuality has a tendency to become mixed up with and replace emotions when men and love are discussed—owing precisely to this notion of naturalness.[73] As the interview comes to a close, the natural is underscored by the Swedish author of the article: "Thus far Miss Talmadge. She should know men, at least American men. But are not all men fairly similar, whether they live in the New World or the Old?"[74]

Writer bell hooks's criticism of the media society for its tendency to talk solely about sex and not about emotions is connected with and explained by this notion of naturalness: "The truth we do not tell is that men are longing for love. This is the longing feminist thinkers must dare to examine, explore and talk about."[75] Let us see, then, how men and love were represented in Swedish film production in the 1920s, positioned between extremes such as Meighan and Navarro.

Love in Earnest

The love-drenched melodrama can be divided into serious dramas and those that tended toward romantic comedy. Beginning at the serious end, we find films such as *The Lady with Camellias* (*Damen med kameliorna*, 1925), *Only a Dancer* (*Bara en danserska*, 1927) and *Sealed Lips* (*Förseglade läppar*, 1927). All of these films contain great emotional fluctuations, set in stories of impeded love meant to cast the moviegoer between tragedy and the possibility of a happy ending. The first-mentioned film, which dutifully follows the 19th-century novel by Alexandre Dumas the Younger, was considered theatrical and rigid.[76] The love story was perceived as unrealistic, because the Camellia Lady's (Tora Teje) tearful sentimentality and recurring fainting fits were thought to be "ridiculous according to modern views."[77] The modern woman of the 1920s was not quite as silly as this. On the other hand, the lead lover, Armand (Uno Henning), gets away with restrained emotions, although he does shed a few tears when the Camellia Lady dies in the end. The few objections rather concerned his lack of "ability to express his emotions."[78]

Only a Dancer and *Sealed Lips* were products of the Swedish-German Isepa collaboration. The melodramatic elements of these films were so numerous that the derogatory term "construction" was often found in the reviews.[79] Moreover, the praise fluctuated depending on the degree of Swedish involvement, which influenced opinions on the melodramatic elements. In *Only a Dancer*, Paul (Walter Janssen) vacillates between an unglamorous marriage and an exciting dancer. And in *Sealed Lips*, the irresolute Frank (Louis Lerch) is torn between loyalty to his lame wife and the woman he loves, who—just to add some melodramatic zest—is preparing to take her vows as a nun. Although the former film is more ordinary and realistic, it was the latter, the one with the most Swedish involvement, that was highly acclaimed by the critics and that was a hit with audiences.[80] The two male lead lovers appeared to be similarly indecisive, which is also reflected in the reviews. German actor Walter Jenssen was not considered "funny with his constant awkwardness,"[81] whereas Austrian Louis Lerch had "all the prerequisites of a charmer."[82] The fact that Lerch is not a Swede was turned into an advantage, as the credit for his acting and suitable appearance was given to Swedish director Gustaf Molander.[83]

Another Isepa film, *Discord* (*Hans engelska fru*, 1927), was one of the greater successes of the 1920s, notwithstanding the fact that the two leading roles, English upper-class lady Cathleen and Swedish forestry boss Birger, were played by German actress Lil Dagover and Finnish actor Urho Somersalmi, respectively. The film alternates between two settings: the English aristocracy and the wilderness of Norrland in northern Sweden. An English society family, deeply in debt to forestry baron Birger, persuades its reluctant daughter to marry him. Before the family has reached its destination, the slender-limbed Cathleen falls into a swift river. She is saved by a coarse and vigorous Norrlander, who takes her to a raftman's hut. There, the timid man, obviously highly embarrassed, removes her wet clothes in a somewhat risqué scene. Naturally, the Norrlander is Birger, and according to the rule that opposites attract, they fall in love and get married.

After a few months, Cathleen begins feeling lonesome in the isolated wilderness. Birger encourages her to pay a visit to London. There, Cathleen returns

Discord **was one of the great romantic films in Sweden during the 1920s. Here, the Norrlander Birger (Urho Somersalmi) and the upper-class English lady Cathleen (Lil Dagover) in the somewhat risqué undressing scene (*Filmjournalen* No. 1, 1927).**

to her glamorous life. A radio broadcast from a dance performance at the Savoy, which Cathleen attends, causes Birger to suspect that his wife is being unfaithful. Raving with jealousy, he goes to London, where the married couple has a furious dispute, the upshot being that they part on bad terms.

More time passes, and Birger sets off south on a train journey. The train stops for a meal break. At that point, Cathleen arrives on a northbound train. They pretend not to see each other. But Birger stays behind his train, and then Cathleen does the same. When the last train has left and they are alone in the restaurant, they book a double room at the railway hotel. Thus, the film ends with an indication that their married life will continue happily.

In the reviews, *Discord* was described as "the old story of a strong man and a weak woman, the man cut out to be a warrior and the woman made to be the source of the warrior's vitality."[84] The film's four key scenes—the rescue from the rapids, the undressing scene, the dispute at the Savoy and the reconciliation at the railway station restaurant—can be seen as melodramatic climaxes that serve to cement traditional gender roles. Given the film's success at the box office, it can be claimed that these gender roles were accepted. But what roles were actually being played out? There can be no doubt that the strong Birger/Urho Somersalmis gave shape to a male ideal. In the reviews, he was characterized as "the strong man from the primeval forest."[85] The film also revealed Birger's soft and more refined sides through scenes showing that he is kind to animals (a substitute for children) and that he is knowledgeable about art and, thus, intellectually sensitive. The "masculine" rescue scene was commented on in *Aftonbladet:* "The courage that he demonstrates [...] in the torrential river is a suitable contrast to his somewhat awkward and embarrassed conduct, which we discern when he finds himself alone in the cabin with the helpless female."[86]

These reactions reveal that it was through these soft contrasts that Birger's strong man deviated from a modern ideal masculinity. At the same time, precisely the same contrasts made this romantic melodrama a working and credible fiction that was appreciated across gender boundaries—which would hardly have been the case had Birger only been presented as the strong man from the primeval forest.

We are thus dealing with the preservation of a traditional gender coding, with the possible addition of the modern woman's independence, which was, moreover, the cause of the marital conflict in *Discord*. Thus, it may be claimed that, at some level, Birger's character was brought up to date in order to tame the modern woman in a way that boyish masculinity would presumably not have been able to manage. At another level, however, the film's ending leaves it to the audience's imagination to determine how the couple's marital bliss will progress. Given how the road to marriage is presented in the film, maintenance of a traditional division of power would not seem to be automatic. The ambivalence thus satisfies both the traditional and the modern attitudes toward marriage and love held by different moviegoers. Even if the ending of this and other films typically means the reestablishment of social norms, one should recall that the path to such endings is equally important—even more important, according to Richard Dyer and others, because it is not the ending the audience remembers, but instead the eventful and turbulent—particularly from a gender perspective—way there.[87]

The Norrtull Gang—Realism and Hyperrealism

The Norrtull Gang, based on Elin Wägner's novel from 1908, is about the life of four self-supporting women who live together in Stockholm. The film's narrative "I" is Pegg (Tora Teje). One of "Stockholm's boundless army of office drudges," she has her 12-year younger brother living with her as a lodger. In the reviews, the film was described as a "women's film in all respects, with very little room for the masculine element."[88] But the masculine element manifests itself even in this film, mainly represented by Pegg's nameless boss (Egil Eide, who played the destructive father in *The King of Boda*).

According to Tom Lutz, the melodramatic moments constituted the fulfillment of a role, but not necessarily the expected or traditional one.[89] The melodramatic elements can be further described as a form of hyperrealism centering on emotions, where the boundaries of what characterizes factual realism are transcended—the latter being the reason the world's film studios are often called dream factories.

The portrayal of a number of current societal issues in *The Norrtull Gang*, e.g., single women's poor finances, the lack of job security, extramarital children and groping bosses, satisfies the demand for realism according to which art should deal with one or more socially important topics. The affair between Pegg and her boss begins realistically but is concluded under the sign of emotional hyperrealism; that is, with a happy ending.

Pegg and her boss appear together in five scenes that illustrate the development of their relationship. Another part of the picture is that the four women in the Norrtull Gang have a "healthy" attitude toward men, meaning that they avoid them like the plague. Their shared apartment is a fortress to which no men have access and whose walls are covered with written notes warning against men and their deeds.

In the first scene, the boss is introduced as a thin-haired man in his fifties. He has difficulties taking his eyes away from the 25-year younger Pegg, who is sitting at her desk. The boss calls her to his office to take dictation. The film switches over to the other female office workers, whose gazes suggest what is going to happen inside the boss's office when the door is closed. The boss makes a pass at her almost immediately, but the experienced Pegg is unresponsive. The boss then asks whether she is in some kind of trouble, as she has seemed absent-minded of late. Pegg hesitates at first, but then tells him that she needs money for a new coat for Putte, whose existence the boss immediately interprets as an extramarital lapse. The boss promises to lend her the money because "he feels lonely and in need of sympathy." He then grabs hold of Pegg, who reacts by hitting him in the face. The boss laughs at her and obtains a kiss by force before she manages to escape. Afterwards, she is not sure whether she should laugh or cry. But when on her own, she catches herself thinking about her boss.

The second scene begins when Pegg, who is on her way home after a late evening, is accosted by a drunken man on the street. A taxi pulls up, the boss gets out and forcibly drives the perpetrator away. The grateful Pegg—"And he thought that I, a 25-year-old spinster and would-be suicide, was young and jolly and that flattered me, so I gave in"—agrees to accompany him to a restaurant. In the restaurant, they converse and, again, get on to the subject of money. One of Pegg's friends in the Norrtull Gang has to cover a deficit in her teller's desk. The boss generously lends her the money without requiring any thanks. Later, however, at the front door leading to Pegg's apartment, the boss makes another abrupt pass, which Pegg returns by pushing him aside. But when he turns to leave, she changes her mind and gives him a kiss. She regrets this later on—does she really love him?

After thinking it over, Pegg hands in her resignation in the third scene. The boss says she is ridiculous to listen to rumors from the other office workers and tries to kiss her. Then Putte comes into the office. The boss finds out that he is Pegg's brother, not her child. Pegg and the boss part with a firm handshake.

In the fourth scene, the boss calls on Pegg—though he doesn't think it is perfectly correct—under the pretext that she cannot quit because there is a lot to do with Christmas approaching. Pegg, realizing he didn't come on account of the job, accepts with a smile.

The crescendo of the fifth scene takes place on Christmas Eve, when the boss comes to Pegg's place wanting to talk to her privately, which means talking in the kitchen of the one-room apartment shared by the Norrtull Gang. Over a pot of porridge, he wants to give an engagement ring to the seemingly indifferent Pegg. As he is about to put the ring on her finger, it falls into the porridge. Pegg's reaction reveals that she is not at all as indifferent as she pretends to be. Like the rest of the film, the ending is emotionally downplayed, with the women of the Norrtull Gang—three of whom are now engaged—enjoying a cozy moment with their men on the floor in front of an open fire.

In Wägner's original novel, the leading female character was forced to escape to relatives in the country to get away from her impertinent boss. The happy ending of the film was criticized by practically all of the reviewers, because it was considered to distort the social content of the novel.[90] As shown, however, the level of social realism was high throughout the film, and was only disturbed by the hyper-realistic, yet emotionally downplayed, ending, when the main threads of love were intertwined in an unrealistic manner. Given the male director and the male scriptwriter, this distortion could be described as an expression of a masculine-domination technique for hiding the oppression of women by proposing the patriarchal patent solution: marriage. Another interpretation is that love and emotions in their hyper-realistic form are experienced as false.

Given that the film's destitute Pegg was "too well-dressed to give the illusion of a female office worker,"[91] Tora Teje was fiercely criticized for her downplayed acting, which is somewhat contradictory considering the understanding of social realism at the time: "In the book, Pegg is an enchanting girl, lively, intelligent, sparkling with humor and gallows humor, sensitive and warm-blooded. In the film, she is none of these things."[92] The occasional critic praised the unaffected acting.[93] But by and large, the reactions demonstrate that the film's realism—especially in relation to even women having to hold back their emotions so as not to be regarded as promiscuous—was not in accordance with the notion of how a woman in love should behave.

Egil Eide's boss, who would be regarded as a sexist lout by today's standards, did not meet with reactions of that type at all. Half of the reviewers felt the character of the boss was "an unusually pleasant and charming one."[94] The negative criticism concerned Eide's unsuitability for the role: he was too old and not sexy enough.[95]

Perceptions expressed at the time present a picture of the boss as a fundamentally good man, whose "benign" passes reveal uncertainty and unmanliness inappropriate for a man in his position of power. In other words, Eide did not evoke the expected image of the self-assured lead lover. Thus, his character did not appear realistic according to the convention—a convention falling within the hyper-realistic sphere: "One might think that Egil Eide, as the powerful boss and irresistible womanizer, won his victories rather too easily. But maybe that is what Don Juan really looks like?"[96]

Older Men's Love for Younger Women

A recurring romantic theme in Swedish films from the 1920s is an older man falling in love with a much younger woman, today referred to as the "Lolita motif" after Vladimir Nabokov's notorious novel from 1955. Several common characteristics of the ill matched couple—appearing in, among other films, *Masterman* (*Mästerman*, 1920) and *Johan* (1921)—include the young woman looking up to the older man as a father, sometimes literally, as the older man had brought up the young woman as his own daughter. The older man, in his turn, is strengthened (or believes himself to be strengthened) by, figuratively speaking, drinking from the young woman's youthful spring—figuratively speaking because such romances bordered on the forbidden already in the 1920s.

The actor who came to excel in the role as the elderly gentleman rejuvenated by romance was Ivan Hedqvist. In four films—*Dunungen* (1919), *She Is the Only One* (*Hon, den enda*, 1926), *Uncle Frans* (*Farbror Frans*, 1926) and *Youth*—he played this role opposite actresses who were between 21 and 33 years his junior. *Dunungen*, which included the character Uncle Theodor, was a great success, particularly in France where Hedqvist was engaged to create a similar role.[97] This role was, in fact, popular in France, but at the same time the performance could be projected onto a less masculine France, as is evident in the commentary in *Våra Nöjen* on Hedqvist's role in *She Is the Only One:* "Otherwise such good uncles only exist in older French novels, and then usually as degenerate roués who gaze with incredible sentimentality at 'the amours of the young.'"[98]

The keyword here is the derogatory "sentimental," a component that, according to convention, was necessary when it came to a forbidden romance that was seldom consummated. In actuality, this meant two things: first, the older man's love can never be permitted to be manifested physically, but must only exist on a chaste level; and second, the romance (but not necessarily the film) must have an unhappy ending. In both cases, there is room for elements dripping in emotions.

Uncle Frans was based on author Jenny Blicher-Claussen's best-selling novel from 1902. In the film, Hedqvist plays Uncle Frans, an elderly teacher who has taken care of Kaja (Inga Tidblad) since she was very young, owing to her mother's untimely death and her father constantly being away on business. When Kaja is engaged to the celebrated stage actor Peter, Uncle Frans is distressed. Contemplating childhood photographs of Kaja in his solitude, he doubts that Peter is really the right man. To him, she had become "youth, life"; to her, he was just Uncle Frans.

The day before the wedding, Kaja says that she wants to share her great happiness with her uncle. Frans misinterprets the utterance, which goes straight to his heart. Realizing that he loves Kaja, he pulls himself together and takes flight. At the wedding, Uncle Frans can only look on with melancholy when Kaja and Peter promise each other their everlasting faithfulness.

Peter, however, turns out to be a libertine who drinks and is unfaithful. This does not change even when Kaja gets pregnant. During Peter's periods of absence, Uncle Frans often goes to visit Kaja, who regards him as an intimate friend. Frans, who is head over heels in love, hides his feelings from Kaja, but not from the audience, who can see the conflicting emotions raging behind his almost-still facial features. One day, when Kaja shows the nursery to her uncle, the truth of the situation comes over them both. Kaja understands that Uncle Frans's feelings are not just those of an uncle, and that she has made a mistake in marrying Peter. The physical expression of this understanding is that they grasp each other's hands, gazing into the air, and that Frans finally kisses Kaja's hand.

When it is time for the child to be born, Peter has gone away with his mistress. Uncle Frans hurries to Kaja and finds her in great pain. Holding his hand at the bedside, Kaja tells him the truth: "Frans, I do not want to die until you know every corner of my heart. I love you!" Then she faints. For several days, Uncle Frans struggles with Death for Kaja. By the time her condition stabilizes, his hair has turned white.

When Peter comes home, Kaja does not let him touch the child. She sues for divorce. Uncle Frans and Kaja can thus get married. They are married for a few years, as indicated by the text: "Days followed, brimming with happiness." When the moviegoer sees them again, they are living in an idyllic countryside setting.

One day when Kaja and her son are out, Uncle Frans is sitting at home looking at photographs of his wife, recent ones as well as some from her childhood. He is happy and kisses the photographs passionately. Suddenly, he suffers a heart attack, falls from his chair and dies with a photograph in his hand. Returning home, Kaja finds her husband. She is beside herself with grief. Her son cannot get her to speak or react for several months. Finally, he pretends to order a telephone call to heaven, where Uncle Frans is. He tells his mother to take the receiver. Then, finally, Kaja wakes up from her slumber and can go on living.

This tips the sentimentality scale. Again we see how the pattern of strong male expressions of emotion sealed behind an iron mask of self-control repeats itself. And because these emotions cannot take on a physical form, the result is a two-fold restraint that seems to be twice as melodramatic. The kissing of the photographs—the symbolic substitute for sex—exemplifies this.

Even though the original novel had been written only 20 years prior, the reviews mentioned that the book was "sentimental beyond words"[99] and that "today's youth prefer something else. The romantic generation is gone and reality counts more and more."[100] The love story in *Uncle Frans* has thus passed over into the hyper-realistic sphere, and the film's sloppy sentimentality can be explained away as belonging to the past. Nevertheless, we are dealing with a contemporary Swedish film, which almost required that the presence of such "French" emotions had to be renegotiated: "As we well know, the novel is marked by great sentimentality, which is also apparent in the film. In the film, however, it has been overcome to produce wholesome moderation."[101] Nevertheless, almost all reviewers reported that there was a great deal of sobbing going on in the movie theatre.[102] And there is no reason to assume that only the women cried. The silent film audiences often vented their emotions more directly than today's filmgoers do.[103]

Like in *Dunungen* and *She Is the Only One*, Ivan Hedqvist received excellent reviews for *Uncle Frans*: "Ivan Hedqvist is, of course, perfectly cut out for the leading part. Using small means—but with a superb mask—he adds another great creation to his many previous ones."[104] One reviewer explicitly referred to this as a male characteristic: "There is a masculine stature and nobility about this Uncle Frans that makes him interesting and touching."[105]

At the same time, there were objections to this masculine reserve, including Inga Tidblad's unaffected acting, which alluded to the film being too "French": "It portrays the story of a woman's life [...] and her new happiness by another man's side in such a quiet and discreet way and in such a low key that one sometimes wishes a breeze of bustling, boisterous life would blow through the closed and barred rooms in which these people abide."[106]

The balance between the good father (or uncle) figure and the romantic lover could be upheld only as long as the physically sexual was unexpressed or at least outside the picture. When Ivan Hedqvist repeated, for the last time, his role as mature gentleman in *Youth*, opposite Brita Appelgren, objections were finally raised. Appelgren was actually only 14 years old, whereas he was 47. This caused several papers to write about this as a very "ill-matched game of love-making," even though it stopped, physically speaking, at the kissing of photographs.[107] Director Ragnar Hyltén-Cavallius explained that everything was going well at the beginning of the filming until, one day, Ivan Hedqvist looked at least 15 years older after suffering a small stroke. As a result, "His worshiping of the flower-like little Brita just as suddenly became preposterous—and repulsive."[108]

Love and Subversive Humor

Throughout the 20th century, humor was a prominent feature of Swedish film. A contributing reason the dramas *Sealed Lips* and *Discord*, but not *Only a Dancer*, became box-office hits was precisely that they contained a dash of humor to counterbalance all the dead seriousness. In both cases, popular Stina Berg played a comical sidekick in supporting parts as a nun and a housekeeper, respectively.

A male counterpart to Stina Berg was Fridolf Rhudin. He began his film career as an extra in, among other films, *The Stroke of Midnight* (*Körkarlen*, 1921), worked his way up to become a comical sidekick in films such as *The People of Närke*, *The Rivals* (*Hon, han och Andersson*, 1926) and *The Ghost Baron* (*Spökbaronen*, 1927), before getting leading roles in *Black Rudolf* (*Svarte Rudolf*, 1928) and the overwhelmingly successful *Artificial Svensson* (*Konstgjorda Svensson*, 1929). The latter film helped to make him one of Sweden's best-paid actors until his death in 1935.[109]

In many of the films, Rhudin's characters fell in love, which gave an easy comical effect as he was regarded to have a "funny appearance."[110] With his oblong rubber face, he was simply considered too ugly for love. In the absence of a handsome film face, there was room for the use of socially subversive humor as a romantic weapon. For example, *Artificial Svensson* begins with a prologue, recorded with sound, in which Rhudin acts in a serious love scene before turning directly to the audience and jokingly asserting that sound film has no future, referring to his nationally known appearance: "Looks like mine speak for themselves; you don't want to waste them on talkies."

In the film, Rhudin plays the inventor Fridolf Ambrosius Svensson, a man who lives on his own with a myriad different inventions, and a female rat as his only companion. By mistake, Fridolf is drafted into military service under a false identity. There, he meets the beautiful canteen cashier Mary (Brita Appelgren)—the unattainable love around whom all the soldiers swarm, including Fridolf's antagonist, strong man corporal Göransson (Weyler Hildebrand).

Fridolf, who cannot compete with the corporal's appearance or muscular power, has to rely on smartness and luck instead. The three characters meet for the first time on a country road, where the corporal's big, shining motorcycle has stopped running due to engine failure. This monstrosity is contrasted with Fridolf's tiny lightweight motorized bike. Also, Göransson is wearing a fashionable cap, turned back to front, whereas Fridolf is wearing a silly crash helmet. Fridolf offers to try to locate the fault while the others wait at a nearby café. After having dismantled the entire motorcycle into its component parts, he finds the fault. The fuel tank is empty. Göransson goes crazy, whereas the unconcerned Fridolf offers Mary a lift to the garrison.

Humor and looks. Even in caricature, actor Enrique Rivero (left) is found better looking than actor Fridolf Rhudin (all others) (*Filmnyheter* No. 36, 1927).

Some time later, a misunderstanding arises when the colonel thinks that his daughter, whose name is also Mary, is romantically interested in Fridolf. The daughter is, in fact, interested in a flier named Smith (played by Greta Garbo's younger brother Sven Garbo), under whose name Fridolf is registered. Fridolf is called to the colonel's office, and when he sees Fridolf, he cannot understand what his daughter sees in such an ugly man.

On the drill ground, Fridolf drags his rifle after him in a very unwarlike manner. When he finds out that Göransson is playing the banjo for Mary, he tries to learn to play as well. He soon realizes that it is impossible. Instead, he hides a gramophone in the bushes outside Mary's window and pretends to serenade her, which she, naturally, believes to be Fridolf's actual voice. Thanks to his false identity as a flier, Fridolf is also forced to participate in an air show, a contest he wins by not knowing how to fly, because the judges on the ground mistake his lack of ability for advanced aviation tricks. The film ends with the ugly Fridolf winning the beautiful Mary, and the victory is sealed with one of the longest film kisses of the 1920s.

All the fun, as well as the subversive elements, arise because Rhudin's various characters deviate from modern ideal masculinity on all levels and, thus, stand out as the substance of ideal masculinity's opposite, i.e., unmanliness. Nevertheless, he always lands on his feet as the winner, especially in love.

Artificial Svensson received dazzling reviews. Above all, several male reviewers expressed a certain relief over the fact that the film went against masculine ideals, for example, by describing Rhudin as "half-foolish and divinely shameless"[111] or claiming that the ugly but charming Fridolf was actually attractive: "Rhudin's ugliness and stupidity both had a personal touch, and it was surely not only his amorous canteen cashier who found him irresistible."[112]

Most of Rhudin's film characters had a somewhat revolutionary message, which for a moment maintained that it was all right to depart from a strict masculine ideal. This is one of the explanations for his great popularity. Owing to his "ugliness," Rhudin was regarded as naturally gifted rather than as artificial, at a time when constructions were condemned as affected—an appraisal that was generally the melodrama's downfall.[113] In other words, the subversive nature of humor permitted presentation of the revolutionary because it was not "for real," while the naturalness ensured that it was nevertheless "for real."

The Battle Between the Sexes

One focus of conflict that was also handled with humor was the struggle between the sexes or between husbands and wives. This conflict was manifested in two ways. There was an old tradition, stemming from the Swedish popular burlesque comedies of the turn of the century, circa 1900, in which the wife was portrayed as the absolute ruler of the home. The bullied, often physically battered, husband found a moment of freedom when he slipped out to drink, hunt or fish. This kind of relationship could be glimpsed in *Boman at the Exhibition*, and it constituted the humorous driving force in a handful of films that have been lost, such as *Dan, Auntie and Little Miss Söderlund* (*Dan, tant och lilla fröken Söderlund*, 1924), *The Österman Brother's Virago* (*Bröderna Östermans huskors*, 1925) and *When Bengt and Anders Swapped Wives* (*När Bengt och Anders bytte hustrur*, 1925). The popularity of this type of film increased temporarily in the 1930s, until the tradition died away with a long succession of Åsa Nisse films produced well into the 1960s.

Tytti Soila writes that the stereotyping of women in melodramas from the 1930s was a direct expression of a patriarchal discourse and that extremely few films contained female characters that deviated from the 12 stereotypes she identifies. Among these stereotypes is *The Virago*, the female domestic dictator "who makes her husband's life miserable." Unfortunately, Soila does not attempt to anchor her results in a context. We are thus provided no answer to the question of why films could become so popular despite the presence of female stereotypes.[114] Moreover, the viragos' husbands, the oppressed men, are not discussed. Through use of the universally operative patriarchy, all female stereotypes are reduced to victims. This becomes apparent in Soila's discussion of love, where she asserts that the female stereotype of *The Colt* "is admirable and interesting, but needs the support (of a real man) to enter into her role as a wife. In a way, she deserves admiration, but also needs to be punished for her tricks and rescued into marriage."[115]

According to Soila, in films from the 1930s, love and marriage were consistently represented as educational and character building for women. Men are active whereas women are passive, and exceptions, such as colts or viragos, are punished due to their deviations from the norm. The problem with this line of reasoning is that it leaves no room for nuances. Two synonyms of Soila's choice of the term *colt* are, e.g., madcap and romp, whose meanings are markedly different from their counterpart in the present work, i.e., the young modern woman. As noted, the young modern woman was not representative of an oppressive stereotype, but, according to the contemporary source material, as something positive, by both women and men. "Punishment" in the form of marriage occurred in films such as *A Housemaid Among Housemaids*, but in both that case and similar cases, there were often divided opinions about who was strong and who was weak in the relationship, irrespective of the films' "patriarchal" endings.

The other, more modern expression of the conflict between the sexes depended on a combination of older women's suffrage feminism and women's new and greater personal freedom in relation to clothes and behavior patterns. The misogyny that Birgitte Søland claims to have found in the contemporary popular culture at the time—which, conversely, is not to be found in the source material on youth—can be said to appear occasionally here, although misogyny is hardly the right word for describing the phenomenon.[116] This was instead a conflict about where to draw the new boundaries between masculine and feminine, not least in connection with love and marriage. Articles mirroring this conflict began to pop up in film magazines in the mid–1920s, as evidenced by, among other things, a statement about men made by Polish-born film star Pola Negri:

> The unmarried man is usually an egoist. He surely is considerate toward women, but primarily toward himself. And he doesn't understand how to be a companion. What we refer to as love is very, very common; what we call friendship occurs very rarely between a man and a woman. But this is all probably just in the spirit of the time. Whereas men used to consider themselves our protectors, their view of us now—except when they are in love—is as competitors. And thus they simply don't want to be different.[117]

Våra nöjen published a number of articles on love and marriage, including discussions of how men and women could possibly deal with these new modern relationships. In these articles, the difference between ladies' men and married men was considered, the gist of the matter being that marriage required self-discipline on the part of men, whereas bachelors were immature because they "think constantly about themselves, their own emotions and moods."[118]

If marriage meant self-discipline for the man, it meant self-denial for the woman. In connection with journalist Anna Nordenström-Law's book on the art of keeping a man, *Våra nöjen* published an excerpt from the book, including several thoughts about the married man's need for love. Here, marriage was described as a roaring emotional journey of bliss that gradually levels out as the man reduces his physical tenderness. We learn that this is perfectly natural, but that "eighty percent of all married women fail to comprehend it"; instead, they begin to worry. In an attempt to bring the marriage back to its happy beginning, the woman may display "a sickening, erotic persistency that annoys the man." Nordenström-Law's advice was to idealize the man instead: "Your obvious duty is to admire and praise your man, to inspire him. [...] Woe betide the woman who finds fault with him or nags at him! If she does this, she will betray his most sacred hope. He will feel deceived, ridiculed, and completely taken in."[119] But time flew by, and an article published about a year later raised the question of the status of men's peace of mind, given that women appeared increasingly to be the active party in initiating relationships. The interviewed men were unanimous in their negative attitude toward women taking the initiative: "Write that a man doesn't like being chased by women. That he prefers to do his own chasing. He is the one to take the first step, not the woman."[120] Another article maintained that women had laid aside the weaknesses that were part of their make-up in the previous century. The new woman has "transformed herself so unprecedentedly" that, these days, she neither faints nor fears rats. And she no longer "turns on the waterworks" if her husband comes home too late. "She simply pays him back in kind."[121]

It was also at this time that the "sensation" of a woman in men's clothing became a reality. Once again, a reporter went out on the town to ask questions about the ladies' new fashion: pants. The male attitude can be summarized as follows: Young women were welcome to wear pants, but such attire was not suitable for older women. However, one woman in long pants had this to say when asked whether it was appropriate for women to wear pants in public:

—Of course! If men wear pants, why shouldn't we? Equality, please.
—Isn't it instead a matter of aesthetics?
—Well, perhaps you don't think they suit me?
(She said, looking at herself with relish in the polished display window.)

> —Let me tell you, she went on to say, that the modern woman is, as it were, created for long pants. Slender and agile with a boyish haircut. And what's more, it's perfectly hilarious to meet an elderly gentleman on the street who casually asks:
> —Listen, my young man, can you tell me the way to the Biology Museum?[122]

Many of the articles and reportages were marked by humor simply because, using humor, one could express truths that might otherwise have been construed as problematic or offensive. The films that dealt with the modern conflict between the sexes were also characterized by humor. In Sweden, the rather antiquated women's suffrage feminism persisted as a subject of ridicule, sometimes interwoven with the modern struggle between the sexes. In *The Norrtull Gang* and *The Girl in Tails,* we see caricatures of older feminists, often portrayed in pants, tie and monocle, and smoking a pipe. These older feminists were frequently depicted as strikingly ugly, a coincidence that Elin Wägner had views on in connection with *The Norrtull Gang.*[123]

In *Getting Married* (*Giftas*, 1926), which was based on one of Strindberg's marriage novelettes from the 1880s, Paul (Olof Winnerstrand) and Signe's (Tora Teje) happy marriage is infiltrated by an older suffragette, Annie (Hilda Borgström). Paul is a naval officer and, thus, often away on maneuvers. Signe is a housewife. After six years of marriage, they are still like newlyweds because they often spend weekends together at a hotel where they can devote themselves to each other.

On her way home from one of these romantic encounters, Signe meets her old friend Annie, who has just finished her new book: "The Martyr in Marriage—A Word of Warning." After reading the book and falling under Annie's influence, Signe soon becomes a dedicated feminist. Her relationship with Paul changes drastically, from affectionate to cold. When Paul comes home, Signe has removed all adornments with erotic motifs from the bedroom. At the breakfast table, Signe and Annie are busy planning how to "check men's wild advances." A bit later, a meeting of mannish women is organized. A few men participate, too, and they are depicted knitting and on the verge of tears.

Paul—who has demonstrated masculine self-restraint by resisting a proposition from a vamp on the train home—realizes that he must do something to put everything right again. He achieves this through male cunning. He has noticed that Annie is interested in him, and therefore ingratiates himself to her to make Signe jealous. Annie begins dressing in modern clothes and has her hair done. In contrast, Signe dresses frumpishly and has stopped caring about her appearance. At a dinner dance, Paul flirts intensely with Annie. This leads to a showdown between Paul and Signe, who both pack their bags before finally reconciling.

Given its narrative contents, the film established that feminism causes men to be tempted by infidelity, as well as the notion that feminists are frigid. The only thing that could remedy frigidity was sex, which is supplied by the man. *Getting Married* could constitute a kind of confirmation of patriarchal dominance in the world of film, if not for the fact that it was hardly representative of Swedish film production. Based on the reviews, which were lukewarm at best, it appears that the film was regarded as very old-fashioned: "But why, in the name of all the gods, an idea that is so unconvincing and has so incredibly little contact with reality. [...] Today's woman would never behave like that, even if she were featherbrained."[124]

In films with no suffragettes, the conflict was given shape in different ways. One film that was mentioned at the time, but that later came to be a uniting symbol, was *The Battle of the Sexes* (1928), a modern comedy by D.W. Griffith, in which the struggle between the sexes concerned where the new boundaries were to be drawn. In this film, a loving father (Jean Hersholt) is seduced by a very purposeful gold-digger, Marie (Phyllis Haver). On the surface, Marie is a prototype of the modern young woman, but as it turns out, she is driven by her love of a male vamp. The father's infidelity results in the collapse of the nuclear family, and the film's true heroine turns out to be the daughter, Ruth (Sally O'Neill). Ruth is observant and finds out about her father's infidelity, physically saves her mother from suicide, and thereafter, goes to Marie's apartment with a revolver to force Marie to leave her father. Via Griffith's characteristic intercutting between two story lines, the film comes to a decisive moment with Marie and the male vamp quarreling in one room, and the father and Ruth quarreling in the next. If the first-mentioned quarrel maintains the traditional gender coding, the second one questions the same coding, as Ruth rejects her father's patriarchal protest—she has pretended to be interested in the male vamp—arguing that she is only following in her father's footsteps.

The melodramatic elements are piled on top of one another, which one reviewer routinely classified as typical "American pandering to the public."[125] The actors, however, especially Sally O'Neil's active Ruth, consistently received favorable reviews.[126]

The same conflict can be found in *Jansson's Temptation*. In this film, Gunnar Jansson (Edvin Adolphson) lives "the bachelor's thoroughly happy and unclouded life" as a farmer, businessman and horse trainer. His farm is adjacent to the estate of a baron. The two men are in the midst of litigation over a waterfall situated on the boundary dividing the two properties. In this rural setting, Gunnar is portrayed as an upright and self-sufficient man's man who stands firm against the despotic baron. Gunnar also has a good, almost fatherly relationship to the young stableboy on his farm.

One day, the baron's daughter Inga (Margita Alfvén) returns home from a boarding school in France. The character is introduced while driving a car at high speed—the baron's driver having been relegated to the passenger seat—intimating that she is an independent, modern woman. On their way, they meet with Gunnar, who is out training a horse. It is a surly first encounter, ending when Inga calls Gunnar a "lout" as neither of them is willing to give up their independence. Thus, the struggle between the sexes has begun.

A little later, Gunnar is invited by Inga to the baron's estate under the pretense that he is to examine a trotting horse. When Inga does not show up, Gunnar walks to the manor house, where he gets lost. Inga laughs at him when he spits superstitiously because a cat has crossed his path. When they are alone in her room, Inga makes a pass at Gunnar, which confuses him. About to take her hand, he learns that a "real gentleman kisses a woman on the hand." Gunnar says that farmers don't do that.

"What do you do, then?," Inga asks.

"Well ... we don't kiss hands.... We go for it right away...," Gunnar replies, with an uncertain smile. Inga continues behaving provocatively, which scares Gunnar; he is apparently not used to aggressive females. Finally, his eyes darken, he throws his hat aside and tries to embrace Inga. She reacts with fear and yells at Gunnar, who is now very confused and runs away. A little later, the scene is repeated in the stable when the unaffected Inga chooses to come down. She continues behaving seductively, but Gunnar is unable to interpret her signals. Finally, he kisses her violently. Inga goes wild and gives his cheek a lash with her riding whip. Gunnar gets angry in his turn, pushes her over onto the hay and walks away.

Naturally, it turns out that Gunnar and Inga are in love with each other. Neither of them, however, is able to express it in a way that the other can understand and accept. Gunnar's "natural" violence—which, at least in the world of film, often turned ladies into jelly in men's strong arms—did not work as a first step. At the same time, Inga shows her independence in a way that irritates Gunnar's masculinely coded sexual drive and that, as Gunnar sees it, gives him "permission" to embrace or kiss Inga without her consent. The clash, and the new conflict between the sexes, could not be clearer.

In *Jansson's Temptation*, the conflict is resolved by Inga and Gunnar first becoming friends and thrashing things out with each other before the film can end with the traditional final kiss. This new phenomenon of both men and women experiencing and playing out hot emotions, initiating relationships and being active as well as passive could be perceived as controversial. This is why the film is a comedy—a context in which such things could be handled more easily.

The fact that Edvin Adolphson played this part puzzled some reviewers

Love and misunderstanding. A scared Inga (Margita Alfvén) and a confused Gunnar (Edvin Adolphson) after his unsuccessful romantic advances in *Jansson's Temptation* (*Janssons frestelse* [1928]/Film AB Minerva/courtesy Swedish Film Institute).

as, during the 1920s, he had chiefly made his name as an eminent villain in, e.g., *The Flying Dutchman* (*Den flygande holländaren*, 1925), *Sealed Lips* and the two parts of *Gustaf Wasa* (1928).[127] This was also the only time in the 1920s that a Swedish actor came anywhere near the rough Meighan type. It may have been the case that Adolphson's dark eyes and bad-guy persona were judged as necessary to counterbalance the young woman's sexual autonomy.

In the reviews, Adolphson was considered top notch, as the "somewhat harsh and rugged well-to-do farmer."[128] Only Lorens Marmstedt had objections, because Adolphson "seems too decked out and polished for his part" and because Jansson "should actually be a rough-hewn child of nature." The same reviewer thought that the scene in which Margita Alfvén hits an insolent admirer in the face with a fish demonstrated "a lack of taste; one is dumbfounded when confronted with such vulgarity."[129] The love scenes, which were unorthodox for Swedish film, were called "violent flirtation"[130] and were regarded as "risqué and difficult to play."[131]

The Rivals is an action comedy in which the gender conflict recurs and which, according to Soila's deterministic approach, ends with an oppressive marriage. But like *A Housemaid Among Housemaids*, *The Rivals* does not follow the patriarchally defined path to marriage. The loving couple in this film consists of two journalists, Harry (Nils Ohlin) and Maud (Vera Schmiterlöw), who are competing for the same scoop.

Harry is a "promising young force" who dresses fashionably, smokes and is initially portrayed as ambitious, daring and agile. He threatens men with a beating when needed, or he charms housekeepers with a smile so they will let him into places where he can ferret out new sensational stories. But his masculinely coded pushiness falls flat when he meets Maud. Maud is even more ambitious and active. She keeps duping Harry until he finally loses his job. Compared to Maud, Harry stands out increasingly as a fumbling wimp, and a credibility crisis arises around the film's two lovers. The scriptwriters are therefore forced to resort to a melodramatic and seemingly patriarchal emergency solution: It is revealed that Maud has been interested in Harry all along, and that the competing is part of her plan to catch him. The effect of this twist, however, is that Maud seems to be even more active compared to the passive Harry, who remains just a pawn in her game.

Toward the end, an attempt is made to restore Harry's halting masculinity in an impressive car chase scene, which ends with Harry saving Maud—who is hanging over a precipice. Still, the film ends when Maud gets Harry a new job at her newspaper and with the line: "You will always be my big silly boy." When Maud initiates the final kiss, the victory of the young modern woman is complete.

Nils Ohlin's love-struck journalist was met with dual opposition in the reviews, which were, of course, written by journalists. *Arbetet*'s critic was particularly upset: "A journalist who betrays his calling for a pair of lovely eyes is not a real journalist. He can just go home and go to bed once and for all. [...] No thank you, Mr. Nils Ohlin, the type of journalist you try to portray for the Swedish film audience does not sit well with us. Our noble profession must not be desecrated by bunglers."[132]

Who is really in charge? Maud (Vera Schmiterlöw) and Harry (Nils Ohlin) in *The Rivals* (*Hon, han och Andersson* [1926]/Värmlandsfilm/courtesy Swedish Film Institute).

Regarding masculinity, an overwhelming majority of reviewers felt that Ohlin was a "much too well-behaved mamma's boy."[133] Vera Schmiterlöw, on the other hand, is "a smart female journalist—she is pretty and cheerful and, above all, her acting in the really exciting scenes the film offers is exceptionally good."[134] The paper *Social-Demokraten* wrote that Schmiterlöw was a "natural, little young lady, one that Stockholm's pen-pusher corps would certainly want to count as a member."[135]

The fact that the film's gender relation—which was upside down according to current norms—functioned as fiction, and that the reviewers generally did not find it offensive or surprising can be seen in the frequent use of adverbs such as "naturally" and "of course" to describe that the woman was the stronger character and that this had become self-evident in a very short time period.[136] This experience came from watching the many American films that portrayed gender in a progressive manner, e.g., *The Battle of the Sexes.* This was a type of Americanization that had undoubtedly influenced *The Rivals* and that, in contrast to the often-reproached artistic Americanization, was thought to be something positive.[137]

The year 1929 saw a crisis in Swedish film production. Not a single film was released during the first nine months of that year. In the fall of 1929, six films were finally produced, five of which were planned to be sound films. In the end, three were shown with some form of sound: *Ville Andeson's Adventures*, *Artificial Svensson* and *Say It with Music* (*Säg det i toner*, 1929). In Swedish film history, *Say It with Music* is usually said to be Sweden's first sound film. But as a matter of fact, both *Ville Andeson's Adventures* and *Artificial Svensson* were released earlier. The book *Svensk filmografi 2* maintains that the final wedding sequence in *Ville Andeson's Adventures* had obviously been intended to feature sound, but "as far as is known, the film has never been shown with sound."[138] However, in his autobiography, director Sigurd Wallén mentions that several songs for the film were recorded on phonograph records, and a reviewer at *Svenska Dagbladet* complained that "the synchronization left a great deal to be desired."[139] A month later, there were further complaints about the synchronization. And at this point, the existence of John Wilhelm Hagberg's recording of "Stockholm, My Childhood Town" was confirmed, as well as the fact that it was played in connection with the film's final wedding sequence.[140] *Ville Andeson's Adventures* was, thus, the first Swedish sound film.

In the last film of the decade, *Say It with Music,* a class perspective on the conflict between the sexes is played out in the story of a poor young man, Olof (Håkan Westergren), and a rich young woman, Lisa (Elisabeth Frisk), who begin a relationship that is looked upon with disapproval by Lisa's parents. This was a common theme in Swedish films from the 1920s, the difference being that the man in the forbidden affair was typically rich and the woman poor. *Say It with Music* seems to mark the beginning of a period of films made in the 1930s in which the financially weaker man must work his way upwards to overcome the female advantage.[141] In the film, this is accomplished when Olof becomes a successful composer of popular songs—songs that were integrated into the film plot and that contributed to the unparalleled success of *Say It with Music*.

Olof lives in the Södermalm area of Stockholm. To support his mother, he works as a streetcar conductor. He doesn't despise his job, but dreams of continuing his studies and of making music. His father, who has worked as a streetcar conductor for 25 years, dies on the very day Olof graduates from high school.

One day at the harbor, Olof witnesses how a dog is close to being crushed by a falling box. Running to save the dog, he pushes his way forward through the jeering dock workers. This is witnessed by Lisa, a modern young woman with short-cropped hair who drives her own car and who, to all appearances, is attracted by Olof's protective qualities.

Early on in the film, Olof is established as a "soft" young man without any "hard" masculine characteristics. Olof's relationship to his mother is very affectionate and he has no problem showing his emotions. This is even given visual space in the film during the lengthy uses of sequences featuring mood-creating music. In contrast to Nils Ohlin in *The Rivals*, Olof does not appear to be a wimp. This is because he is portrayed as a sensible and honest young man who never preens himself or tries to dominate others, least of all women. This becomes obvious in the first love scene with Lisa, in which Olof holds her hand, watches the sunset, sings, looks deep into Lisa's eyes and kisses her hand—until Lisa initiates the first kiss. The difference from Edvin Adolphson's brusque seduction tricks in *Jansson's Temptation* could not be greater. Thus, Olof embodies a new modern masculine ideal on the threshold of the 1930s—an ideal that is in good accordance with what the young modern women in Søland's study were looking for in a perfect husband: trust, shared responsibilities and leisure interests as well as physical intimacy.[142]

4

Sexuality and Popularity
Queer Moments and Gösta Ekman's Androgynous Masculinity

In an article from 1927, two gentlemen discussed the phenomenon of the modern woman and her consequences for marriage, reproductive choice, the spirit of the time, and men:

> Marry a mannish woman—i.e., one who doesn't consider herself a finer and nobler being than yourself, but who wishes to be your equal in everything—and we shall see if conflict doesn't steal into your marriage. Because to her the rule is: Equal rights for equal individuals. By making demands for equality, she descends to a lower plane, steps down from the elevated position she has over the fray, a position the man, in his gallantry, wants to give her. [...] Life loses some of its romance and becomes more realistic, drastic and coarse. [...] And in addition, there are the domineering women, whose number is probably growing rather than diminishing, and who prefer to marry good-natured and peaceable men whom they can rule. This is how feminized masculinity is rewarded. But do you think real men derive any pleasure from all this? No, of course not. But instead, we can be glad on behalf of these effeminate men. They seem to get married more easily now than before. [...] It could be said, with a slight exaggeration, that we live in the golden age of mannish women and effeminate men.[1]

Apart from the fact that the two gentlemen consider themselves to be "real" men, their world of ideas is dominated by heterosexual partner relationships that in no way include homosexuality. The thought that mannish women or effeminate masculinity could amount to female or male homosexuality never crosses their minds. Everything is, instead, a matter of the influence of reversed gender roles on marriage, a state that is unavoidable. The article is not unique. After 1925, the film magazines poured out articles, film reportages and caricature drawings under headings such as "Woman or man?,"[2] "Man or woman?"[3] and "If they were women."[4] Also, films problematizing the experienced shifting of gender codes were common, e.g., *The Girl in Tails* or the American movie *Man Crazy* (1927), to mention but two.

At one level, the ongoing attempts to explain and put into order the new masculinities and femininities could be said to exemplify the hegemony of the heterosexual matrix. The question is whether such a simplification is possible, particularly in view of the fact that, from today's perspective, the obvious opposite of heterosexuality—homosexuality—was never part of the equation. At another level, therefore, we can ask whether the phenomenon at issue—homosexuality—was at all necessary in order to constitute heterosexuality, or the heterosexual matrix, as has often been claimed.[5]

"If they were women": male film stars (clockwise from upper left) Douglas Fairbanks, Rudolph Valentino, Richard Barthelmess, Gösta Ekman, Buster Keaton and Harold Lloyd (center) (*Filmjournalen* No. 9, 1925).

There is a loose connection between an official and a more general level of thinking, because earlier research on homosexuality has usually relied on sources such as medical literature, trial records and legal texts, but less frequently on sources from popular culture.[6] The medical term *homosexuality* was coined in 1869 by Swiss physician Karoly Maria Benkert. In the Swedish research, however, the "homosexual breakthrough" is usually considered to have taken place in 1907, when a certain Nils Santesson was prosecuted for fornication with another man. This resulted in further spreading of the terms *homosexual* and *homosexualism* by the scandal-hungry press corps.[7] This does not mean that the term functioned as it does today. Moreover, there are those who claim that it did not acquire its present meaning until the 1950s and 1960s, whereas what we now call homosexual acts have always existed.[8] The distinction lies between what is considered an isolated act and what is considered an established sexual disposition. Because if homosexuality did not "exist" in the latter sense, at least not outside medicine and the courts, then it takes on great importance for how men and women, as well as their bodies and sexuality, were discussed and depicted in the 1920s.

According to Michel Foucault and others, a paradigm shift in views on sexuality took place during the 19th and at the beginning of the 20th century. This was primarily a question of sexuality having slipped out of the Church's moralizing grip, instead ending up under the microscope of science, where it was medicalized as a truth in moralizing forms. Sexuality within marriage was still recommended. However, medical science's pursuit of truth resulted in an increase in the number of sexualities, most of which were described as deviations from the norm. Among these sexualities, the medical term *heterosexuality* (coined in 1868) was mentioned in particular. This did not stand for the opposite of homosexuality, but designated the perverted practice of having sex for pleasure. Therefore, according to Foucault, the notion of the Victorian era as a reserved and repressive period in relation to sexuality is not correct, the reason being that scientific findings on masturbation, prostitution, hysterics, homosexuality, heterosexuality, etc., trickled down as increasingly permanent truths, which at once elucidated and cast suspicion on almost all forms of sexuality.[9]

David Tjeder has made rather similar observations indicating that this medical way of thinking was timely in relation to Swedish middle-class men's relation to sexuality during the 19th century. Continence was proclaimed as the ideal, but in practice, the seducer, or the Don Juan ideal, served as the true model for most men.[10]

In medical terms, a Don Juan type was classified as perverted, but this model could nevertheless function as a prevailing ideal. For this reason, Foucault maintains that the repressive view of sexuality also gave rise to an impetus, where power and pleasure interacted and reinforced each other and where resistance to power—the medical truth—was itself capable of producing pleasure. By embracing the Don Juan ideal, one could oppose predominant morals, marriage and family formation.[11] However, the degree of resistance an individual could afford was linked to criteria such as gender, class, ethnicity and generation, factors that Foucault hardly touched upon at his high level of abstraction and that have literally delimited the relevance of Tjeder's results to concerning middle-class men, while, e.g., women and working class men had a different relation to power and pleasure.

Foucault discusses yet another distinction that he considers specific to Western society: that between *ars erotica* and *scientia sexualis*. Historically, there have been two approaches to producing and teaching the truth about sexuality. Almost all the great civilizations, such as those of China, Japan, India, Rome and the Muslim societies, have utilized *ars erotica*—erotic art. In contrast, according to Foucault, early modern Western society was the only civilization to practice *scientia sexualis*—a scientific approach that stands in opposition to illusory art and that discloses the truth about sexuality through confession: "In any case, next to the testing rituals, next to the testimony of witnesses, and the learned methods of observations and demonstration, the confession became one of the West's most highly valued techniques for producing truth. We have since become a singularly confessing society."[12] The old Western tradition of confession as a means of achieving truth has become part of the science of sexuality. With time, it has taken the form of pedagogy in order to elucidate the relations between adults and children, family circumstances, medicine and psychiatry. Also, the element of confession's link to truth has resulted in sexuality gradually becoming an object on which suspicion is cast, the reason being that the confession/revelation per se contains a stage of concealment out of which only science seemed to be able to entice the truth. However, Foucault poses the question of whether *scientia sexualis*, concealed under the guise of prudish positivism, hasn't come to function as *ars erotica* after all, at least since the 19th century.[13]

Leaving the sphere of medical literature and jumping down into the barrel of popular culture, using film as our example, it doesn't take too long until we meet *ars erotica*'s cousin, pornography—a film genre that began immediately after the film camera was invented. There can be no doubt that pornography borders on *ars erotica*, and that it teaches sexuality to a higher degree than medical literature does and without this body of literature's euphemisms. Up until the late 1960s, the distribution of pornographic films was insignificant in Sweden, owing to very strict censorship.[14] This does not mean that such films were not shown in Swedish cinemas in the 1910s and 1920s. It is, however, difficult to determine the extent to which they were shown. Unannounced performances clearly took place, a circumstance that was related to (as well as strengthened) the secretiveness surrounding sexuality.[15]

To fill in the gap, as it were, a large number of *Aufklärungsfilme* (instructional films) came to Sweden, first from Germany in the 1910s and then from the Soviet Union in the 1920s. These films combined the pedagogical and confessional elements. These instructional films used the melodramatic format to handle and discuss problems such as pacifism, alcoholism, venereal diseases, prostitution and, in a few cases, homosexuality. One common feature of the films was that they attributed a social status to individual and sexual problems—a social status that was later linked to several different moral declarations.[16] The way in which these social problems were given shape often bordered on the downright sensational. But owing to the fact that the films were shown under the guise of enlightened pedagogy—in combination with the strong confessional element—they were able to make their way through the Swedish censorship process conspicuously often. Many instructional films were highly successful features of the Swedish cinema repertoire,[17] e.g., the German *Falsche Scham* (1926), which was marketed as both a visual, pedagogical warning and an audience sensation, later to be shown separately for men and women. Another film was the Russian *Prostitutka* (1926), which was marketed with drawings of nude women and as "a box-office magnet like few others!"[18] *Stockholms Dagblad*'s reviewer wrote: "A genuine film with a purpose, ruthless and clearly produced with the best intention to be informative regarding venereal diseases, which are depicted by means of, among other things, tables and gruesome, living examples." *Aftonblandet* noted that the "tempting title had attracted a full house."[19]

No Swedish instructional films of this kind were produced, particularly on the subject of sexuality. On the other hand, the feature films *The Stroke of Midnight* and *Storgårds-Anna's Suitor* (*Storgårds-Annas friare*, 1927), with alcoholism and *tattare* as their respective themes, can be said to border on this kind of film, one with a social overtones. There are also clear analogies to the large number of documentary short and feature-length films from the 1920s dealing with non–Swedish racial and ethnic groups, particularly regarding the occurrence of nakedness and insinuated sexuality, features that were allowed to pass by the censor due to their scientific quality.

"This season's big surprise!" Advertisement for *Falsche Scham* (1926), one of many German and Soviet *Aufklärungsfilme* (instructional films) whose success at Swedish cinemas was due to their sensationalist appeal (*Biografägaren* No. 11, 1926).

Thus, in combination with the medical literature, and probably to an even greater extent than that literature, the films helped to produce and teach truths about sexuality during the 1920s. Film culture, in particular instructional and pornographic films, belong somewhere between *ars erotica* and *scientia sexualis*. Even the impetus involving power and pleasure mentioned by Foucault can be found here—such that the visual and emotional experience utilized in a cinema—contains both elements.[20] It should be emphasized, however, that the dual process of seeing and making various acts visible contributed to creating notions of gender and sexuality for which the scientific truth had perhaps not yet been cemented, e.g., the case of homosexuality. Through the pluralism of film, a subversive representation of sexuality was sometimes made possible in ordinary Swedish feature films. This representation modified how the seemingly rigorous boundaries between the sexes were drawn up.

Masculinity and Queer Studies

The focus of research on modern ideal masculinity, as well as the prevailing view that masculinity is mainly a homosocial construction, has led to a discussion of men's sexuality that seldom questions the naturalness of heterosexuality. In this discussion, homosexuality is often represented in an unproblematic manner as a subordinate and "natural" opposite of heterosexuality. As a consequence, all shifts between the sexes—for example the phenomenon of cross-dressing—are transformed into deviations from the "natural" and other possible meanings are rarely even considered.[21]

How, then, are such shifts between the male and the female to be discussed without fixing and normalizing? Is it possible to move outside the frames of reference for a while so as to nuance the "normal"? In this context, the theoretically complex field of *Queer Theories* (QT) is of immediate interest. The principal purpose of QT is to scrutinize the heteronormative matrix for deviations and obvious constructions that are able to show that the norm is neither natural nor fixed in time and space, but rather a historical and social construction.[22] In contrast to poststructuralist theories, according to which social gender is a construction that is placed on top of biological gender, QT holds that biological gender is socially constructed as well. This line of thought includes an emancipatory signification, the consequence being that nothing exists that is naturally male or female. Instead, there is an infinite number of different sexualities. At this point, the critics of QT usually begin to rant about the dissolution of morality and society, because "anything goes." It is possible, however, to reverse this reasoning and to claim that postmodernity is, in fact, a moral era in the sense that its aggressive questioning of power structures points an ethical finger at all the social injustices caused by these structures.[23]

If we start from the assumption that there are no fixed categories at all, it may be difficult to have a discussion. However, whereas all of the sciences depend on evidence that is clearly linked to empirical results, QT can be said to be engaged in a search for deviations from these chains of proof—deviations that, by definition, consist of exceptions. QT theoretician Donald E. Hall therefore maintains that QT's most important task is *not* to build its own chains. Rather, if one is to attack the stable hetero-/homosexuality dichotomy, one's task must be to try to understand the contradictory and to permit immoderation in interpretation.[24]

It is therefore justified to raise the question of whether QT doesn't read too much into the analyses. Hall holds that precisely this sort of response—when walls of defense are built up to guard "normalcy"—may be a sign that the researcher is on to something very interesting. A more concrete observation, however, is that the researcher must always keep in mind the firm social resistance against which, e.g., "homosexual" filmmakers work. Analyzing a film from the early 1900s is not the same as analyzing a film like *Brokeback Mountain* (2005), with its openly portrayed homosexuality. The reason is that any possible homosexual theme could not be shown outright at the beginning of 20th century, but had to be hidden behind a smoke screen of secret codes. It is, therefore, easy to cast suspicion on the excavation of a forgotten and "secret" cultural history and to depict such practices as excesses in interpretation. Another example of an approach that may be accused of employing overinterpretation is the study of *queer moments* in texts and films. Queer moments are those which strongly disturb the heteronormative narrative, in the sense that they suddenly crop up, momentarily splitting the dichotomies male/female and hetero-/homosexual in an otherwise normal context. This intention may be conscious or unconscious on the part of the actor or producer, but what is interesting is that queer moments do occur, and of particular interest are the reactions to which they give rise.[25]

It is not my intention to survey homosexuality in Swedish film culture from the 1920s. Instead, the discussion will focus on the male-versus-female codes tied to certain bodies and on how these were discussed on the basis of the sexuality of the time and what was popular at the time—which will, to some extent, include the possible existence of homosexuality. It would, thus, be rash to attempt—for political reasons—to theorize away the categories male/female so as to avoid dichotomies, as is done by some currents within QT.[26] It would seem better to be aware of the problem and to call attention to the fact that such concept pairings contain so much more, which is particularly important when looking at a time when the meanings of the terms heterosexuality and homosexuality had not yet been solidified. Or, in the words of QT theorist Nikki Sullivan:

> Since queer need not be simply equated with same-sex relations, and sex between men and women need not necessarily be heteronormative, then queering what we usually think of as "straight" sex can allow the possibility of moving away from stabilized notions of gender and sexuality as the assumed foundations of identity and social relations.[27]

I will now present a relatively comprehensive case study of the actor Gösta Ekman, who, in the Swedish research, is often held up as the example *par excellence* of a new soft and sensitive masculinity[28]—one in which shifts between male and female, as well as heterosexuality and homosexuality, are found. First, however, I have a few words to say about cross-dressing and its ties to some queer moments in Swedish films from the 1920s.

Queer Moments

The phenomenon of cross-dressing, when men put on women's clothes and women put on men's clothes, is only found in nine Swedish films from the 1920s. It was, thus, fairly uncommon, although it cannot be considered to have been sensational at the time. There was, after all, a long historical tradition including, among other things, carnival antics and other more obvious occurrences, such as the burlesque shows staged in Stockholm.

In QT research, cross-dressing has become next to synonymous with a—later on aggrandized—thesis presented in *Gender Trouble* by Judith Butler. In her view, the phenomenon displays a discord between sex and performativity, sex and gender, as well as between gender and performativity, because the "sex" of the person who performs in drag is not the same as the gender that is displayed. Gender is, thus, only a parody—and not even a parody of the original, but of the very idea that an original exists at all.[29] Because cross-dressing is primarily associated with humor and exaggerated behavior on the part of what is being parodied, e.g., sexuality, ethnicity and class, it contains, as does all humor, a subversive potential for undermining "normality," in the sense intended by Butler. But what is it, exactly, that makes a parody a parody? Is it a parody if it isn't read as such?[30] In other words, what is the meaning of these clothes swappings when they are seen in their various contexts? There is, for example, a huge difference in meaning between a performance by professional transvestites on the stage or in a film and a man in women's clothes on the street. Both can be considered parodies of "the norm," but whereas professional entertainers are protected stars, the male transvestite on the street may be risking his life. There is, thus, both permitted and forbidden cross-dressing within normality—a normality that is, furthermore, historically changeable.

Both *Black Rudolf* and *The Tale of Fritiof* (*Fritiofs saga*, 1924) are comedies that, on the surface, contain the permitted variant of cross-dressing. In both films, however, there are queer moments that modify the heteronormative narrative by erasing the boundary between what is allowed and what is prohibited.

In *Black Rudolf*, Fridolf Rhudin plays Rudolf Carlsson, a filmstruck man who lives his life on the borderline between dream and reality. Among other things, he views himself as a screen hero à la Valentino, practicing his kissing technique on clothes dummies at the department store where he works. Rudolf, who has written a screenplay about bootleggers, is prepared to do anything to get into the movie business. He visits a ball at which film and dance artist Molly Sisters performs, and immediately invites her to his table, hoping to convince her to perform in his film. Molly Sisters, however, is a drag queen—a man (Gunnar Tannefors) in women's clothes. This is revealed early on, both for the movie audience and for the audience at the annual ball, within the cinematic space of a brief scene in which another man thumps Molly Sisters on the back when he is done with his feature, saying: "Well done, Gösta! You dance like a man!" The fact that Rudolf did not see through all this constitutes the joke.

When Molly Sisters accepts the invitation, the filmmakers choose to add another emphasis with the text: "Molly Sisters met his destiny like a man," to avoid any misunderstandings. Sitting at the table, however, Molly Sisters does not behave in an exaggeratedly womanly manner. Moreover, he does not look like a man dressed in women's clothes. It could well be a woman sitting next to the happy Rudolf. After a while, another man approaches, wanting to ask Molly Sisters to dance, but Rudolf shoos him away and asks his guest to join him for a dance. Out on the crowded dance floor, Molly Sisters's wig suddenly falls, causing him to rush out, while Rudolf remains and is a laughingstock. There is then a brief cut from behind the stage in which Molly Sisters does not laugh maliciously along with the man who thumped him on the back. Instead, he throws down his wig indignantly, expresses despair and almost bursts into tears.

Here, another queer moment arises, one with unusually great scope for alternative interpretations. I am thinking of the other man who asked Molly to dance. Did he know whether Molly was a man or a woman? And the "wrong" reaction behind the stage—what did it mean if not an interest in Rudolf on the part of Molly Sisters himself?

A comparison with the screenplay reveals that some remarkable changes were made that both reinforce and weaken what may be "queer" about the sequence. First, the "revealing" scene in which Molly Sisters is slapped on the back was different in the original manuscript: "PICTURE BEHIND THE STAGE: Two guys congratulate the dancer, overly delighted. The dancer says with exaggerated seductiveness: 'Vicke, my darling, hand over a cigarette.' Her request is granted and she is chivalrously assisted with lighting the cigarette." Second, the film scene in which Molly Sisters is in despair was changed from the first version, in which Molly Sisters and the other man are collapsing in fits of laughter after tricking Rudolf. However, this was deleted and changed to: "ON THE STAGE: 'The dancer' tells a few guys about his adventure," which is also not in accordance with the final version.[31] In other words, a very brusque (male) version was changed to a more subtle (androgynous) version when the filmmakers weeded out most of the exaggerations needed to make the parody permissible. It is impossible to say why these changes were made. And, unfortunately, not a single reviewer commented on the sequence.

The Tale of Fritiof was one of three carnival films made by students at Lund University in the 1920s. The film is a students' farce that makes fun of the controversy surrounding Stiller's free screen adaptation of Selma Lagerlöf's *The Legend of Gösta Berling* from the same year. Esaias Tegnér's poem *Fritiof's Saga* was used in the same "free" spirit. The film, thus, takes place in the Viking Age, but modernity is nevertheless highly present in the form of motorcycles, automobiles, daily newspapers and urban environments.

The cross-dressing in *The Tale of Fritiof* is represented by Ernst Alexandersson, who plays the mannish Viking broad Ingeborg in the exaggerated, permitted manner. However, the film's queer moment occurs when the conventional final kiss is to be executed by Ingeborg and Fritiof (Axel Möller)—i.e., by two men and in a manner that exceeds the limit of what is allowed. It is even more interesting that the kiss is followed by the intertitle: "Thus the tale ended. The fact that Ring in Tegnér's poem marries Ingeborg, that he cuts himself to death in his old age, etc., that Balder's fire is quite a different story, etc.—we thought that these things, like the poetic drivel, have nothing to do with film art. We just show the following, edifying final scene":

The intertitle is followed by a close-up of the two men tenderly leaning their heads toward each other, holding hands and, then, giving each other a long kiss. Swedish film from the 1920s does not get more queer than this, but thanks to the carnival-like setting, no reviewer raised objections to this obvious provocation. Instead, they understood and wrote: "Ingeborg was so fair that it was at first difficult for the audience to determine her—or his—sex."[32] The fact that there was room for prohibited cross-dressing in the jaunty student sphere is also observed in films such as *Boman at the Exhibition* and *Charley's Aunt* (*Charleys tant*, 1926), where the men in women's clothes mention that they have previously dressed as women in connection with students' farces. However, with regard to the men in *The Tale of Fritiof* and the subtle sequence in *Black Rudolf*, there is definitely room for alternative interpretations.

Gösta Ekman

> Axel himself is played by Gösta Ekman, who has both good and bad sides. His looks and boyishness are on the good side—Gösta Ekman is after all a man, not a Miss like most of our screen heros. Unfortunately, his manliness is little cultivated. [...] He is not a film actor either: the Caroline soldier does not smell of blood, gunpowder, horse or wet leather, but of make-up and theater dust.[33]
>
> Many have imagined a soldier in the service of Charles XII quite differently from the one represented by Gösta Ekman. Caroline soldiers and their "feats"—where did you go? Nobody has imagined a sugary mother's boy dressed up like a warrior. A more pitiful expression than the one Gösta Ekman puts on when he gets the assignment to bring the King's letter to the Stockholm Council can hardly be imagined.[34]
>
> With due deference to Gösta Ekman, however, it must be said that it is difficult to come to terms with a slicked-back ladies' favorite as a bold Caroline. It cannot be helped that one finds a consolidated chasm between a spoilt dandy from 1924 and one of the more robust warrior figures of the 18th century.[35]

These were some of the judgments made about Gösta Ekman and his interpretation of the heroic part in the now-lost historical adventure film *Charles XII's Courier* (*Karl XII:s kurir*, 1924). The literary original was Esaias Tegnér's heroic poem "Axel." In the film, Axel Roos—"The bravest of the brave"—is charged by Charles XII himself with bringing a secret dispatch to Stockholm. On his way there, he is waylaid by seventeen "Polish ruffians" whom he fights alone with his back against a tree. He meets the beautiful Maria Sobieska and lies with her. Having reached Stockholm, Axel Roos organizes the peasants against the Russian and Polish troops foray raids along the Swedish coast: a "helping angel in distress: his breast is steel, his arm is death."[36]

At first glance, it seems as if Gösta Ekman failed miserably at creating a "bold Caroline" because he could not act. But Gösta Ekman was no commonplace actor. He was a celebrated stage artist in Stockholm and a very popular film star in Sweden in the 1920s. He received lucrative offers from the Continent as well as from Hollywood.[37] So what were the reviewers criticizing, really? Above all, it was his looks. The sugary, slick and spoilt dandy Gösta Ekman was, according to the critics, much too pitiful to give shape to their historical fantasies about what an 18th-century warrior of the Caroline kind should look like. He was a mother's boy who had not developed his manliness, implying that he did not have a sufficiently muscular body or coarse appearance and, above all, that he had too little dirt under his fingernails. In other words, he was not a man according to the ideal definition that emphasized strength, courage and strength of character—inner traits that, according to popular physiognomy, should have been reflected on the exterior, i.e., his body.

The fierce attacks against Gösta Ekman's creation of the Caroline Axel

Roos can be interpreted in many ways. It is notable that he was not considered to be a film actor, but rather a theater actor with feminized attributes, such as make-up and theater dust. Here, a direct connection can be made to the contemporary notion of ideal boyish masculinity that was so strongly associated with the American screen hero Douglas Fairbanks. Gösta Ekman was, despite his boyishness, not manly enough to meet expectations—those created by adventure films and historical writing, and held by some reviewers—regarding how a male historical film hero should conduct himself. All the talk about him being the ladies' favorite and a dandy became a way to make him less masculine, owing to his looks and escalating popularity with women. However, Ekman was never explicitly marketed as a womanizer, and he very seldom played that role in his films. Instead, he often got to create roles that were strikingly asexual in character, e.g., in comedies such as *Puss in Boots* (*Mästerkatten i stövlar*, 1918) and *The Gyurkovics Family*, or in dramas like *Mortal Clay* (*Vem dömer*, 1922). Whether this was a conscious strategy or mere chance I would not like to say. However, the fierce attacks against his masculinity in connection with *Charles XII's Courier* reveal that there were things about Gösta Ekman that troubled the critics.

Looks, Popularity and Genre

Gösta Ekman was popular, and his looks were an asset. In Swedish film magazines from the late 1910s and throughout the 1920s, he was the most written-about Swedish film star, despite the fact that the theater was his true passion up to the time of his death in 1938. In an interview from 1924, he gave a diplomatic answer to a question about the competition between film and theater. He said that "for really good theater, film is not a 'dangerous' competitor," and that "both are good in their own ways."[38]

Already in 1910, the gossip magazine *Figaro* named Gösta Ekman "Sweden's most handsome actor"—an epithet that was to haunt him and of which he strongly disproved, because it cast a shadow over his achievements as an actor.[39] But the popularity he had achieved on the stage would be multiplied by his leading roles in *Puss in Boots* and *The Gyurkovics Family*, owing to the enormous impact of the film medium. According to newspaper reports, he became a national celebrity more or less overnight, as well as the favorite of the female members of the audience.[40] It was said after *Puss in Boots* that "this film all at once made him as dangerous for all Sweden's young women as he has been for all of Stockholm during his career at the Svenskateatern."[41] In connection with the national breakthrough that can happen to a "favorite of the audience," playwright August Brunius wrote a sort of defense article in which he claimed that the favorites "are not as divine as they seem to the wide-eyed girls in the isles." And about Gösta Ekman: "I do not wish to claim that he was born unsentimental: When he came to Stockholm eight years ago to replace Gunnar Wingård, who was of a much broader and more mature nature, he not only seemed thin but also sweetish and soft. One could fear a good amount of impersonal sweet stuff from this young man, who looked so cute."[42]

Here, appearance and youth are turned against Gösta Ekman. In other words, a pretty face is regarded as unmanly. We saw the same reaction in the reviews of *Charles XII's Courier.* Ekman's biographer and friend, Per Lindberg, analyzes his looks and their negative connection to masculinity in the following way:

> The reason why he was interesting to the young ladies does not need to be analyzed—he was "terribly sweet." Why did he so offend some critics? There might have been something too soft and unmanly and superficially extrovert[ed], something too thin that seemed to reveal a lack of natural breadth, and people thought he wanted to hide this shortcoming with poses and charming manners. People thought he laid it on thick to hide an inner thinness—God, his beauty was annoying, his delicacy un-Swedish![43]

Again, we see traces of the popular physiognomy. Gösta Ekman was considered to suffer from such a want of masculinity that he could even be regarded as un-Swedish, perhaps the most derogatory term that could be used in the 1910s and 1920s. In addition, Ekman's appearance and acting were seen as an attempt to conceal shortcomings in masculinity and talent behind a curtain of poses and charming manners. This did not tally well with Foucault's notion of a Western confessional culture, and it cast suspicion on Ekman in relation to that culture. I could go on enumerating examples of the negative connection between a handsome appearance and lack of masculinity, as well as examples of Gösta Ekman's lifelong resistance to this predicament. But though it seems as if he was irretrievably lost in a quagmire of unmanliness, pursuing the analysis a bit further may be worthwhile, as he was not regarded as thoroughly unmanly owing to his looks, neither by women nor by men.

Gösta Ekman, c. 1925, dressed fashionably with white gloves, cane and expensive clothes (*Filmnyheter* No. 36, 1925).

The shifting between a positive and a negative view on Gösta Ekman's supposed unmanliness depends on several factors. First, discussions in the 1920s distinguished between genuine and artificial stars, a genuine star being able to create a platform of popularity through his or her own work and intrinsic development. The success of an artificial star, on the other hand, could not be attributed to talent. Such a star was thought to have been created by unscrupulous film producers who were trying to make easy money on the star's publicity value: "It is a distortion of real values, a counterfeiting against which the audience is heard to react sometimes, but all too seldom."[44]

Here, once again, we see how the distinction between the authentic and the constructed comes to light, or the strong contemporary current that differentiated between art and trash in film culture as well as in society at large. The question is, then, what significance this had for Gösta Ekman. The answer can be found in Brunius's equivocal defense article in which Gösta Ekman, despite his slickness, was characterized as genuine because he was not created by some dubious film producer, but had met with the audience's adoration through no fault of his own. According to Brunius, this was due to the audience's demand for superficial heroic parts, and to the fact that Gösta Ekman actually mastered the "sound" technique needed to create "deeper qualities"; on the other hand, "such a change in the repertoire can hardly be expected these days."[45] Thus, Gösta Ekman was regarded here as a genuine star, whereas his unmanliness was partly accounted for by the parts he played.

An article about leading lovers of Swedish film, or rather the lack of them, may further elucidate the art/trash dichotomy and explain its connection to masculinity. According to the article, the "Swedish film actor, whether he is a *père noble* or leading lover, is primarily a character actor. This may to some extent be due to the kind of films Swedish film studios have produced." The writer held that the reason Sweden did not have a male star such as Fairbanks or Valentino was that Swedish film was equivalent to art, because "we hardly make any comedies [...] and not a single adventure film in the proper sense of the word."[46] When the article was written, in 1923, adventure films such as *Charles XII's Courier* were still uncommon. On the other hand, if we look at comedies and farces, they were, by far, more frequent than the prestigious dramas. The writer simply disregarded the actual state of affairs, thus throwing all Swedish comedies onto the rubbish heap. Based on this, we can construe that the genre was of considerable importance to how masculinity was viewed and judged.

Up until *Charles XII's Courier*, Gösta Ekman had mostly taken part in comedies, with the exception of *Mortal Clay*. He had, thus, ended up in roles that were predetermined to be light and superficial. This did not mean, however, that looks were only regarded as negative in the comedy genre, particularly not by the audience. But even the critics did not put the same negative emphasis on his looks as they did in the case of *Charles XII's Courier*, although mentioning his appearance seemed unavoidable: "In the guise of Géza, Gösta Ekman appeared as the great favorite of the ladies he really is, and many of his old female admirers were surely delighted to see his features again"[47] (*The Gyurkovics Family*). "Gösta Ekman creates his usual film hero. [...] But he is amiable and well-dressed—and, of course, he is Gösta Ekman"[48] (*Family Traditions/Familjens traditioner*, 1920). "Instead, Gösta Ekman, as the fortune hunter, is so much prouder and so much more alluring, a dazzling vision of course"[49] (*A Fortune-Hunter/En lyckoriddare*, 1921). Here, he got away with his looks. But even in the comedy genre there were less kind opinions, e.g., that he was "slick, sugary and empty."[50]

During the same year as *Charles XII's Courier*, Gösta Ekman acted in a car film, *The Young Count Wins the Girl and the Prize*. Referring to that film, one reviewer expressed an opinion about Ekman's masculinity that deviated from those of the other reviewers: "As the young count, Gösta Ekman is the central figure of the performance. An actor with more manly power would certainly have been better suited to the task. In some situations, it is hard to distinguish Ekman's face from that of his leading lady—sometimes she is almost more masculine than he is. But both their faces are a bit stiff. Though the girl is pretty."[51]

Here, a queer moment occurs when the lovely looks of the insufficiently masculine Gösta Ekman made the reviewer unable to see the difference between him and his leading lady, Anita Dorr, who, moreover, was considered almost more masculine than Ekman.

This was not a way for the reviewer to belittle the film, as the review was otherwise very positive.[52] Also, it cannot be a question of the reviewer actually having had difficulty distinguishing between the two actors, because the difference is clear from the film. On the other hand, it may be a reaction to the phenomenon of the modern woman and the unusual degree of equality represented in the film—that is, the same type of reaction expressed by the two gentlemen cited at the beginning of the chapter with regard to the spirit of the time and the reversed gender roles. As we see, it is his fair appearance that once again feminizes Gösta Ekman. None the less, Anita Dorr is made masculine on the same grounds—by virtue of her fair looks. How can we make sense of this? Or does it make sense at all? Pretty looks, which are primarily gender coded as feminine, fall between two stools, so to speak, in relation to the masculine/feminine dichotomy.

As far as the more prestigious Swedish drama productions are concerned, Gösta Ekman took part in Victor Sjöström's *Mortal Clay*, including the customary gala première on New Year's Day. *Mortal Clay* was the first collaboration between Hjalmar Bergman (who wrote the screenplay) and Gösta Ekman. It was set during the Renaissance and contained strong elements of religious symbolism and mysticism. In the film, Gösta Ekman plays Bertram, a handsome young man who is in love with Ursula (Jenny Hasselqvist). But Ursula is married to the much older Master Anton (again Ivan Hedqvist), who, during the course of the film, discovers that Ursula and Bertram are meeting behind his back. In sheer desperation, Ursula tries to poison her husband. He dies, but from the shock, not from the poison, which has been replaced with a harmless substance. When Ursula is accused of murder, Bertram offers to drink from the poisoned cup to prove her innocence, but she knocks the cup from his hand. Ursula is then taken to the court of God. She is sentenced to walking through fire as a means of determining whether or not she is guilty. Once again, Bertram offers to sacrifice himself for her, and his offer is accepted. At the last moment, however, Ursula changes her mind—she has realized her guilt—and she carries out the divine sentence on her own. Because her deceased husband forgives her with a kindly smile from heaven, she can be reunited with Bertram on the other side of the pyre.

One cannot claim, even with the best intentions, that the film's representation of Bertram has anything to do with modern ideal masculinity. Bertram is not only handsome, he is also a yearning and dreaming young man in tights and puffed sleeves. The self-sacrificing elements are reminiscent of *The Sorrows of Young Werther*. The love affair with Ursula is portrayed in the same passionate manner. In addition, he is humiliated by Master Anton for his literary interests. When Bertram draws his sword to defend Ursula against the mob, it is only pathetic proof of the fact that he cannot fight.

On the whole, *Mortal Clay* received cool reviews and was not the success it was expected to be. The leading man's acting was not exactly praised—"Gösta Ekman is weaker, a rather bloodless and tame lover"[53]—although it should be stressed that many reviewers realized the role's limitations: "The role as a lover gives him few opportunities to show more than his pretty Raphaelesque face and his agile, beautifully attired figure."[54] As usual, Ekman's looks were in focus. However, one critic chose to strongly question the meaning of this handsome masculinity:

> Both [i.e., other actors who were praised] in liberating contrast to the pretty virgin Gösta Ekman, who would be irresistible in suitable girls' roles, but who becomes impossible and insufferable even as a f a i r y t a l e hero. How this superficially cute dandy has become the adored hero of the w o m e n ' s w o r l d is a sexo-psychological mystery greater even than the mystery of the woman herself![55]

In contrast to the other reviewers, who pointed out the frailty, boyishness and beauty of a weak masculinity—but still masculinity—this critic took a giant step, high-handedly changing Gösta Ekman's sex. He was feminized as a fair virgin. The writer asked indignantly how Swedish women could be interested in another woman or, at least, in a man without the slightest trace of real or modern ideal masculinity. Here is yet another queer moment, raising the question of whether the male reviewer saw Gösta Ekman as a threat in the form of a homosexual, or whether his statement had another meaning. Before tackling these questions, I will take another turn in the analysis, thus complicating the picture even more.

A Hyper-Masculinity with Queer Elements

At the same time as *Charles XII's Courier* and *The Young Count Wins the Girl and the Prize* had their respective opening performances, Gösta Ekman was given the leading role in the six-hour-long, historical monumental film *Karl XII* (1925)—hands down the most expensive film production of the 1920s. Considering all the harping on his feminine beauty, dandyism and lack of Swedishness, shouldering the part of Charles XII himself—"one of the greatest Swedish men who has ever lived"[56]—was downright spectacular. Even his friend Per Lindberg expressed a certain wonder, writing: "The fact that the delicate, handsome dandy Gösta Ekman managed to create a good likeness of Charles XII's outer appearance was in itself worthy of respect."[57]

By this time, Gösta Ekman had already created a large number of dramatic roles on the stage, and he is said to have been given the role of Charles XII as a "compensation" for having lost the struggle for the principal part in *The Legend of Gösta Berling* (*Gösta Berlings saga*, 1924) to Lars Hanson, who was considered more masculine.[58] Yet this reasoning is untenable because common sense, or rather the economic sense of the financiers behind the extremely expensive *Karl XII* production, should make it clear that Gösta Ekman got the part because he was a respected actor and, in particular, because he was so immensely popular with the filmgoing audience. In a high-risk venture such as this, his stardom served as a financial guarantee—which clearly shows that his looks, per se, were not judged as solely negative, but that they could even function as a very real and economic asset.[59]

This time, however, it was not Ekman's good looks that touched the right chord with or, more to the point, that triggered the entire symphony orchestra of the critics. *Karl XII* was received as "the Swedish national film above all others by virtue of the national and heroic character of the subject matter as well as the force and dignity of the rendering."[60] Despite some flaws, Charles XII stood out in the film as hegemonic masculinity personified in comparison with his antagonist, Czar Peter, the main difference between the two being that the Swedish king could control his passions, whereas the Czar yielded to them, making him appear more unmanly, at least according to the male ideals of the time.[61]

"A monster of valor": Gösta Ekman as King Charles XII, the man above all other men in Sweden's historical consciousness during the 1920s (*Filmjournalen* No. 15–16, 1925).

Charles XII's flaws were mainly that he, according to legend, did not drink alcohol and that he was only moderately interested in women. In the film, this aspect was emphasized in relation to the promiscuous drunkard Czar Peter. However, this caused some male reviewers to feel obliged to point out that Charles XII could indeed "drink wine like a real man"[62] and that "he also was not [...] as afraid of women as has been presented"[63]—objections that demonstrate the discrepancy between male ideals and experienced reality.

What happens, then, if emphasis is put on the fact that it was the "fair virgin" Gösta Ekman who played this hyper-masculine role? Surprisingly little, really. By using very lifelike make-up and toning down his acting, which "was able to capture the proud, humble, bitter, lonesome, idealistic soul of the warrior king,"[64] Ekman seems to have caused the reviewers to forget his earlier efforts and his looks. Instead, it is only a matter of him creating "the will, the tenacity and the irrepressible courage of the solitary man at the head of the realm and the army.[65] In other words, Gösta Ekman succeeded in portraying Charles XII as "a monster of valor."[66]

But how does this accord with the earlier, and as we have established, very strong picture of Gösta Ekman as unmanly and even feminine, particularly given that he was now in the "wrong" genre, one in which this unmanly and feminine image was regarded as more of an encumbrance than when it appeared in a "less serious" comedy? Was the character of Charles XII itself so strong that it could gloss over the previous image? A close reading of the many and long reviews reveals that there are, in fact, a few deviations from the flood of superlatives—in the form of gibes blurted out in subordinate clauses. Carl Björnberg, writing for *Nya Dagligt Allehanda*, praised the film and, at first, Gösta Ekman. But then he could not refrain from writing: "It is only occasionally that the actor's own personality shines through."[67] At the première of the second part of *Karl XII*, artist Gustaf Cederström was commissioned to write the review in the same newspaper. The review was very positive, and at first this also applied to Gösta Ekman's efforts: "His acting has acquired a livelier, more masculine character [...] which one might think would be rather foreign to Gösta Ekman, given his disposition."[68] The clauses stating that Gösta Ekman's personality shone through and that masculinity was foreign to him thus allude to the notion of popular physiognomy, in the sense that Gösta Ekman was unable to hide his inner, "true" self. But what, then, of what does the "true" self consist? The third and final gibe may provide an answer to that question:

> The King's increasing introversion, his insensitivity to the people's suffering, his toughness and, in all his zealotry, his magnificent perseverance in battle are hardly seen. Likewise, the disguise is probably somewhat too good a likeness. And do not forget that we have seen a Karl Gerhad revue show since then [i.e., after the first part of the film].[69]

The critic's point that the disguise had become too lifelike could imply that Gösta Ekman was hiding something. This "something," from a revue show by Karl Gerhard, obviously disturbed the image of harsh masculinity imagined by the reviewer, Herbert Grevenius, as he sat in the movie theater. In addition, he had previously expressed the opposite opinion about the first part of *Karl XII:* "Gösta Ekman plays Charles XII in an excellent disguise, delicately and discreetly, at times in a touching manner. His rendering of the role is what one primarily takes away from the film."[70]

During the 1920s, Karl Gerhard, a close friend of Gösta Ekman's, performed a number of popular revue shows on the Stockholm stage, making fun of current events and well-known personalities in satirical songs and allusions.[71] These allusions often stole the show by creating reversed-gender roles with very risqué texts, implying that certain feminine young men, the so-called jazz boys (and others from Stockholm's circle of celebrities) had an inclination for their own sex. Karl Gerhard, himself a homosexual, thought, among other things, that Gösta Ekman was much too effeminate, calling him "the blond male diva of the group."[72]

We may, thus, assume that Herbert Grevenius's illusions about Gösta Ekman in the disguise of Charles XII had changed between the two parts of *Karl XII*, and that this happened at a revue show alluding to Gösta Ekman's sexual orientation. Consequently, this could also explain the two clauses mentioning "personality" and "Gösta Ekman's disposition" in a way that does not really conform to the image of the hyper-masculine Charles XII. Isn't it possible that this "something," this "homosexual disposition," also constitutes the decisive explanation for all the animosity directed at Gösta Ekman's person, acting and appearance? And if that explanation was correct, isn't it directly contrary to the thesis that homosexuality did not "exist" in the 1920s? Given only the three last-mentioned objections, and possibly the queer moments that turned up, we could take the easy way out and make this assumption. But, then, we would also have to disregard the fact that these examples constitute only a negligible part of all the talk about unmanliness that was not linked to homosexuality. In order to sort this out further, it may be a good idea to discuss the existence of established homosexuality in relation to the image of Gösta Ekman and whether this can be traced at all in Swedish film culture.

(Homo)Sexuality

It is not easy to study Gösta Ekman based the criterion of sexuality. In 1914, he married Greta Sundström, and the year after they had their first child, Hasse. According to the five biographies written on Ekman, they lived happily together until his death in 1938. If we examine the same biographies looking for the attraction to men that so disturbed Herbert Grevenius's visit to the cinema in 1925, the result is meager. However, it is possible to see a development from absolute silence to a partial elucidation connected to the changed attitudes in society. In his autobiography from 1928, Gösta Ekman did not mention this or the addiction to cocaine he incurred in Berlin while filming *Faust* (1926).[73] It was primarily the absence of the latter "confession" that caused the daily press to try to make a sensation out of the autobiography.[74] In 1938, Gösta Ekman's son, Hasse, wrote about his father's cocaine addiction in greater detail, but nothing about his father's sexuality.[75] The same silence can be found in the commemorative book that was published the same year.[76] On the other hand, Per Lindberg's biography from 1942 was more outspoken, particularly regarding Ekman's cocaine addiction, but also in mentioning that, from time to time, Ekman fell in "love through a window" with various young men, among others actor Sture Lagerwall.[77] This literary euphemism may require an extra digression. *Kärlek genom ett fönster* ("Love Through a Window") was a short story, written in 1925 by Hjalmar Bergman, about a lonely lady, with paralyzed legs, who sits at her window, looking out over a square. At a distance, she falls in love with men and boys, not because of their "personalities, but because [they] had a beautiful face, curly hair, a powerful figure, merry eyes, a smiling mouth, nice teeth."[78] Significantly, Gösta Ekman once expressed that "the man who has written this short story is closer to me than any other author of our time."[79]

Lindberg also wrote about a scandal involving Gösta Ekman in Copenhagen at the beginning of the 1930s when he was accused of having had "a disastrous influence on some Danish youth." This resulted in a police report and a brief work ban in Norway, until the inquiry was dropped.[80] Bengt Forslund largely based his biography, written in 1982, on previously published biographies. He raises the question of whether there was something to all the rumors, and cautiously arrives at the conclusion that Gösta Ekman had "a more or less latent homosexual orientation [that] may have attracted him to young men."[81]

The emerging picture of Gösta Ekman's sexual disposition was, in many respects, hush-hush, which could explain the few explicit (disposition) and the many implicit (unmanly) attacks on him. The question is, however, whether this historiography is correct, considering the tactfulness that surrounds all the talk about "love through a window?" After all, homosexual acts were prohibited in Sweden up until 1944. Jumping forward to the 1990s, however, a completely different picture of Gösta Ekman appears in an interview with actress Annalisa Ericsson: "We always had homosexuals around us, of course. Gösta Ekman senior was incredibly courageous, already at that time. He would go into town wearing a fur coat and carrying a purse. He was not afraid. Homosexuality was nothing you paid attention to or thought of as extraordinary."[82]

This picture is also verified by Lindberg's vivid description of Gösta Ekman's arrival to Oslo for one of his many guest performances. "It was spring, the lilacs were coming into leaf and the sun was shining over Karl Johan Avenue when G.E. came to Oslo in an elegant green velvet suit—it always annoys somebody!—in a diamond bracelet that was lost and then found—with dark black rings around his eyes, his fingers flapping nervously with nails painted red."[83]

There is also evidence in the form of live film sequences, such as the documentary boxing film *Harry Persson–Bud Gorman* (1927), where, apart from the actual boxing, showing well-known personalities in the audience to moviegoers was a clear attraction. The private person Gösta Ekman was so spectacular in his dashing outfit that the photographer and the editor returned only to him, and not to the other celebrities present.

In brief, we have two pictures of Gösta Ekman. One is open and extravagant, the other more subtle. There are, thus, four possible answers that are, to some extent, interrelated and that are all supported by the analysis: (1) Many people knew that Ekman was attracted to men; (2) it was difficult to define him as homosexual, because the term homosexual had not yet been established; (3) nobody cared; and (4) few people knew about it.

We return once again to Brunius's defense article, in which he wrote: "No—this actor is not sentimental. He doesn't even try to sound sentimental, although it would undoubtedly be rather lucrative in such a vulgar time as this one." The vulgar spirit of the time, thus, rewarded sentimentality, and here Brunius denies that Gösta Ekman made use of it. But elsewhere in the text, Brunius nevertheless points out there was "quite a bit of impersonal sweet stuff" to be found in this cute youth.[84]

Sentimentality is a topic that Eve Kosofsky Sedgwick discusses in relation to homosexuality and femininity. In her view, in the 20th century, sentimentality has been regarded as negative, as feminine, and, if associated with men, as homosexual:

> The strange career of "sentimentality," from the later eighteenth century when it was a term of high ethical and aesthetic praise, to the twentieth when it can be used to connote, beyond pathetic weakness, an actual principle of evil—and from its origin when it circulated freely between genders, through the feminocentric Victorian version, to the twentieth century one with its complex and distinctive relation to the male body—is a career that displays few easily articuable consistencies; and those few are [...] consistencies of subject matter.[85]

Kosofsky Sedgwick also comments on the dualism that characterized sentimentality up until the 20th century, linking it to a discussion of Oscar Wilde's novel *The Picture of Dorian Gray.* Today, we find it difficult to separate Oscar Wilde and homosexuality. But when the novel was published in 1891, the public disclosure was still four years away. Kosofsky Sedgwick, therefore, considers that *The Picture of Dorian Gray* is "a perfect rhetorical distillation of the open secret, the glass closet, shaped by the conjunction of an extravagance of deniability and an extravagance of flamboyant display."[86] The similarity with the dual image of Gösta Ekman is suggestive. It becomes even more interesting when we consider that all the biographies have spoken of him as a Dorian Gray figure. This was primarily due to his appearance, but also to the fact that his drug abuse and superhuman working pace did not seem to affect him—he was perpetually young.[87] Does this mean that the dualistic Dorian Gray figure had already acquired its homosexual patina by that time? The answer is both yes and no. Studies of the self-image and identity of homosexuals have shown that they were the first to adopt the term homosexual, often long before it had become common.[88] This awareness can be linked to the fact that Gösta Ekman flatly denied the comparison the first time he heard about it.[89] In a letter from Hjalmar Bergman, himself a homosexual, to Ellen Key, this awareness becomes even clearer:

> Some time ago, I happened to reread Dorian Gray and was again touched—though perhaps less strongly than before—by this morbid, yearning thirst for beauty. And I thought: Who is he? He loved a young man—thus a freak of nature, incomprehensible to most, strange, a bit "crooked" if you wish, but still in no way immoral. This love was perhaps all that was pure and real about him.[90]

I will now leave Gösta Ekman for the time being, widening the perspective to include the film culture and society at large, to see whether this awareness extended that far.

Film Culture and Fäderneslandet

If we begin with the images intended for the public, we can quickly establish that there is not a single explicit description of a "homosexual" character in the

Swedish films preserved from the 1920s. The reason may be that "homosexuality" did not exist, or that the subject was much too controversial and thus censored—even though this is not a matter of tangible intervention on the part of The Swedish Board of Censorship. However, even if homosexuality had not yet been constituted, this doesn't mean that no one experienced an attraction to their own sex, or identified themselves as "homosexual."

In a historical account of lesbian and homosexual films, Richard Dyer claims that the Swedish film *The Wings* (*Vingarna*, 1916), directed by Mauritz Stiller, was probably the first film in the world to include a homosexual theme.[91] However, *The Wings* does not belong to the category of films that openly show homosexuality. Instead, the film presents a subtle picture: the secret codes, dual motifs and allusions. It relates how the sculptor Claude Zoret got the idea for his sculpture *The Wings* in connection with meeting the young and beautiful painter Mikael. Zoret adopts Mikael. A few years later, the beautiful Princess Lucia de Zamikow enters their lives. A triangle drama is enacted in which Mikael begins an affair with the princess, despite Zoret's objections. However, Lucia is more interested in the money for which Mikael must repeatedly ask his adoptive father. Zoret falls seriously ill after having talked in private with Lucia, saying among other things: "Give me my child back." The princess replies to this: "You are old and you no longer understand love." When Mikael learns about the illness, he rushes home. But it is too late—Zoret is already dead. Then, at last, the truth dawns upon Mikael and he breaks off his relationship with Lucia. *The Wings* is also surrounded by a frame story, in which the actors and the director play themselves, first while the film is being planned, and, later, showing their reactions to the film when the lights come up in the movie theater after the opening performance.

Homosexuality researcher Fredrik Silverstolpe has identified many of *The Wing*'s codes, which can be regarded today as part of cultural history. He points out the presence of bronze statuettes in Zoret's home as a typical sign of wealthy homosexuals of the period. In addition, he claims that Zoret was thoroughly homosexual, as he was unable to render the tempting erotic glow in Lucia's eyes when painting her. Mikael, on the other hand, was able to do this. Also, the film's use of the Ganymede myth clarifies the dual motif. Last but not least, the film's use of an actual statue by Carl Milles, *The Wings*—a homoerotic icon—must be emphasized.[92] In his analysis, Dyer attaches great importance to the fact that many of the people involved were themselves homosexual and that many around them should have been aware of that fact. He also claims that the benefactor-recipient relationship between Zoret and Mikael was a highly idealized form of homosexuality at the time, although today it may seem like an embellishment. In this way, the homosexual Stiller was able to throw up something of a smoke screen, relating one story to the general audience, while the initiated interpreted the film quite differently.[93]

Although *The Wings* may seem to have sent out strong homoerotic signals as seen from today's vantage point, these signals were not mentioned in the contemporary reviews. On the whole, the film reviews were negative, mostly because the frame story was considered to have a defusing and dissociative effect that broke the illusion of the film.[94] It is clear that the frame story managed to distract attention from the "secret" theme of the film. This becomes particularly evident in the prologue, when the homosexual actor Nils Asther, who is looking for work, reads the following advertisement signed by Stiller: "Young, intelligent man with attractive appearance wanted for shooting of a film." The real persons involved and the advertisement's connotation to a contemporary homosexual personal ad should, in fact, have been more revealing than the film itself.[95]

After *The Wings*, Dyer's history lifts its gaze, landing in Germany during the Weimar Republic, which, at the time, had close cultural, political and economic ties to Sweden. Part of this lively exchange was the import and export of silent films. In contrast to the almost anemic absence of "homosexuality" in Sweden, its presence was somewhat greater in German films. On the whole, there was greater openness in relation to sexuality in German film. This was evident particularly through the production of instructional films, but also through the explicit nakedness found in so-called culture and health films. Even if the decadence of Berlin in the 1920s is exaggerated, Dyer claims that the city had earned its reputation as "sex capital of the world." It is, therefore, conceivable that this openness created an awareness on a popular cultural level as well. Even so, only three films were produced during this period that openly and centrally dealt with male and female homosexuality, respectively: the instructional films *Different from Others* (*Anders als die Andern*, 1919) and *A Man's Girlhood* (*Aus Eines Mannes Mädchenjahren*, 1919), and the melodrama *Mädchen in Uniform* (*Maedchen in Uniform* 1931).[96]

Different from Others was unique. It created an unholy alliance between the famous German sexologist Magnus Hirschfelt and the notorious director Richard Oswalt, who specialized in "sensational" instructional films. Hirschfelt was one of many German scientists who claimed that homosexuality was natural; that is, a disease, and therefore not a criminal offense.[97] He must, thus, have seen in the film medium a chance to create public opinion against § 175 of the German penal code (criminalization of sodomy). Oswalt, on the other hand, must have thought that the subject had commercial potential. The leading character was created by the then-rising star Conrad Veidt. The film is about love between two men and its possible consequences under the threat of criminalization, namely blackmail and suicide. The stagings, which included presentations of several different homosexual subcultures, were interspersed with illustrative lectures by Hirschfelt, who also collaborated with Oswalt in writing the screenplay.

Here, Dyer provides a reading of Veidt who, like Gösta Ekman, had a favorable appearance and was on his way to becoming a star—a reading in which beauty is dualistically combined with a grim tragic nature à la Dorian Gray—a man with a secret that leads to grief and death for those around him and, eventually, for him. In the home of Veidt's character, too, we find the typical statuettes of naked men, which Dyer interprets more explicitly than Silverstolpe does: "It is sometimes argued that the cult of the athlete was just a cover for the desire to look at naked men. No doubt in some cases this was so, but the athlete was also the actual form that desire took. People were not pretending to be turned on by athletic features—they were the turn-on."[98]

The notion that homosexuals were doomed to a life of torment, suffering and loneliness, which would lead to suicide, stemmed from the medical literature, in which such outcomes were regarded as "natural" developments of the disease homosexuality. After World War II, this picture was established in the popular culture as well.[99] However, the film *Different from Others* shows that the stereotype was established as early as 1919. It is, thus, not surprising that the stereotype can be found in several well-known German silent films from the 1920s, among others in the two parts of *Dr. Mabuse, the Gambler* (*Dr Mabuse, der Spieler*, 1922). In that film, the character Spoerri, one of the degenerate underlings of the master criminal Dr. Mabuse, is portrayed as a weak and delicate barber with a strong cocaine addiction—an addiction that served as a symbol of the homosexual's need to alleviate his "natural" loneliness.

Dyer also mentions that vampire symbolism was used as a way to rewrite the dualism of homosexuality. This image can be found in *Nosferatu* (1922), where count Orlok both dresses and moves like a lady, whereas Thomas Hutter is masculine and broad shouldered—a variant of the notion of the inverse femme/butch orientation.[100]

From a Swedish point of view, then, one might expect that an influx of German films would have increased, in one way or another, awareness of an established (mainly male) homosexuality. This was, however, not the case. First, in contrast to the general openness concerning sexuality found in the film studios of Berlin, both open and subtle representations of "homosexuality" were unusual. Second, both the *Dr. Mabuse* films and *Nosferatu* were totally prohibited by the Swedish censors, although this was not on the grounds of their homosexual connotations.[101] More interestingly, however, *Different from Others* was not purchased by a single Swedish distribution agent. Today, we can only speculate about the reason for this. But it is puzzling, in view of the popularity of the instructional genre and the fact that no less than 27 films by the notorious Richard Oswalt were imported to Sweden between 1915 and 1929 (seven of which were totally prohibited).[102]

Returning to the Swedish film industry, it can be observed that Stiller and several individuals surrounding him were exposed in the magazine *Fäderneslandet* (*The Fatherland*). According to Greger Ekman, *Fäderneslandet* was just a scandal sheet that, lacking all ambitions to be an objective news service, reveled in such articles in the late 1910s and throughout the 1920s.[103] However, *Fäderneslandet* had many readers and also brought up a number of taboo topics about which the established daily newspapers did not write. *Fäderneslandet*'s writings about "homosexuality" probably monopolized much of the production of general conceptions among the large majority of people who did not read the medical literature. When *Fäderneslandet* celebrated its 70th anniversary in 1923, it published a blacklist of topics that it "had been obliged to treat with kid gloves" for the public's sake. Under the heading "Perverted figures," one could read the following:

> In principle, *Fäderneslandet* holds nothing against the poor persons who by law of nature have a "perverted" disposition. But the paper has always insisted that they not be permitted to cause *damage* or *public offense*. And we have also pilloried, to the same degree, those who *do business* with perverted eroticism, for example aristocratic officers in the Guards and "aide-de-camps" who "dishonor their uniforms" by publicly displaying their filthy inclinations and, in order to satisfy these inclinations, abuse their "disciplinary authority."[104]

Here it would seem as if the "natural," medical explanation had caught on. The term homosexuality was not used, however. Instead, *Fäderneslandet* maintained that it wished to pillory "perverted" public deeds. Thus, we still find ambivalence concerning the definition of homosexuality as a disposition and as an isolated, perverted action. Even the strongly disapproving stance against the acts being carried out in public was ambivalent, as the paper did not seem to mind if such acts took place in the private sphere. In other words, it was a question of the "infection risk" attached to homosexuality, mainly from the 1940s and onward. There was a fear that the younger generation would be seduced by adult individuals—which, in itself, contradicts the notion of the "naturalness" of homosexuality.[105]

The Dual Personality of Gösta Ekman

Gösta Ekman's extroverted public personality, as described by, among others, Annalisa Ericson, should reasonably have made shivers run up and down the spines of the people at *Fäderneslandet*. However, a survey of the paper from 1922 to 1925, one of Gösta Ekman's most active film periods, has yielded a very meager result. One single article is about Gösta Ekman or, more specifically, his pants. The writer behind the pseudonym "The Black Hand" made fun of the consequences of celebrity status when he told a tall story about how he had gotten hold of a used pair of Ekman's pants, which he subsequently sold through an advertisement. On the day after the advertisement appeared, the "staircase was full of females of all ages and standings, from young backfisches to old ones on wooden legs!" After a quarter of an hour, he had sold the pants for the tremendous sum of 187 crowns! Gösta Ekman himself was described in the article as "Stockholm's handsomest man" and as "the ladies' idol," which takes us back to square one.[106]

We can thus establish that, in some respects, Gösta Ekman's looks and popularity singled him out as unmanly and feminine, but that exactly the same appearance gave rise to an immense popularity, primarily among women, but also among men. Paradoxically, it was his unmanly physiognomy that—via his popularity—placed him in the boots of the super-masculine Charles XII, boots that he, according to contemporary judgments, filled better than Gustaf IV Adolf could have done. This, in turn, can be ascribed to the modern woman's influence (at the box office), which created real scope for a more androgynous masculinity, in contrast to modern ideal masculinity. As Gösta Ekman was not marketed as a lady-killer and Don Juan, the actual marketing was even more logical in that it used several reportages from his home to emphasize "soft" ideals such as fatherhood and family.[107]

With regard to the way in which Gösta Ekman's sexuality influenced the public picture and discussion of him as an actor and as a person, the image that emerges is somewhat ambivalent. Apart from the view of him as a good-looking charmer and family man, there were two additional images: the extravagant and the subtle. The fact that Gösta Ekman displayed an androgynous, unmanly and, in some respects, feminine image in his choice of clothes and paraphernalia did not seem to affect his popularity in the slightest, with just a few exceptions. It could provoke reactions among the "initiated," such as Karl Gerhard. But, in general, Gösta Ekman's "disposition" was not discussed. Was the reason it could not be discussed be that homosexuality did not "exist?" Or was it that few knew about it, or possibly, as pointed out by Annalisa Ericson, that few cared? The question is actually impossible to answer. But it should be emphasized that the frequent objections concerning unmanliness and femininity never had connotations to what is characterized as homosexuality today. It rather seems as if Gösta Ekman's extravagant masculinity, in fact, falls back on the older notion of the heterosexual but outwardly very feminine dandy, rather than pointing forward to the modern hetero-/homosexual dichotomy.[108] The queer moments that appeared in the reviews singled him out as feminized but still as a man,

GÖSTA EKMAN HEMMA HOS SIG

Gösta Ekman, hans charmanta fru och lille son

»Är det fråga om intervju?» säger Gösta Ekman, när vi, beväpnade med kamera och övriga moderna intervjuare-utensilier kliva in i hans vackra hem vid Nybrogatan och på husfaderns inbjudan slå oss ned i salongen, där marssolen just silar in genom de körsbärsfärgade gardinerna och ljuset bryter sig gnistrande i en kristallvas med härliga djupröda rosor. »Ja, vet ni vad, jag är i allmänhet inte pigg på att yttra mig och i synnerhet inte att yttra något om mig själv, varken om min första filmroll eller min sista. Den insats jag hittills gjort inom svensk filmkonst har ju varit, anser jag själv, än så länge ganska obetydlig. Jag har försökt att ge publiken ett gott humör och jag vill att publiken skall vara glad med mig. Har jag lyckats med det är jag mycket belåten. Men jag hoppas att i framtiden få tillfälle att försöka även i större, djupare saker. Att jag är belåten med mitt arbete i filmens tjänst och intresserad av det, det kan jag försäkra.»

Och med utsökt älskvärdhet visade han oss så omkring i sin med konstnärlig smak inredda våning, från vilken vi här presentera några bilder.

Lille Hans kommer säkert att bli en duktig ryttare.

Gösta Ekman själv.

I tankar, vid skrivbordet.

— 111 —

One of several at-home peeks at Gösta Ekman's, where softer masculine ideals, such as fatherhood and family, are highlighted (*Filmjournalen* No. 4, 1920).

whereas the three subordinate clauses in connection with *Karl XII* were the only statements that may have touched upon his sexual orientation. Once again, it deserves mentioning that these reproachés are so few that they drown in the remaining material.

Through his extravagant mode of expression, and as a happy family man,

Gösta Ekman also deviated from the picture of the "homosexual" as a pathological recluse, a picture that had been created in the medical literature (and in film). This was true despite the fact that he had acquired an addiction to cocaine in Berlin during the filming of *Faust*. The reportages from the filming in Berlin did not express one word about decadence. Rather, they dealt with the pride and anxiety felt over the fact that Swedish stars were achieving success on the Continent.[109] The symbolic equivalence that Dyer establishes between cocaine and "homosexuality" have no bearing on the public image of Gösta Ekman.

As regards to Ekman's "dual nature," there is yet another film worthy of attention, as its structural prerequisites are similar to those of *The Wings*. After their initial encounter and collaboration in connection with *Mortal Clay* and, subsequently, *Karl XII*, in the summer of 1927 Gösta Ekman asked Hjalmar Bergman to write a screenplay solely for him. Ten days later, Bergman presented the idea for *A Husband of Proxy* (*En perfekt gentleman*, 1927). The film was directed by Ekman himself in collaboration with Vilhelm Bryde, and it had a traditional, magnificent Boxing Day (December 26) première that same year. According to Per Lindberg, during the preparatory period the homosexual Bergman began to regard Gösta Ekman as a "typical Bergman character—in witty capriciousness and imaginative dialectics." This is said to have contributed to the fact that Gösta Ekman got to play dual roles in the film.[110]

On the surface, *A Husband of Proxy* is an internationally oriented drawing-room comedy in which Gösta Ekman initially plays Marquis Robert de Luny. Robert belongs to the old, venerable aristocracy. But he is without means and has therefore "sold himself" and his manor-house to the *nouveau riche* upstart Charlotte Ponson, to whose granddaughter he is now married. The film's comical strokes are illustrated when Ponson shows the manor-house and its contents to relatives, eagerly pointing out how old everything is and how much it has cost. They finally reach the smoking-room, where Robert is sitting in an armchair. He is also pointed out as one of the manor-house's fixtures, with "the bluest blood of France" running through his veins. Robert is horrified to see how the relatives push themselves up against the smoking-room's glass doors to get a glimpse of the nobleman, and this literally turns him into an beast in a cage, into an object.

Robert displays all the signs of a degenerate nobleman: He wears a monocle and dresses in either a tuxedo, smoking-jacket or silk pajamas; he is generally blasé, has an ironic attitude toward everything and doesn't care about anything except the expensive clothes and footwear that have been custom made for him. He behaves disrespectfully toward Ponson's relatives and his treatment of his wife is thoroughly ice-cold—despite the fact that she does everything in her power to get him sexually interested in her. Robert's lack of interest is brought to a head when one of his acquaintances, Jacques Renard, interprets his indifference as weakness and takes the opportunity to accost Hortense. Robert comes upon them, and custom demands that a duel be fought. But instead of being upset, Robert shows no feelings at all. This is reflected physically when the ritual blow that is supposed to confirm the duel doesn't turn out to be more than a limp pat. When the duel is about to be fought, it is agreed that the outcome will be determined when the first blood is drawn. Robert and Renard begin fencing, and suddenly one of the seconds shouts that Robert is injured. Surprised, he examines himself without finding any wound. Finally, the second must go up and show the "wound," which is nothing more than a pinprick. "Yes, I am literally bathing in blood," Robert says ironically. He takes nothing seriously.

In the next scene, he arrives at the Nobility Club with his arm in a sling. However, everyone at the club freezes him out because Renard has spread the rumor about his wife and "the wound." When Robert confronts Renard, Renard insults him by looking at "the wound" through a magnifying glass rather than the customary monocle.

Here, the film takes a new turn. Robert takes flight into the countryside, crashes his car and wakes up in the home of the peasant Jean Coubert (Gösta Ekman's second role in the film). Jean turns out to be his double in appearance, which suggests that somebody in the de Luny family had taken a turn on the bedstraw with a country girl. Jean's connection to the "healthy" countryside automatically makes him more physically vital than Robert is. This is never illustrated in the film, but it was taken for granted that the contemporary audience would see it that way. Robert therefore convinces his lookalike that they should change places, because, before fleeing, Robert had promised his mother-in-law that he would turn up as a new man at her lawyer's office to withdraw his appanage.

A number of comical complications follow from this, Jean having certain difficulties stepping into the shoes of the jaded marquis. Robert's butler, who knows of the conspiracy, offers a great deal of good advice that reveals the difference between degenerate and healthy masculinity in a very direct manner; for example, he tells Jean not to stand up straight and to try to "look ill!" In the meantime, Robert has a hard time adjusting to his new role as a peasant. This is illustrated by the fact that he cannot milk a cow. He simply puts the milk can under the udder and politely asks the cow for half a liter—please—in the belief that the milk is going to stream down by itself.

However, the comedy soon turns into a drama with sinister undertones when Renard, still believing that the Marquis is a pathetic coward, makes an outright attempt to rape Hortense. However, when the new Robert finds them in the bedroom, the reaction is different. This vital Robert pushes the surprised

Renard up against the wall, knocking him down with a few forceful blows, before throwing him out of the manor-house with a crash. Hortense, likewise surprised, throws herself into "Robert's" arms. Jean now gives proof of yet another sign of health when he shows a sexual interest in the mistress of the house. And to top it all off, his honor prevents him from taking advantage of the situation. Instead, he confesses to the plot. As he is about to leave, Hortense stops him at the door, trying to kiss his hand. When he draws it away she asks: "Why can I not kiss the hand that has defended me?"—which shows that her heart now belongs to Jean.

In the meantime, the real Marquis has come home and overheard the entire conversation while hidden behind a curtain. Thoughtfully, he saunters into the smoking-room where Renard's two aides-de-camp are waiting. The three settle the details of the unavoidable duel. Robert, who takes Jean's place on his own initiative, states that it is "a life-and-death struggle and it must take place within an hour!" After the duel, the injured Robert is moved to the manor-house. On his deathbed, he gives Hortense his blessing. The films ends with Jean returning to the manor-house.

Robert, as interpreted by Gösta Ekman, exhibits a number of traits that could easily be mistaken for "homosexuality," e.g., his disinterest in his wife, clothes snobbery, delicacy and solitariness. Jean, in his turn, represents quite the opposite of these characteristics, thus showing a more forceful, "natural" masculinity to which Hortense is sexually attracted. The point is, however, that Robert is, if anything, asexual in his dandyism. The degenerate streak in his masculinity has, in other words, no contemporary link to "homosexuality"—a view that also permeates the reviews. It is true that, in *Stockholms-Tidningen*, Arthur Nordén wrote about Robert as a "drawing-room lion à la Oscar Wilde who cracks irreverent jokes, a dandy with the heroism of irony." But further on, he none the less expressed his surprise over the film having been specially written for Gösta Ekman because "even the well-shaped wholesomeness of his face and the bright flashes of intelligence contradicted previous statements as to his pitifulness."[111]

Because there were very slight differences in visual appearance between Robert's and Jean's two masculinities, it should be noted that the postulated difference nevertheless had a great emotional impact in the reviews. The peasant was perceived as "sympathetic, upright and handsome,"[112] whereas the Marquis stood out as "decadent, a wretch and a sissy."[113] The change of identity in the film can be summarized in the words of Per Johan Enström: "A man has now been made of him."[114] On one level, the reactions show how incredibly small physiognomic deviations can distinguish a sissy from a man. On another level, however, the reactions are also due to action *versus* passivity. There are mainly two factors that make Robert a sissy, whereas Jean, in the same situation, is a man. The first is Robert's passivity in the face of his wife's sexual advances, something that was hard for most reviewers to accept.[115] The second is his passivity in reaction to the first attempt to rape Hortense. In addition, several reviewers wondered whether Robert hadn't actually encouraged Renard.[116] Note that this was one of the few occasions on which the reviewers did not elect to talk about Gösta Ekman's pretty looks.

A few years later, according to Per Lindberg, when Gösta Ekman "had become more conscious of his own dual nature," he placed *A Husband of Proxy* over all the other films he had made.[117] This suggests that there may have been a "secret" motive for the dual roles in films such as *The Wings* or *The Picture of Dorian Gray*, but this was nothing that, at the time, was linked to the hetero-/homosexuality dichotomy.

In his memoirs, film director Ragnar Hyltén-Cavallius, himself a homosexual, wrote that he had heard through the grapevine that Gösta Ekman "had not been very pleased with something that I, in perfect innocence, called a complimentary article" in *Våra nöjen* in 1925. Hyltén-Cavallius suspected that it was his description of Gösta Ekman as a "Titus," which may have been misinterpreted as a "pleasure boy from the days of antiquity,"[118] that had caused Ekman's displeasure—in other words, he suspected he may have slandered him.

Hyltén-Cavallius's memoirs were written in 1960. A considerable number of years had thus passed since the article was written, which explains, among other things, that Hyltén-Cavallius mistook the year. As a matter of fact, the article was published in 1928, and it is easy to understand why Gösta Ekman became so cross. First, the young Hyltén-Cavallius wrote almost exclusively about how "implausibly fair" Gösta Ekman was. And, second, the article was imbued with double-edged allusions to Ekman's sexuality. It was concluded in the following way:

> But one day, perhaps, the dandy will throw off his mask. Maybe once, behind the Dorian Grayish image, the sharp and passionate features of a mature artist will appear, burning with eagerness to reach the highest peaks. Nobody knows, perhaps not even the charming youth Gösta Ekman himself, whom the Graces once kissed on both forehead and mouth, who enjoyed the kisses with such self-evident assurance, and who wandered on, finally becoming, like Titus, if not mankind's then at least Sweden's and Stockholm's love and sensual pleasure.[119]

A Husband of Proxy is fascinating because, in the part as Robert, Gösta Ekman represents the publicly created picture of himself (handsome, unmanly, fashionmonger), whereas Jean symbolizes the real self, or the masculine man. Per Lindblerg also holds that Gösta Ekman "had become entangled in webs of secrets such that he needed one over-exertion after the other, and constant multiple tasks, to conjure away the image of the life he was living."[120] Thus, where Gösta Ekman's sexuality is concerned, certain parallels can be drawn to Kosofsky Sedgwick's discussion of a "glass closet." With a few exceptions, however, Gösta Ekman's sexuality was not discussed in terms of homosexuality, but alternately as unmanly, feminine and masculine. The occasions on which he was exposed to slander were few and usually limited to the euphemisms of the already initiated, while the uninitiated used a terminology that did not include the modern hetero-/homosexuality dichotomy—thus indicating that "homosexuality" did not yet exist as an easily accessible conceptual category.

5

Among Savages and Wild Beasts
Racial Stereotypes and Ethnicity

In his dissertation on the Swedish picture of America and on how Americanization influenced Swedish cultural life during the interwar period, Swedish historian Martin Alm claims that "a special aspect of American culture was the question of race. This question could not be directly transferred to Sweden, as Sweden was still quite ethnically homogeneous."[1] The claim that Sweden was ethnically homogeneous at the time in question is neither new nor totally incorrect, even though it could be argued that the Swedish population was probably a cultural mishmash owing to the numerous waves of immigration and emigration during the course of history. It is nevertheless interesting that the ideological notion that Sweden was ethnically homogeneous is used to explain why "the question of race" could not be transferred to a Swedish context. This implies that there has existed an undivided white race in Sweden, and that race was an issue only in countries with several "races"; that is, it implies that conceptions of "race" came from abroad, in particular from the U.S.

Statistics show that approximately 62,000 individuals immigrated to Sweden in the 1920s. Of these, 31,500 came from other Nordic countries as well as from other parts of Europe, whereas 27,500 came from the U.S., most of them returning emigrants. The remaining 3,000 emigrated from other parts of the world—270 from Africa, most of them probably returning missionaries.[2] Seen in an overall "White" European perspective, Sweden was relatively ethnically homogeneous in the 1920s. But this did not do a great deal to stop Swedes from entertaining a variety of notions about other ethnic groups or "races," both within and outside national borders. It should be pointed out at this juncture that race and ethnicity are partially overlapping cultural concepts. I will not use these terms in their pseudoscientific, "biological" sense, however, but rather as social constructions associated with contemporary notions of, primarily, gender.[3]

Apart from the idea that Sweden used to be ethnically homogeneous, there has been a reluctance to examine the use of racial stereotypes in Swedish culture during the 1910s, 1920s, and 1930s, and this includes, to a great degree, the writing of Swedish film history. This "cultural heritage" tends to be erased from historical memory. The fact that use of racial stereotypes has been made invisible is a consequence of the division of culture into art and the mainstream, which is illustrated by film studies' focus on the style and form of a few films, but also by the fact that racism and racial stereotypes are in very poor accordance with "art." In no other area is there a greater discrepancy between the myth surrounding the films of the Swedish Golden Age and the real state of Swedish film during the 1920s. Statements to the effect that Swedish silent films made no use at all of explicit racial references are not uncommon.[4]

According to historian Lars M. Andersson, history research has demonstrated a reluctance and an inability to see anti–Semitism, the reason being that historians have typically used semi-official sources in which anti–Semitism did not occur after 1870, the year in which Jews were given rights of citizenship in Sweden. However, Andersson's summary of studies that have been carried out clearly shows that anti–Semitism existed on all social strata: in science, politics, religion, art and the press.[5]

Andersson, who has studied the Swedish humor press, refers to and relies on two film scholars who, in his opinion, have been pioneering in the research on Swedish anti–Semitism in popular culture.[6] In *Folkhemmets bilder*, Per Olov Qvist has conducted a systematic survey of Swedish film from the 1930s. He has, among other things, come to the conclusion that one film in ten contained an anti–Semitic character. However, anti–Semitism or xenophobia has not at all been Qvist's main object of study. Moreover, Qvist claims that anti–Semitism was a typical phenomenon of the 1930s, as, in his view, only one clear case occurred in the 1920s, namely in *The Million Dollars* (*Dollarmillionen*, 1926).[7]

In *The Visible Wall*, American Scandinavist Rochelle Wright takes her point of departure from Swedish films of the 1930s, establishing decade by decade, up until 1995, which type of ethnic outsider has occurred most frequently. It was Jews in the 1930s, Travelers ("tattare") in the 1940s and 1950s and, to a lesser extent, the Sami and Finns during the same decades. In the 1960s and 1970s, Wright claims that ethnic stereotypes disappeared from Swedish film and were replaced by a more serious discussion of ethnic matters. According to her, this was a consequence of the quality improvement resulting from the 1963 film agreement, which only granted support to "serious" films. Wright interprets the fact that the very high box-office figures for Swedish film decreased concurrently from hundreds of thousands to tens of thousands as reflecting a disinterest in or dislike of serious subjects on the part of the Swedish audience. In this way, she implies that serious themes cannot be dealt with within the framework of popular culture, but only by serious art.[8]

Wright claims, without having seen any Swedish films from the 1920s and by referring to Qvist (who also had not seen them), that the Jews were not portrayed in an anti–Semitic spirit either before or after the 1930s. This, she maintains, demonstrates a clear correspondence to the period—that is, that the German Nazism of the 1930s had an intellectual influence.[9] Returning to Andersson, he is also unable to explain why Swedish film from the 1920s, according to Qvist and Wright, did not contain the same degree of anti–Semitism that he had found in extensive circulation in the humor press. The truth is, however, that he is on the tracks of the answer in his discussion about using alternative sources in history and film studies to discover the non-official and, thus, overlooked notions circulating in a society.[10] For example, an examination of Leif Furhammar's survey of Swedish film reveals that anti–Semitism in films from the 1930s was seen as "naive"; it was a matter of "thoughtlessness" rather than "inciting racial hatred." The flagrant anti–Semitic portrait in *The Million Dollars* is not even mentioned.[11]

The fact that Swedish films from the 1920s were full of malicious portraits of Travelers was not mentioned either. On the other hand, Furhammar devotes one line to the phenomenon in *Svensk filmografi 2*, raising the question of "why, in 1924, the fear of Travelers recurs in one film after the other."[12] However, he is unable to answer the question, thus missing the fact that *tattare* were used as a dramatic motor in 11 films dealing with the problem of "racial mixture" between Swedes and non–Swedes, often including elements strongly reminiscent of the American use of blackface in relation to black people.[13]

I will return to Andersson, Wright and Furhammar, because Swedish films from the 1920s included many more countertypes than the single anti–Semitic portrait in *The Million Dollars*. In fact, Swedish films from this period are teeming with racial stereotypes, many of which are tied to men or masculinity. This observation is also made by Wright in her temporally more comprehensive study.[14]

Swedish Racial Thought

Furhammar and others have characterized Swedish anti–Semitism as "naive," whereas Wright distinguishes between what she calls a conscious and an unconscious anti–Semitism during the 1930s, the only conscious anti–Semitism having appeared in *Panic* (*Panik*, 1939). This film pursues the thesis that the Swedish match king Ivar Kreuger did not commit suicide, but was subjected to a Jewish conspiracy and murdered.[15] Andersson explains the anti–Semitism found in the humor press as part of a modernization process that had very little to do with Swedish Jews. The phenomenon is said to have been a matter of teaching who the Other was through codes, which could be used to help orient new city dwellers in an otherwise incomprehensible environment.[16] However, Andersson claims that the modern anti–Semitic tradition was already established around the year 1900. But at that time, only 1.1 of Sweden's 5.1 million inhabitants lived in cities.[17] In addition, Wright maintains that the anti–Semitic elements of films from the 1930s derived their iconographic inspiration from the humor press. There was also a clear intertextual connection between these two mass media as well as between other visual mass media at the time.[18]

These explanations are inadequate. To widen the perspective, all of Swedish society, as an integral part of the Western sphere of ideas, must be denounced as having been extremely racist. Johan Fornäs holds that open "racism and xenophobia constituted a considerable political force during the interwar period" and that "explicit racist thinking was part of common sense."[19] In other words, it is not enough to show that anti–Semitism and other racist notions only existed in film, the humor press and other popular culture media. Based on the insights I have gained into "the spirit of the time" in Sweden, I would like to claim that society was permeated by racist thinking that is, in many ways, inconceivable and perhaps difficult to understand today. I am, thus, clearly hesitant about characterizing the ideas about race that prevailed in Sweden during the first half of the 20th century as naive or unconscious. By choosing the "naive" perspective, today's scholars are simply censoring out less pleasant memories from Swedish history. Also, thinking in terms of race was hardly as unconscious or innocent as present-day projections stipulate. Such thinking was, instead, a state-sanctioned science that identified Swedes as pure, and others as impure or inferior.

In 1921, Sweden was the first country in the world to establish an Institute for Racial Biology. This is not mitigated by the fact that racial biology and its dark epigone, eugenics, were international phenomena associated with the modernization process and science's increasingly important role in society, because, after all, this discipline was constantly the subject of dispute. Nor was the Institute for Racial Biology created single-handedly by the historical scoundrel Herman Lundborg. Establishing such an institute had been under discussion for some ten years, which meant that the doctrine had had time to establish itself in Swedish society already before World War I. When the bill was introduced in 1920, it was signed by all parties represented in the Swedish Parliament, the Riksdag, from right to left—demonstrating a degree of political consensus that was rare at the time.[20]

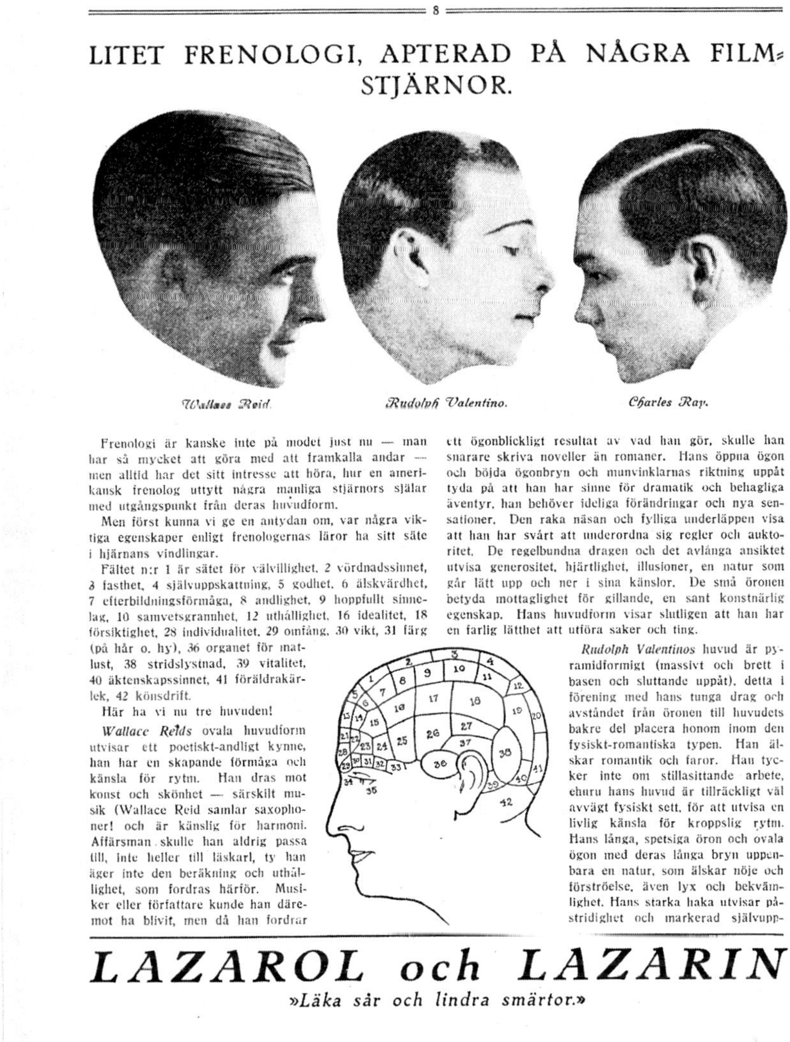

8

LITET FRENOLOGI, APTERAD PÅ NÅGRA FILM-STJÄRNOR.

Wallace Reid. Rudolph Valentino. Charles Ray.

Frenologi är kanske inte på modet just nu — man har så mycket att göra med att framkalla andar — men alltid har det sitt intresse att höra, hur en amerikansk frenolog uttytt några manliga stjärnors själar med utgångspunkt från deras huvudform.

Men först kunna vi ge en antydan om, var några viktiga egenskaper enligt frenologernas läror ha sitt säte i hjärnans vindlingar.

Fältet n:r 1 är sätet för välvillighet, 2 vördnadssinnet, 3 fasthet, 4 självuppskattning, 5 godhet, 6 älskvärdhet, 7 efterbildningsförmåga, 8 andlighet, 9 hoppfullt sinnelag, 10 samvetsgrannhet, 12 uthållighet, 16 idealitet, 18 försiktighet, 28 individualitet, 29 omfång, 30 vikt, 31 färg (på hår o. hy), 36 organet för matlust, 38 stridslystnad, 39 vitalitet, 40 äktenskapssinnet, 41 föräldrakärlek, 42 könsdrift.

Här ha vi nu tre huvuden!

Wallace Reids ovala huvudform utvisar ett poetiskt-andligt kynne, han har en skapande förmåga och känsla för rytm. Han dras mot konst och skönhet — särskilt musik (Wallace Reid samlar saxophoner! och är känslig för harmoni. Affärsman skulle han aldrig passa till, inte heller till läskarl, ty han äger inte den beräkning och uthållighet, som fordras härför. Musiker eller författare kunde han däremot ha blivit, men då han fordrar ett ögonblickligt resultat av vad han gör, skulle han snarare skriva noveller än romaner. Hans öppna ögon och böjda ögonbryn och munvinklarnas riktning uppåt tyda på att han har sinne för dramatik och behagliga äventyr, han behöver ideliga förändringar och nya sensationer. Den raka näsan och fylliga underläppen visa att han har svårt att underordna sig regler och auktoritet. De regelbundna dragen och det avlånga ansiktet utvisa generositet, hjärtlighet, illusioner, en natur som går lätt upp och ner i sina känslor. De små öronen betyda mottaglighet för gillande, en sant konstnärlig egenskap. Hans huvudform visar slutligen att han har en farlig lätthet att utföra saker och ting.

Rudolph Valentinos huvud är pyramidformigt (massivt och brett i basen och sluttande uppåt), detta i förening med hans tunga drag och avståndet från öronen till huvudets bakre del placera honom inom den fysiskt-romantiska typen. Han älskar romantik och faror. Han tycker inte om stillasittande arbete, ehuru hans huvud är tillräckligt väl avvägt fysiskt sett, för att utvisa en livlig känsla för kroppslig rytm. Hans långa, spetsiga öron och ovala ögon med deras långa bryn uppenbara en natur, som älskar nöje och förströelse, även lyx och bekvämlighet. Hans starka haka utvisar påstridighet och markerad självupp-

LAZAROL och LAZARIN

»Läka sår och lindra smärtor.»

Race biology found some followers in the 1920s. The science of phrenology is here applied to American film stars Wallace Reid, Rudolph Valentino, and Charles Ray (*Filmnyheter* No. 10, 1922).

Historian of ideas Gunnar Broberg has shown that work at the institute was characterized by an anthropologically oriented inventory of the Swedish population and by energetic propaganda activities that served to popularize scientific findings. This was done by touring the country and offering well-attended lectures (which were diligently reported in the press), exhibitions, pamphlets and books such as *Svensk raskunskap* (Swedish Racial Anthropology, 1927),[21] in which anthropological photographs were used to give a twisted view of the Swedish racial inventory. For example, pictures of middle-aged Sami and Nordic youth were placed side by side to demonstrate the inferiority of the Sami. The institute was also asked to provide expert knowledge in connection with the production of a dramatic film as well as an instructional film with a eugenic theme. Both these projects came to nothing, however.[22]

What we will concentrate on here is the dissemination of "scientific" knowledge. Through intense popularization, this knowledge won respect among Swedes from different social strata, because it was most likely rather agreeable for everyone to find out that Sweden and the "Aryan," "White" or "Germanic" race always, without exception, came out on top of the scientific diagrams and tables produced by the Institute for Racial Biology. Had Sweden been found at the bottom, I suspect that racial biology would not have had anywhere near the same impact. This racial thinking was most clearly expressed in positive terms, both implicitly in the constant talk about the healthy, agile, sound, well-built and natural Swedish body (both male and female), but also explicitly in film critics' frequent praise of Swedish actors for their "genuine Nordic origins"[23] as an aspect of their contribution to the films. Another example of the impact of popularization was *Filmnyheter*'s publication of an article on phrenology, which used a diagram, photographs and numerical data to categorize a number of well-known American actors into types.[24]

In the 1920s, racial biology was regarded as a mixture of physical anthropology, medicine and dismal cultural observations. The use of, e.g., craniometry was not considered odd. Instead, according to Broberg, racial biology could "for very good reasons regard itself as one of the progressive forces of the time and as scientifically modern." The ethical discussion was far from absent. Yet it adopted the role of a scientifically founded morality of sorts that encouraged reflections on race, nation and family because, in Herman Lundborg's view, mankind had thrown the laws of nature off balance.[25]

Nevertheless, the institute's operations were sometimes subjected to criticism. After having read Lundborg's publication *Degenerationsfrågan* (1922) (The Question of Degeneration), future member of the Swedish Academy Torsten Fogelqvist sarcastically wrote: "The idea that, from a racial biological point of view, lack of patriotism, godlessness, individualism and egoism are phenomena or symptoms of degeneration is very interesting news."[26] Now and then, objections to the use of racial stereotypes in Swedish film cropped up, but these views often drowned in the racial-nationalistic torrent of positive talk about Swedishness.

Nationalism, Swedishness and Film as Representation

In 1922, *Biografrevyn* reported that Mexico had stopped importing American films because Hollywood had used Mexicans as villains in too many movies. The conflict had been going on for half a year, and the American film moguls had taken the issue as far as to the Mexican president, Álvaro Obregón, in an attempt to have the ban revoked. They received the cutting reply: "Mexican scoundrels as permanent fixtures in American films had caused much offense in Mexico, as it was known that the films were distributed around the world, thus giving rise to erroneous ideas about the Mexican national character."[27]

This article is interesting in many ways. First, because an "entire country" had taken exception to a distorted picture of its national characteristics being spread over the globe, which demonstrated great awareness of the impact of the film medium—and a resistance that minorities within a country would have a harder time achieving. It is also interesting that a Swedish magazine chose to report on the incident. This supports the thesis that silent films were international in character. This type of articles did not disappear with the sound films. However, in the 1910s and 1920s, there was a strikingly large number of such articles, as seen from the extensive reporting on the march of Swedish films abroad during the Golden Age years.

Under the telling heading, "Swedish film as national advertising. How the Swedish Film Trust proposes to conquer the world," the director of the Swedish film production company Svensk Filmindustri (SF), Nils Bouveng, said in an interview in 1919: "Second-rate, mass production must be foreign to Swedish film. Why is it that our country's film industry has been able to create a leading position on the world market? Simply because it is a Swedish product, Swedish in the best sense of the word: a quality product."[28]

Sweden should not distribute mass productions, as America did, and this would be guaranteed by the constantly recurring, but vaguely defined, notion of the "Swedish." In view of the successful export of Swedish film during these years, it should be emphasized that it was not only the heavy dramas that sold well, but also lighter comedies, such as *The Bomb* (*Bomben*, 1920).[29]

In 1920, SF's new CEO, Charles Magnusson, was interviewed. He, too, called attention to the film industry's potential to create publicity for Sweden abroad, particularly concerning Swedish nature environments, but also through a "living portrayal of various aspects of life in our country, of our national character."[30] For example, *The Stroke of Midnight* was praised in a number of articles from, among other places, Britain, France, Belgium and Switzerland.[31] In France, the magazine *Le Cinéma* even published a special issue devoted to Swedish film.[32]

To be sure, tributes to the Swedish continued up until 1924, but after *The Stroke of Midnight*, protests began to appear. A Swedish clergyman in Buenos Aires thought, among other things, that *The Stroke of Midnight* "is likely to convey the idea to a Catholic audience that Swedes are a morally primitive people." In contrast, *Filmnyheter*'s columnist took the view that the assertion was completely in error, advancing the commercial argument that *The Stroke of Midnight* had been sold with good profit to Spain, France and Italy—all Catholic countries.[33] On the other hand, when a Swiss newspaper accused Swedish film of becoming American with "the empty noise of gigantic mass effects," it was defended as being art without "histrionic manners."[34]

At the end of 1924, *Svensk filmtidning* summarized the period:

> Here at home, we have for quite some time flattered ourselves by saying that Swedish cinematography is outstanding in the world, that nowhere are there as good actors and directors, even as good photographers and technicians as ours—but first and foremost that no film producing countries have so much culture in their films as we do. And we have explained the matter quite correctly: we have, here at home, an ancient spiritual culture to build on [...] Counting ourselves as at least one of the world's most prominent film countries is, thus, not a form of conceit.[35]

We are further told that the whole world has embraced Swedish film, except the U.S. "where people on the whole lack an understanding of our special art."[36] It was, in fact, at this stage that the Swedish Golden Age came to an economic halt, owing precisely to the overwhelming competition from the U.S. At the same time, reports on Swedish film changed character, as a number of Swedish directors and actors flocked to the Continent, particularly to Germany, only later to continue across the Atlantic. Articles about the successes of Victor Sjöström, Mauritz Stiller, Greta Garbo, Lars Hanson, Nils Asther and Einar Hanson were not at all as frequent as in earlier reporting, and these individual were now almost regarded as traitors to their country.[37] From 1927 onwards, the discussion was not about Swedish-versus-American film. It was, instead, concerned with the fact that European film was now beginning to compete with American film through European co-operation.[38]

The meticulous coverage of and commenting on foreign reactions to Swedish film show that the Swedish film industry was very much aware of film's function as a display window toward the rest of the world. In contrast to Mexico, Sweden was able to decide what would be shown in films that were distributed across the entire known world.

The fact that not everything was considered acceptable is made clear in an article from 1921 entitled "Incorrect Designation of Origin." It turned out that a recently formed company, located in Sweden but with a German director, had produced a film that was marketed with the following words: "Since Swedish film has become famous abroad as *'intellectual,' we propose to pursue this traditional line*, each year releasing a number of quality programs." The editor of *Filmbladet*, Karl Lundegård, argued passionately in the same article that Swedish film is "a Swedish shrine." He was, therefore, of the opinion that "the good name and reputation of Swedish film should not be discredited before the rest of the world by clever, second-rate producers."[39]

I have been able to identify the title of the film, which was not mentioned in the article, as the now-lost *The Bimbini Circus* (*Cirkus Bimbini*, 1921). It was produced in Sweden with Swedish actors and technical staff, but under the name of the film company Baltisk filmindustri.[40] The interesting thing here are the reactions caused by the film, which once again demonstrate awareness of the impact of film on the surrounding world, but also on moviegoers in one's own country. In other words, Swedish film contributed to the visual construction of national characters and races on the silver screen. And just as Mexico protested against the American image of Mexican scoundrels, some images in Swedish films triggered protests in other countries, Finland among others.

Blacks

> But for the time being it must be considered a wonderful thing that a film can reproduce in a few hours this number of historical facts, which would otherwise require a rather thorough study. And this has been done in a way that removes all doubts about the correctness of the representation.[41]

The above is an excerpt from one of the Swedish reviews of D.W. Griffith's *The Birth of a Nation* (1915) in connection with the film's opening performance in Sweden in the fall of 1918. Another reviewer wrote that the film "rightfully deserves to be incorporated into a film archive as a historical document."[42] A third wrote: "What immediately catches the moviegoer is [the film's] warm humanity."[43] The representation of the film's black, mainly male characters was not even mentioned.

At the Swedish revival of *The Birth of a Nation* in 1963, there was a different tone, but still the reviewers could not refrain from mitigating the film's grossly racist contents

> as a historical account, the film is implausible. [...] However, the extremely reactionary tendency seems to be a manifestation of prejudice rather than of racial hatred and evil. Griffith was incapable of giving a reasonably balanced account of the events he depicted. His film is a terrifying sample of the grossest and most commonplace racial and social prejudices that have survived in the South until our

> time. [...] The Negroes are faithful servants who turn into a wild mob as soon as they acquire their freedom and public influence. The Ku Klux Klan are portrayed as the administrators of law and justice.[44]

Forty-five years after its première, *The Birth of a Nation* was no longer seen as a historical document that researchers could simply fetch from the archive shelf. In the second round of reviews, the artistic significance of the film still outshines both its contents and its real historical significance as a contemporary portrayal of blacks as the countertype. It is the same principle as that underlying the canonization of Swedish Golden Age films, which were primarily discussed as art. If they "happened" to contain race-baiting stereotypes, these were reduced to the "prejudices of the time."

The Birth of a Nation is a typical example of what Martin Alm means when he says that the "question of race," as far as black people were concerned, came from outside, in this case from the U.S.[45] It is, thus, justified to ask why blacks in particular represent by far the most frequently occurring racial stereotype in Swedish films from the 1920s. Black characters appear in 22 films, which results in a higher percentage than the 10 percent Qvist claims to be the incidence of anti–Semitic characters in Swedish films from the 1930s. As we shall see, very small sections of the Swedish population, such as Jews, could cause anxiety that led to stigmatization. However, as far as blacks were concerned, the actual number of residents in Sweden must have been practically nil.[46]

Historian Gerald R. Butters, Jr., questions the view of early film as an ostensibly innocent form of entertainment. Early films were incredibly racist in relation to blacks, who were quite simply characterized as subhuman, a construction primarily directed against black men. Between 1896 and 1915, blackface was constantly used to portray blacks in movies. This tradition derived from 19th-century vaudeville performances, in which white men blackened their faces, imitating black culture by performing derisive song and dance numbers. The blackface stereotypes can be divided into two main types: (1) "Happy Darkies" or "Uncle Toms," who came from the country (the South) and recognized their "natural" place as slaves, and (2) "Zip Coons," who came from the city (the North) and tried to act white.[47]

The most common markers in portrayals of "Black" men, women and children in films were their insatiable appetite for watermelons, which was primarily thought to symbolize black men's sexuality, that they were "naturally" musical and keen on dancing, as these were regarded as non-white, exotic behaviors, and that they were notorious chicken thieves, which, again, symbolized their sexual appetite, but which was primarily a sign of black people's "natural" inclination toward criminality. Moreover, they were represented as lazy, superstitious and infantile.[48]

One of the Swedish Banana Company's numerous 1920s advertisements featuring "humorous" caricatures of black people (*Våra Nöjen* No. 7, 1926).

For obvious reasons, these distorted stereotypes were met with opposition from Afro-American society in the U.S. After *The Birth of a Nation*, which was the last straw, a black film industry began to produce its own *race films*, between 1916 and 1929, to counteract the negative image of blacks. After the war, blackface disappeared from American mainstream film, as it was no longer regarded as realistic. The exceptions were a number of popular musical films, beginning with *The Jazz Singer* (1927). Black actors now got to play minor roles in which they served whites as, for example, valets, cooks or porters. This cemented the "Uncle Tom ideal." It was also common for blacks to play the Other: the primitive, exotic native, the Indian and, markedly often, the cannibal—the ultimate Other.[49]

The Documentary Representation of Black Men

The use of blackface was very rare in Swedish silent films, and in Swedish society, blacks were all but non-existent.[50] Nevertheless, the image of blacks was common in daily newspapers, commercial advertising and films as, e.g., "savages" or as stereotypical caricatures in banana ads.[51]

Representations of black people in feature films can be categorized into three groups: (1) the exotic savage or cannibal, (2) the musician with rolling eyes, and (3) the subordinate Uncle Tom servant. However, the greatest attention at the time was paid to Swedish documentary films about various exploring expeditions around the world. Leif Furhammar calls this "the first period of greatness of Swedish documentary film." He points out, however, that "the way in which foreign peoples were depicted aimed more at amazement than at understanding" and that it was "difficult to distinguish the genuine from the provoked."[52] However, Furhammar discusses neither the fact that representations of blacks in the documentaries clearly referred back to portrayals of blacks in feature films, nor the fact that documentaries, in contrast to feature films, had a longer lifespan. Within the framework of the great investments made in educational film, which was meant to raise the standing of the Swedish film industry, the documentaries continued to be circulated for decades as scientifically correct accounts.[53]

In *Watching Wildlife*, media researcher Cynthia Chris argues that, during the past hundred years, wildlife film has been judged as superior to feature film, the reason being that the wildlife film genre provides access to cultural capital: We watch wildlife films or nature programs on TV in the belief that we are learning something, in contrast to when we "passively stare at" feature-film entertainment. By virtue of the documentary qualities of wildlife films, the genre has been perceived as neutrally objective, even though it, just like any other type of film, is full of ideology that touches upon and creates notions of nature, animals, race, gender, sexuality, etc.[54]

The feature-length documentary films *Among Savages and Wild Beasts* (*Bland vildar och vilda djur*, 1921) and *On Safari in Africa with Prince Wilhelm* (*Med prins Wilhelm på afrikanska jaktstigar*, 1922) were the results of Svenska Bio's (later SF) African expedition in 1919–1920, and of Prince Wilhelm's expedition to Central Africa in 1921. Already, the title of the former film reveals a patriarchal Swedish attitude toward "Black" Africa. The difference in kind between savages and animals is articulated as a mere difference in degree. The films' existence is a manifestation of colonial thinking, according to which the Swedish expeditions brought white, masculinely coded knowledge to uncivilized nature.

Today's wildlife films usually treat one species of animal, such as lions or elephants, and less often look at a whole habitat. In cases where an entire area is described, the indigenous population is usually left out, because filmmakers wish to avoid the risk of comparing humans to animals. Another difference is that today's wildlife films frequently attempt to convey an ecological understanding and knowledge of animals' manner of living by, for example, following a pride of lions throughout a year.[55] Wildlife films made in the 1920s were completely different. They dealt with the whole habitat, primarily aiming to "discover" and display rather than to portray and create understanding. This was evident from the white men's constant engagement in big game hunting—a phenomenon that would never be included in a wildlife film of today. In this way, people, animals and nature were reduced to commercial attractions and sensations, all under the guise of documentary science.[56]

It is, therefore, difficult to understand why Furhammar cannot distinguish between what is arranged and what is "genuine" in these films, because the outcome, achieved through individual takes, editing and intertitles, is so obviously both arranged and interpreted without the slightest consideration of the people involved. As a matter of fact, the films are purposefully organized to show how scared and funny the "blackies" are compared to the white Swedes—which served to stereotype both blacks and Swedes in general, as it became a literal comparison between black and white.

The first of a number of tribes "discovered" in *Among Savages and Wild Beasts* are the Kikuyu. First, the film shows pictures of people working in a field. Then it cuts to a picture of a man climbing into a tree-hut, which is followed by the text: "The men's less taxing day's work consists of guarding the plantations from look-out huts in the trees." The next images are of a pack of baboons, followed by: "But even the baboons are on the alert, always stationing a sentry to warn against dangers." Next we get to see pictures of a group of black men sitting in a ring and discussing something, which is accompanied by intertitles such as "Trials are the idle Kikuyu gentlemens' diversion" and "A lawyer distorts justice until he himself believes what he is saying." In this way, we learn that black men are not only lazy—which has already been emphasized by contrasting pictures of working women—but that they are also irrational.

The last tribe to be visited are the Maasai, who are presented as cowardly and in need of white protection. In connection with this visit, lions, hippopotamuses and crocodiles are hunted, and it is always the white Swedish men who shoot the animals. Without exception, the scenario is one in which the fearful black men ask the white men to help them kill "the beasts." Their helplessness is emphasized by intertitles that make fun of a group of black men who are having difficulties hauling ashore an over four-and-a-half-thousand-pound hippo from a swift river. Another significant scene recurring in all the films depicts a group of black men who first appear in the background and then carry the quarry forward, humbly laying it down in front of the camera.

The film ends with a rhinoceros hunt. First, a few takes of a rhinoceros are shown, and a text explaining that it will not leave the area. The next cut shows how the black men run away and climb up a tree. A cut back to the rhino, now with a Swedish man holding a rifle in the foreground: "But the Swedish hunter's hand did not shake." The scene is then constructed so that the "heroic" Swede shoots the advancing rhino at such close range that it drops on top of the camera stand! This is a trick with perspective in which the stand (take note: without the camera) has obviously been put into place later.

On Safari in Africa with Prince Wilhelm didn't only have a royal luster; it was also a real zoological expedition, commissioned by the Swedish Museum of Natural History to collect plants and animals, primarily fourteen mountain gorillas (which were placed under protection already at that time). Back home after the journey, Wilhelm wrote *Bland dvärgar och gorillor* (*Among Dwarfs and Gorillas*), a travel book that gives some insight into Western thinking about Africa and that makes the same allusion to the relation between humans and animals as in *Among Savages and Wild Beasts.*[57]

The film contains the same mixture of sensational presentations of animals and humans as that found in *Among Savages and Wild Beasts*. We see pictures of "funny" hairstyles, stretched-out lips, adornments and several dancing scenes—"Wherever we came, the arrival of the white Prince was celebrated with dances and festivities"—the dancing often taking place under Wilhelm's supervision. The way in which the dancing scenes are presented implies that the blacks take every opportunity to dance rather than work. *Among Savages and Wild Beasts* contains a dancing scene in which it looks as if the black people are performing a jumping dance. To emphasize the exotic element, the scene is cranked at a higher than normal speed. In *On Safari in Africa with Prince Wilhelm* there is a dancing scene with a text that shouts "Shimmy!," followed by a long take showing a group of dancers with their backsides sticking out. The scene ends with the sarcastic intertitle: "The Western dance culture still has a great deal to learn from the Blacks."

The dancing is followed by scenes of sleeping black men and the text: "The men's main occupation." Once again, the next images are of working women. The two most distasteful scenes are those in which black men are edited together and compared with animals. In one scene, a couple of mountain gorillas that have been shot are first displayed in a degrading manner. Then the Swedish filmmakers have arranged the scene so that the audience can see the back of a dead gorilla that is sitting upright beside a black man. The text—"Two backs"—informs the moviegoer about the "humorous," striking similarity between the black man and the dead gorilla. In another scene, pictures of a group of black men cutting up an elephant are cross-cut with those of a group of vultures eating from the same carcass. The symbolism is unmistakable: the blacks constitute an uncontrollable horde that poses a threat to the small number of white men. This simile, or horde metaphor as I have chosen to call it, returns in several other contexts, both in connection with black people and in descriptions of other menacing ethnic groups.

In the films, nudity occurs very frequently, both naked men and naked women. This is a matter of a literal nakedness, including breasts, pubic hair and "full frontal" nudity that the censors would not allow to pass through until the end of the 1960s. In view of the strict censorship rules at the time—and the fact that film reviews could frown with disapproval when white women "overexposed" themselves by wearing a nightgown[58]—allowing this degree if nudity would, on the face of it, seem to be a bit contradictory. However, the explanation is that blacks were regarded as being one with nature. Black women and men were simply thought of as such extremely ugly and primitive beings that they could not entice the same kind of sexual reactions that a white woman's bare leg or shoulder could—which was emphasized by the fact that the films were not only intended for a general audience, but were even marketed as films for children and families.[59]

Wilhelm's travel book teaches the reader that black men have no concept of time, that they are lazy children of nature who, if you allow them to come too close and show them kindness, immediately become insolent, demanding and shameless. All they understand is "the commanding, strong hand that leads them and forces them to work—even with the help of the *kiboko* (the hippopotamus whip)."[60] This laziness can be contrasted with the fact that both of these hunting and filming expeditions used hundreds of African men to carry supplies, by order of the British and Belgian colonial authorities. Wilhelm's recurring, sarcastic talk about "lazy blackies" and escaping black carriers becomes a bit thick when constantly compared with the trials and hardships of the white expedition members, particularly because several of the carriers died during the course of the expedition. The black men carried baggage weighing about 55 pounds, whereas Wilhelm and the other white men did not so much as carry their own rifles—even during the hunt for mountain gorillas living at an altitude of nearly 10,000 feet.[61] In other words, the "White man's burden" made Wilhelm—and the films—blind to what they describe in a schizophrenic manner, which follows

The "superior" white hunters and "lazy" black Africans at work in *On Safari in Africa with Prince Wilhelm* (photographer unknown/*Med prins Wilhelm på afrikanska jaktstigar* (1922)/Svensk Filmindustri/courtesy Swedish Film Institute).

from the notion that blacks are hardly human, just a notch above the animals being killed in massive numbers.

The fact that this is presented as a "burden" becomes visible in connection with the hunting. Hunting has always been portrayed as heroic and exciting, but as Wilhelm nonetheless paradoxically claims, it is a duty he would rather have been spared, had it not been for its scientific purpose. While describing himself as a great nature lover who is upset about seeing the old Africa disappear and the wild game becoming scarce, he doesn't give a thought to the fact that he himself has participated in this to the highest degree.[62]

Bengt Berg, the only Swedish documentary filmmaker to achieve worldwide fame in the 1920s, also made a couple of feature-length nature documentaries in Africa, including *Abu Markúb and the Hundred Elephants* (*Abu Markúb och de hundrade elefanter*, 1925).[63] Purely documentary portrayals of birds and animals are predominant in Berg's films, but even so, the same type of disparaging representations of black inhabitants recur. The black assistants are constantly held up to ridicule, getting the blame for anything that goes wrong. This is contrasted to white, manly courage, for example, when elephants are filmed at close range and the intertitle boasts that the audience should "count the blades of grass" between the camera and the elephant herd. Also in the documentary *With Fellow-Country-men in America* (*Bland landsmän i Amerika*, 1925)—to which I will return in the section on anti–Semitism—black people are seen in passing.

All of these films were received with the highest of praise. The reviews stress that the films were "scientific" and "instructive,"[64] and virtually all reviewers mentioned how "entertaining" and "amusing" they were, particularly the "Shimmy" and the other dance scenes.[65] Others reported that "the scenes with blackies bumping around and jumping with both feet together [were received] with roars of laughter."[66] From the point of view of masculinity, we can also gather that the films were successful in representing black men as lazy.[67]

As regards the films' veracity, some memorable opinions were voiced. In view of the regularity of wildlife films in the repertoire, frequently in the short film format, *Stockholms-Tidningen* wrote that the "thrilling hunting episodes should absolutely not be suspected of having been arranged for the camera, as has been the case with so many other such episodes."[68] Tora Garm in *Stockholms Dagblad* came straight to the point, asserting:

> No one can go home from this wilderness drama in two long parts without superlatives about the unquestionable importance of film aspiring to be at its best. The picture wins a decisive victory over the word, which has already described the land of the blackies in thick volumes, descriptions that have not, however, always gained credence, that have remained in our imagination as stereotypical images and that have, moreover, been corrupted by the fancy of the individual reader.[69]

Thus, here we have the pure and genuine truth about "the blackies," and it was the documentary vision, through the "objective" camera, that made the pictures on the silver screen credible, because moviegoers themselves got to see the "reality." The social reputation of the wildlife documentary, its cultural capital, functions as a guarantee that the films were scientifically correct and perceived as such—irrespective of their sensational content. In addition, many of the Swedish film expeditions resulted in a very large number of documentary short films that, along with the feature-length films, were circulated at the movie theaters as shows that were especially appropriate for children. These films were then used in the schools as scientifically reliable instructional material until long after World War II. Against this background, it is evident where a great many prejudices against blacks have their origins in the "ethnically homogeneous" Sweden.

It should be emphasized that the "humorous" depiction of blacks in these films was not without its commercial motives. The Swedish government did not interfere with or support the Swedish film industry until the 1960s. This meant that SF's great investment in documentary film should preferably pay off in the cinema repertoire before the feature-length and short films were used in educational film showings.[70] Making the films "amusing" was, thus, a highly conscious narrative device used to entice the family audience to the cinema, because documentary wildlife films had a reputation for being deadly dull in comparison with common feature films.[71]

Exotic Cannibals and Black Musicians

The "cannibal" did not appear in the Swedish documentary films. On the other hand, an abundance of ethnographic films flourished at Swedish cinemas under titles such as *Shipwrecked Among Cannibals* (1920). This film was classified by the censors as a culture film for general audiences, and marketed by SF, using the following words: "Intrepid explorers may even today run across live man-eaters in some of the darkest corners of our beautiful world. Unfortunately, it is not always possible for them to return to civilization."[72] This sounds like and, in fact, is the same type of exploitation as that found in the infamous Italian cannibal horror films from the 1970s and 1980s, e.g., *Cannibal Holocaust* (1980). The major difference is, however, that the films from the 1920s were marketed as scientific ethnological studies.

Modern social anthropology questions whether cannibalism has ever existed anywhere on earth, except in times of extreme food shortages. Cannibalism has instead been used by "civilized" cultures to assert their power over "primitive" cultures. Showing that the Others ate one another was a way to demonize them.[73]

The worldwide fame of the Swedish Golden Age films also included Victor Bergdahl's animated short films about Captain Grogg, which were sold around the globe between 1916 and 1921. Bergdahl mentioned in an interview that the films were met with cheers everywhere, but that in "the British colonies, Grogg films featuring niggers could not be shown—I suppose the blackies cannot bear to see caricatures of themselves."[74]

Animations were found in Swedish feature films, as well. In the comedy *Robinson in the Archipelago* (*Robinson i skärgården*, 1920), the fat banker Agathon ends up by mistake on a desert island in the archipelago, where he is forced to live like Robinson Crusoe. The first night, Agathon has a nightmare in which he is "chased by savages and other wild animals,"[75] as one reviewer put it. In the animated dream sequence, Agathon is captured by black male cannibals who later perform a wild war dance around the cauldron. The cannibals are caricatured as black, ghostlike beings in grass skirts, carrying spears, but lacking individuality. Their faces are completely dominated by enormously oversized lips and staring eyes. The nightmare ends abruptly when Agathon, who is scared stiff, falls down from the tree in which he had sought protection.

All of the reviewers mentioned Paul Myrén's animations with approval,

Paul Myrén's depiction of black cannibals in *Robinson in the Archipelago* (*Filmjournalen* No. 14–15, 1920).

and although no one believed they represented the true picture of black men, the connection to the cannibal myth and to ethnology is nevertheless clear.

Exotic black men appeared in three additional Swedish films from the 1920s. In Mauritz Stiller's well-known comedy *Just Like a Man* (*Erotikon*, 1920), the principal characters go to the opera to watch a performance containing black eunuchs. And in the comedy *Charley's Aunt*, the only example of blackface is found in a brief scene. In *Just Like a Man*, the opera scene is of great symbolic importance to the film plot. Therefore, the scene was mentioned by most reviewers, both as a success and a failure, but primarily as "exotic"[76] and "oriental,"[77] which demonstrates that the black element served its purpose.

Already in the advance stories about *First-Mate Karlsson's Sweethearts* (*Styrman Karlssons flammor*, 1925), it was touted that director Gustaf Edgren would use "genuine Negroes" whom he had found in Marseille, as they "are, of course, rather far and few between in our country." In three full articles, the father and daughter, Albert and Yvonne Lesti (who were not allowed to speak for themselves), are described, and we learn that the "Negroes" from the South of France will have the rare honor of becoming Swedish film stars. Albert Lesti was proudly introduced as "a wash-proof Negro." And as for Yvonne, we find out that "the camera work was mostly merry play." Because, as everybody knows, "most Blacks are good actors with a lively power of imagination."[78] Here, the black actors were represented as natural and childish. It was also pointed out that they should be grateful to the Swedish film industry.

In brief, *First-Mate Karlsson's Sweethearts* is about the he-man, first mate Karl Alfred Karlsson (Ernst Rolf), who is cheated on by his flame in Gothenburg. He then sets off on a sailing trip around the world that takes him to places like Marseille, Rio and Sidney, where he meets other women. After a violent scuffle in a tavern on Barbados, Karlsson returns to the brig. There, he dreams about courting the Black South Sea princess Naoma (Yvonne Lesti).

Behind the scenes of *First-mate Karlsson's Sweethearts* where Albert and Yvonne Lesti were referred to as "wash-proof negroes" by Swedish film journalists. From left to right: Albert Lesti, Ernst Rolf, Yvonne Lesti, Fridolf Rhudin, unknown extras (*Styrman Karlssons flammor* [1925]/Värmlandsfilm/courtesy Swedish Film Institute).

The eight-minute sequence begins with Naoma dancing for Karlsson—a clear parallel to Wilhelm's white indulgence with the black dancers in the documentary films. The father, King Tamotu (Albert Lesti), watches in secret from behind a tree. After a while, he summons some 15 warriors, black men in grass skirts and carrying spears, who steal through the tall grass. At the same time, second mate Augustsson (Fridolf Rhudin) is courting another "little Negro girl," who kisses his cheek, which makes Augustsson feel uncomfortable when he conjures up an image of the girl's lips having left an enormous mark on his face. In the meantime, King Tamotu demands that Karlsson marry his daughter. Karlsson refuses. This leads to a fight in which he keeps the attacking horde of black natives at bay for a long while. Augustsson hears the turmoil and brusquely throws his "Negro girl" aside to come to Karlsson's rescue. But Augustsson then runs into a terrifying cannibal in full war paint who threatens him with a spear and an angry face. He flees, but the savage chases him. In the meantime, Karlsson has been overpowered and tied to a tree. Under supervision of the contented and laughing King Tamotu, the cannibals perform a war dance around Karlsson. Suddenly, the dance ends and all the blacks begin shooting arrows at the tied-up Karlsson. After a while, the arrows form a halo around his head. He gets angry and tries to get loose. All of a sudden, he wakes up, entangled in his bedclothes.

Apart from Naoma's dancing, what we have here is a straight line of images, from the black "cannibals" to the Captain Grogg animations, the ethnographical cannibal films and the Swedish documentaries in which menacing hordes of black men appear in grass skirts, with spears and oversized lips. This was also reflected in the reviews.

Despite all the publicity surrounding Albert and Yvonne Lesti, no one mentioned them by name. One reviewer wanted to see more of "the cannibals' reception preparations,"[79] whereas another complained that the dream was much too "disguised, but that could be blamed on the good first mate's lack of imagination and ethnographical knowledge."[80] In other words, the reviewer wanted it all to be more "realistic." Carl Björnberg, too, was convinced by the "authentic framework." According to him: "The scenes from the South Sea island with the many authentic blackies seem especially convincing."[81]

As regards the exotic element, *The Bimbini Circus* also had a "circus Negro" in its cast, who was said to have had an affair with a white woman in the film. This may have contributed to the ample use of adjectives such as "grotesque" and "disgusting" in the devastating reviews,[82] which can be compared to the fact that none of the reviewers had any objections when two white men—Karlsson and Augustsson—courted black women in *First-Mate Karlsson's Sweethearts.*

The dancing and "natural" musicality of black people are found in three Swedish films from the 1920s. All three take up the decadent influence of "Negro jazz," with clear links to the primitive sex drive shown in the documentaries' "mating dances."[83] In 1921, the bandleader and conductor Hjalmar Meissner warned that "jazz is a terrible infectious disease that is approaching our healthy shores at a neck-breaking pace." The music was described as "animal sounds.

Particularly popular is the bellowing of oxen, but the crowing of roosters, the meowing of cats, the braying of asses and the croaking of frogs are also at a premium." Musicians who play jazz "infallibly become idiot[s]," and Meissner even suggested that Sweden set up "institutions for quarantine and delousing so that we might avoid the epidemic that is now running rampant in our poor, afflicted Europe."[84]

But Sweden did not establish "delousing institutions." Jazz made its breakthrough in the same or possibly the following year.[85] Already in 1922, black male musicians can be glimpsed at a seaside resort in *Thomas Graal's Ward*. And *A Housemaid Among Housemaids* is about young modern women and their morning-time dancing at a club called Jazzil, where a white jazz band led by a black man serves up the musical enticement. *On Safari in Africa with Prince Wilhelm* also referred "humorously" to the new dancing fad, the shimmy, a "dance style that has attracted numerous fans and keen practitioners of late, even in Stockholm."[86] All in all, this illustrates film's instinctive feeling and propensity for picking up on contemporary social phenomena.

In 1926, *She Is the Only One* was released. This was the first film within the framework of the Isepa collaboration that aimed to produce films set in an international and modern age.[87] In the summer of the same year, the "Negro cabaret" The Black People, with solo dancer Maud de Forest, performed at the Vasa Theater in Stockholm.[88] The Black People were engaged for a big show number in *She Is the Only One*, where they played and danced at yet another seaside resort, this time in a fictitious Biarritz, as the film was set in France. This was a typical musical show number that put the film's plot on "pause," a feature that was to become very popular when talkies made their breakthrough a few years later.[89] The purpose of such features is to display rather than to narrate. According to director Gustaf Molander's instructions, we get to see how the black male band plays and groves wildly, while the black female dancers, led by Maud de Forest, do their show dancing under the white audience's supervising gaze. For a Swedish silent film, unusually fast cuts are used between the musicians and the dancers to give the illusion of a high tempo. De Forest dances fiercely, characteristically rolling her eyes, while the black band plays with such excitement that a white man in the audience grabs a guitar and starts playing. During a solo, the drummer suddenly squeezes one of the drumsticks in between his nose and upper lip—an explicit connotation to the primitive cannibal with a bone through his nose. The number ends when de Forest folds herself up and rolls backwards out of the camera's optical field.

Here, the black element constitutes a purely exotic attraction. In all likelihood, the rolling of eyes and the drumstick were the result of Molander's and photographer Julius Jaenzon's directions. This was commented on in a couple of newspapers: the "skillfully edited scenes with The Black People [...] have an agility and a speed that promise the best for Molander's continued production."[90] Whether or not these elements were actually part of The Black People's repertoire, the effect was the same: exoticizing blacks by linking them to the primitive.

As far as jazz music was concerned, a certain ambivalence arose in connection with the arrival of the first sound films in Sweden from the U.S. in 1929. In *Biografbladet*, one writer expressed concern about the music now being synchronized with the film. This could present a danger to Swedish culture, because "Negro jazz" used to be moderated by the fact that it was played by Swedish musicians in the cinemas, without "Negro syncopations." On the other hand, the writer felt that "in a way, this is fun: you get to hear jazz that is more pure and real than before."[91]

The Uncle Tom Servant—The "Civilized Negro"

In Swedish films from the 1920s, the largest and, symptomatically, most invisible single group of black characters appeared in the role of subordinate servants of white superiors. A black servant is found in the 18th-century historical film *Two Kings* (*Två konungar*, 1925). In addition, a "Negro manservant" figures in *The Silk Stocking* (*Silkesstrumpan*, 1921).[92] A black bellboy appears in *The Million Dollars*, and in *The Doctor's Women* (*Parisiskor*, 1928), we catch a glimpse of a black male doorman and a black errand boy in connection with a restaurant visit. In *Discord*, a charity party is organized to benefit black children. This is marked briefly by an intertitle that floats down the screen: "When Negro children freeze," followed by a short documentary picture of a naked black child, which Herbert Grevenius felt was an "apt transition."[93]

Desdemona Schlichting's role as a lady's-maid in *A Husband by Proxy* is interesting in two respects. It was without a doubt the most important role for a black character during the 1920s. And the film reproduced an iconographic image of black submissiveness that would come to be very familiar. The plot of *A Husband by Proxy* was related in detail in the previous chapter. In the film, Schlichting plays the role of Hortense's lady's-maid. In Schlichting's first scene, Ponson is running about showing the historic manor-house to her imposing friends. When Ponson wonders where Hortense is to be found, the party proceeds to her quarters. A guest opens the door leading to the bathroom. There, the daughter is sitting half-naked on a chair, having her feet dried off by the lady's-maid, who is kneeling and dressed in her maid's uniform. Schlichting smiles at the guest, who yells and slams the door. The scene with the black lady's-maid and the white woman was soon reproduced in ads for "Björktvål Prins av Parma" (a brand of soap), a picture that was widely distributed for years in film magazines and daily newspapers.[94]

Desdemona Schlichting (left) as the maid of the lady Hortense (Lary Jana) in *A Husband by Proxy* (*En perfekt gentleman* [1927] Film AB Minerva/courtesy Swedish Film Institute).

In her next scene, Schlichting warns Hortense, saying: "Madame Ponson is coming—!!!" Hortense and the lady's-maid run to their quarters. However, the film's villain, Colonel Renard, follows them. He knocks on the door. Hortense persuades the lady's-maid to stand behind the door, and as a consequence, the Colonel mistakenly embraces the black woman—with clear intertextual reference to Edwin S. Porter's film *What Happened in the Tunnel* (1903). In the meantime, Hortense has locked herself up in another room. Schlichting mockingly shows the key to the Colonel, who tries to take it by force. He gets her in an arm lock and, after some wrestling, takes the key. Later on, Schlichting is first to discover that there are two Gösta Ekmans, and toward the end of the film, the lady's-maid informs Hortense that her husband has been brought home, fatally wounded.

In view of the relatively important role she played, it is remarkable that not a single reviewer mentioned Schlichting or her character. Some even enumerated several minor, white roles. In other words, considering that the reviews of *A Husband by Proxy*, which was counted as an important film, were ample in number, these reviewers must have left her out on purpose. On the other hand, Vera von Kraemer carried out a short interview with Schlichting, informing her readers that the actress came from Abyssinia, but that she now spoke German

The iconographic image of black submission from *A Husband by Proxy*, which was reproduced in advertisements for Björktvål Prins av Parma for years to come (*Filmnyheter* No. 17, 1928).

and resided in Berlin. Other things stressed by Kraemer were that Schlichting was a "thoroughbred Negro woman" and that one "understood why a marquise would want someone of her race as a lady's-maid." Asking about Schlichting's family, Kraemer admitted to being "shocked" by the answer: "My daughter is studying music and my son—my son is a medical student."[95]

Kraemer's astonishment might have been based on the highly stereotypical images of black men, women and children that were in circulation in Sweden in the 1920s. Martin Alm writes that "even those [in Sweden] who made appreciative statements about Blacks' contributions to culture could entertain notions about their having different racial traits."[96] In other words, black people were exoticized, seen as infantile and as having a vivid imagination, based precisely on the notion that they constituted another race.

The question then arises of whether there were any objections to or deviations from the stereotyping of black people in the Swedish (film) culture. I have not found a single direct example of this, but I have found two indirect examples. The first example is a notice in *Biografbladet:*

> American filmmakers are not lacking in fearlessness. Now one company has resolved to use film to prove the untenability of Darwin's theories! To this end, seven expeditions are to tour the world for three years to film every tribe that inhabits a spot on our earth. The purpose is to show that there are people living today who have less intelligence than the apes. Thus, we could not be descended from the apes! This is simple and easy to understand. But why make such a big business out of it, looking for proof so far away, when, to all appearances, such proof can be found quite close to the head office of the company in question?—a sarcastic reporter asked.[97]

The second example is found in *Fire on Board* (*Eld ombord*, 1923), a film about seamen in which two black sailors form part of the crew of the schooner *Framtiden* (The Future). The two black men only appear in the background, as they are subordinate to the main characters, the white captain and the white first mate. However, they are portrayed as equals in the group of white sailors. This becomes particularly evident when, toward the end of the film, the crew raises a mutiny and captures the captain, who has gone mad and intends to blow up the schooner. The black sailors' contribution is just as valuable as the white sailors.' Afterwards, they celebrate together. When the schooner *Framtiden* is on the point of exploding, they escape with the white sailors in the lifeboats—without the film singling out the black men as particularly scared or cowardly.

Fire on Board is all the more remarkable when compared to the revisionist big-budget American film of the period, *Uncle Tom's Cabin* (1927), which was intended to redeem the image of blacks. The advance stories about the film began a full year ahead of the film's première in Sweden, when it was reported that the cost of filming had amounted to two million dollars, an astronomical sum at the time.[98] Several articles attempted to place Harriet Beecher Stowe's novel in a historical context. It can be gleaned from the use of terms such as "mediaeval slavery" that the social theme of the novel was regarded as belonging to the past.[99] A large advertisement introduced the gallery of film characters, using photographs and brief presentations, e.g.: "Uncle Tom, honor and generosity personified," "George Harris, a gentleman in all but the color of his skin," "Eva, a little blond ray of sunshine," "Topsy, a coal-black little whirlwind," and "Simon Legree, a monster in human shape."[100] The presentations emphasized that the blacks are black, but not that the whites are white.

The film does recreate, however, every possible cliché in relation to the representation of blacks. In an early scene, a group of black children are running after a wagon filled with watermelons. A melon falls off and the children pounce upon it. Two seconds later, only the gnawed-off rinds remain on the ground. Uncle Tom (James B. Lowe) is portrayed as completely submissive despite extreme hardships—which explains why "Uncle Tom" subsequently came to be an insult among Afro-Americans in the U.S. In addition, all of the black characters are portrayed as childish and unintelligent. For commercial reasons, the film company had even considered using blackface throughout so that the film could be shown in the South. Instead, they chose a mixture of black and fair-skinned black actors. The film's subsequent distribution in the South was very limited.[101]

The little "whirlwind" Topsy (Mona Ray), however, was played in blackface by a white girl in what must be one of the most racist scenes that has ever been shown in a film. Topsy is the film's comic relief. She is portrayed as thievish, constantly lying and with rolling eyes. In a central scene, the white girl Eva tries to make Topsy see reason. Topsy, however, argues that there is a "natural" explanation for her behavior: "I could't be nuthin' but a nigger if I wuz ever so good." "If I could be skinned and come out white, I might be good." Topsy then tells Eva that nobody likes a "nigger." Eva replies that she loves Topsy anyway, and at that very moment, a halo appears around Eva's head, while Topsy bursts into a flood of tears.

The film is sentimental, but also very violent, containing several vicious whipping scenes. In one of these, the villain of the film, Simon Legree, whips Uncle Tom to death. The censors released the film for adults only and shortened the violent scenes considerably.[102] This did not prevent a reviewer from stating that the entire slavery story was "exaggerated, of course."[103]

With one exception, none of the Swedish reviewers mentioned any of the black actors by name. The exception is the white Mona Ray, who was described as "the little black Mona Ray, she seems to be temperamental—it won't be easy to forget her grotesque little face, swollen with weeping, and her stiff braids sticking out from her head like spikes."[104] It seems as if the reviewer failed to notice the use of blackface. Also, all of the reviewers complained about the film being much too sentimental, which they thought was bad, and indicated that the literary original had now "become a children's book that little girls devour breathlessly, with excitement and tears."[105] This chain of understanding—the past-sentimental-exaggerated-children's book—in combination with the enormously stereotyped but, at the time, "natural" portrayal of blacks, causes the film to lose its possible revisionist message, and the Swedish reviewers to accept the film's representation of blacks as realistic.

Uncle Tom's Cabin was followed by several popular sequels in a series of films in which the Topsy and Eva characters were lifted out from the original story. In Sweden, these films were marketed as highly appropriate for children, e.g., *Topsy and Eva* (1929)—a film described by Butters Jr. as "a racist joke from beginning to end."[106]

All of these films and their black characters say a great deal about a "White" Sweden. If the existence, as well as the notion, of a modern ideal masculinity could be called into questioned in previous chapters, it is both present and indubitable here. As a contrasting effect, a Swedish masculinity was created that existed on an adventurous, imperialistic and patriarchal level, where white was really white and black was really black. The idea of "the Black" was so strong that nothing can be found in the source material to contradict it. In addition, the fact that so many Swedish films utilized and created their own images of blacks contradicts the notion that such images primarily came from abroad. What is particularly Swedish is illustrated by the fact that the threat, with the exception of the horde metaphor in the documentaries, was conspicuous in its absence. In addition, the common watermelon- and chicken-eating clichés were not recreated even once in Swedish film—which implies that, despite its frequent occurrence in American films, this symbolism was not intellectually rooted in Swedish society. In other words, the cultural presence of blacks in combination with their factual absence in society eliminated the need for the big-city–based, threatening Zip Coon stereotype in Swedish film. It should also be pointed out that the disparaging picture of blacks in Swedish film was not the result of innocent unawareness. It was a highly purposeful construction, commercially motivated to attract a wide audience with "humor." Another reason was that blacks functioned as exotic symbols in films that were supposed to take place in an international setting.

The extensive stereotyping of blacks is not completely lacking in intrinsic nuances. However, the power of stereotyping and its overall social function make it difficult to talk about the phenomenon as merely a contrasting effect for the creation of modern ideal masculinity. The construction is masculine coded, but at the same time its expression spills over to comprise all of what is conceived of as "White" Sweden. Accordingly, women, too, are included as part of, and as the co-creators of, the social construction of blacks as countertypes. In other words, it is not possible to only talk about this as a homosocial construction, a notion that becomes even clearer when the creation of countertypes comes closer to home and, thus, is transformed into a more tangible threat.

Jews

The fact that the anti–Semitic portrait in *The Million Dollars* were the only one to appear in Swedish film from the 1920s has been reiterated in Swedish film history for decades. However, anti–Semitic portraits in films from the 1930s had a prehistory reaching back to Emile Stiebel's grotesque representation of a "pawnbroker Jew" in *Emigrant* (1910), one of the very earliest Swedish feature films. *Emigrant* presents a nightmarish vision of how Åke, a young Swedish man, immigrates to the U.S., where he perishes in the loud and noisy metropolis of New York. The pawnbroker Jew cheats Åke, taking his last belongings before he dies of starvation and destitution, all alone in a charitable hospital. The film was made in connection with the immigration issue, which was highly topical at the time.[107] The male Jew thus functions as an explicit threat, showing what awaited emigrants in the United States.

A companion film to *Emigrant* was the documentary *With Fellow-Countrymen in America*. By 1925, the immigration issue, as well as immigration itself, had ebbed. In the film, successful Scandinavians were lined up in front of the camera.

On only one occasion does the film leave these success stories for a visit to the slums of Philadelphia, which is introduced by the text: "Fortunately, no Swedes live on the South Side, but that many more Negroes and haggling Jews." The camera pans over a street scene including people and market stalls. The film cuts over to cages with poultry and then a new text: "On the South Side, *der* David and *der* Moses attend to their trade with used toothbrushes and other *sheyn* rarities." Then we see pictures of people standing around a table with merchandise, discussing prices. "Demijohns, kegs, stills—everything needed to get around the inconvenience of prohibition is available here."

Although immigration had petered out and the film's attitude toward Swedish-Americans is very positive, Jews and blacks are pointed out as groups with whom Swedes "fortunately" have no contact. The documentary representation is interesting, as Jews are identified as such only in the intertitles, with names such as David and Moses, but also by means of a stylistic "Jewish" accent. This is then linked to a less positive word for small trade—haggling—which is coupled to the Jews, followed by allegations that they sell suspicious merchandise, such as used toothbrushes and illegal equipment for home-distilling. Distinguishing Jews from non–Jews based on the visual sequences is, however, impossible, as the characteristic features of the Jewish stereotype—well known to the contemporary Swedish audience through the humor press and feature films—are conspicuous in their absence. Like the representation of Jews in the humor press, the film sequence has a humorous function. In this way, the tangible threat in *Emigrant* has been transformed into ridicule.

Anti-Semitic images of the Jew in films from the 1930s were defined by ethnic markers such as dark, curly hair, hooked noses, exaggerated gestures, unfamiliar names and a foreign accent. Their most characteristic feature was greed. And on the whole, they only played roles as money-lenders, usurers or bankers. In addition, almost all Jews in Swedish films from the 1930s were represented as men without a family, which meant that they were isolated both from Swedish society and from their own group. According to Wright, Jewish men were portrayed according to two models: (1) as harmless, farcical characters; or (2) as a threat to the Swedish community—by implying the possibility of racial mixture, but primarily by depicting them as a threat to the economy.[108]

Lars M. Andersson writes, following in Mosse's footsteps, that the Jew was defined in the humor press in relation to "the predominant masculine ideal, the modern stereotype, the national body," according to which the Swedish man was characterized as tall and well-built, with fair hair, blue eyes, self-control, strong nerves and hard muscles. The Jews constituted the countertype: spool-shaped, stout and stooping, with big hooked noses and oversized lips. Andersson holds that the male Jew was deliberately portrayed as feminine and cowardly, and as though he only thought about money.[109]

Since the middle of the 18th century, the Jews had constituted only a very small minority in Swedish society. However, around the turn of the century, circa 1900, the number of Jews doubled as large groups of emigrants left Eastern Europe. During the 1920s, there were about 6,500 Jews living in Sweden. Whereas a large part of the older German-Jewish population had assimilated, though they were still conspicuous owing to their achievements in business, the press or academia, the new waves of immigration drew renewed attention to the Jewish population, due in part to the formation of ghettos in Sweden's major cities. In the 1920s, Sweden was the country with the greatest proportion of marriages between Jews and other Swedish citizens.[110] Thus, one might think that this new visibility and the many marriages would have had an impact on film. But during the 1920s, the Jewish man was never represented as a sexual racial threat, only as a greedy man with money on the brain.

Shylock—The Modern Capitalist

The Shylock image, originating from Shakespeare's play *The Merchant of Venice*, is one of many anti–Semitic stereotypes. Shakespeare's portrayal of Shylock was in no way that of a modern capitalist. But even 300 years later, the stereotype remains a personalization of usury and avarice. There is also a contemporary connection between feature films and the emigration of Eastern European Jews, as many of the great Hollywood studios had been started and were being run by immigrant Jews. I do not believe this contributed to the bad reputation of film. But many influential people, Henry Ford among them, attempted to discredit the industry as a Jewish conspiracy: "Henry Ford has found a new fad. He claims that the world's film production is controlled by Jews. In his newspapers, he has started a campaign against the Jews as well as film. [...] Henry Ford has succeeded in most of his undertakings. [...] But he will fail miserably in his anti–Semitism and hatred of film."[111] As we can see, there was an awareness of anti–Semitism at the time. The question is whether this awareness included representations of the Shylock stereotype in Swedish films from the 1920s.

The Shylock Jew appeared briefly in four films.In *Laughter and Tears*, we see him as an elderly male pawnbroker (actor unknown) with a hooked nose, a long beard and a cap without a bill. The Jewish pawnbroker has given a loan on a stolen necklace. When the Swedish man, Bernhard, wants to buy it back, the pawnbroker refuses at first, making the characteristic "que-sais-je" ("What do I know?") gesture with his hands.[112] Berhard then gives the pawnbroker a good shake, and the pawnbroker, under the threat of violence, submits in a cowardly manner. When Berhard has paid and left, the film—remaining with "the Jew" cuts to half-shot and shows with great clarity how he counts the money with immoderate greed.

The Jewish pawnbroker returns in the lavish venture *The Lady with Camellias*. Never appearing on camera, he is only referred to in the intertitles, which reveal that he grossly underpaid a female pawner despite her being an acquaintance from his youth. In *Erik XIV* (1928), he flashes by as a hunchbacked "haggling Jew" in an early-modern setting, once again making the *que-sais-je* gesture. In the now-lost *Getting Baron Olson Married Ltd (A.-B. gifta bort baron Olson*, 1928), it is the ruthless money lender Efraim Kahn (Bror Bergner) who starts the company, and thus the intrigue that drives the plot, in order to get back the money that Baron Olson owes him.[113]

In *Life in the Country* (*Livet på landet*, 1924), Axel Hultman plays the unfeeling profiteer Pomuchelskopp, who forces the film's leading characters to leave their home and property. *Life in the Country* has been lost, too. This is unfortunate, because the film contains the only positive portrait of a Jew, Moses from Ranstadt, who helps the leading characters with money, allowing them to keep their home.[114] Curiously enough, Moses was played by Emile Stiebel, the same actor who created the evil pawnbroker in *Emigrant*.

Two years later, *The Million Dollars* was released. Here, Axel Hultman returns to another "Jew" role, this time in the form of the villainous Simon Jakobovsky.[115] *The Million Dollars* is a comedy. The plot is as follows: The Swede Richard Bergin lives in Paris. Bergin has engaged a lookalike to avoid being drafted. At home, the false Bergin has become engaged to Fylgia, daughter of the perpetually indebted merchant Falkman (Fredrik Hedlund), who—when we meet them for the first time—refuses to buy her a mourning dress. The tight-fisted father eagerly awaits the arrival of a batch of patented German collars, which would settle his bad finances. However, as Falkman is about to collect the collars at the customs office, it appears that they have been water damaged and turned into glue.

At home, Falkman's business partner and creditor Jakobovsky is waiting. The first picture we see is a close-up of a hand impatiently shaking a bundle of bonds. This is followed by the text: " 'District judge' Simon Jakobovsky, private

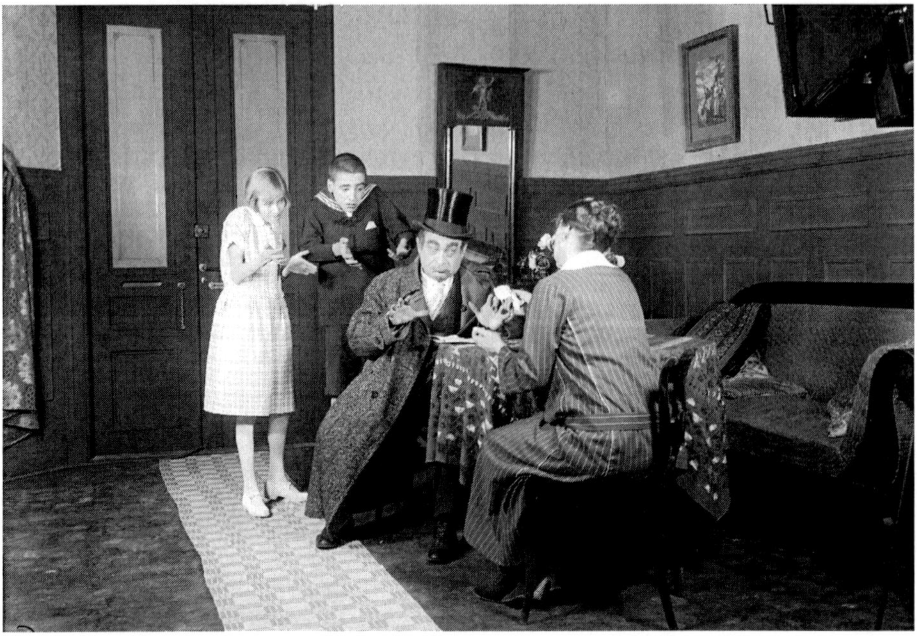

Anti-Semitism for fun: Axel Hultman as the capitalist Jew Jakobovsky in *The Million Dollars*. Behind his back the family's two children mock his accent and mimic the stereotypical *que-sais-je* gesture (*Dollarmillionen* [1926]/Film AB Minerva/courtesy Swedish Film Institute).

banker by birth and by force of habit, was a most successful combination of Västerlånggatan,[116] Poland and Jerusalem." Then the man himself is shown. Hultman is grotesquely made up to bring out the character's coarse features, above all his big nose. He is stocky and wears a black top hat: the symbol of capitalism. Mrs. Falkman asks him to have a seat. The film then takes the opportunity to cut to a close-up of Jakobovsky's hands making the *que-sais-je* gesture over the bonds. The family's two children enter the room saying: "Kutafternoon, uncle, for ve may say uncle, may ve not?" Then they mimic the *que-sais-je* gesture until Mrs. Falkman drags them out by their ears.

In the meantime, Falkman has discovered that the deceased Bergin is the heir to a million dollars and that a search is on for his next of kin. Because Fylgia has been engaged to Bergin, he gets the idea that she should claim the money. Back home again, he persuades Jakobovsky to become his partner. This causes the otherwise-tight fisted Jew to open wide his wallet. It should be noted that Falkman and Jakobovsky appear to be equally covetous of the million dollars. Moreover, they start spending money like never before. In a scene characteristic of the period, we see how the Falkman nursery is filled with new toys, how the youngest daughter listens to jazz records on her new gramophone, and how the son sits beside his new wireless set listening to a broadcast by Prince Wilhelm.

Falkman and Jakobovsky buy a new, expensive car, and they engage a driver who happens to be the real Bergin. During a drive in town, they meet Fylgia, who is out riding her new horse, accompanied by a suspicious baron who is interested in her because of the million dollars. Falkman immediately begins bragging about the fine qualities of the car and the fact that the driver can speak ten languages, while Jakobovsky boasts about the car having cost fifty thousand and the driver costing five thousand a year.

On account of some infidelity questions involving the baron, who is keen on getting married, Fylgia arrives one day at Jakobovsky's office on Vasterlăng-gatan. There, the two partners are drinking expensive cognac, smoking fine cigars and chuckling greedily about money. When Fylgia tells them she no longer wants to be part of their charade, Jakobovsky goes wild. He runs around, tearing at his thin hair until it stands on end, and throwing cognac bottles all about. In addition, the "Jewish" accent becomes extreme in the dialogue texts. Falkman tries to persuade his daughter, but she persists. When she leaves, Jakobovsky grabs Falkman, shakes him ferociously and pushes him down into an armchair. After a short while, we see Jakobovsky crying uncontrollably, while Falkman sits next to him with an empty expression on his face.

In the meantime, Bergin—who has fallen in love with Fylgia, who, in turn, has fallen in love with him—decides to reveal his true identity and to accept his punishment. He tells Fylgia that he will present himself at the Falkmans.' As the time approaches, the family is sitting and waiting. Jakobovsky, on the other hand, is busy noting the more valuable items in the Falkman household in his notebook, while at the same time filling his pockets with silver spoons and other things to cover his costs in the company. The films ends with Bergin disclosing his true identity to Fylgia. He asks for her hand in marriage, which suggests that the Falkmans' financial situation will straighten itself out after all. It should be noted that Jakobovsky is not excluded from the plot of *The Million Dollars*. At the glad news, Falkman simply stops what he is doing, dragging Jakobovsky and the family into an adjacent room to give Bergin and Fylgia a chance to execute their final kiss in peace.

Axel Hultman's role as Jakobovsky is the most clear-cut anti–Semitic portrait to be found in any Swedish film from the 1920s. Jakobovsky was created as a caricature in every detail, beginning with the stressed syllable "bov" in his name, the grotesque make-up, the "Jewish" accent, the *que-sais-je* gesture, his capitalistic interest in money and, last but not least, his emotional outburst as the million dollars slips through his fingers. According to Wright, the shape "the Jew" was given was solely determined by the Jews' function as an incarnation of the Other, which implies that the psychological nuances used to make a character deeper were not needed.[117] On one plane, this is in good accordance with the stereotypical representation of Jakobovsky. On another plane, however, a complication arises: Although both Wright and Andersson assert that the only function of the Jew was to emphasize the "Swedish," Jakobovsky's business partner, the Swedish man Falkman, is hardly held up as "the prevailing masculine ideal."[118] Falkman is just as greedy as Jakobovsky. He takes advantage of his own daughter to lay hands on the money.

The reviews of *The Million Dollars* were mainly caustic, but they all had one thing in common. No one said a single word about Axel Hultman's portrayal of Jakobovsky being anti–Semitic. On the contrary, Hultman's performance was singled out as the only amusing feature in an otherwise-clumsy film: "Axel Hultman performs an excellent study of a Semitic district judge, always looking at every penny, but willing to open his wallet as soon as the prospects of multiplied profit present themselves."[119]

The purpose Jakobovsky serves is to provide humor. But he was seen as a representation of a caricature, whereas depictions of blacks were regarded as representations of reality. This does not make things better, however, as it is an anti–Semitic portrayal nonetheless. But it may explain the absence of any objections to the character.

One final caricature of a Jew can be found in *New Pranks by Andersson's Kalle*. In this sequel, Kalle begins doing business with an "electricity machine." The machine is obtained at a junk store owned by the Jew Isaksson, who is introduced in the screenplay as "a greasy man of Jewish appearance," and with the line: "I karantee, Mr. Andersson, tat wis tis solid machine you vill nefer get olt." As Kalle counts out the money, the scriptwriters manage to use three different adjectives—"the interested Jew," "the fawning Jew" and "the sneering Jew"—to really drive home the notion of his greed. As soon as Isaksson appears later on in the film, the writers take pains to make long and detailed descriptions of his "Jewishness."[120] In the finished film, Isaksson is called "the Jew of Kvastmakarebacken." He was played by Sven Ingels, whose appearance resembles that of the pawnbroker Jew in *Laughter and Tears:* an elderly man with a big nose and a long beard. He, too, gets his "punishment" in the film when he engages Kalle to mend galoshes. Through one of his pranks, Kalle completely demolishes the junk store.[121]

Only two reviewers chose to mention "the Jew": "Sven Ingels is also worthy of warm recognition for his Jew of Kvastmakarebacken."[122] However, *Folkets Dagblad* wrote that "the unsavory ingredients that were seen in *Andersson's Kalle* are almost gone, with the exception of a rather disagreeable caricature of a Jewish salesman."[123] This is the only objection I have discovered to the anti–Semitic caricatures found in Swedish films from the 1920s.

Why did no one else choose to protest? The fact that the Jew was portrayed as a representation of a caricature is not an adequate answer. What needs to be emphasized is that all representations of Jews in films from the 1920s (including Jakobovsky who was described as a capitalist) were of Jews from the East who had recently immigrated and who had an "abnormal" appearance. This may well answer the question of why the danger of racial mixture was not represented in film. It was mainly assimilated Jews who married Swedes. However, there is an indirect link between the successful, real Swedish Jews and the fictitious Eastern European Jews who appeared in films, i.e., the strong notion of the Jew's "intrinsic" eye for money, manifested through use of the Shylock stereotype. According to the interpretation of the Bible made by the Swedish Church—an interpretation that was of great importance to the spread of anti–Semitism—the Jews were destined to suffer. But this image was at odds with reality, because the assimilated Jews were comparatively successful in Swedish society.[124] The Shylock stereotype works as a way to fuse the two groups, thus discrediting all Jews through the obscure connection it makes between "race" and a "natural" feeling for money.[125]

Moreover, the biased representation of the Jew as a money-grubber also eliminates the religious aspects as an explanatory basis. Like films from the 1930s, those from the 1920s depicted all Jews as men without a family. This was probably because filmmakers, who were mainly men, had a hard time imagining anyone other than male actors playing parts meant to portray economic threats. For this reason, there was no possibility to place the "Jewish" woman on a higher level and, thus, to belittle Jewish masculinity in the way in which black masculinity had been belittled.

The Shylock stereotype served not only to emphasize the "Swedish," but also to make fun of Swedish male characters such as Falkman. Given that *The Million Dollars* was a popular comedy, it is possible to adopt a class perspective, such that an upper-middle-class character like Falkman is ridiculed in tandem with an easily ridiculed "Jewish type" like Jakobovsky, the probable purpose being to invite the huge working-class audience to laugh just as reassuringly at the economic threat posed by the entrepreneurial class. In view of the pluralism of film, it is quite possible filmmakers imagined that the middle-class audience would laugh at "themselves" when they saw Falkman, because, as shown by David Tjeder with regard to Swedish middle-class masculinity at the turn of the century, circa 1900, the threat did not only come from external countertypes. On the contrary, it existed to the highest degree within the middle class, where Swedish men constantly risked falling outside the stereotyped framework of what characterized modern ideal masculinity.[126]

The Sami and "Primitive" People

In addition to blacks, other "primitive" people appeared in Swedish feature films and documentaries from the 1920s. In the now-lost parts of *Prince Wilhelm's Expedition to Central-America* (*Prins Wilhelms expedition till Central-Amerika*, 1921), Indians and blacks were presented. Five years after the première, these parts were combined to make an educational film for use in the schools.[127] Prince Wilhelm's journey inspired students at Lund University to produce a carnival film, *Indians in Lund* (*Lunda-Indianer*, 1920), in which an expedition sent to South America to collect Indian ethnographic material is attacked by Indians. *With Fellow-Country-men in America* contains a brief interview with the two then-oldest-living Swedes in the U.S., who say: "We had to watch out for those Indian scum all the time," which was illustrated by a picture of a male Native-American in ceremonial dress.

In 1923, SF and Albert Bonnier's publishing company sponsored an 11-month-long round-the-world trip with cinematographer Gustaf Boge and author Sigfrid Siwertz. The trip resulted in a now-lost feature film, *With Malays in Sumatra* (*Bland malajer på Sumatra*, 1925), a number of short films about Fiji that remained on SF's list of educational films for many years, and the travelog *Lata latituder* (Lazy Latitudes). The very title of the travelog gives some indication of Siwertz's patriarchal view of "the natives." The trip took almost a year, covering the route London-North America-Hawaii-Fiji-Sydney-Indonesia-Sumatra-Cairo-London. It gives a broad insight into a Swedish attitude toward the rest of the world. In the course of the account, Siwertz finds time to designate New York a "city of Jews," to be fascinated by the Ku-Klux-Klan and to denounce Fijian men as lazy and unreliable, but also as naively happy "children of nature," drawing direct parallels between apes and humans on several occasions. Moreover, we learn that Sydney suffers from "a terrible lack of culture" and that "the Australian Negro" is the "lowest of all human creatures."[128] During his stays in Hawaii, Fiji, Indonesia and Sumatra, the author constantly refers to cannibals to heighten his prospective reader's excitement.[129]

The same patriarchal attitude characterized the short films as well as *With Malays in Sumatra*, which is evident from the following review extract: "It is hard to tell whether it is the people with their unfamiliar, often superstitious customs or the depiction of the world of plants and animals that is the most captivating. Everything merges into an extraordinary whole!"[130]

However, Swedish filmmakers did not always need to travel around the world to portray "primitive people." In their native land, there were the Sami, or "Lapps," as they were always called in the 1920s. If the Jews were seen as an inferior race within the human species, the Sami were dangerously near being categorized on the same "natural" bottom level as the blacks. This connection is made explicit in a conversation between Prince Wilhelm and a Belgian colonizer in Central Africa: "He began the conversation with savages, but soon transitioned to tales from the war years in Belgium and to an analysis of [...] Maeterlinck, G. Hauptmann and others. I replied in the same vein with Lappish troll-drums, neutrality guard and Selma Lagerlöf."[131]

The Sami were of particular interest to the Institute for Racial Biology. They had long been regarded as Sweden's native population. But when the racist explanatory models caught on, this notion became increasingly difficult to accept. The Institute for Racial Biology carried out extensive anthropological studies of the Sami, measuring them (including skull measurements) and photographing them individually—schoolchildren through coercion and the adults in return for a photograph.[132] In *Rasfrågor i modern belysning* (*Questions of Race in a Modern Light*), the racial features of the Sami were described thoroughly, the conclusion being that the "Lappish race can hardly be counted as one of the more advanced. On the contrary, it is a backward developmental form of human being."[133]

Wright compares the Sami's conflict over land with Native Americans' corresponding struggle in the U.S. According to her, this conflict was an important motif in Swedish feature films from the 1950s that included a Sami theme. She also points out that Lapland was established as an exotic environment already in the 1930s. During that period, several semi-documentary films were produced in which the narrator's voice and the audience remained outside observers. However, Wright asserts that the Sami were portrayed in a more positive light than other stereotyped groups were.[134]

Sami people can be found in two Swedish feature films from the 1920s, where they primarily serve as exotic ingredients. In *The Triumph of the Heart* (*Hjärtats triumf*, 1929), ethnic Swede Waldemar Wohlström plays a minor role as the "mysterious Laplander Heikka." Heikka is offered alcohol so that he will reveal the location of an old buried treasure, a parallel of the "redskins and firewater" theme found in American Westerns. The second film was the prestigious production *The Blizzard*. In a 15-minute-long action scene, the film's hero, Gunnar Hede, is shown moving a reindeer herd down from the high mountains in order to make a quick profit. For this scene, the filmmakers used documentary footage, which were identified by several reviewers as having been taken from a Norwegian film.[135] The documentary pictures were spliced together with takes of Gunnar Hede, three male "Lapps" and a reindeer. When a storm blows up, however, the reindeer becomes difficult to handle. Hede and the leading "Lapp," as he was called in the film, have considerable problems keeping the animal in check. When the "Lapp" is about to scout the area, he falls into a hole in the ice. As a consequence, Hede loses control of the reindeer, which rushes off, dragging Hede behind it.

Because the documentary and the fictitious film sequences were shot on different occasions, the suspicion arises that the three "Lapps" in *The Blizzard* were not played by Sami actors, but by Swedish extras in a Sami version of blackface. This suspicion is further supported by the fact that the "Lapps'" faces are extremely dark compared to the white coloring of Einar Hanson's face, whereas everyone's hands are light.

The great action scene was mentioned in all the reviews. Characteristically, no one chose to talk about the "Lapps," the reindeers or mountain sceneries per se, but instead everything is lumped together into one exotic dough.[136] One reviewer, who felt that the reindeer-moving scene "constitutes the most beautiful and valuable part of the film," called it "the only Swedish feature."[137] The recognition of Lapland as Swedish was due to loud complaints about the fact that Selma Lagerlöf's literary original, *En herrgårdssägen*, was thought to have been adapted too much to foreign tastes, with a view to exporting the film.

In the documentary genre, two longer films were produced: *Where the Northern Light Burns* (*Där norrskenet flammar*, 1923), only fragments of which have been preserved, and *In the Land of the Mountain People* (*I fjällfolkets land*, 1923), which has been saved in its entirety. The latter film was photographed by Gustaf Boge. It is mainly a portrayal of the life of one Sami family, focusing on the woman, Inka Länta. Footage of reindeer keeping is alternated with footage of life in and around the tent. The men and the reindeer are always filmed at a distance, probably so the reindeer cannot knock over the camera, whereas women and children are portrayed more intimately. We see Inka Länta waking up, making coffee, preparing food, working with handicrafts and looking after the livestock. The children go to school under the supervision of a female Sami teacher.

Whereas the footage of the men is "authentic" for practical reasons, the one of Inka Länta is arranged. She is thus acting in front of the camera, and having obvious problems controlling her laughter and the neophyte's tendency to look directly into the camera lens. Like in the sound films from the 1930s, the intertitles in these two films resemble an added-on narrator voice that displays rather than explains the life of the Sami, without letting them speak for themselves. When Inka Länta puts on boots lined with straw, we are told that "socks are despised by the mountain-dwellers." As a group of male Sami wade across a stream, it is said that "the vigor of the Laps bears witness to the race's vital force."

The film presents the Sami as something exotic, as a different, but not necessarily inferior, race. In contrast to the documentaries featuring blacks, the filmmakers do not poke fun at the Sami. The men's masculinity is not minimized and, above all, the film producers are never shown—which prevents a comparison that, given the spirit of the time, would have positioned the Sami as inferior. This dilemma is illustrated toward the end of the film when Inka Länta and her husband walk down from the mountain to purchase provisions in the Swedish-owned store. There, they are invited to have coffee. The intertitle—"Inka is welcome to have coffee at the home of the chief engineer himself"—leaves no doubt as to who ranks highest.

The reviews were positive: "A very good and instructive description of the life of the Lapps. [...] It is probably the best film about the Lapps made to date. The opening-night audience applauded the show, deeply moved by the final scene."[138] If we disregard for the moment the constantly present exoticism, it is clear that the film, and the reactions to it, differed strongly from the Institute for Racial Biology's scientific conclusion that the Sami are subhuman. This is even clearer in view of the reactions to the other documentary, *Where the Northern Light Burns:* "Moreover, despite its completeness of detail, it is not complete enough; it also suffers from misleading accounts and, finally, the text is intolerably naive, trivial and frequently meaningless."[139] Both these films were distributed as educational films. *In the Land of the Mountain People* was so successful that a follow-up was immediately produced for use in the schools.[140]

Whites

Reacting to American Madison Grant's denouncement of Scandinavians as "completely intellectually anemic" in his renowned study *The Passing of the Great Race,* Josef Almqvist philosophized in a column about Sweden versus foreign countries: "The American and the Norwegian have a boisterous conceit, the Englishman a platitudinous one, the Finn an inveterate one, the Frenchman a feminine one, the German a blend of a little of everything, and the Italian one that is completely beyond description. What is wrong, then, with our proud, indolent self-righteousness, as dignified as the Spaniard's, as considerate as the Austrian's?"[141]

As can be seen, along with masculinely coded nationality followed clear distinctions between the various national characters. Or, to be historically precise and consider the period, between the different races of people. On one level, at the time white people were regarded as a specific race in relation to encounters with the Other. Subsequently, whites were divided into several different races of people, where national characteristics were frequently thought to derive from racial rather than cultural differences. An example of this line of thinking can be found in an article on the colossal American film *Ben-Hur: A Tale of the Christ* (1925), the production of which was interrupted in Rome.

The production in Italy had been dragging on, and the last straw was when thousands of extras demanded a pay raise. The Americans said no, and the extras, convinced that they were indispensable, went on strike. As a consequence, the Americans packed up their things and returned to Hollywood, despite the fact that they had already spent millions. One Swedish writer, describing the event, relied on racial psychology to explain the debacle: "The difference between the American and the Italian mentality has been too great. They have not understood one another." The Italians, we are told, are "the most unthinking people there are, and the least ambitious ones to boot. With a few hundred lire in their pockets, they think they're made of money." In contrast, the American could "not take in Europe. He doesn't have the right antennae. If an American has seen the Colosseum once for five, ten minutes, all right, then he's seen it, and that's it. Over and done with! Sentimental values do not exist for them."[142]

In *White*, Richard Dyer wishes to make the "White" foreign by discussing white people from various points of view, among them race. Being white, he claims, is equivalent to being invisible, in the sense that white people have not been characterized as belonging to any particular race. Owing to a number of historical influences, such as Christianity and imperialism, being white has come to be normalized as the naturally human state. The automatic consequence of which is that "black," "yellow," and "red" are not regarded as normal. This invisibility means that white can be everything and nothing at the same time, which gives rise to flexibility, such that determination of who will be included or excluded is synonymous with power.[143]

An example of this sometimes-paradoxical flexibility is that the Irish and the European Jews, who have a white complexion, have sometimes been considered white, sometimes black. Dyer further claims that, when everything is said and done, only two colors count—white and black—and the important thing is to which color category one belongs. The strong symbolism according to which white represents good, and black evil, has been extremely stable throughout history. Owing to Western dominance, white has come to be transformed into the universal good, which just happens to match the complexion of white people, in a neutral manner.[144]

In the 1920s, the superiority of the white race was discussed openly in relation to the Other—blacks, Jews and Sami—who thereby became symbolically "black." But within the white race, too, distinctions were made, some groups receiving a higher rank than others. Swedish films from the 1920s included a large number of "White" nationalities, with Swedish actors playing Norwegians, Estonians, Hungarians, Danes, Americans, Englishmen, Germans, Spaniards, Russians, Finns, Italians and Poles. However, it also occurred in Swedish films that Germans were played by Englishmen, Frenchmen by Russians, and Swedes by Austrians, just to mention a few examples. This was also the case in other European film countries where, e.g., Swedes got to play Germans and Americans in German films. In other words, feature films helped establish notions of and prejudices about the white races of people.

In this connection, I will limit my presentation to three different examples—Finnish, Russian and Southern European—of how white races of people were constructed in Swedish films from the 1920s. This should be enough to reveal the often-paradoxical flexibility involved in characterizing the "White."

Finnish Men—Literary and Primitive Masculinity

The Finns were also presented with a text in the anthology *Rasfrågor i modern belysning* (*Questions of Race in a Modern Light*), wherein we learn that the Finnish race consists of four different, intermixed races and that there exists "a certain kinship with the Nordic race."

> The science of racial psychology is still too young [...] to determine which character traits [...] are Finnish. One could possibly—but with considerable hesitation—call attention to the Finns' predominantly literary and humanistic disposition. [...] In general, the Finnish national character could be described as more introverted, reserved, heavy and inert than the Swedish. The Finn has far less initiative and drive than the Swede does. But in some respects he is more idealistically inclined, more easily carried away by an idea—even though the fascination can sometimes be transformed into blind fanaticism, which finds far from idealistic but simply terrifying, abominable expressions, as was the case during the Red Rebellion. [...] The most serious weakness of the Finnish racial disposition is their insignificant capacity to organize and their lax notions of social order and law.[145]

According to this characterization, the Finnish man has a literary and introverted disposition. He is a dreamer, lacks the ability to organize, and is less energetic than the Swede, although his dreaming can sometimes turn into violent eruptions that reveal his disregard for law and order. The emotional Finnish man is compared to an imaginary ideal Swedish masculinity emphasizing character, hard work and the importance of organization—which can be summarized in terms of what the Finn lacks: male self-control.

In Swedish films from the 1940s and 1950s, the Finn was associated, according to Wright, with the "primitive." Finnish men, in particular, were represented as having an overwhelming sex appeal, which served to accentuate the erotic manly courage of the Other, often expressed through the cliché that Finnish men readily fought with knives. The image of the Finns was also influenced by whether the film was set in Sweden or Finland. In Finland, Swedish Finns were represented in a less favorable light than were Finnish Finns[146]—a distinction not found in the same way in Swedish films from the 1920s.

The Realm of the Rye (*Rågens rike*, 1929) is the only film to use the cliché of the knife-carrying Finn. Set in Norrland in northern Sweden, it is a heated film about country life, stylistically inspired by Soviet film, which attracted a great deal of attention in Sweden during the second half of the 1920s.[147] In brief, the plot is that of a well-to-do farmer, Mattias, and his farmhand, Markus, who share an interest in the same woman, Klara. The Finn, who bears the telling name of Pecka the Knife (played by the Finlander Axel Slangius), has a small but pithy role. In the district, there is an ongoing conflict between the lumbermen in the woods and the farmers in the settled countryside. Pecka the Knife is the lumbermen's boss. At the beginning of the film, he is with his fellow workers, getting ready for the Saturday night dance. It comes out during their conversation that he has "dibs on" Klara as his woman for the evening. At the same time, the farmers have discovered that the lumbermen are coming to the dance. They therefore prepare themselves for a "double waltz on the dance floor."

As the dance begins, Pecka the Knife leaves because he says he has a few small things requiring his attention. He sits down, leaning against a tree with a bottle of schnapps, and waits for Klara. When she comes, they start walking together. She is unconcerned. She is first afraid when Pecka the Knife forces himself on her. She puts up a good deal of resistance, and while they are wrestling, they are seen by a passing maid, who runs to the dance pavilion to get Markus. In the meantime, Pecka the Knife tears Klara's clothes apart. When she faints, he looks around and then carries her away to a glade, where he lays her on the ground to consummate the rape. Then Markus comes to the rescue, and a wild, five-minute-long fight ensues. Klara wakes up during the fight, and both she and the cinema audience become onlookers, viewing the event from a female perspective. Pecka the Knife draws his knife. The fight ends when Markus is stabbed in the arm and Pecka the Knife runs away.

As Pecka the Knife disappears from the film story, the scene serves to emphasize Markus's masculinity through his accomplishment of a manly deed. In short, Pecka the Knife—the Finn—is demonized. In the final analysis, however, Pecka the Knife does not conform to this stereotype. First, the mere sight of him does not scare Klara. Second, he is equal to Markus in that neither of them really wins the fight.

The third and most striking deviation from the stereotype appears later on in the film. After having lost a snaps duel over Klara to the well-to-do farmer, Markus flees to the lumbermen in the woods, who eventually accept him. One day, Pecka the Knife steps into the cabin after an eight-month-long prison sentence. All the men except Markus cheer Pecka the Knife, who walks over and stands in front of Markus, who is seated. "Thanks a lot, you scoundrel! You got me rent-free lodging that time—until now!" he says arrogantly, while the film cuts back and forth between the men standing around him, whose faces are filled with eager expectation. The two men stare menacingly at each other, until one man says that Markus now hates "the country bumpkins" as much as they do. This causes Pecka the Knife to hold out a hand of reconciliation. After a moment of hesitation, Markus takes Pecka's hand and they become friends.

Here, Pecka the Knife is undemonized in a male-bonding scene that can be interpreted either as Pecka becoming "Swedish," or as Markus becoming one of "them." In this way, both can be said to belong to a kind of "primitive" northern Swedish masculinity, defined by "male" activities such as boozing and fighting, which finds its contemporary counterpart in a film like *The Hunters* (*Jägarna*, 1996).[148] Thus, the problem of the rape is, unfortunately, played down in a way that transforms it into a "natural" part of uncontrollable masculinity. Or, as one male reviewer put it: "It is a harsh, headstrong Swedish nature one encounters in this character portrayal."[149]

There is one other film with a Finnish man in a Norrland environment. In *Johan*, the farmers have a problem with log-driving. They therefore engage people from outside the community to dig a log canal. Some of them, such as the Stranger (Urho Somersalmi), get to stay with Johan, an elderly farmer who lives with his domineering mother and who is about to marry a young woman, Marit.

The Stranger is young, tall and strongly built. He has dark hair and dark eyes, which are emphasized by his high cheekbones. Dressed in high boots, a bandanna and a black hat, he is the first person to be seen in the picture, poling a boat through the swift rapids. Upon coming ashore, he immediately begins flirting with three young housemaids. He even lifts one of them straight up to show off his strength. Not far away, Marit watches longingly. Somewhat later, the Stranger meets with Marit's approval when he defends her against some lumbermen who verbally abuse her. When the lumbermen have left, the Stranger stays. He ingratiates himself with Marit, who is obviously flattered. During the summer, the cocksure Stranger continues to make passes. He finally forces Marit to kiss him, but she boxes his ears in response. In the midst of it all, the canal is completed and he leaves.

Johan marries Marit, and time rolls on. One day, the Stranger returns to the farm. He brings gifts, brightening up the life of the ill-matched couple. Marit, in particular, is delighted. As the Stranger begins making passes again, her resistance becomes weaker. He makes fun of her because she lives with a ramshackle "old buffer." He tempts her by saying, "I will liberate you." What decides the matter is a dispute between Marit and Johan's mother. When the Stranger leaves this time, Marit follows him on an adventurous descent of the rapids, which takes them to a remote island where he has a hut. She experiences a moment of happiness, and when the Stranger renews his passes, she submits.

However, Marit discovers that the Stranger has a habit of having a "girl for the summer," and she bitterly regrets her actions. In the meantime, Johan, believing that the Stranger has kidnapped his wife, has discovered their location. He suddenly storms into the hut, calls the Stranger a "wild beast," and begins beating him with a piece of wood. The Stranger desperately persists in claiming that Marit followed him voluntarily, and that is what saves him. Heartbroken, Johan staggers out of the hut, and Marit confirms the Stranger's story. When Johan is about to push off from the shore, Marit clings to him, imploring him to take her along. Thus, security defeats adventurousness, and the Stranger is left on the beach.

In this film, Urho Somersalmi plays the Finnish man with a primitive sexual power of attraction, something that is made explicit in the reviews: "He has an imposing appearance, a genuinely Nordic, manly vigor about his entire form,"[150] and he is "deadly handsome with his frizzy hair and his triumphant smile."[151]

From Mosse's theoretical perspective, the representation of the Finnish man as sexually primitive can be interpreted in terms of him serving as a countertype, because he lacks masculinely coded self-control. This, then, would position him as subordinate to a hypothetical ideal Swedish masculinity, represented in the film by the hard-working Johan. In fact, Johan was "victorious" in the end. However, reactions at the time showed that the Don Juan ideal was hardly used to condemn Finnish men; if anything, just the opposite.

Somersalmi, who was engaged by the Finnish National Theater in Helsinki, returned a few years later in *Discord*, where he played a quiet, strong Swede in a barren northern Swedish environment. It was said again that "Urho Somersalmi, that strong man, will certainly take the female audience by storm"[152] and that "a woman must give in to him."[153] Others even referred to him as a Swede: "The tall, angular yet truly kind-hearted Swede, with the broad shoulders and strong fists."[154]

Thus, the image of the Finnish man in Sweden turns out to have been essentially positive, and when it comes to the image of the Finnish man in Finland, even more positive. Finland's historic destiny was portrayed in a handful of films: The Finnish War 1808–09 in the two parts of *Stories of Lieutenant Stål* (*Fänrik Ståls sägner*, 1926), the Cossack riots in 1902 and the murder of the Russian Governor-General Bobrikov in 1904 in *Johan Ulfstjerna*.

Stories of Lieutenant Stål served more as illustrations of Johan Ludvid Runeberg's cycle of poems than as an independent film. It was built up with a frame story, in which the young Runeberg visits Lieutenant Stål, who recites a number of the poems. The Finns, led by von Döbeln (Edvin Adolphson) and Sven Dufva (Alex Slangus), are represented as enormously courageous throughout. When the announcement of war is read in the villages, the reaction is: "Where should we go, and where are the weapons? Do we get to fight tomorrow?" And on the battle field: "A Finn always feels good when he gets to fight!" And in relation to masculinity: "A real man is not forced to defend his country, he does it of his own accord!" Besides this, *Stories of Lieutenant Stål* is teeming with images of marching, positioned and fighting soldiers who accomplish one heroic deed after the other, one example being Dufva clubbing Russians with the butt of his rifle on Virta Bridge. In fact, the Finnish-Swedish armies seem to win everything, making the endings of the respective films—the surrender of Sveaborg and the final defeat leading to the division of Sweden and Finland—stand out as quite remarkable in a cinematic context, but not from a Finnish nationalistic perspective.

While being made, *Stories of Lieutenant Stål* encountered heavy criticism in Finland, as it was thought that the film medium per se would commercialize and trivialize Runeberg's heroic epic. Yet the final production could not be accused of failing in patriotism or criticized for its representation of Finnish masculinity. Accordingly, the film met with formidable success in Finland. In 1939, *Stories of Lieutenant Stål* was even released in a re-edited Finnish version with an added sound track.[155] The Swedish reviewers were, likewise, extremely careful in emphasizing the Finnish aspects of the film or the two countries' common history. Because the films did not contain any true leading roles, the reviewers avoided discussing individual performances. However, one review did describe Edvin Adolphson's von Döbeln as "an exceptional man of action."[156]

Even *Johan Ulfstjerna*, which was based on a Swedish play by Tor Hedberg, was met with hard resistance in Finland when news came that it was about to be adapted to the screen. Finnish chief librarian Allan Törnudd objected forcefully:

> Tor Hedberg's work is valuable as a psychological drama but it is not a historical drama, and the deviation in the external plot is already too great. Moreover, the entire environment described in the play and the atmosphere that animates it is Finnish to such a small degree that, as a matter of fact, its "localization" has lost all significance to the value of the whole project. [...] Is it the intention [...] that this shortcoming [...] should be remedied in the film by photographing certain public buildings and places, Cossack riots interspersed into the action, and other scenes from the *real* history of our country, which could certainly be made "reasonably true" by the use of Finnish extras?[157]

On one level, Törnudd's criticism targets the historical falsification achieved by merging two historical events—the Cossack riots and the murder of Bobrikov—into one. On another level, the criticism is a protest against the masculinity in the play/film, a masculinity that is in good accordance with the "literary masculinity" attributed to Finnish men in *Rasfrågor i modern belysning* (*Questions of Race in a Modern Light*), which ultimately denounces them as incapable of organizing their own country.

In the film, this takes the form of a theatrical struggle between the father, Johan Ulfstjerna (Ivan Hedqvist), a poet who had written patriotic appeals for liberty as a young man but who has now grown old and indolent, and his son Helge (Einar Hanson), who entertains revolutionary dreams of liberty. The conflict between old and young is introduced when Ulfstjerna receives a letter from the Russian Governor-General, thanking him for important services, which causes Helge to look upon his father with disapproval. When it becomes known that censorship has been imposed, Helge accuses his father of supporting the Russian oppressors. Ulfstjerna rejects this criticism, asserting that he must provide for his family. Helge replies, defiantly: "I would rather die of starvation than eat my oppressors' bread!"

Helge's romantic inclination is fulfilled by his membership in a secret revolutionary group. After the Cossack riots, which were brought about by protests against the introduction of censorship, the revolutionary group decides to murder the Governor. Helge is chosen by drawing lots. In the meantime, Ulfstjerna has developed a bad conscience. He decides to hand in his letter of resignation, to which his wife objects. When he is about to resign, he is interrupted by the Governor, who informs him that Helge will be employed as a secretary. Back home, Ulfstjerna happens to find the Browning that Helge has hidden in his father's desk drawer. After rummaging around a bit, the father uncovers the revolutionaries' plans. He decides to take over the assignment without his son's knowledge.

In the meantime, Helge is turning into a nervous wreck. He is anxious, irritable, and black rings are forming under his eyes. Yet at the same time he is very proud of his honorable assignment. When he arrives for the interview in the Governor's palace, he finds, to his surprise, his father in the reception hall. His father's hair has turned completely white. Before there is time for any discussion, some Russian officials rush into the room announcing that a conspiracy has been uncovered and that every visitor must be searched. Ulfstjerna persuades Helge to give him the Browning. When Helge is led away to the interview, Ulfstjerna, who does not need to be searched because he is a loyal servant, enters the Governor's office and shoots him. Ulfstjerna is arrested immediately. On his way to the prison carriage, his heartbroken son asks why, and receives an answer: "I must die so that you may live." In the street, the crowd that has gathered take off their hats to Ulfstjerna, who is completely self-possessed compared to Helge, who is nearly hysterical.

In the reviews, it is the stoic Ivan Hedqvist/Ulfstjerna who received praise. "Some of the scenes are stupendous; he murders and captivates, so that the entire movie audience is in tears, thinking they've been transported to a dismal, poignant reality."[158] There was more hesitation with regard to Helge. "It is natural

Finnish literary and, at the same time, hyper male masculinity: the father, Johan Ulfstjerna (Ivan Hedqvist), has just shot the Russian Governor Bobrikov in order to save his son in *Johan Ulfstjerna* (*Filmjournalen* No. 41–42, 1923).

that the young student, in choosing between his call to martyrdom and his love of life and his betrothed, should shows signs of hesitation and nervousness. But the actor overemphasizes his irresolution and appears to be more of a weakling than a champion of liberty."[159]

In *Johan Ulfstjerna*, both father and son suffer from "literary masculinity." But the reviews imply that action is everything, while indecision makes a man seem like a wimp. The fact that many held up Ulfstjerna's "sacrifice" as the most manly is in full parity with the modern masculine ideal. It is also a parallel to Warriorhood, which, according to historian Sanimir Resic, is the historically timeless and, thereby, most important link in the construction of ideal masculinity.[160]

Although Helge is a bit out of character, there is a trace of envy in many of the Swedish reactions to Finnish masculinity. To return to Almqvist's discussion of Sweden versus foreign countries:

> Reputation can be bought for money. For a couple hundred thousand, some energetic cultural attachés could probably increase the value of our reputation stock to a level comparable to that of Switzerland or Florida. But that is not the issue. It is a matter of living. If one wants to live and create something new, one cannot be a countryman in the universe, indifferent to one's own welfare and that of others. No, one must as [...] Finland have lived through a time of national struggle, or one must feel like a member of the group of great nations that perceive their actions, their destinies as historic.[161]

Russian Men—Cossack Hordes, Bolsheviks and Europeans

The Swedish perception of Russians as a hereditary foe has a history dating back to the middle of the 16th century and the series of wars fought against Russia until 1808–09. It was also during this time that the image of "Mongolian barbarism" was created. From a contemporary historical perspective, the relation between Sweden and Russia was tense. The Russification of Finland around the turn of the century, circa 1900, was seen as an aggressive policy of expansion, and there was great concern about Russian spies. Conversely, Sweden's rearmament during the period 1895–1914, as well as the many contacts with Germany, caused the Russians to suspect mischief. This found concrete expression at the beginning of World War I, when the Russian fleet was ordered to destroy the Swedish fleet, an order that was later canceled. The subsequent Russian revolution caused Swedish entrepreneurs to leave Russia, losing both money and property. This, in combination with Soviet financial support to the Swedish communists, helped to create a negative view of Soviet Russia.[162]

In the 1920s, a number of historically inspired as well as contemporary films appeared in which Russians were represented by means of the threatening horde metaphor, e.g. *Stories of Lieutenant Stål.* In the film, Russian men, in the form of Cossacks (wearing false beards) attack the civilian population with sabers and knouts. The Russian lieutenant colonel Kulneff (Adolf Niska) disapproves of this. He orders that the civilian population shall not be harmed. Nevertheless, in the next scene a group of Cossacks attack civilians. The action is repeated once more in the second part when the Cossacks attack a church, slaughtering the civilian population before the Finns come to their rescue. In *Charles XII's Courier*, the ravages of the Russian fleet along the Swedish coast are also recreated. All cities between Gävle and Luleå were burned to the ground, giving rise to a great, still-surviving Russophobia.[163]

The two parts of *Karl XII* are teeming with Russian Cossacks, represented as cruel and completely out of control, as in the scene from the Russian camp before the Battle of Narva in 1700. The scene is introduced by the text: "In the Czar's camp, no thought was paid to the Swede. Life went on as usual—." Then the Russians/Cossacks are displayed as an unbridled horde indulging in wild Cossack dances and unrestrained boozing, and these images are cross-cut with pictures of straight ranks of Swedish troops lined up with their flags fluttering in the wind. Here, representation of the male Cossacks as a horde has a clear connotation to that of blacks in Swedish documentary films.

The "Mongolian barbarians" are thereby stereotyped as being "naturally" evil. Consequently, the only figures who seem to have any control over these barbarians are the "White" Russian men, who, thus, stand out as Europeans; e.g., Kulneff in *Stories of Lieutenant Stål* and Peter the Great (Nicolai de Seversky) in *Karl XII.*

Peter the Great is interesting because his masculinity is sharply contrasted with that of Charles XII, using the yard stick of the modern masculine ideal. Whereas Charles XII, according to legend, refrained from sexual extravagances and alcohol, Peter willingly diverted himself with a number of women even though he was married. The filmmakers also made sure to show Peter drinking alcohol in all scenes except two. As a result, Charles XII is in control of his pas-

Czar Peter the Great (Nicolai de Seversky center) in *Karl XII*, where elements of white, Western-based masculinity are blended with so-called oriental and barbarian characteristics (*Karl XII* [1925]/Historisk Film AB/courtesy Swedish Film Institute).

sions, whereas Czar Peter is depicted as a degenerate habitual drunkard and ladies' man, without any self-control whatsoever. On the other hand, Peter, despite his enormous alcohol intake, appears to be a hard-working European who wishes to lift Russia out of its oriental backwardness. He is unceasingly making plans, military as well as civil, such as construction of the new capital Saint Petersburg. At the same time, he must resort to blows and threats to keep a close check on his lazy and reluctant "Asian" subjects. On one occasion, he even cuts off the beard of a boyar who objects to moving the capital from Moscow. Peter's element of "White" masculinity almost makes him Western by disposition. But only "almost," because, time and time again, the film emphasizes Peter's "oriental, barbarian characteristics" on the grounds that he cannot control his aggressions; in other words, he lacks manly, Western self-control.[164]

Only one objection to representing the Russians/Cossacks as a threatening horde can be found in reviews of the historic films, namely the scene before the Battle of Narva—a scene that was regarded as exaggerated.[165] Nicolai de Seversky as Peter the Great received unreserved praise for his portrayal. Naturally, the fact that he was also a genuine Russian was not a disadvantage: "He gives Czar Peter inner latitude, power and violence [...] so spontaneously that one is transported back to a historic reality."[166]

However, the historiography of the films was problematized in two reviews. In *Folkets Dagblad Politiken*, Bernhard Bengtsson protested: "The best component is the rendering of Czar Peter by Russian actor Nikolaj Severski, even though the Czar was obviously not the halfwit or coward that the actor, following the scriptwriter's instructions, had to make him out to be."[167] Even Russian author Vladimir Semitjoff, a resident of Stockholm, wrote an article about the respective renderings of Charles XII and Peter the Great in the *Karl XII* film. In the article, we learn that Semitjoff had grown up with Russian textbooks in which Peter the Great was presented as the "Czar-Carpenter, Czar-Soldier, Czar-Scientist":

> And I am searching through the pages of my textbook for the image of Czar Peter's strong adversary—as powerful, gallant and commanding as Peter himself. I am searching for—Charles XII. But in vain. [...] Now I can see both Charles XII and Czar Peter on the screen in a grand film drama. [...] And a remarkable metamorphosis impinges on my previous notions [...] in front of me, Czar Peter's powerful figure is overshadowed and disappears, leaving room for another—etched as hard as flint, cast-solid from top to toe—Charles XII. Peter is not present on the screen. I can see an absurd character, a wimpish quasi-dramatic hero, the leading lover in a mediocre operetta, a braggart from a market theater, whatever—but not a trace of either the Czar-Genius or the Czar-Carpenter, even less the Czar-Commander. [...] now it is the Swedes' turn to ask where the dignified opponent of their heroic king is, and why those remarkable Russians call their Peter—as he appears on the screen—"the Great." What greatness can be found in this neurasthenic?[168]

As can be seen, the Swedish filmmakers succeeded in their contrasting representation of Swedish and Russian masculinity. But the article also shows a fragile proximity: The two white masculinities did not really differ. From a Russian point of view, Czar Peter and King Charles simply changed places on the ladder of modern ideal masculinity.

Two films were set during or just after the Russian revolution. First released was the now-lost hit *In Self Defence* (*De landsflyktige*, 1921), a love story and courtroom drama, with the revolution as its backdrop and the Bolsheviks as the villains.[169] It was at this time that the word "Bolshevik" became an insult without any direct link to the real Bolsheviks.[170]

The second film to have the revolution as its backdrop was the Swedish adventure film *When Millions Are Squandered...* (*När millionerna rulla...*, 1924). The film was directed by Lasse Ring and was based on his experiences during the troubled years 1918–19, when he was stationed as a captain at the northern border between Sweden and Finland. This was a time when profit mongers made big money by smuggling people, weapons and luxury items. *When Millions Are Squandered...* dramatizes the course of events using a sea of different nationalities and elements such as espionage, wild chases, and a romantic element.

The story is as follows: Irma, the daughter of a Polish count, is engaged to the Russian count and general staff officer Marantoff (Sven Hasselström). She keeps a mysterious music album containing information about gigantic money investments abroad that constitute the financial nucleus of the Polish liberation movement. When the war breaks out, Irma ends up as a war refugee in Sweden, where her husband—who turns out to be a Russian agent—steals the album. In Sweden, however, two Swedish profit mongers come to her assistance.

Apart from Marantoff, who is portrayed as a villain of the European type, a number of Russian men appear. As usual, the Cossacks are portrayed as a group, this time as frontier guards. In one scene, they get to show their cruelty by shooting a group of Finnish refugees in the back. However, the Russian consul in Haparanda, Bitvargsky (Elias Ljungqvist), and his metamorphoses during the course of the film are more interesting. There is no doubt that Bitvargsky is modeled on Lenin. Ljungqvist's face has the same shape as Lenin's, and his appearance has been altered by means of the characteristic beard, a thin-haired coiffure, and a three-piece suit. As Russian consul, Bitvargsky does business with the Swedish profit mongers, constantly coming dangerously close to being stereotyped as a Shylock Jew, which is visualized through his accent and incessant hand-rubbing.

When the revolution breaks out, however, he puts on a cap, à la Lenin, which transforms him into a "working-class revolutionary." After the revolution, Bitvargsky presides over a court assigned to interrogate Irma. Around him is a group of theatrically portrayed Bolsheviks—dressed in a mishmash of workers' clothes and uniforms—who, from that point onward, take over the Cossacks' role as a Russian horde. Bitvargsky, however, is still only interested in money. He orders that Irma be tortured, and she is forced to reveal that her father knows how to decipher the music album. In the following scene, Bitvargsky has thrown off his cap and worker's clothes, and he is thus transformed into a member of the bourgeois. He kidnaps Irma's father and takes him to an isolated cabin, where he, in his turn, is overpowered by one of the Swedish profit mongers. Sitting there trembling, with his hands held up over his head, Bitvargsky makes a brief *que-sais-je* gesture, which, again, may indicate that he is a Jew.

According to the conception of Jews as cosmopolitans, where opposites such as capitalism and communism could be ascribed to "the Jewish," it is not unreasonable to assume that the filmmakers chose to borrow some well-known stereotypical features that would associate Bitvargsky with "the Jew." However, the main point would not have been to denounce him as a Jew in an anti–Semitic sense, but to blacken Soviet Russian masculinity by linking "the Jewish" to the representation of Bitvargsky as Lenin. The intention to portray the character as a Russian rather than a Jew can be discerned from the caricatured "Russian" name and from the fact that the strong accent lacked certain features characteristic of a "Jewish" accent.

There is no doubt that the description of the setting and the types of people were considered authentic, largely due to the fact that Ring, the director, was regarded as a historical witness.[171] In other words, the Russian men were accepted as they were portrayed: "All this is done with extraordinary accuracy [...] above all the Russian consul in Haparanda"[172] and "the entire thing [...] often gives the impression of truthfully mirroring what was once a singular reality."[173]

What we see here is a transfer of Russophobia from Cossack to Bolshevik, the difference being that the Western-minded "White" Russian male leaders, such as Czar Peter and various officers, were no longer able to control the Russian horde, as they were themselves turned into Bolsheviks with a horde mentality. The concrete effect of the visual confusion between Cossacks and Bolsheviks became evident in the infamous Swedish "Cossack election" of 1928, when the youth league of the Conservative Party set up election posters that depicted brutal, male Bolshevik Cossacks using their characteristic knouts to threaten defenseless Swedish women and children.[174]

All things Russian were not dismissed, however. As noted, Russian film caught on and was greatly admired in Sweden during the second half of the 1920s. For example, *Mat* (*Mother*, 1926) was voted one of the best films of 1927.[175] After having seen Sergei Eisenstein's *The Battleship Potemkin* (*Bronenosets Potjomkin*, 1925) in Germany, journalist Gerda Marcus was the first to report on the new sensation:

> Even the worst slanderers of film agree that "The Battleship Potemkin" is great art. [...] It is not a Bolshevik film really, it is more a revolutionary film in the deepest, most original sense of the word. [...] The crowd scenes in "Karl XII" are "mild" compared to the immense scenes enacted in this film. [...] Hardly a scene is shown without the audience, night after night, breaking out in endless applause "with the curtain up." And serious businessmen, who are not normally touched by anything in the world, except possibly a fateful fall on the stock market, walk around for days on end as if they were sleepwalkers. The images give them no peace.[176]

One month later, *The Battleship Potemkin* was totally prohibited in Sweden on the grounds that it was "inflammatory."[177] It would nevertheless be seen by thousands of Swedes because workers' associations around the country circumvented censorship by organizing "private" performances, supported by a statute on private parties.[178] From the point of view of masculinity and with the horde metaphor fresh in memory, *The Battleship Potemkin* and other Russian films from the 1920s, e.g., *Ten Days that Shook the World* (*Oktjabr'*, 1927), are interesting because many of them were based on crowd scenes in which the horde, mainly men, was represented as something positive. Thus paradoxically, Russian filmmakers corroborated a negative and already-existing Swedish-made notion of the threatening Russian horde. From a leftist perspective, this could be seen in another light.[179] Yet as shown by the example of *The Battleship Potemkin*, this positive way of presenting the horde was not accepted by the Swedish establishment, here represented by state censorship.

The image of Russian masculinity was thus divided in two, both parts having a clearly negative ring. In line with the threatening horde metaphor, the majority of Russian men were represented as non-white Cossacks and Bolsheviks. In contrast, the European Russian men, such as Peter the Great, were portrayed as individuals whose task was to control the non-white Russian horde. However, a more in-depth treatment of individual characters did not entail an emphasis on positive aspects. If anything, a number of negative, masculinely coded properties were stressed that subordinated these Russian characters to a hypothetical Swedish ideal masculinity. The two images of Russian masculinity also tended to merge in films depicting a period fairly recent in time against the backdrop of the menacing rumble of the Russian revolution.

Southern Masculinity—Rudolph Valentino and Enrique Rivero

In the 1920s, *Filmjournalen* published recurring reports from cinema life in other countries. It was said about South America:

> The audience are like children, and the cinema owners buy films accordingly. Polite society is rarely seen in the cinemas. There is no great demand for good taste and artistic quality. Douglas Fairbanks has never been seen here and neither have, of course, any of the loftier products of recent times. If a Chaplin film appears, then it's so scratched up it looks like it's raining and you're tempted to turn your coat collar up. What you get, in contrast, is William Fox and William Fox again, with revolvers and the Wild West and sentimentality and mass murder—that is the Song of Songs in South America. Unfaithful husbands and wives, poison and spies, cheating at cards, trials and hysterical women, all that is candy to the Peruvians, and William Fox treats them to huge bags of it.[180]

This generalization is interesting as a Swedish projection, because it reduces the whole of South America to a continent with bad and superficial taste. It represents the "White" outlook on a distant part of the world as the Other. This outlook, however, is not without its complications, nor is it black or white from the perspective of masculinity, which is evident in SF's hiring of South American actor Enrique Rivero to serve as Sweden's own Rudolph Valentino.

In the U.S., there was something of an erotic thrill in not regarding Valentino as white. Also, the negative reactions were an expression of pure racism, which, in light of the discussion on racial biology, warned of "race suicide" if white women continued desiring non-white immigrants.[181] According to Swedish film scholar Mats Björkin, Rivero did not give rise to the same threat in Sweden, because the ethnic and erotic elements were toned down. However, Björkin comes to this conclusion without considering the material used by SF to launch Rivero as Sweden's Valentino.[182] Before looking at the introduction of Rivero, therefore, it may be a good idea to examine the Swedish outlook on Valentino.

Rudolph Valentino had his great breakthrough in *The Four Horsemen of the Apocalypse* (1921). When the film came to Sweden the following year, *Filmnyheter*'s front cover featured a large picture of Valentino. In the same issue, an attempt was made to explain to a Swedish audience the Valentino craze that had broken out in the U.S. Vera von Kraemer claimed that Valentino was being idolized because he could fill a film with life and soul—he made the spectator feel something. He was no matinée idol, however, because such an actor is only good-looking in a slicked-back way, like a surface without contents. Instead, Valentino was a full-fledged actor. But like small pinholes in his enormous popularity, some Americans had reacted negatively: "The Americans do not quite understand him. He is a bit too refined for those naive Americans. He is not 'hearty' and not a boxing expert." In Europe, however, the audience was less unsophisticated, for "we are children of a more ancient culture, and Valentino's shading of expression is received with greater appreciation here."[183]

In Sweden, Valentino, who was born in Italy but marketed as having had a mysterious past in South America, is not at all regarded as non-white, but as an urbane European, and thereby white, man. Gaylyn Studlar discusses Valentino's masculinity as one created by and for women. His films were very popular among women, and by exercising their consumer power at the ticket office, women thus helped to create a male ideal based on their own desires. This "feminized" masculinity, combined with the threat of racial mixture, stirred up appreciable anxiety in the U.S. of the 1920s. Valentino's consumption-based masculinity was often contrasted to its remedy; that is, a return to a "natural" boyish masculinity, à la Douglas Fairbanks.[184] However, in another Swedish article, written in connection with Valentino's death in 1926, even this dichotomy was turned upside down, when the writer wondered: "How can anybody call such a boyish being feminine?"[185]

What about Rivero, then? Was he regarded as white or non-white? Everyone was aware of the real Valentino's persona. Thus, if SF wished to launch Rivero as a Valentino type, it is quite likely that they played on both ethnic and erotic themes to conjure up the attractive danger of a non-white Latino lover.

As early as March 1927, five months prior to his Swedish début in *Youth*, Enrique Rivero was introduced on the front cover and in an article in SF's magazine *Filmnyheter*. Under the cover picture, the following hopeful question was printed in boldface: "The new Valentino?" From the article, we learn that Rivero is Argentinian, slightly more than 20 years of age, and that he had been "discovered" in Paris.

> Judging from the photographs—see especially the front cover picture!—Enrique Rivero's appearance resembles that of Valentino in many ways. Like Valentino, he is also a Southern Latin—the extent to which these countries recruit film lovers these days is striking. [...] Rivero is not a new name on the silver screen. He has been in three French productions. [...] Facts about Enrique Rivero are still scarce, but we know that his person radiates a youthful charm, and that he is dark as is becoming a son of the Argentine. The South American paired with the blond Nordic beauty Margita Alfvén—wouldn't that be an attractive constellation! [...] Besides, Enrique Rivero is unmarried, a circumstance that will probably not lessen the ladies' interest in him.[186]

This is a professional launching in the best Hollywood style, a rare event in Swedish film in the 1920s, where discovery, glamorous photographs, rumors of romance and coming roles are all components of the creation of a new star.[187] Here, apart from his resemblance to Valentino, Rivero's ethnic qualities are emphasized and linked to the erotic element, not only in relation to the blond Alfvén and the remark that he was unmarried, but also, by association, with reference to the erotic city of Paris. Like today's talk about "Swedish sin," a notion spread by film, in the 1920s the same kind of talk was about "French sin."[188]

During the filming of *Youth* in the summer of 1927, an interview was conducted with Rivero, in which his answers were noticeably twisted so as to make him appear excessively interested in the opposite sex:

> —Bonjour, monsieur Rivero! You are studying Swedish film direction?
> —As you can see. —Isn't that girl beautiful?
> —Very! —What's your opinion of our Swedish film?
> —Look at how delightfully graceful her movements are...
> —Yes, but...
> —... she is like a doe, the little one. But you were saying? That...[189]

In the article, Rivero changes nationality to become Chilean, making his past more mysterious. Also, the erotic element is intensified through his inflated interest in women, a connection is made between women and Paris, and Rivero is said to have made "interesting discoveries" with Swedish women during a car trip. Thus, the entire article, now without any references to Valentino, substantiates the notion that a man of the South is more passionate and more interested in sexual excesses.

During the filming of *The Ghost Baron*, a report was published in which the writer begins by following up the erotic theme, wondering whether female readers would not like a "South American man in a Swedish naval officer's uniform." The article then starts making ironic remarks about Rivero's lack of knowledge of Swedish customs during a restaurant visit, the upshot being that Rivero seems very awkward for someone who is supposed to be "The new Valentino."[190] Later in the fall, after *Youth* and *The Ghost Baron* had been released, Rivero was interviewed on account of his returning to Paris:

> —Tears will be shed now that you are leaving, monsieur Rivero.
>
> The nice boy looks embarrassed.
>
> —I really cannot help it. I've been living in peace and quiet. Can I help that I look like a Southern Latin! I was born down there. And you cannot blame me because there are foolish little girls who must have some film artist as their "hero?"—Do you know what happened to me on this very day? I was walking quietly on Stureplan when I suddenly heard a couple shouts: "Monsieur! Monsieur!" Turning around, I saw two young, very young ladies coming after me. They said something in French. I didn't catch what. I hurried up to the point of half running, and managed to get into Anglais.
>
> —Did you ever hear anything like it! we said. Have our women in Stockholm, notorious for their erotic frostiness, become so hot-blooded? Then life must be quite spirited in Paris.
>
> —Don't mention it.
>
> And Rivero turns up his coat collar—not just against indiscreet gazes, it was a cold day too—slipping away into the anonymous crowd.[191]

Behind his back, then, a rumor is related according to which Rivero was accosted by a female admirer in a Paris movie theater, ending in him running away with his tail between his legs.[192]

Whereas the ethnic markers had now disappeared, the erotic ones had not been abandoned. However, the Don Juan ideal had backfired, making Rivero appear unable to control his "masculine" behavior, his looks, or the women around him. It is quite possible that Rivero was pursued in the streets of Stockholm, but the combination of running away from little girls and the incident at the movie theater reduces him to a pretty surface, a matinée idol without contents, in precisely the same way as Valentino was dismissed by his critics. Consequently, during his short period of exposure, the media image of Rivero's masculinity was transformed from a dangerous Latino lover variant of (non-white) masculinity into a femininely coded, consumption-based (white) masculinity.

Rivero's media image comprised three Swedish films in which he took part, which premièred between August 1927 and February 1928. But given that the launching of his person had begun in March 1927, we can observe that the films' image and reception are out of step with the image of Rivero that had already been conjured up.

In *Youth*, Rivero flickers by in a three-minute-short role as Count Juan di Mitjana, attaché of the Spanish ambassador. The themes of the film pit youth against old age. An older man falls in love with a young girl. He is prepared to leave his wife, Agnes, to once again experience the vitality of youth. At a garden party, Agnes is also tempted by this force when she is courted by the young Juan.

Juan is introduced in a scene that shows him smelling flowers. When Agnes walks by, he looks at her with a conceited smile, then follows her and sits down at her table. When they are alone, he looks around, then leans forward saying: "I never see you so pretty, so desirable like today, Madame!" Agnes gives a start of surprise, looking at Juan. At this point, the film begins to use Point of View (POV), which allows us to see, from Agnes's point of view, a close-up of Juan, who, in turn, gives Agnes a very penetrating look, gazing at her from top to bottom. He kisses her hand, saying: "I you adore!" To be sure, Agnes is flattered, but she shakes her head slowly, pointing out matter-of-factly the 20-year difference between them. The film returns to POV, showing Juan as he ponders this. "Love makes miracles!" he finally says, but she answers: "No, it does not!" The scene ends with another POV take, in which Juan looks very dejected.

Here, the ethnic and erotic elements are emphasized through the names of the characters, the foreign accent in the dialogue texts, the actors' appearance and the fiery courting—all with connotations to an imagined southern masculinity. The many close-ups of Rivero's face are illustrative, as their only function was to display and exploit his looks. This did not always fall on fertile ground, however, as close-ups were considered vulgar. Rivero's function in *Youth* would be very clear if it weren't for a small glitch in the machinery—Juan fails most seriously in "conquering" the older Agnes. Thus, in a twinkling, southern masculinity is transformed into something pathetic instead of manly.

Given the secondary nature of his role, it may seem remarkable that Rivero/Juan was mentioned in more the half of the reviews. The explanation is related to the massive advance publicity, which was turned against Rivero: "On the other hand, it seems to us as if Enrique Rivero has been highly overrated. If he is not able to achieve more than what we saw last night, then he will probably be a disappointment to those who engaged him."[193] Here, the uncertainty and erotic failure of his role as Juan is already combined with exploitation of the person Rivero in a way that classifies him as belonging to consumption-based masculinity.

In the comedy *The Ghost Baron*, Rivero has a somewhat larger role, appearing in a total of five scenes. Considering how he was launched as a Latino lover, however, it is remarkable that he plays Swedish naval lieutenant Gösta Bramberg. The question is, then, how the filmmakers went about presenting Rivero as Swedish, and a military officer at that, a role strongly associated with an ideal warriorhood masculinity.

In the first scene, Gösta is found with his sweetheart, Gurli, on board the armored vessel *Baltic*. Gurli is there to say farewell, because she is being forced against her will to marry a rich baron (Fridolf Rhudin) to settle up the family's bad finances. Gösta is dressed in a uniform, his black hair slicked back. During the scene, the unhappy Gösta is turned away from Gurli most of the time, but when she is about to leave, he gives her a fiery kiss that is transformed into an awkward kiss when she breaks loose from the embrace.

After a knock on the head during his stag party, the rich baron is afflicted with severe memory loss and, through mistaken identity, ends up as a sailor on the *Baltic*. In the second scene, Lieutenant Bramberg is looking dreamily at a photograph of Gurli when a non-commissioned officer leads "Larsson," with whom the baron has been mixed up, into the room. Not knowing where he is, "Larsson" is confused, but Lieutenant Bramberg mistakes his behavior for a hangover. Bramberg gets angry, bangs his fist on the table and demands improved conduct. When "Larsson" has gone, the film dwells upon the lieutenant, who smiles into the camera.

Then the *Baltic* sets out for the sea, and the film turns its focus to comic elements when "Larsson" learns to be a proper seaman. In the following scenes, all of the seamen surrounding "Larsson" are authentic Swedish sailors, made available for SF by the Swedish Armed Forces. In addition to the men, even the armored vessel *Sverige*, the *Baltic* in the film, had been provided.

Considering the contemporary symbolism and the military connection to masculinity, it is striking that the filmmakers did not incorporate Rivero into these scenes, which would have provided a good opportunity to depict him as Swedish. Instead, in the third scene, Bramberg gets a letter from Gurli in which she writes that the baron has been officially declared dead and that her family, who has now sorted out their finances, has bought the baron's villa at an auction. She also tells him that her mother has agreed to their engagement, which provides yet another opportunity to show an idle Rivero leaning against a railing, a dreamy smile on his lips.

Following a shore leave, during which "Larsson" meets a new sweetheart, the *Baltic* sails without him. He tries to catch up with the ship in a rowboat, but the rowboat sinks. To avoid drowning, he clings to a floating mine. The mine turns out to be a hollow hiding place for smuggled liquor. "Larsson" climbs into it. The next morning, the mine is sighted by the *Baltic*'s captain, who instructs Lieutenant Bramberg to shoot it to pieces. In this fourth scene, Rivero is standing on the bridge in full uniform, wearing white gloves and a pair of binoculars hanging around his neck. He looks determined when he gives the order to fire. This is cross-cut with pictures of real sailors sighting the ship's cannons, then beginning to fire on the mine. After some ten missed shots, the lieutenant realizes that there is somebody in the mine. He suspends the firing and makes sure a boat is sent out to pick up "Larsson."

When the *Baltic* returns to Stockholm, "Larsson" gets another bang on the head, causing his memory to return. He immediately sets off for his villa, where Bramberg, now in civilian clothes, is telling ghost stories to Gurli, her mother, and some friends. When the baron arrives, Gurli's mother has already gone to bed. Entering the bedroom, he is taken for a ghost. The mother screams, and in the parlor, the others wonder what is going on. The baron enters the parlor, and Bramberg immediately recognizes him as "Larsson." The lieutenant scolds "Larsson," believing he is drunk. The baron, in his turn, tells Bramberg off because he wonders what they are doing in his home. The situation comes to blows. Bramberg and the other male guest wrestle the baron to the floor and tie him up. After the turmoil, Rivero gets to utter his only funny line in this comedy. When Bramberg enters the bedroom, the mother exclaims: "Did you see him? Conrad! The dead walk again!" He arranges his tie, saying: "Yes, Auntie dear, and he'll walk out again soon!" A cut over to a smiling Rivero: "It was only a ghost from the *Baltic* still walking the earth!"

After this scene, Rivero disappears from the film, which is remarkable. After everything has been sorted out, the film ends with the traditional final kiss between the baron and his new sweetheart. According to convention, Bramberg and Gurli should also have been included in the final scene.

Apart from the Swedish character name and the lack of a foreign accent in the titles, it is not entirely clear what makes Rivero a Swedish man. If anything, this is achieved by not stressing the preconceived characteristics of southern masculinity. Gone are the fire and the sexual brazenness from *Youth*. These qualities have been replaced by dreaming inactivity that could have characterized Swedish masculinity, but not an ideal one, especially not in the military setting in which Lieutenant Bramberg found himself. The military environment, including authentic Swedish sailors, actually serves to accentuate Rivero's consumption-based masculinity, and his elegant uniform only functions instrumentally to bring out his looks, though not as a marker of an inner, ideal warriorhood masculinity. This inconsistency was also reflected in the reviews:

> However, Enrique Rivero was less pleasing in the role of a naval officer. He was much too weak and tame for that part. I should have liked to see the lieutenant who, while at sea and especially in the summer, makes an appearance on the bridge clad in dazzlingly white kid gloves—he would have had a merry time in the gun-

room afterwards! Otherwise, the young man was "easy on the eyes," and he no doubt charmed the female audience in his becoming naval officer's uniform.[194]

The Ghost Baron was a huge hit and like all hits, it made a "crossover"; that is, by virtue of its pluralism, the film managed to capture the attention of many different groups in society, some of which found the entire film pleasing; others, only parts of it. Enrique Rivero contributed to the film's success by functioning as an advertisement pillar for male beauty, which—based on SF's intentions and the unanimous reactions to his performance—in all probability drew, particularly, women to the cinemas. This further undermined Rivero's image as a masculine man or dangerous Latino lover.

His third and final film, *His Royal Highness Does the Shingle*, is a romantic adventure comedy. This time, Rivero plays one of the main characters, Nickolo, the grandson of an immigrant barber from the fictitious country of Tirania.

It is midsummer in the small seaport of Salthamn, and Nickolo returns home in his white student's cap. His grandfather, André (Hans Junkermann), is

Enrique Rivero as the charming Nickolo in the shop-window scene in *His Royal Highness Does the Shingle* (*Hans kunglig höghet shinglar* [1928]/AB Isepa/courtesy Swedish Film Institute).

dismayed to learn that Nickolo has trained himself to be a hairdresser. But Nickolo immediately takes the initiative, putting a placard in the shop window advertising the shingle haircut. A group of young women gather outside to have a look at the handsome Nickolo, who is thereby literally transformed into an object. But he soon has plenty of work because everyone wants a shingle haircut. In the meantime, the young, modern woman Astrid (Brita Appelgren) pulls her car up outside the barber shop. Curiously peeking inside, she meets a woman on her way out, who says: "Isn't he enchanting, the new barber?" Nickolo catches sight of Astrid, but she plays hard to get and drives away. Looking longingly after her, he asks a customer if he could be introduced, but is told he "must be at least a count" to be interesting to her. Astrid's mother, who is a wealthy lady (Karin Swanström), wants her daughter to marry an elderly count. But Astrid wants to marry for love.

During the evening's midsummer celebrations, Nickolo and Astrid meet again. Nickolo is asked to dance by a female customer, but answers frankly: "No, thank you; I don't dance!" Then he finds Astrid who, wishing to avoid the insistent count, agrees to dance with him. One thing leads to another, and they decide to go for a row to a nearby island. As they are talking, they catch sight of a ship. Astrid asks about the strange flag the ship is flying and is told that it is the Tiranian flag: "My native country."

"Are you not Swedish?" Astrid wonders, wanting to know more.

Nickolo then tells her that he came to Sweden as a child, and during the conversation that follows, they get to know each other better. When they are about to row back, they find the boat has drifted out from the shore. Astrid misinterprets the situation, believing it to be a base seduction trick. This annoys Nickolo, who takes off his hat and jacket, plunges into the water, swims out to the rowboat and rows it back in. Astrid realizes that she has made a mistake, but Nickolo is too proud to accept her apologies. She gets to row back home on her own. On the shore, he puts on his hat and jacket, adjusts the handkerchief in his breast pocket, and then jumps back into the water again to swim home. Passing Astrid, he politely lifts his hat. She says: "If you don't catch a cold from this you can come and do my hair tomorrow."

The introduction is different from that of the previous films. To be sure, Rivero becomes an object to be stared at in the shop window scene, but both before and after, Nickolo is represented as an active, young and successful man. Also, his profession as a hairdresser, who can do a shingle haircut on women, should not be interpreted anachronistically as unmanly. In the 1920s, young women went to male barbers because the female hairdressers refused to cut off their long hair.[195] And the rendering of this film is also strikingly different with regard to the ethnic and erotic markers. First, the character of Nickolo is allowed to develop his background. Second, it never occurs to Astrid that he might not be Swedish. When she discovers that he isn't, she doesn't turn him away point-blank, but wants to know more. In addition, the forward southern style is gone, as is, paradoxically, the passivity, which has been replaced by active, but respectful, courting. In connection with the rowboat incident, no reference is made to Nickolo's ethnicity. Instead, Astrid interprets it from a class perspective: "What else could you expect from a simple barber?"

The next day, Nickolo comes to the palace to give Astrid a shingle haircut. When he is halfway through, Astrid's mother enters the room, becomes raging mad and throws him across the room like a rag doll. Shortly afterwards, however, she has a reason to change her mind when André informs her that Nickolo is of royal descent. It turns out that his grandfather brought Nickolo to Sweden in the belief that he is the true heir to the throne of Tirania. This is, in fact, a bluff. For the past 20 years, two Tiranian swindlers have been cheating André out of money. Now, they claim they have come to bring Nickolo home to reinstall him. They need huge amounts of money for the *coup d'état*, which is also the reason André approaches the rich mother. At the prospect of Astrid becoming a queen, the mother does an about-face and gives André the money.

In the meantime, the following scene

Advertisements for hairdressers who specialize in the shingle. The phenomenon started in the mid–1920s, and in the beginning it was mostly male hairdressers who shingled the hair of trend-following young women (*Våra Nöjen* No. 12, 1926).

is enacted in the barber shop: Nickolo is standing around, yawning indifferently, because it is the third time he has given the woman who found him enchanting at the beginning of the film a haircut. Suddenly, an angry Astrid drives up so that he can finish the shingle haircut he started. Seeing her, he begins flirting with the customer to make Astrid jealous, and it works. To give him a bit of his own medicine, Astrid pretends to call the count to thank him for the nice evening she had yesterday, which causes Nickolo to start. But then he pulls himself together, because the count is seated in another room in the barber shop. When Astrid begins talking about marrying the "count," Nickolo says self-assuredly, "May I congratulate you," and starts whistling the wedding march. It all ends with them kissing and making up. Because they still believe that Astrid's mother is against the relationship, they decide to run away together, then escape with the boat to Tirania.

The scene in which they make their escape is a parody of *Romeo and Juliet*, with elements of slapstick. Nickolo first climbs a ladder to the balcony where Astrid is waiting. But the ladder breaks, and he slides down, breaking off every rung on the way. Astrid then decides to steal down the stairs. She stumbles, of course, rolling down the staircase with a great hullabaloo. Meanwhile, they are constantly being watched by the mother and André, who smile contentedly, pleased that the young couple have taken a fancy to each other without their interference.

Thus, when Nickolo and Astrid climb onboard the boat, the mother, grandfather and the two villains are already waiting with the Tiranian royal crown. The young couple fails to grasp the situation at first, but then misunderstanding number two arises when Nickolo gets the idea that Astrid only wants him because of his "royal" descent. To prove that this isn't true, Astrid suggests that they escape once more, and they say to the movie audience: "We abdicate!" During their escape, they run across the two villains who are about to bolt with the money. Nickolo wrestles the first villain down, then steals upon the other one and takes his pistol. The villain puts up resistance and a fierce fight breaks out. Nickolo finally wins. With his shirt torn to pieces and his tie askew, he and Astrid reveal the plot to the mother and André. The film ends with the four of them moving to Paris, where they open a luxurious barber shop. The mother enters the room, asking: "Where is my son-in-law?" and André replies contentedly: "His royal highness is doing the shingle," which is followed by the final scene in which Nickolo intimately cuts Astrid's hair. Final kiss.

Here, Nickolo is actively included in the comical plot. He gets a bit dirty in the fight and he also marries Astrid. The question is, then, whether this more active masculinity is able to overshadow Rivero's consumption-based masculinity image in the media?

In *Nya Dagligt Allehanda*, the shop window scene and the scene in which the couple runs away were considered the most amusing: "In the young Chilean, Enrique Rivero, [Astrid] had a sympathetic person to play opposite to, he will no doubt make himself known in the charmer branch."[196] And: "The young Chilean, Enrique Rivero, [...] was a pleasant acquaintance, played soundly and heartily, and it is understandable that the young ladies gladly let him give them a shingle haircut a couple times a day."[197]

The active Rivero thus received a more positive reception than he had before. On the face of it, we could conclude that the activity, with its ties to modern ideal masculinity, counterbalanced the image of consumption-based masculinity and all the talk about Rivero's looks. It should be noted, however, that almost all of the reviewers linked this heartiness and liveliness with Rivero's ethnicity, by pointing out that he is a Chilean or Argentinean.[198]

However, *Stockholms-Tidningen*'s reviewer was of a different opinion: "Enrique Rivero has a noble, racially defined face, and the whole of this stylish, self-controlled young man expresses culture. But does he have sufficient fire and vitality to carry off the part of a lover? This film leaves the question unanswered, and he has very little humor."[199] His noble, racially defined face and his self-control bring Rivero into the "White" fold, while his lack of fervor once again reduces him to the preconceived image of southern masculinity.

During Rivero's brief sojourn in Sweden, the image of his masculinity underwent several metamorphoses. First, SF tried to create a southern, erotic and non-white masculinity, whose "danger" was meant to attract mainly women to the movies houses. However, it was clear from the outset that Rivero, like Valentino, was not seen as a threat in Sweden when it came to the risk of racial mixture, because he was regarded as a white man. A non-white masculinity was also not emphasized in the films, the exception being the failure Juan in *Youth*. Instead, the focus came to be on Rivero's looks, something that undermined the image of his masculinity.

The three examples above show that the white race, or white masculinity, was not an undivided whole—neither on the group nor on the individual level. Finnish men, described as "literary" on the official racial biological level, were represented in a positive light in films emphasizing "primitive" masculinity. In many cases, this spread a shadow of ridicule over an imagined Swedish ideal masculinity, which lacked war experience. Even geographical and historical explanations had an influence on how Finnish and Russian masculinities were represented in the films.

With the exception of the Cossacks, who seem to be inherently prone to rape, the threat of racial mixture is also conspicuous in its absence. On this level, the white race thus stands out as an undivided whole. This creates a tremendously contrasting effect in relation to the Cossacks—but also in relation to blacks, Jews and the Sami—as it literally divides people into white and black, just as Dyer points out. The strength of this classification becomes particularly clear if we consider SF's complete failure to construct and launch Rivero as a non-white and, thereby, threatening Latino lover, corresponding to the role Valentino played in the United States.

Conclusions

Swedish society underwent great changes during the first decades of the 1900s, and as a symptom of these quite evident changes, the new consumption and entertainment culture came under fire. The older generation projected its own uncertainty about societal developments primarily onto children and youth, but also onto women and the working classes, the reason being that these groups had become symbols of the forces that had broken down traditional structures and values. These groups were also rhetorically pinpointed as the principal users of the new film medium. The visible public presence of children and youth resulted in loud criticism on the part of established society, and this concern was the main reason for the introduction of state-controlled film censorship in Sweden in 1911. In the 1920s, however, the criticism did not go beyond argumentation, an important reason being that the concern was not shared by all, or that it was even doubted by many. This is evident when we consider the following circumstances: (1) The film industry defended itself, using the same kind of experts employed by the moralists; (2) many parents sent their children to the cinemas; and (3) as witnessed by the high box-office figures, young people as well as their parents went to the movies.

One overall goal of *Masculinity in the Golden Age of Swedish Cinema* has been to challenge both the enduring image of modern ideal masculinity and the seemingly unshakable dichotomies between masculine and feminine that have been depicted in gender studies. Another goal has been to question Swedish and international historiography dealing with the so-called Golden Age. This has been accomplished by locating the study's sociological space in the heterosocial setting that is film culture, as well as by considering all feature films and feature-length documentaries produced in Sweden in the 1920s, thus moving beyond the strict canon of the Swedish silent films.

Gender is a fundamentally relational concept. It is created in relation to both masculinity and femininity, but it also depends on a number of other factors, each specific to their respective time period. The present focus has been on the film medium as a vital part of the emerging consumption and entertainment culture, including the impact of film on the construction of gender. The consumption of entertainment has often been regarded as something that dulls the intellect, which is reflected in the sharp division into art films and mainstream films made in film studies. Gender-oriented sociological film studies have undoubtedly been influenced by this culture-critical classification, in the sense that there exists a strong notion that art films contain more acceptable representations of gender, sexuality and ethnicity, while mainstream films, during the more than 100 years of film history, are thought to have recycled a handful of unchanging stereotypes so as to paint a simpler picture of the world. But because only a handful of films are regarded as art and, thus, paid attention to in the research, the majority of all films produced have been ignored. This canon formation limits our cultural knowledge and historical memory because it gives an incomplete picture of both the film culture and the society in which the films are produced.

In the present study, the films and the culture surrounding them have not been treated as art, but as commercial products. Introduction of the concept of the pluralism of film has thus served to break down the dichotomy between art and mainstream film, instead analyzing the films from a contextual perspective. The pluralism of film is based on the following three facts: (1) Films are made by many individuals whose different ideas affect the end results; (2) films are extremely expensive to produce; they must, therefore, largely conform to the public preferences of the time; and (3) films are intimately tied to a realism that requires them to be true to life, and through this connection, the human raw material—the actors—function as representations of a number of contemporary notions and prejudices concerning, e.g., gender and ethnicity. Taking this as a theoretical point of departure, the study's analyses of the film culture of the 1920s have been carried out thematically, with a focus on four areas, which share the fact that they have seldom been addressed in Scandinavian or Anglo-Saxon masculinity studies: (1) children and youth, (2) fatherhood and love, (3) sexuality and popularity, and (4) racial stereotypes and ethnicity.

Relational Gender Research and the Meaning of Diversity

An important result of these analyses is that they have revealed the great variety of masculinities portrayed in all the films. Another result is the sometimes very complex social constructions of these different masculinities. The existence of a modern ideal masculinity, which according to George L. Mosse has had a great influence on Western men during the past 200 years, seems at first to be somewhat out of place in the Swedish context of the 1920s.[1] Swedish films from the 1920s contain very few examples of male characters that can be said to express modern ideal masculinity. Exceptions can be found in *The Strongest*, the two parts of *Karl XII* and *Stories of Lieutenant Stål*, respectively, although the latter film contained representations of an ideal Finnish masculinity. But not even in this case was the ideal completely fulfilled. Instead, the most evident presence of modern ideal masculinity can be found in the discussion of racial stereotypes and ethnicity in Chapter 5. It was mainly the documentary genre that, by virtue of its flagrant "scientific" footage of the Other, evoked an imaginary Swedish hegemonic masculinity that corresponded well with the colonial discourses of the time.[2] The lack of concrete expressions of modern ideal masculinity is connected to the fact that it is just an ideal, not a reality. If modern ideal masculinity very seldom materializes—even in the "dream-world" of film—of what significance is this ideal? Does the actual absence of macho men in Swedish film from the 1920s mean that Sweden is different from other countries? Or was the time period special in this case? In my view, the difference between this study and previous research depends on several factors, among others the present study's almost complete inclusion of available film sources, resulting in a much more complex picture of masculinity. Film studies specializing in gender research have mainly used a narrow film selection based either on factors such as popularity or artistic quality, or on longer time periods, often with the specific aim to pinpoint predominant gender ideals.[3] However, representations of ideals tend to be discussed uncritically as representations of reality by later researchers, the consequence being that the picture of masculinity and gender becomes distorted. In this light, the lack of representations of modern ideal masculinity in Swedish films from the 1920s would appear to be neither conspicuous nor divergent. Thus, Sweden is not a special case. And if research continues to look beyond the artistic and commercial canon, the picture of modern ideal masculinity and other stereotypes will probably be further problematized.

An example of this is the existence of and struggle between two masculine ideals during the first decades of the 1900s, where the so-called civilization process of established society was equivalent to middle-class masculinity, while the "enemy" of this process was the notion of the "natural" man who had not yielded to civilization and bureaucratization. Following Sally Robinson's thesis, I would like to claim that it is in the competition between these two ideals that the general notion of Western masculinity can be found, and thereby not in the singular modern ideal masculinity.[4] If we abandon the idea of the existence of an ideal, a more dynamic view of masculinity and social gender construction appears, and this view, per se, helps to broaden our understanding of a complex process that goes beyond the generalizing dichotomies.

But what about the time period? The 1920s and the entire interwar period are often singled out as particularly problematic for masculinity, and as a time of crisis. The issue of a masculinity crisis seems to be constantly topical in the academic as well as mass media world. However, media specialist John Beynon has raised the question of whether the crisis exists at all, or has it simply been reproduced so often that it has become a fact. And is the frequent talk about a masculinity crisis of any value to gender studies, or is the "crisis" trotted out too casually to explain changed relations between men and between men and women? In Beynon's opinion, each time period has a tendency to perceive the "crisis" as something new. Also, its definition is imprecise in the sense that everything negative is lumped together with masculinity in a stereotyped way.[5] Unquestionably, all men are not in a crisis all the time.

In the source material, we find discussions to the effect that the social civilization process was equivalent to feminization, which, for example, was thought to influence boys and men—all according to the motto "things used to be more masculine." But was this influence only negative? On a superficial, ideal level, the new consumption culture, and the modern young woman's liberating use of it, could be interpreted as a crisis for masculinity. But what is it exactly that characterized this crisis? Was it that consumption quickly came to be coded as something feminine and thus inferior, or that women took up more room in public life? Using a relational perspective, I have shown, among other things, that consumption did not designate women as weaker and that the shift in gender relations, brought on by the new feminine element in public life, was very quickly normalized, often because young men adapted themselves to suit young women. This "adaption," too, has been interpreted as something negative, like a crisis. During the 1920s, however, it was generally regarded as positive by both men and women.

My criticism of the homosocial thesis is also of relevance in this context. By adopting a relational perspective that includes women and femininity in the social construction of men and masculinity, three facts can be made clear: (1) Women have a considerable influence on the formation of masculinity; (2) masculinity is not primarily a homosocial construction, with the possible exception of already strongly homosocial settings, such as the military; and (3) a relational perspective may suggest alternatives that go beyond ideal constructions, thus providing a way out of the impasse at which much of gender and masculinity research presently finds itself.

The relational perspective does not only entail a shift in focus from gender as a homosocial or hierarchical power construction to a heterosocial one, but it also includes the insight that the social construction of gender is affected by a number of relational power factors, such as generation, class, ethnicity, sexuality and consumption—factors that must sometimes be allowed to overshadow the primary gender criterion to avoid evoking a misleading contextual understanding of the relation in question. The dual themes of the present study—children and youth, on the one hand, and fatherhood, on the other—have demonstrated the existence of a generational conflict, but not a crisis of masculinity or fatherhood, as a consequence of societal changes. In contrast, if fatherhood had only been discussed from a homosocial or power hierarchical perspective, as has often been done in previous research, it is very likely that the results would instead have concerned some kind of theoretical crisis.

The many different and transformative masculinities that appear in Swedish films from the 1920s were products of their time. They constitute evidence that the reshaping of society both dissolved old boundaries and established the new ones for what was to be coded as masculine and feminine, respectively. From a gender-historical point of view, the early decades of the 1900s were particularly interesting, because the historical and constant "struggle between the sexes" entered an unstable phase, which, in fact, created many alternatives for what were regarded as traditional gender relations. Many of the constructions and solutions that were tested have survived to this day in modified forms, providing the basis for modern gender relations. Many others, however, were rejected. By using source material such as the film culture in historical research one is able to get at the many alternatives found beyond the official and prescribed. Herein also lies what is important and vital about revealing the alternative, because the alternative, per se, shows that change is possible, which may inspire us to achieve greater equality.

Considering the great number of so-called alternative masculinities presented here, and in view of the absence of pure incarnations of modern ideal masculinity, it may even be possible to turn previous gender research upside down, and to ask whether these alternative masculinities do not, in fact, constitute masculinity. There is no doubt that modern, ideal, hegemonic or true masculinity constitutes the yardstick for masculinity in the Western world, but in the long run, can it really be fruitful to only look at the yardstick and to relate the "alternatives" to a norm that few men can or even want to live up to?

The Writing of Film and Gender History

By way of introduction, I raised the tentative question of why the adult man who was fooled in *L'arroseur arrosé* has so seldom been discussed in gender-oriented film studies. In the course of the study, several answers have crystalized: (1) As a consequence of the theoretical influence in the field, film studies has primarily concentrated on discussing male ideals and bodies as well as a normative male gaze; (2) alternative masculinities and dominating femininities have been treated as anomalies or symptoms of a male crisis in the world of film, too often disregarding the period-specific context[6]; and (3) this culture-critical view, which has largely been built around the defense of film as an academic discipline, has entailed a persistent and unfortunate division, or canonization, of film into art versus mainstream, which influences both the selection of material and the results.

Swedish film history includes many black holes that are tentatively bound by a general historiography. Up to now, the history of Swedish films from the 1920s has constituted such a hole, temporarily held together by the mythological story of the Golden Age. But the Golden Age has consisted, at best, of some 20 films, which have been discussed in a repeated cycle for 80 years, whereas the remaining hundreds of films produced during the same period have been "forgotten" because they have not been considered artistically sophisticated. That may be all right if the researcher chooses to study films in terms of their style and form. But if the study is to deal with some form of representation, a selection based on "artistic" criteria will unavoidably lead to a number of misleading and flawed conclusions.[7] Where Swedish films from the 1920s are concerned, there is a strong notion that some filmmakers' integrated use of nature in the narrative constituted a Swedish national characteristic, which has later been taken to represent "Swedishness."[8] But if we consider the whole of Swedish film production, this use of nature was merely a deviation, more related to individual filmmakers than to an entire film culture. Looking back, it is possible to discern a kind of national pride over the successful export of Swedish films all over the world in the aftermath of World War I. However, a closer look at these exports reveals that it was not only the artistic Golden Age films that were sold, but also now totally forgotten, light comedies and blatantly racist animated short films. If a specific "Swedishness" can be said to have permeated Swedish film culture, it was not a love of nature, but instead racism and xenophobia. Moreover, Swedish ideal masculinity and "Swedishness" were at their most salient in the innumerable representations of the Other.

Studying film at the national level, perhaps particularly silent films, can be called into question. The Swedish film culture of the 1920s, as well as film culture in general, should be investigated in a more international perspective than has been the case thus far, owing particularly to the considerable and more equal export and import of films—and the people who work with film—between and within both Europe and the U.S. For instance, racism wasn't only a Swedish cultural trait; instead it was a vital part of society in the entire Western cultural sphere. In a Swedish context, however, expressions of racism were specific in some cases, as a consequence of social factors. For example, the absence of black people in Sweden influenced Swedish film's visual treatment of this group, and likewise, the presence of Afro-American in the U.S. came to affect how they were depicted in American film productions. Moreover, a national focus results in large parts of film consumption—through which people *de facto* see, understand and finally create film based on these experiences—being greatly neglected. In this way, there is a risk that complex nuances will disappear and that, instead, results will be painted too broadly. This is the case with the downfall of the Swedish Golden Age of film, which is usually explained as a consequence of the so-called Americanization of Swedish film.[9] Such a statement can only be made if actual financial and contextual factors are disregarded, e.g., the fact that Sweden found itself in a unique export situation with the rest of the world at war. Moreover, Swedish film producers made more mainstream than art films both before, during and after the Golden Age period.

In the present study, I have claimed throughout that film culture constitutes a heterosocial sphere that can capture the relational aspect more completely than can studies of homosocial spheres. Against this claim, one can pose the strong view that film is a masculine sphere. On some structural levels, the film medium has historically been an enterprise dominated by men. This has particularly been the case with regard to directing and scriptwriting. Between 1910 and 1929, 441 films were produced in Sweden. Of these, about 200 were shorter one- and two-reel films produced prior to 1917. Of all these films, 13 were directed by five women, whereas slightly more than 10 percent of all screenplays were written by women.[10] These figures are low at first glance, but nevertheless higher than during the decades to follow. Considering the pluralism of feature films and documentaries, which was necessary at the time owing to the financial realities of the industry, we cannot reduce filmmaking to a matter of auteurship, with its customary focus on the director. Film culture is imbued with an inclusive pluralism, where relatively equal factors such as actors, audience, reviewers, and the authors of literary sources, e.g., Selma Lagerlöf and Elin Wägner, and their actual influence on filmmaking and film culture seldom can be explained away by using abstract theories such as psychoanalysis.[11]

With the present study, I join the growing number of researchers—for instance, Gaylyn Studlar and Ben Singer—who stress the strongly heterosocial qualities of early film, in the sense that the concrete female influence on film and film culture was greater during this formative period than during subsequent years. This is manifested, among other things, by the modern young woman, the fact that women played the role of the protagonist and, thus, the hero without problems, and that the woman was not automatically subordinated to male characters in the films.[12] Here we also find an example of what I have called positive Americanization, i.e., the naturalness with which these female characters were received in the Swedish context, which was undoubtedly a consequence of having seen the many serial-queen melodramas and other American movies with progressive gender portrayals that were so popular in Sweden during the 1910s and 1920s. From the perspective of equality, what followed was a decline that, at least in the American context, can be explained by the implementation of the Hays Code of 1934, which contained production regulations that, by threatening to obstruct distribution, in one stroke steered film production onto a more conservative path with regard to the representation of gender relations.[13] This was primarily the case with the great Hollywood production companies, the majors and the minors, whereas the smaller companies, the so-called Poverty Row studios, could go on dealing with politically sensitive topics and more progressive gender portrayals, though on a smaller scale.[14] The lessons we can learn from this are that (1) the film culture's depictions of gender and gender relations are not static, but can instead be characterized as having moved like a wave, rising and falling, during the course of film history; (2) the traditional classification of male and female characters into a small number of stereotyped pigeonholes seldom provides any adequate answers; and (3) film and gender analyses are dependent on a context that transcends artistic criteria.

Chapter Notes

In the 1910s and 1920s, most Swedish film reviewers wrote under various, often cryptic pseudonyms, such as XXX, —lin, Marfa, etc. These have been retained in the notes as author names and, where possible, the writer behind the signature has been identified in brackets.

Introduction

1. David Bordwell and Kristin Thompson, *Film History: An Introduction* (New York: McGraw-Hill, 1994), 9–10.
2. Perry Nodelman, "Making Boys Appear: The Masculinity of Children's Fiction," *Ways of Being Male: Representing Masculinities in Children's Literature and Film*, John Stephens, ed. (London and New York: Routledge, 2002), 1–14.
3. See Robert Bly, *Iron John: A Book About Men* (London: Ebury Press, 2001).
4. The Lumière brothers did not "invent" film all by themselves; film historians usually regard the invention as an international process. In the U.S., for example, Thomas A. Edison took out a patent already in 1891; see Bordwell and Thompson, *Film History*, 3–24. Janet Staiger, "Combination and Litigation Structures of US Film Distribution 1896–1917," *Early Film: Space, Frame, Narrative*, Thomas Elsaesser, ed. (London: BFI, 1997), 189–191.
5. See, e.g., Ingrid Lindell, *Att se och synas: Filmutbud, kön och modernitet* (Gothenburg: Makadam förlag, 2004) and *Män, män, män och en och annan kvinna*, edited by Vanja Hermele (Stockholm: Svenska filminstitutet/Arena, 2002).
6. Joan W. Scott, *Gender and the Politics of History* (New York: Columbia University Press, 1999), 28–52. *Male Trouble*, eds. Constance Penley and Sharon Willis (Minneapolis and London: University of Minnesota Press, 1993).
7. See, e.g., Anna G. Jònasdóttir, *Kärlekskraft, makt och politiska intressen: En teori om patriarkatet i nutida västerländska samhällen* (Göteborg: Daidalos, 2003) and Sylvia Walby, *Theorizing Patriarchy* (Oxford: Blackwell, 1990).
8. Gerry Holloway, "Writing Women: The Development of Feminist Approaches to Women's History," *Historical Controversies and Historians*, William Lamont, ed. (London: UCL Press, 1998), 177–187. Sharon Rider, "Teoribygget sätter krokben för feminismen," *Svenska Dagbladet* (Stockholm), 26 October 2002.
9. See, e.g., Ronny Ambjörnsson, *Mansmyter: en liten guide till manlighetens paradoxer* (Stockholm: Ordfront, 1999); Bly 2001; Stephan Mendel-Enk, *Med uppenbar känsla för stil—ett reportage om manlighet* (Stockholm: Atlas, 2004); Jørgen Lorentzen, *Blikk på mannen gjenom litteratur og film* (Oslo: Spartacus, 2004); Susan Faludi, *Ställd: Förräderiet mot mannen* (Stockholm: Ordfront, 2001).
10. The history of male ideals mainly derives from two studies: George L. Mosse, *The Image of Man: The Creation of Modern Masculinity* (New York: Oxford University Press, 1998) and Michael Kimmel, *Manhood in America: A Cultural History* (New York: Free Press, 1996).
11. See, e.g., Kimmel, *Manhood in America*; R. W. Connell, *Masculinities* (Cambridge: Polity Press, 1999); Mendel-Enk, *Med uppenbar känsla för stil*; Faludi *Ställd*.
12. Mosse, *The Image of Man*, 17–24.
13. Ibid., 24–45.
14. Ibid., 44, 107–119.
15. Ibid., 56–76.
16. Ibid., 77–106.
17. Connell, *Masculinities*, 2–44 (citation 70).
18. Ibid., 67–81.
19. Ibid., 36–39, 67–81.
20. The theory includes the power relation to women, though on a subordinate plane. Ibid., 81–86.

21. See, e.g., Thomas Johansson, *Det första könet? Mansforskning som reflexivt projekt* (Lund: Studentlitteratur, 2000) and Sune G. Dufwa, *Kön, lön, karriär: Sjuksköterskeyrkets omvandling under 1900-talet* (Göteborg: Växjö University Press, 2004).

22. Claes Ekenstam, "Män, manlighet och omanlighet i historien," *Män i Norden: Manlighet och modernitet 1840–1940*, eds. Jørgen Lorentzen and Claes Ekenstam (Stockholm: Gidlunds förlag, 2006), 44.

23. See, e.g., Ekenstam, "Män manloghet och omanlighet i historien," 33, 44; Kimmel, *Manhood in America*; *Masculinities in Politics and War: Gendering Modern History*, Stefan Dudnik, Karen Hageman and John Tosh, eds. (Manchester and New York: Manchester University Press, 2004).

24. See, e.g., Thomas Sörensen, *Det blänkande eländet: En bok om kronprinsens husarer i sekelskiftets Malmö* (Malmö: Lund University, 1997); Sanimir Resic, *American Warriors in Vietnam: Warrior Values and the Myth of the War Experience During the Vietnam War 1965–73* (Malmö: Lund University, 1999); Anders Ottosson, *Sjukgymnasten—var tog han vägen? En undersökning av sjukgymnastyrkets maskulinisering och avmaskulinisering 1813–1934* (Göteborg: Göteborg University, 2005); Jens Ljunggren, *Känslornas krig: Det första världskriget och den tyska bildningselitens androgyna manlighet* (Stockholm: Symposion, 2004); David Tjeder, *The Power of Character: Middle-Class Masculinites, 1800–1900* (Stockholm: Stockholm University, 2003); Henrik Berggren, *Seklets ungdom: Retorik, politik och modernitet 1900–1939* (Stockholm: Tidens förlag, 1995); Tomas Berglund, *Det goda faderskapet i svenskt 1800-tal* (Stockholm: Carlssons, 2007); Patrik Steorn, *Nakna män: Maskulinitet och kreativitet i svensk bildkultur 1900–1915* (Stockholm: Norstedts Akademiska förlag, 2006).

25. For further criticism of this, see Yvonne Hirdman, "Konstruktion och förändring—genus och vetenskap," *Kvinnovetenskaplig tidskrift* 3, 4 (1998), 10.

26. Joan W. Scott, "Woman's History," *New Perspectives on Historical Writing*, Peter Burke, ed. (University Park: Pennsylvania State University Press, 1991), 47–55. See also, bell hooks, *The Will to Change: Men, Masculinity, and Love* (New York: Washington Square Press, 2004), xi–xvii.

27. David Tjeder, "Maskulinum som problem: Genusforskning om män," *Historisk tidskrift* 3 (2002), 481–483.

28. *Svensk filmografi 2 1920–1929* (Stockholm: Svenska filminstitutet, 1982), 9.

29. Leif Furhammar, *Filmen i Sverige: En historia i tio kapitel och en fortsättning* (Stockholm: Dialogos and Svenska filminstitutet, 2003), 386.

30. Tytti Soila, "Sweden," *Nordic National Cinemas*, Tytti Soila, Astrid Söderbergh Widding and Gunnar Iversen, eds. (London and New York: Routledge, 1998), 3, 152–169.

31. See, e.g., Gösta Werner, *Den svenska filmens historia: En översikt av* (Stockholm: P. A. Norstedt & Söners förlag, 1978), 14–61. See also Elisabeth Liljedahl, *Stumfilmen i Sverige—Kritik och debatt: Hur samtiden värderade den nya konstarten* (Stockholm: Proprius, 1975) and Robin Hood [Bengt Idestam-Almqvist], *Den svenska filmens drama: Sjöström och Stiller* (Stockholm: Åhlén & söner, 1939).

32. Furhammar, *Filmen i Sverige*, 91–125. *Svensk filmografi 2*, 52–53.

33. Furhammar, *Filmen i Sverige*, 95–98, 123.

34. Bo Florin, *Den nationella stilen: Studier i den svenska filmens guldålder* (Stockholm: Aura förlag, 1997).

35. Bordwell and Thompson, *Film History*, 65. For a survey of international research on Swedish film from the 1920s, see Florin, *Den nationella stilen*, 51–66.

36. See, e.g., Larry Langman, *Destination Hollywood: The Influence of Europeans on American Filmmaking* (Jefferson, NC: McFarland, 1999).

37. Bordwell and Thompson, *Film History*, 229–231.

38. Andrew Higson, "The Concept of National Cinema," *Film and Nationalism*, Alan Williams, ed. (New Brunswick, NJ: Rutgers University Press, 2002), 52–67.

39. Orsi Husz, *Drömmars värde: Varuhus och lotteri i svensk konsumtionskultur 1897–1939* (Stockholm: Gidlunds förlag, 2004), 264. Ulf Boëthius, "Högt och lågt inom kulturen. Moderniseringsprocessen och de kulturella hierarkierna," *Ungdom och kulturell modernisering*, Johan Fornäs and Ulf Boëthius, eds. (Stockholm: Symposion, 1994), 59–93.

40. See, e.g., John Tosh, "Hegemonic Masculinity and the History of Gender," *Masculinities in Politics and War*, Stefan Dudnik, Karin Hagemann and John Tosh, eds. (Manchester and New York: Manchester University Press, 2004), 43–44; hooks, *The Will to Change*, 52, 125; Louis Althusser, *Essays on Ideology* (London: Verso, 1984), 21–42.

41. For further discussion, see Tommy Gustafsson, "Ett steg på vägen mot en ny jämlikhet? Könsrelationer och stereotyper i ung svensk ungdomsfilm på 2000-talet," *Solskenslandet: svensk film på 2000-talet*, Erik Hedling and Ann-Kristin Wallengren, eds. (Stockholm: Atlantis, 2006), 180–182.

42. Claire Johnston, "Women's Cinema as Counter-Cinema," *Movies and Methods: An Anthology*, Bill Nichols, ed. (Berkeley and London: University of California Press, 1976), 208–217.

43. For example, Mats Björkin, *Amerikanism, bolsjevism och korta kjolar: Filmen och dess publik i Sverige under 1920-talet* (Stockholm: Aura, 1997) and Göran Bolin, *Filmbytare: videovåld, kulturell produktion & unga män* (Stockholm: Borea, 1998).

44. For example, Louise Wallenberg, *Upsetting the Male: Feminist Interventions in the New Queer Wave* (Stockholm: Edita Norstedt, 2002); Monica Dofs Sundin, *Rödluvan i filmens tidsålder: sagospår och filmversioner 1901–2001* (Uppsala: Filmförlaget, 2003); Therése Andersson, *Beauty Box: filmstjärnor och skönhetskultur i det tidiga 1900-talets Sverige* (Stockholm: Acta Universitatus Stockholmiensis, 2006).

45. Laura Mulvey, "Spelfilmen och lusten att se," *Modern filmteori 2*, Lars Gustaf Andersson and Erik Hedling, eds. (Lund: Studentlitteratur, 1995), 30–43.

46. Tytti Soila, *Kvinnors ansikte: Stereotyper och kvinnlig identitet i trettiotalets svenska filmmelodram* (Stockholm: Stockholms universitet, 1991), 29.

47. Ibid., 24–34.

48. Ibid., 45–79.

49. Ibid., 119–174, (citation, 172).

50. For the same type of criticism, see, e.g., Ashton D. Trice and Samuel A. Holland, *Heroes, Antiheroes and Dolts: Portrayals of Masculinity in American Popular Films, 1921–1999* (Jefferson, NC: McFarland, 2001), 5–6.

51. William Hughes, "The Evaluation of Film as Evidence," *The Historian and Film*, Paul Smith, ed. (Cambridge and New York: Cambridge University Press, 1976), 49–79.

52. See, e.g., Trevor McCrisken and Andrew Pepper, *American History and Contemporary Hollywood Film* (New Brunswick, NJ: Rutgers University Press, 2005), 34, 125 and Ulrika Holgersson, *Populärkulturen och samhället: Arbete, klass och genus i svensk dampress i början av 1900-talet* (Stockholm: Carlssons bokförlag, 2005), 127–138.

53. Erik Hedling, "Filmen som historiograf eller som historisk källa?" *Historisk tidskrift* 2 (2002), 76–77.

54. See, e.g., John Fiske, *Television Culture* (London: Methuen, 1986) and Douglas Kellner, *Media Culture: Cultural Studies, Identity and Politics Between the Modern and the Postmodern* (London: Routledge, 1995).

55. Miriam Hansen, *Babel & Babylon: Spectatorship in the American Silent Film* (Cambridge and London: Harvard University Press, 1991), 60–65; Miriam Hansen, "Early Cinema—Whose Public Sphere?" *Early Cinema: Space, Frame, Narrative*, Thomas Elsaesser, ed. (London: BFI, 1997), 228–246.

56. Ben Brewster and Lea Jacobs, *Theatre to Cinema: Stage Pictorialism and the Early Feature Film* (New York: Oxford University Press, 1997), 6.

57. Richard Dyer, *Stars* (London: BFI, 2004), 20–25, 127. Trice and Holland, *Heros, Antiheros and Dolts*, 1–4. McCrisken and Pepper, *American History and Contemporary Hollywood*, 42. Murry Smith, *Engaging Characters: Fiction, Emotion, and the Cinema* (Oxford: Oxford University Press, 1995), 142–186.

58. Gerald R. Butters Jr., *Black Manhood on the Silent Screen* (Lawrence: University Press of Kansas, 2002), 1–40. Richard Dyer, *Now You See It: Studies in Lesbian and Gay Film* (London and New York: Routledge, 2003).

59. Mats Jönsson, *Film och historia: Historisk hollywoodfilm 1960–2000* (Lund: Lunds universitet, 2004), 1.

60. See, e.g., the analysis of *The Merchant of Venice* (2004) in Tommy Gustafsson, "Filmen som historisk källa. Historiografi, pluralism och representativitet," *Historisk tidskrift* 3 (2006), 487.

61. Jönsson, *Film och historia*, 15, 38–39, 50, 177, 213.

62. Siegfried Kracauer, *From Caligari to Hitler: A Psychological History of the German Film* (Princeton and Oxford: Princeton University Press, 2004), 61–128.

63. See, e.g., Robert L. McLaughlin and Sally E. Perry, *We'll Always Have the Movies: American Film During World War II* (Lexington: University Press of Kentucky, 2006).

64. Birgitte Søland, *Becoming Modern: Young Women and the Reconstruction of Womanhood in the 20s* (Princeton, NJ: Princeton University Press, 2000), 3–17; Björkin, *Amerikanism, bolsjevism och korta kjolar*, 199–202.

65. Janet Staiger, *Interpreting Films: Studies in the Historical Reception of American Cinema* (Princeton, NJ: Princeton University Press, 1992), 7–15.

66. Birgit Pettersson, "Journalistyrkets långsamma professionalisering," *Sylwan II: Tema: Presshistoria: Den svenska pressens historia*, Karl Erik Gustafsson and Per Rydén, eds. (Göteborg: Göteborgs universitet, 2002), 43–45.

67. The decoded signatures were collected from *Svensk filmografi 2*, 402–407; Björkin, *Amerikanism, bolsjevism och korta kjolar*, 312–316; Liljedahl, *Stumfilmen i Sverige*, 321–330; Florin, *Den nationella stilen*, 251–253, complemented with further decodings made by the author. In total, this has yielded 120 decoded signatures for 105 different individuals, 31 of whom are women.

Chapter 1

1. Eva Silvén-Garnert et al., eds., *Storstadsungdom i fyra generationer* (Stockholm: Tiden, Folksam and Stockholms stadsmuseum, 1991), 31.

2. Ulf Boëthius, *När Nick Carter drevs på flykten: Kampen mot "smutslitteraturen" i Sverige* (Södertälje: Gidlunds, 1989), 23–24, 245; Viviana A. Zelizer, *Pricing the Priceless Child: The Changing Social Value of Children* (New York: Basic Books, 1985), 37–46.

3. Søland, *Becoming Modern*, 16–17, 172.

4. Thomas Englund, "Skolans samhällsbild—elevernas medborgarfostran via folkundervisningens samhällsorientering," *Från folkskola till*

grundskola: Tio forskare vid Pedagogiska institutionen, Uppsala universitet, belyser utvecklingen under 150 år i anslutning till folkskolejubiléet, Erik Wallin, ed. (Uppsala: Uppsala universitet, 1998), 139–164. Zelizer, *Priceing the Priceless Child*, 47–50.

5. Orsi Husz and Amanda Lagerqvist, "Konsumtionens motsägelser. En inledning," *Förbjudna njutningar—spår från konsumtionskulturens historia i Sverige*, Peder Aléx and Johan Söderberg, eds. (Stockholm: Podium, 2001), 9–26.

6. See, e.g., Matthew Hilton, *Consumerism in 20th-Century Britain: The Search for a Political Movement* (Cambridge: Cambridge University Press, 2003) and Conrad Lodziak, *The Myth of Consumerism* (London: Pluto Press, 2002).

7. See further Thomas Krogh, *Frankfurtskolan: en introduktion* (Göteborg: Daidalos, 1993).

8. Peter N. Stearns, "Stages of Consumerism: Recent Work on the Issues of Periodization," *The Journal of Modern History* 69:1 (1997), 102–117.

9. Johan Fornäs, "Senmoderna dimensioner," *Ungdom och kulturell modernisering*, Johan Fornäs and Ulf Boëthius, eds. (Stockholm: Symposion, 1994), 17–18.

10. Husz and Lagerqvist, "Konsumtionens motsägelser," 26.

11. Tom Gunning, "The Cinema of Attractions: Early Film, Its Spectator and the Avant-Garde," *Early Cinema*, 56–62.

12. Furhammar, *Filmen i Sverige*, 17–25; Bordwell and Thompson, *Film History*, 26–38; Michael Chanan, "Economic Conditions of Early Cinema," *Early Cinema*, 174–188.

13. Gunning, "The Cinema of Attractions," 56–62.

14. Furhammar, *Filmen i Sverige*, 21–23. Jan Olsson, "I offentlighetens ljus—några notiser om filmstoff i dagspressen," *I offentlighetens ljus: Stumfilmens affischer, kritiker, stjärnor och musik*, Jan Olsson, ed. (Stockholm: Symposion, 1990), 219–227.

15. See, e.g., Tom Gunning, *D. W. Griffith & the Origin of American Narrative Film: The Early Years at Biograph* (Urbana and Chicago: University of Illinois Press, 1994); Mark Jancovich, Lucy Faire and Sarah Stubbings, eds., *The Place of the Audience: Cultural Geographies of Film Consumption* (London: BFI, 2003); Yuri Tsivian, *Early Cinema in Russia and Its Cultural Reception* (Chicago and London: University of Chicago Press, 1998).

16. Boëthius, *När Nick Carter*, 22–23, 62–100, 129–218.

17. Marie Louise Gagner, *Barn och biografföreställningar: Ett föredrag av, jämte ett uttalande i samma ämne av professor B. E. Gadelius* (Stockholm: Lars Hökerberg förlag, 1908), 2–3, 7–8.

18. Gagner, *Barn och biografföreställningar*, 10 (original italics).

19. Stanley Cohen, *Folk Devils and Moral Panics: The Creation of Mods and Rockers* (London and New York: Routledge, 2007), 19–26.

20. Olsson, "I offentlighetens ljus," 239–246, 252–253.

21. Quotation from Erik Skoglund, *Filmcensuren* (Stockholm: Pan/Norstedts, 1971), 18.

22. Ibid., 17, 21–25, 99–100.

23. Olsson, "I offentlighetens ljus," 253.

24. Skoglund, *Filmcensuren*, 45–52.

25. –dt, "De ungas brottslighet," *Filmbladet* 1 (1918). See also, Carl Göran Andræ, *Revolt eller reform: Sverige inför revolutionerna i Europa 1917–18* (Stockholm: Carlssons, 1998).

26. Quoted in Halfdan G. Liander, *Biografen: Ett ord till fackets män samt till föräldrar och lärare* (Lund: Pedagogiska skrifter utgivna av Sveriges allmänna folkskolelärareförenings litteratursällskap, 1922), 71.

27. Gagner, *Barn och biografföreställningar*, 3. Liander, *Biografen*, 7, 35.

28. Good examples of children who "know about film" are to be found in R.L. Ring, *Kallprat om film* (Stockholm: A-B Tullbergs films förlag, 1928), 126–132.

29. Berggren, *Seklets ungdom*, 27–33.

30. David Tjeder, "Borgerlighetens sköra manlighet," *Män i Norden: Manlighet och modernitet 1840–1940*, Jørgen Lorentzen and Claes Ekenstam, eds. (Stockholm: Gidlunds, 2006), 60–61.

31. Gunning, *D. W. Griffith*, 85–129; Furhammar, *Filmen i Sverige*, 67–70.

32. Boëthius, *När Nick Carter*, 127–150.

33. See, e.g., the fanciful numerical examples in Liander, *Biografen*, 8–12, 61–62.

34. See, e.g., Karl Lundegård, "Strykpojken biografen," *Filmbladet* 5 (1918) and [Unsigned], "Barnfrågan," *Biografägaren* 6 (1926).

35. Furhammar, *Filmen i Sverige*, 45.

36. Swedish Government Official Reports. *Ungdomen och nöjeslivet*, Ungdomsvårdskommitténs betänkande del III, Vol. 22 (Stockholm, 1945).

37. Stockholm City Archive (SCA), Archives of the Stockholm's Elementary School Board (SFA), "Brev från Sveriges biografägareförbund till Konungen," *Handlingar angående elevers biografbesök* 2 (1929), 1–3.

38. [Unsigned], "Hur barnen gå på bio. En redovisad skolundersökning i Stockholm," *Filmbladet* 6 (1918).

39. Karl Lundegård, "Ungdomens förvildning och dess orsaker," *Filmbladet* 6 (1918) and Karl Lundegård, "Biografen och ungdomens brottslighet," *Filmbladet* 30 (1922).

40. [Unsigned], "Hur barn gå på bio."

41. e.g., Liander, *Biografen*, 65.

42. SCA, SFA, "P. M. över undersökning rörande folkskolebarnens biografbesök" and "Förteckning å Stockholms biografer och filmer," *Handlingar angående elevers biografbesök* 2 (1929), 1–5 and 1–7, respectively.

43. SCA, SFA, Överlärarnas sammanställningar, *Handlingar angående elevers biografbesök* 2 (1929).

44. SCA, SFA, "P. M. över undersökning rörande folkskolebarnens biografbesök," *Handlingar angående elevers biografbesök* 2 (1929), 4–5.
45. SCA, SFA, Remissvar till Kungliga Skolöverstyrelsen, *Handlingar angående elevers biografbesök* 2 (1929), 1–6.
46. SCA, SFA, "P. M. över undersökning rörande folkskolebarnens biografbesök," *Handlingar angående elevers biografbesök* 2 (1929), 2.
47. Quoted from E [M. Enderstedt], "Barn på bio," *Biografägaren* 18 (1929).
48. SCA, SFA, "Uppgifter angående barns biografbesök, Judit Schäring, Värtans folkskola," *Handlingar angående elevers biografbesök* 1 (1929).
49. See, e.g., [Unsigned], "Film är icke synd. De frikyrkligas skuggrädsla för allt, som stöter på biograf, kommer snart att upphöra," *Filmnyheter* 10 (1920); [Unsigned], "En vetenskapsman som försvarar biografen. Läxar upp kritiken," *Filmbladet* 3 (1922); [Unsigned], "Filmen i kyrkans kulturella verksamhet. Ett gott betyg från stadsmissionen i Stockholm," *Filmnyheter* 2 (1923).
50. Åsa Jernudd, "Educational Cinema and Censorship in Sweden 1911–1921," *Nordic Explorations: Film Before 1930*, John Fullerton and Jan Olsson, eds. (Sydney: John Libbey, 1999), 152–162.
51. [Unsigned], "En million svenska barn på skolfilmsbio," *Filmnyheter* 23 (1923).
52. Boëthius, "Högt och lågt inom kulturen," 76.
53. Björkin, *Amerikanism, bolsjevism och korta kjolar*, 145–203.
54. Søland, *Becoming Modern*, 3–17.
55. Eva Blomberg, *Vill ni se en stjärna? Kön, kropp och kläder i* Filmjournalen *1919–1953* (Lund: Nordic Academic Press, 2006), 197.
56. Søland, *Becoming Modern*, 44–61. See also Ben Singer, *Melodrama and Modernity: Early Sensational Cinema and Its Contexts* (New York: Columbia University Press, 2001), 221–262.
57. Husz, *Drömmars värde*, 36; Jancovich, Faire and Stubbings, *The Place of the Audience*, 42.
58. Søland, *Becoming Modern*, 67–79.
59. Ibid., 80–89.
60. Ibid., 97–106.
61. Mark Abrams, *The Teenage Consumer* (London: London Press Exchange, 1959).
62. David Fowler, *The First Teenagers: The Lifestyle of Young Wage-Earners in Interwar Britain* (London: Woburn Press, 1995), 7, 23, 93–103. Søland, *Becoming Modern*, 70–73. Silvén-Garnert et al., *Storstadsungdom i fyra generationer*, 31, 37–42, 171–173. Linda Lane, *Trying to Make a Living: Studies in the Economic Life of Women in Interwar Sweden* (Kungälv: Göteborgs universitet, 2004), 99–100, 118–119.
63. See, e.g., "Edra förlovningsringar. Juvelerare H. Karefelt," Advertisement, *Filmnyheter* 45 (1921); "Dans varje afton i Ceders salonger," Advertisement, *Filmnyheter* 7 (1922); "Mot pormask, röd näsa. Bomans Myrrhatinktur," Advertisement, *Filmnyheter* 10 (1922); "Nutidens modernaste tandkräm, som bleker tänderna genast. Chlorodont," Advertisement, *Filmnyheter* 22 (1922); "Regissör John Lindlöfs Filmskola," Advertisement, *Filmnyheter* 17 (1928).
64. Examples of diatribes from the ecclesiastical camp: [Unsigned], "Diakonistatistik," *Biografbladet* 15 (1922); [Unsigned], "Det farliga nöjet," *Biografägaren* 3 (1926). From political quarters: [Unsigned], "Fem farliga f—och ett sjätte. Förargelseklippan filmen: förebråelser, fakta och förvarsförsök," *Filmjournalen* 15 (1921). From the academic world: [Unsigned], "Kulturchauvinism. Nya attacker mot amerikansk film," *Filmjournalen* 15 (1927).
65. Referenced and quoted from [Unsigned], "Svenska Morgonbladets 'kristliga' kärlek till filmen. En sensationell hetsartikel i stället för ett objektivt referat," *Filmbladet* 21 (1923).
66. Quoted from [Unsigned], "Svenska Morgonbladets 'kristliga' kärlek till filmen."
67. See, e.g., "Juveler och pärlor. AB Nordiska Kompaniet," advertisement, *Filmnyheter* 39 (1922); Pälsvaru-A.-B. Alaska," Advertisement, *Filmnyheter* 44 (1922); "Vid Ludvig XV:s hov. Automobilcentralen. Fiat," Advertisement, *Filmnyheter* 40 (1925); "J. O. Baumgarts pianofabrik. Tillverkar Flyglar och Pianon," Advertisement, *Filmnyheter* 38 (1927).
68. Berggren, *Seklets ungdom*, 120–130, 143–162. Boëthius, *När Nick Carter drevs på flykten*, 154–167, 265–271. Husz, *Drömmars värde*, 81.
69. See, e.g., "Biografbesökare! Läs Social-Demokratens recensioner!" Advertisement, *Filmnyheter* 14 (1921).
70. See, e.g., "Biografägare! Ett effektivt organ för reklamering av Edra filmer är utan tvivel Social-Demokraten," Advertisement, *Filmbladet* 44 (1921).
71. Søland, *Becoming Modern*, 44–45, 58–61. See also Andersson, *Beauty Box*.
72. From 1921, *Filmjournalen* ran the standing page "New fashions from stage and film." For dieting, see, e.g., [Unsigned], "Tio minuter om dagen ha vi råd att offra for att hålla vår kropp i form," *Filmnyheter* 21 (1923); [Unsigned], "Ett par kilo i stjärnhullet kan betyda mycket. Hur man fetmar eller magrar i Los Angeles," *Filmnyheter* 27 (1923); [Unsigned], "Medeltida tortyr går igen i våra dagars skönhetshygien," *Filmnyheter* 21–22 (1929).
73. Husz, *Drömmars värde*, 24, 34, 99. Ann-Sofie Ohlander, "Ekonomisk makt och ekonomiskt ansvar—två skilda storheter," *Mot halva makten—elva essäer om kvinnors strategi och mäns motstånd*, Ingrid Hagman, ed. (Stockholm: SOU 113, 1997), 3–14.
74. Jonas Liliequist, "Från niding till sprätt. En studie i det svenska omanlighetsbegreppets historia från vikingatid till sent 1700-tal," *Manligt och*

omanligt i ett historiskt perspektiv, Anne Marie Berggren, ed. (Stockholm: Forskningsrådsnämnden, 1999), 85–88.

75. Ragnar Bentzel, *Den privata konsumtionen i Sverige 1931–65* (Stockholm: Almqvist & Wiksell, 1957), 11–12, 215–216.

76. See, e.g., David Tjeder, "Konsten att blifva herre öfver hvarje lidelse. Den ständigt hotade manligheten," *Manligt och omanligt i ett historiskt perspektiv*, Anne Marie Berggren, ed. (Stockholm: Forskningsrådsnämnden, 1999), 177–182; Mosse, *The Image of Man*, 77–106; Kimmel, *Manhood in America*, 40–99; John Horne, "Masculinities in Politics and War in the Age of Nation-States and World Wars," *Masculinities in Politics and War: Gendering Modern History*, Stefan Dudnik, Karen Hagemann and John Tosh, eds. (Manchester and New York: Manchester University Press, 2004), 32.

77. See, e.g., [Unsigned], "Mitt manliga ideal—och mitt kvinnliga. Filmstjärnor av båda könen ha ordet," *Filmnyheter* 17 (1921) and Maudlin [Vera von Kraemer], "Det manliga koketteriets arsenal. Filmen förser den oavbrutet med nya vapen," *Filmjournalen* 18 (1922).

78. [Unsigned], "Ett par kilo i stjärnhullet kan betyda mycket. Hur man fetmar eller magrar i Los Angeles," *Filmnyheter* 27 (1923).

79. See, e.g., [Unsigned], "Douglas Fairbanks gör en österländsk storfilm. Motivet hämtat ur 'Tusen och en natt,'" *Filmnyheter* 24 (1923) and [Unsigned], "Douglas Fairbanks muskler," *Filmnyheter* 26 (1923).

80. See, e.g., the photography of John Barrymore stripped to the waist in [Unsigned], "Manlig kraft och skönhet—ur filmens stora bilderbok," *Filmnyheter* 10 (1928).

81. See, e.g., "George O'Brien," Fan picture, *Filmjournalen* 11 (1927) and [Unsigned], "Malmöflicka dyker upp på amerikanska filmfirmamentet," *Filmnyheter* 29–30 (1928).

82. [Unsigned], "Våra nöjens programförklaring," *Våra nöjen* 5 (1925).

Chapter 2

1. E [M Enderstedt], "Barn på bio."

2. Gunnar Bjurman, "Barnprogrammen. Dr Gunnar Bjurman är av en annan mening än 'Biogubbe,'" *Biografägaren* 2 (1929).

3. Biogubbe, "Barnprogrammen: 'Biogubbe' är icke omvänd," *Biografägaren* 4 (1929), (original italics).

4. Sally Robinson, "'Emotional Constipation' and the Power of Damned Masculinity: *Deliverance* and the Paradoxes of Male Liberation," *Masculinity: Bodies, Movies, Culture*, Peter Lehman, ed. (New York: Routledge, 2001), 133–147.

5. Gaylyn Studlar, *This Mad Masquerade: Stardom and Masculinity in the Jazz Age* (New York: Columbia University Press, 1996), 1–9.

6. Ibid., 19, 87, 150–153.

7. Ibid., 12–13, 23.

8. Ibid., 25–27.

9. Ibid., 30–41.

10. Silvén-Garnert et al., *Storstadsungdom i fyra generationer*, 101–108.

11. Bo Nilsson, Maskulinitet. Representation, ideologi och retorik (Umeå: Boréa, 1999), 44–60.

12. Emil Norlander, *Anderssonskans Kalle: Pojkstreck och kärringskvaller* (Stockholm: Christofers bokförlag, 1960).

13. Studlar, *This Mad Masquerade*, 86–87.

14. Karl Lundegård, "Emerson och Doug," *Filmbladet* 24 (1922).

15. *Svenska Dagbladet*, 27 November 1923.

16. Norlander, *Anderssonskans Kalle*, 50, 72.

17. *Svensk filmografi 2*, 136; Furhammar, *Filmen i Sverige*, 109–114; Sigurd Wallèn, *Revydags: Tystnad—tagning—kamera går* (Stockholm: Medéns förlag, 1944), 117–18.

18. See further, Diana Serra Cary, *Jackie Coogan, the World's Boy King: A Biography of Hollywood's Legendary Child Star* (Lanham and Oxford: Scarecrow Press, 2003).

19. *Svensk filmografi 2*, 135.

20. Emil Norlander, *Anderssonskans Kalle*, Film manuscript (1922), *Swedish Film Institute Archive* (SFI); *Anderssonskans Kalle: Pojkstreck i fem akter*, Program Note (Stockholm: B Wahlström, 1922).

21. Swedish Board of Censorship Archive (SBC), Censorship card 29632.

22. Norlander, *Anderssonskans Kalle*, Film manuscript. The whole of reel 3 is cut out, and the new reel 6 is added afterwards.

23. Norlander, *Anderssonskans Kalle*, Film manuscript.

24. e.g., *Stockholms-Tidningen*, 5 September 1922.

25. Eva, *Arbetaren* 4 September 1922.

26. e.g., *Folkets Dagblad Politiken*, 5 September 1922.

27. [Unsigned], "Anderssonskans Kalle—ett dåligt föredöme för ungdomen. Maskiningeniör Rosborg går skarpt tillrätta med filmen—andra personer anse den relativt ofarlig," *Filmbladet* 27 (1922).

28. Ibid., *Svensk filmografi 2*, 136.

29. Wallén, *Revydags*, 117.

30. Ibid., 116.

31. Ibid., 116.

32. *Aftonbladet*, 5 September 1922.

33. Marfa [Elsa Danielsson], *Dagens Nyheter*, 5 September 1922.

34. Norlander, *Anderssonskans Kalle*, Film manuscript.

35. Norlander, *Anderssonskanks Kalle*, 46–51; Norlander, *Anderssonskans Kalle*, Film manuscript.

36. For the period's opinions on the early Chaplin, see Liljedahl, *Stumfilmen i Sverige*, 177–184.

37. [Unsigned], "Anderssonskans Kalle."

38. Emil Norlander, "Pappan till 'Anderssonskans Kalle' uttalar sig," *Filmjournalen* 14 (1922), (original italics).

39. See, e.g., "Anderssonskans Kalle torde väl vara Sveriges mest bekanta och populära tjuvpojke," Advertisement, *Biografbladet* 7 (1922) and "Kärleken är en farlig makt, som nogsamt röntes av bilden här," Advertisement, *Biografbladet* 10 (1922).

40. See, e.g., [Unsigned], "Jackie Coogan, sjuåringen, i ny roll," *Filmnyheter* 26 (1922); [Unsigned], "En intervju med en treåring!" [Baby Peggy], *Filmnyheter* 31 (1922); [Unsigned], "Jackie Coogan hemma hos sig. En rörande amerikansk skildring av 'underbarnets privatliv,'" *Filmnyheter* 6 (1923); "Årets verkliga pojkfilm blir naturligtvis Mälarpiraterna efter Sigfrid Siwertz' friska äventyrsbok," Advertisement, *Filmbladet* 14 (1923).

41. Zelizer, *Pricing the Priceless Child*, 7–19, 56–112.

42. *Folkets Dagblad Politiken*, 5 September 1922.

43. Eva, *Arbetaren*, 4 September 1922.

44. [Unsigned], "Ur pressen. Osmaklig och skadlig 'stjärnkult,'" *Filmbladet* 15 (1923).

45. Norlander, *Anderssonskans Kalle*, Film manuscript.

46. Emil Norlander (adapted by Sam Ask), *Anderssonskans Kalle på nya upptåg*, Film manuscript (1923), SFI; *Anderssonskans Kalle på nya upptåg*, Program note (Stockholm: B Wahlström, 1923).

47. *Ny Tid*, 2 September 1923.

48. e.g., *Dagens Nyheter*, 28 August 1923.

49. xxx [Johannes Lindberg, Vera von Kraemer, Knut Jeurling], *Stockholms-Tidningen*, 28 August 1923.

50. *Svenska Dagbladet*, 28 August 1923.

51. *Aftonbladet*, 28 August 1923.

52. "Mälarpirater, ohoj! Ett erbjudande till käcka ungdomar att spela film i sommar," Advertisement, *Filmnyheter* 14 (1923); [Unsigned], "Med ljus och lykta efter mälarpirater," *Filmnyheter* 17 (1923); [Unsigned], "Nya filmengagemang till Råsunda. John Brunius besätter rollerna i 'En piga bland pigor.' Einar Hansson som mälarpirat," *Filmnyheter* 21 (1923); *Svensk filmografi 2*, 177.

53. Sigfrid Siwertz, *Mälarpirater* (Stockholm: Lind & Co, 2002); *Svensk filmografi 2*, 177.

54. Siwertz, *Mälarpirater*, 39.

55. *Stockholms Dagblad*, 30 October 1923.

56. –ck, *Social-Demokraten*, 30 October 1923.

57. e.g., *Aftonbladet*, 30 October 1923.

58. e.g., Jens Flik [Carl Björnberg], *Nya Dagligt Allehanda*, 30 October 1923.

59. Marfa [Elsa Danielsson], *Dagens Nyheter*, 30 October 1923.

60. Marfa [Elsa Danielsson], *Dagens Nyheter*, 30 October 1923.

61. e.g., *Stockholms Dagblad*, 27 November 1923.

62. e.g., Bes [Bernhard Bengtsson], *Folkets Dagblad Politiken*, 27 November 1923.

63. *Svenska Dagbladet*, 27 December 1923.

64. e.g., *Aftonbladet*, 27 December 1923.

65. Farbror Åbergsson, "Samtal med en diva," *Filmnyheter* 26 (1923).

66. Serra Cary, *Jackie Coogan*, 81, 89, 94.

67. –lin [Vera von Kraemer], "Två sidor om filmens pojkar. Som ett apropos till Gustaf Molanders mönstring av Stockholms ungdom nu på söndag," *Filmnyheter* 14 (1923).

68. e.g., L-n, *Dagens Nyheter*, 22 September 1929.

69. e.g., *Aftonbladet*, 22 September 1923.

70. [Unsigned], "Pernod—den amerikanska pojken sådan han verkligen är," *Filmnyheter* 15 (1921).

71. Esko, "Förståndiga ord om film ... Tror åtminstone författaren...," *Filmjournalen* 4 (1927), (original italics).

72. [Unsigned], "Våra studenter och andra. Ivan Hedqvists överliggare," *Filmnyheter* 11 (1920).

73. An academic in Uppsala, "Studenterna och erotiken. Några randanteckningar till 'Carolina Rediviva' av en uppsaliensare," *Filmjournalen* 4 (1921).

74. See, Horne, "Masculinities in Politics and War in the Age of Nation-States and World Wars," 31 and Sörensen, *Det blänkande eländet*.

75. *Dagens Nyheter*, 21 September 1920.

76. Jens Flik [Carl Björnberg], *Nya Dagligt Allehanda*, 21 September 1920.

77. XXX [Johannes Lindberg, Vera von Kraemer, Knur Jeurling], *Stockholms-Tidningen*, 10 October 1922.

78. Marfa [Elsa Danielsson], *Dagens Nyheter*, 10 October 1922.

79. *Social-Demokraten*, 10 October 1922.

80. Tjeder, *The Power of Character*, 39–63.

81. Ibid., 97–128, 236–269.

82. See, e.g., Maudlin [Vera von Kraemer], "Det manliga koketteriets arsenal"; Carl Forsstrand, "Modedårskap och hjältemod," *Våra nöjen* 11(1925).

83. Nixon & Partner [Nils Horney and oth ers], *Social-Demokraten*, 2 December 1924.

84. e.g., R-l [Ragnar Lindqvist], *Aftonbladet*, 2 December 1924.

85. e.g., *Göteborg-Posten*, November 25, 1924.

86. Marfa [Elsa Danielsson], *Dagens Nyheter*, 2 December 1924.

87. P, *Arbetet*, 2 December 1924.

88. Nixon & Partner [Nils Horney and others], *Social-Demokraten*, 2 December 1924.

89. *Stockholms-Tidningen*, 2 December 1924.

90. Studlar, *This Mad Masquerade*, 86–87.

91. M W-r [Magnus Wester], "De unga som filmkritici: Intressanta jämförelser mellan biografen och teatern i höstens studentskrivningar," *Filmbladet* 3 (1924).

92. Björkin, *Amerikanism, bolsjevism och korta kjolar*, 145–203.

93. Quelqu'une [Märta Lindqvist], *Svenska Dagbladet*, 2 January 1923.

94. e.g., *Göteborgs-Posten*, 2 December 1924.

95. Björkin, *Amerikanism, bolsjevism och korta kjolar*, 11–13; *Svensk filmografi 2*, 16–18; Ragnar Hyltén-Cavallius, *Följa sin genius* (Stockholm: Hökerbergs bokförlag, 1960), 240–262.

96. [Unsigned], "Sedligheten beror ej blott på kjolarna?" *Dagens Nyheter*, 12 October 1926.

97. Miss Shingle, "Där fru och fröken Stockholm shinglas. En titt bakom kulisserna på Grands 'hårbar,'" *Våra nöjen* 42 (1925).

98. [Unsigned], "Är filmens unga flicka efter sin tid? Hon är alltför snäll och oskuldsfull, menar en amerikansk tidning," *Filmnyheter* 1 (1923), (original italics).

99. e.g., Bes [Bernhard Bengtsson], *Folkets Dagblad Politiken*, 1 April 1924.

100. e.g., *Aftonbladet*, 1 April 1924.

101. e.g., Marfa [Elsa Danielsson], *Dagens Nyheter*, 1 April 1924.

102. Robin Hood [Bengt Idestam-Almquist], *Stockholms-Tidningen*, 1 April 1924.

103. e.g., *Aftonbladet*, 7 September 1926.

104. *Stockholms Dagblad*, 7 September 1926.

105. Jerome [Göran Traung], *Dagens Nyheter*, 7 September 1926.

106. *Stockholms Dagblad*, 7 September 1926.

107. Tallak Moland, "Konstruksjon av mandighet i det nordlige landskapet. Om Fridtjof Nansens polferder ved århundresskiftet," *Manligt och omanligt i ett historiskt perspektiv*, Anne Marie Berggren, ed. (Stockholm: Forskningsrådsnämnden, 1999), 213–221.

108. [Unsigned], "Vita hår och gömda tragedier i filmvärldens 'old atmosphere,'" *Filmnyheter* 37 (1923).

109. Heather Addison, "'Must the Players Keep Young?': Early Hollywood's Cult of Youth," *Cinema Journal* 4 (2006), 3–10.

110. Kå, *Folkets Dagblad Politiken*, 6 September 1927.

111. See, e.g., *Göteborgs-Posten*, 23 August 1927.

112. *Stockholms Dagblad*, 6 September 1927.

113. Jerome [Göran Traung], *Dagens Nyheter*, 6 September 1927.

114. Søland, *Becoming Modern*, 127–138.

115. *Social-Demokraten*, 22 January 1924.

116. Robin Hood [Bengt Idestam-Almquist], *Stockholms-Tidningen*, 22 January 1924.

117. *Social-Demokraten*, 22 January 1924.

Chapter 3

1. Liander, *Biografen*, 33 (original italics).

2. Claes Ekenstam, "En historia om manlig gråt," *Rädd att falla: Studier i manlighet*, Claes Ekenstam et al., eds. (Södertälje: Gidlunds, 1998), 50–123.

3. hooks, *The Will to Change*, 3–7, 39, 140.

4. See, e.g., Mosse, *The Image of Man*; Connell, *Masculinities*; hooks, *The Will to Change*, 38–54 and Ingemar Gens, *Från vagga till identitet: Hur flickor blir kvinnor och pojkar blir män. Teorin bakom pedagogiken på förskolorna Björntomten och Tittmyran* (Jönköping: Seminarium, 2003).

5. hooks, *The Will to Change*, 125–134.

6. Mulvey, "Spelfilmen och lusten att se." Krogh, *Frankfurtskolan*.

7. Stella Bruzzi, *Bringing Up Daddy: Fatherhood and Masculinity in Post-War Hollywood* (London: BFI, 2005), xvi–xviii.

8. See, e.g., Penley and Willis, *Male Trouble*, Hansen, *Babel & Babylon* and Yvonne Tasker, *Spectacular Bodies: Gender, Genre and the Action Cinema* (London and New York: Routledge, 1993).

9. Milette Shamir and Jennifer Travis, "Introduction," *Boys Don't Cry? Rethinking Narratives of Masculinity and Emotion in the U.S.*, Milette Shamir and Jennifer Travis, eds. (New York: Columbia University Press, 2002), 1–21.

10. Jørgen Lorentzen, "Federne," *Män i Norden: Manlighet och modernitet 1840–1940*, Jørgen Lorentzen and Claes Ekenstam, eds. (Stockholm: Gidlunds, 2006), 138–139, 144, 158.

11. John Tosh, *A Man's Place: Masculinity and the Middle-Class Home in Victorian England* (New Haven: Yale University Press, 2007), 170–195.

12. Barbra Hobson and David Morgan, "Introduction," *Making Men into Fathers: Masculinity and the Social Politics of Fatherhood*, Barbra Hobson, ed. (Cambridge: Cambridge University Press, 2002), 1–19.

13. Lorentzen, "Federne," 154–155, 166; Berglund, *Det goda faderskapet*, 25–49.

14. Tjeder, *The Power of Character*, 278; Berglund, *Det goda faderskapet*, 216. See also Eva Helen Ulvros, *Fruar och mamseller: Kvinnor inom sydsvensk borgerlighet 1790–1870* (Lund: Historiska media, 1996).

15. Berglund, *Det goda faderskapet*, 13, 183–184, 192, 201–202, 311.

16. Ann-Kristin Wallengren, *En afton på Röda Kvarn: Svensk stumfilm som musikdrama* (Lund: Lund University Press, 1998).

17. Rick Altman, *Film/Genre* (London: BFI, 2004), 5. Soila, *Kvinnors ansikte*, 35–44. For criticism of melodramatic elements, see, e.g., Kracauer, *From Caligari to Hitler*; McCrisken and Pepper, *American History in Contemporary Hollywood*, 11.

18. Altman, *Film/Genre*, 71–77.

19. Singer, *Melodrama and Modernity*, 37–51, 197–198, 221–262.

20. Soila, *Kvinnors ansikte*, 169–174. See also, Mary Ann Doane, *Desire to Desire: The Woman's Film of the 1940s* (Bloomington: Indiana University Press, 1987).

21. Tom Lutz, "Men's Tears and the Roles of

Melodrama," *Boy's Don't Cry? Rethinking Narratives of Masculinity and Emotion in the U.S.*, Milette Shamir and Jennifer Travis, eds. (New York: Columbia University Press, 2002), 185–190.

22. For further reading, see Ien Ang, *Watching Dallas: Soap Opera and the Melodramatic Imagination* (London: Methuen, 1985).

23. Lutz, "Men's Tears and the Roles of Melodrama," 191–204.

24. Studlar, *This Mad Masquerade*, 90–145.

25. Sally Robinson, "Men's Liberation, Men's Wounds: Emotion, Sexuality, and the Reconstruction of Masculinity in the 1970s," *Boy's Don't Cry? Rethinking Narratives of Masculinity and Emotion in the U.S.*, Milette Shamir and Jennifer Travis, eds. (New York: Columbia University Press, 2002), 205–229.

26. Hugo Münsterberg, *The Film: A Psychological Study* (New York: Dover Publications, 1970), 48–56.

27. Bruzzi, *Bringing Up Daddy*, xv–xviii, 12.

28. Tjeder, "Konsten att blifva herre öfver hvarje lidelse," 183–188; Merle W. Longwood, "Changing Views of Fathering and Fatherhood: A Christian Ethical Perspective," *Redeeming Men: Religion and Masculinities*, Stephen B. Boyd and Mark W. Muesse, eds. (Louisville: Westminster John Knox Press, 1996), 241–242; Howard Eilberg-Schwartz, "God's Phallus and the Dilemmas of Masculinity," *Redeeming Men: Religion and Masculinitis*, Stephen B. Boyd and Mark W. Muesse, eds. (Louisville: Westminster John Knox Press, 1996), 40.

29. Berglund, *Det goda faderskapet*, 184, 201, 311.

30. [Unsigned], "Varför överge männen hemmen?" *Filmnyheter* 24 (1924).

31. Robin Hood [Bengt Idestam-Almqvist], *Stockholm-Tidningen*, 18 September 1928.

32. *Folkets Dagblad Politiken*, 18 September 1928.

33. Masque [Tora Garm], *Stockholms Dagblad*, 18 January 1921.

34. Marfa o Comp [Elsa Danielsson and others], *Dagens Nyheter*, 18 January 1921.

35. Bruzzi, *Bringing Up Daddy*, 42.

36. Day and Mackay referenced in Bruzzi, *Bringing Up Daddy*, 42.

37. A Lbk, *Stockholms Dagblad*, 17 November 1928.

38. –r, *Stockholms-Tidningen*, 18 November 1928.

39. M N, *Aftonbladet*, 14 December 1920.

40. Robin Hood [Bengt Idestam-Almqvist], *Stockholms-Tidningen*, 22 September 1929.

41. M [Nils Edgren], *Social-Demokraten*, 22 September 1929.

42. Marfa o comp [Elsa Danielsson and others], *Dagens Nyheter*, 2 September 1924.

43. Jens Flik [Carl Björnberg], *Nya Dagligt Allehanda*, 2 September 1924.

44. *Aftonbladet*, 2 September 1924.

45. *Folkets Dagblad Politiken*, 2 September 1924.

46. For further reading, see Björn Horgby, *Egensinne och skötsamhet: Arbetarkulturen i Norrköping 1850–1940* (Stockholm: Carlssons, 1993) and Ronny Ambjörnsson, *Den skötsamme arbetaren: Idéer och ideal i ett norrländskt sågverkssamhälle 1880–1930* (Stockholm: Carlssons, 1998).

47. Per Olov Qvist, *Folkhemmets bilder: Modernisering, motstånd och mentalitet i den svenska 30-talsfilmen* (Lund: Arkiv förlag, 1995), 77–79, 261–264.

48. See, e.g., –d, *Folkets Dagblad Politiken*, 4 December 1923; Jens Flik [Carl Björnberg], *Nya Dagligt Allehanda*, 30 October 1923.

49. See, e.g., Op, *Folkets Dagblad Politiken*, 29 October 1929; Robin Hood [Bengt Idestam-Almqvist], *Stockholms-Tidningen*, 29 October 1929. See also, "Ishavsfilmen Den starkaste," Advertisement, *Filmjournalen* 17–18 (1929).

50. [Unsigned], "Filmarna som jagade björn och säl i Ishavet," *Filmnyheter* 25 (1929).

51. W, *Arbetet*, 19 November 1929.

52. Robin Hood [Bengt Idestam-Almqvist], *Stockholms-Tidningen*, 29 October 1929.

53. Jerome [Göran Traung], *Dagens Nyheter*, 29 October 1929.

54. e.g., W, *Arbetet*, 19 November 1929.

55. Bruzzi, *Bringing Up Daddy*, 62–63.

56. Ragn [Ragnar Lindqvist], *Aftonbladet*, 3 February 1920.

57. Quelqu'une [Märta Lindqvist], *Svenska Dagbladet*, 20 September 1923.

58. *Folkets Dagblad Politiken*, 2 November 1920.

59. –sque [Tora Garm], *Stockholms Dagblad*, 2 November 1920.

60. Ann-Kristin Wallengren, "Kultur och okultur—bilden av landsbygdens folk," *Solskenslandet: Svensk film på 2000-talet*, Erik Hedling and Ann-Kristin Wallengren, eds. (Stockholm: Atlantis, 2006), 51–54.

61. Marina Dahlqvist, "Snow-White: The Aesthetic and Narrative Use of Snow in Swedish Silent Film," *Nordic Explorations: Film Before 1930*, John Fullerton and Jan Olsson, eds. (Sydney: John Libby, 1999), 236–237.

62. Robin Hood [Bengt Idestam-Almqvist], *Stockholms-Tidningen*, 28 October 1928.

63. See, e.g., A Lbk, *Stockholms Dagblad*, 28 October 1928.

64. Berglund, *Det goda faderskapet*, 182–183.

65. *Svensk filmografi 2*, 12.

66. [Unsigned], "Inte uteslutande kärlek," *Filmnyheter* 12 (1920).

67. For a small selection, see, e.g., [Unsigned], "Äktenskapet och stjärnorna: 'Gift er aldrig!' säger Elinor Glyn—men de flesta amerikanska filmstjärnorna protestera," *Filmnyheter* 12 (1921); [Unsigned], "Mitt manliga ideal—och mitt kvin-

nliga: Filmstjärnor av båda könen ha ordet," *Filmnyheter* 17 (1921); [Unsigned], "Filmens Romeo har modärniserats," *Filmnyheter* 45 (1921); [Karl Lundegård], "Kvinnan och kärleken. Och i någon mån även äktenskapet," *Biografägaren* 11 (1927).

68. David Bagare, "Thomas Meighan om kvinnan och kärleken," *Filmjournalen* 14 (1921).

69. Warren G. Harris, *Clark Gable: A Biography* (New York: Three Rivers Press, 2002).

70. Bagare, "Thomas Meighan om kvinnan och kärleken."

71. Inga Gaate, "Om kvinnorna och kärleken: Vad Ramon Novarro har att säga om det viktiga problemet," *Filmjournalen* 29 (1924), (italics in the original).

72. Ala, "Männen och kärleken: Constance Talmadge berättar om varför männen lätt bli förälskade i skådespelerskor," *Filmjournalen* 12 (1925).

73. Robinson, "Men's Liberation," 225–226.

74. Ala, "Männen och kärleken."

75. hooks, *The Will to Change*, 4.

76. Refil [Ragnar Lindqvist], *Aftonbladet*, 13 October 1925.

77. E. F. [Ebba Frendius], *Stockholm-Tidningen*, 13 October 1925.

78. Jerome [Göran Traung], *Dagens Nyheter*, 13 October 1925.

79. See, e.g., E [Nils Edgren], *Folket Dagblad Politiken*, 8 March 1927.

80. *Svensk filmografi 2*, 317.

81. Damsel [Siri Thorngren-Olin], *Stockholms-Tidningen*, 8 March 1927.

82. Refil [Ragnar Lindqvist], *Aftonbladet*, 4 October 1927.

83. See, e.g., P J E [Per Johan Enström], *Nya Dagligt Allehanda*, 4 October 1927.

84. E-m, *Nya Dagligt Allehanda*, 18 January 1927.

85. Jerome [Göran Traung], *Dagens Nyheter*, 18 January 1927.

86. Refil [Ragnar Lindqvist], *Aftonbladet*, 18 January 1927.

87. Dyer, *Stars*, 57; Altman, *Film/Genre*, 165.

88. Quelqu'une [Märta Lindqvist], *Svenska Dagbladet*, 27 December 1923.

89. Lutz, "Men's Tears and the Roles of Melodrama," 185–190.

90. Elin Wägner, *Norrtullsligan* (Stockholm: En bok för alla, [1908] 1994). See, for example, Marfa [Elsa Danielsson], *Dagens Nyheter*, 27 December 1923.

91. Pardners [Nils Horney and others], *Social-Demokraten*, 27 December 1923.

92. Marfa [Elsa Danielsson], *Dagens Nyheter*, 27 December 1923.

93. See, e.g., *Stockholms Dagblad*, 27 December 1923.

94. e.g., *Stockholms Dagblad*, 27 December 1923.

95. e.g., Quelqu'une [Märta Lindqvist], *Svenska Dagbladet*, 27 December 1923.

96. *Aftonbladet*, 27 December 1923.

97. Thure Dahlin, "Onkel Teodor blir onkel Constantin: Ett sammanträffande med Ivan Hedqvist i Paris," *Filmjournalen* 8 (1921).

98. Arbiter & Co [Martin Martelius and others], "Nytt liv i den svenska filmen," *Våra nöjen* 46 (1926).

99. Biopatrullen, *Arbetet*, 16 March 1926.

100. Refil [Ragnar Lindqvist], *Aftonbladet*, 16 March 1926.

101. *Nya Dagligt Allehanda*, 16 March 1926.

102. See, e.g., Refil [Ragnar Lindqvist], *Aftonbladet*, 16 March 1926.

103. Bo Halvarson, "Anteckningar kring det filmiska stjärnsystemets uppkomst," *I offentlighetens ljus: Stumfilmens affischer, kritiker, stjärnor och musik*, Jan Olsson, ed. (Stockholm: Symposion, 1990), 298–299.

104. *Svenska Dagbladet*, 16 March 1926.

105. *Stockholms-Tidningen*, 16 March 1926.

106. Jerome [Göran Traung], *Dagens Nyheter*, 16 March 1926.

107. e.g., A N, *Stockholms-Tidningen*, 6 September 1927.

108. Hyltén-Cavallius, *Följa sitt genius*, 263.

109. *Boken om hela Sveriges Fridolf* (Stockholm: Åhlén & Åkerlund, 1935), 17.

110. Valdemar Dalqvist, "Fridolf och jag av," *Boken om hela Sveriges Fridolf* (Stockholm: Åhlén & Åkerlund, 1935), 13.

111. Bom [Bengt Ahlbom], *Stockholms-Tidningen*, 15 October 1929.

112. B [Nils Beijer], *Nya Dagligt Allehanda*, 15 October 1929.

113. *Boken om hela Sveriges Fridolf*, 23, 32. [Unsigned], "'Hon, han och Andersson'—en Fridolf Rhudinfilm," *Filmnyheter* 30 (1926).

114. Soila, *Kvinnors ansikte*, 56–75.

115. Ibid., 58 (boldface in the original).

116. Søland, *Becoming Modern*, 97–106.

117. [Unsigned], "Ett och annat från filmvärlden. Pola Negri om männen," *Svensk filmtidning* 1 (1924).

118. Pajazzo, "Fruntimmerskarlar och gifta män: Resonemang om Don Juan," *Våra nöjen* 40 (1927).

119. [Unsigned], "Konsten att behålla en man. Ett kapitel om erotisk efterhängsenhet," *Våra nöjen* 10 (1927).

120. Péra [Anna Odher], "Hur är det med mansfriden?" *Våra nöjen* 3 (1929).

121. Péra [Anna Odher], "Ingen längre svag ... Kvinnan har maskuliniserats och lagt bort en hel del av sina gamla svagheter—Istället har hon fått nya," *Våra nöjen* 25–26 (1929).

122. La Fleur, "Böra damerna ha långa byxor?" *Våra nöjen* 28 (1929).

123. Elin Wägner, "'Norrtullsligans' författarinna om 'sin' film," *Filmnyheter* 1 (1924).

124. e.g., Damsel [Siri Thorngren-Olin], *Stockholms-Tidningen*, 2 March 1926.

125. J-e [Göran Traung], *Dagens Nyheter*, 26 March 1929.

126. Bom [Bengt Ahlbom], *Stockholms-Tidningen*, 26 March 1929.

127. e.g., *Folkets Dagblad Politiken*, 27 December 1928. See also, Alexis, "En gång filmbov—alltid ... Edwin Adolphson trivs i bovfacket men vill gärna byta," *Filmjournalen* 19 (1927).

128. *Göteborgs-Posten*, 27 December 1928.

129. Siglon [Lorens Marmstedt], *Svenska Dagbladet*, 27 December 1928.

130. *Folkets Dagblad Politiken*, 27 December 1928.

131. Jerome [Göran Traung], *Dagens Nyheter*, 27 December 1928.

132. *Arbetet*, 5 October 1926.

133. For example, *Göteborgs-Posten*, 12 October 1926.

134. Hake [Harald Hansen], *Svenska Dagbladet*, 5 October 1926.

135. –J, *Social-Demokraten*, 5 October 1926.

136. See, e.g., *Folkets Dagblad Politiken*, 5 October 1926.

137. E-m, *Nya Dagligt Allehanda*, 5 October 1926.

138. *Svensk filmografi 2*, 351.

139. Wallén, *Revydags*, 165. Alter, *Svenska Dagbladet*, 22 September 1929.

140. [Unsigned], "'Synkroniseringen' av Ville Andesonfilmen," *Stockholms-Tidningen*, 29 October 1929.

141. Soila, *Kvinnors ansikte*, 55–56.

142. Søland, *Becoming Modern*, 115–140.

Chapter 4

1. G N-d, "Kvinnan och mannen just nu. Ett samtal om tidsandan," *Våra nöjen* 29 (1927).

2. [Unsigned], "Kvinna eller man?" *Filmnyheter* 29 (1926).

3. [Unsigned], "I modets marginal. Kvinna eller man?" *Våra nöjen* 44 (1926).

4. Gry Berglöw "Om de voro kvinnor," Caricature drawing, *Filmjournalen* 9 (1925).

5. See, e.g., Mosse, *The Image of Man*, 56–76; Sara Edenheim, *Begärets lagar: Moderna statliga utredningar och heteronormativitetens genealogi* (Stockholm: Symposion, 2005), 106; Jonas Liliequist, "Sexualiteten," *Män i Norden: Manlighet och modernitet 1840–1940*, Jørgen Lorentzen and Claes Ekenstam, eds. (Stockholm: Gidlunds, 2006), 167, 206.

6. e.g., Edenheim, *Begärets lagar*; Jens Rydström, *Sinners and Citizens: Bestiality and Homosexuality in Sweden 1880–1950* (Stockholm: Stockholm University, 2001); Michel Foucault, *The History of Sexuality Volume 1: An Introduction* (New York: Vintage Books, 1990); Donald E. Hall, *Queer Theories* (New York: Palgrave Macmillan, 2003).

7. Greger Ekman, "1907: Det homosexuella genombrottet," *Sympatiens hemlighetsfulla makt: Stockholms homosexuella 1860–1960*, Göran Söderström, ed. (Stockholm: Stockholmia, 1999), 149–164.

8. See, e.g., Nikki Sullivan, *A Critical Introduction to Queer Theory* (New York: New York University Press, 2003), 2 and Arne Nilsson, *Såna & riktiga karlar: Om manlig homosexualitet i Göteborg decennierna kring andra världskriget* (Göteborg: Anamma, 1998), 122, 222–226.

9. Foucault, *The History of Sexuality*, 36–49, 54–69; Don Kulick, "Är måsar lesbiska? Om biologins relevans för mänskligt beteende," *Res Publica* 1–2 (1997), 221–232; Liliequist, "Sexualiteten," 167.

10. Ljeder, *The Power of Character*, 160–173, 238–250.

11. Foucault, *The History of Sexuality*, 39, 45–49.

12. Ibid., 59.

13. Ibid., 53–71. See also, Steorn, *Nakna män*, 106–112, 207.

14. Skoglund, *Filmcensuren*, 151–186.

15. Tommy Gustafsson and Mariah Larsson, "Porren inför lagen. Två fallstudier angående den officiella attityden till offentligt visad pornografisk film 1921 och 1971," *Historisk tidskrift* 3 (2009), 445–465.

16. Dyer, *Now You See It*, 23–29.

17. "Säsongens stora överraskning?" Advertisement, *Biografägaren* 11 (1926). SBC, Censorship card 37426.

18. "En ny rysk film i stil med 'Den gula biljetten,'" Advertisement, *Biografägaren* 11 (1929) and "Prostituerad," Advertisement, *Biografägaren* 13 (1929).

19. "Prostituerad," Advertisement, *Biografägaren* 13 (1929).

20. See David Bordwell and Kristin Thompson, *Film Art: An Introduction* (New York: McGraw-Hill, 1997) and Mulvey, "Spelfilmen och lusten att se."

21. See, e.g., Connell, *Masculinities*, 67–81, 113–114, 145, 188; Mosse, *The Image of Man*, 56–67; Ekenstam, "Män, manlighet och omanlighet i historien," 32–33; Liliequist, "Sexualiteten," 167, 206–207.

22. Hall, *Queer Theories*, 1–7.

23. Zygmunt Bauman, *Life in Fragments: Essays in Postmodern Morality* (Cambridge: Blackwell, 1995), 42–43.

24. Hall, *Queer Theories*, 130–132, 166–167.

25. Sullivan, *A Critical Introduction to Queer Theory*, 191–194; Tiina Rosenberg, *Byxbegär* (Göteborg: Anamma, 2000), 15–20.

26. See, e.g., Andrea Dworkin, *Intercourse* (London: Secker & Warburg, 1997).

27. Sullivan, *A Critical Introduction to Queer Theory*, 134.

28. See, e.g., Blomberg, *Vill ni se en stjärna?* 135.

29. Judith Butler, *Gender Trouble: Feminism and the Subversions of Identity* (New York: Routledge, 1990), 138.
30. Sullivan, *A Critical Introduction to Queer Theory*, 90, 193.
31. Sölve Cederström and Gustaf Edgren, *Svarte Rudolf*, Film manuscript (1928), SFI.
32. *Arbetet*, 19 March 1924.
33. Robin Hood [Ragnar Idestam-Almqvist], *Stockholms-Tidningen*, 8 April 1924.
34. *Folkets Dagblad Politiken*, 8 April 1924.
35. *Arbetaren*, 8 April 1924.
36. Rudolf Anthoni, *Carl XII's kurir*, Film manuscript (1924), SFI; *Carl XII's kurir: En berättelse för filmen i fem akter fritt efter Esaias Tegnérs dikt "Axel,"* Program note (Stockholm: Wernqvist & C:is boktryckeri, 1924).
37. Bengt Forslund, *Från Gösta Ekman till Gösta Ekma:. En bok om Hasse, far och son* (Borås: Askild & Kärnekull, 1983), 40–47.
38. Sascha, "Gösta Ekman om film och filmning: En intervju med den store favoriten," *Svensk filmtidning* 12 (1924).
39. Forslund, *Från Gösta Ekman till Gösta Ekman*, 23; Gösta Ekman, *Den tänkande August* (Stockholm: Albert Bonniers förlag, 1928), 140.
40. Hasse Ekman, *Gösta Ekman* (Stockholm: Albert Bonniers förlag, 1938), 118–139; Forslund, *Från Gösta Ekman till Gösta Ekman*, 33, 41. See for example *Göteborgs-Posten*, 21 September 1920.
41. "Gösta Ekman," Fan picture, *Filmjournalen* 3 (1919).
42. August Brunius, "Gösta Ekman," *Scenen* 15 (1921).
43. Per Lindberg, *Gösta Ekman: Skådespelaren och människan* (Stockholm: Natur och Kultur, 1942), 21.
44. O Maurice, "Konstgjorda stjärnor eller äkta. Var ligger felet i stjärnsystemet?" *Filmjournalen* 4 (1923). See also, Dyer, *Stars*, 2004.
45. Brunius, "Gösta Ekman."
46. [Unsigned], "Svenska filmens första älskare. Många yngre karaktärsskådespelare i svensk film, men ont om unga 'filmhjältar,'" *Filmjournalen* 15 (1923).
47. *Göteborgs-Posten*, 21 September 1921.
48. Quelqu'une [Märta Lindqvist], *Svenska Dagbladet*, 7 December 1920.
49. Clement, *Stockholms Dagblad*, 15 March 1921.
50. Rl, *Folkets Dagblad Politiken*, 7 December 1920.
51. P, *Arbetet*, 2 December 1924.
52. Ibid.
53. *Folkets Dagblad Politiken*, 2 January 1922.
54. Quelqu'une [Märta Lindqvist], *Svenska Dagbladet*, 2 January 1922.
55. Crasnij Diavel, *Arbetet*, 2 January 1922.
56. *Stockholms-Tidningen*, 17 November 1925.
57. Lindberg, *Gösta Ekman*, 34.
58. Margit Siwertz, *Lars Hanson* (Stockholm: Norstedts, 1947), 79–80, 191–194; Forslund, *Från Gösta Ekman till Gösta Ekman*, 51–53.
59. Dyer, *Stars*, 9.
60. *Stockholms-Tidningen*, 17 November 1925.
61. Tommy Gustafsson, "Nationell ära och manlighet i *Karl XII* (1925)—en historisk filmanalys," *Scandia* 1 (2005), 66–71.
62. Ax [Axel Andersson], *Folkets Dagblad Politiken*, 17 November 1925.
63. Oswald Kuylenstierna, *Aftonbladet*, 3 February 1925.
64. Robin Hood [Bengt Idestam-Almqvist], *Stockholms-Tidningen*, 3 February 1925.
65. Jerome [Göran Traung], *Dagens Nyheter*, 17 November 1925.
66. Bes [Bernhard Bengtsson], *Folkets Dagblad Politiken*, 3 February 1925.
67. Jens Flik [Carl Björnberg], *Nya Dagligt Allehanda*, 3 February 1925.
68. Gustaf Cederström, *Nya Dagligt Allehanda*, 17 November 1925.
69. Gvs [Herbert Grevenius], *Stockholms Dagblad*, 17 November 1925.
70. Gvs [Herbert Grevenius], *Stockholms Dagblad*, 3 February 1925.
71. Forslund, *Från Gösta Ekman till Gösta Ekman*, 22; Ekman, *Den tänkande August*, 81–85; Karl Gerhard, "Den siste historionen," *Gösta Ekman: Människan: Konstnären*, Gösta Tranströmer, ed. (Stockholm: Åhlén & Åkerlund, 1938), 24.
72. Göran Söderström, "Ögonvittnen," *Sympatiens hemlighetsfulla makt: Stockholms homosexuella 1860–1960*, Göran Söderström, ed. (Stockholm: Stockholmia, 1999), 363–364.
73. Ekman, *Den tänkande August*.
74. E Z & G T-s, "Gösta Ekman som författare. 'Den tänkande August'—en rolig och en fin bok. Varför dagspressen gjort sensation av densamma?" *Våra nöjen* 50–51 (1928).
75. Ekman, *Gösta Ekman*, 157–164.
76. *Gösta Ekman: Människan: Konstnären*, Gösta Tranströmer, ed. (Stockholm: Åhlén & Åkerlund, 1938).
77. Lindberg, *Gösta Ekman*, 50, 81, 132, 188–189, 263. See also, Sture Lagerwall, "Hans vänskap svek aldrig," *Gösta Ekman: Människan: Konstnären*, Gösta Tranströmer, ed. (Stockholm: Åhlén & Åkerlund, 1938), 53.
78. Hjalmar Bergman, "Kärlek genom ett fönster," *Eros' begravning: Kärlek genom ett fönster och andra berättelser* (Stockholm: Albert Bonniers förlag, [1925] 1954), 263–278.
79. Lindberg, *Gösta Ekman*, 189.
80. Ibid., 150–152.
81. Forslund, *Från Gösta Ekman till Gösta Ekman*, 96–97.
82. Söderström, "Ögonvittnen," 361.
83. Lindberg, *Gösta Ekman*, 241.
84. Brunius, "Gösta Ekman."
85. Eve Kosofsky Sedgwick, *Epistemology of the*

Closet (New York: Harvester Weathleaf, 1991), 142–150.

86. Kosofsky Sedgwick, *Epistemology of the Closet*, 49, 161–166.

87. Ekman, *Den tänkande August*, 11; Per Lindberg, "Samarbete med Gösta," *Gösta Ekman: Människan: Konstnären*, Gösta Tranströmer, ed. (Stockholm: Åhléns & Åkerlund, 1938), 8–12; Lindberg, *Gösta Ekman*, 39, 82, 141, 188, Forslund, *Från Gösta Ekman till Gösta Ekman*, 17.

88. Jens Rydström, "Polisen och de perverse: Klagomål och angivelser rörande homosexualitet 1925–1944," *Sympatiens hemlighetsfulla makt: Stockholms homosexuella 1860–1960*, Göran Söderström, ed. (Stockholm: Stockholmia, 1999), 385.

89. Ekman, *Den tänkande August*, 11.

90. Citation from Lindberg, *Gösta Ekman*, 188.

91. Dyer, *Now You See It*, 8.

92. Fredrik Silverstolpe, "Mauritz Stiller och den första homosexuella spelfilmen," *Sympatiens hemlighetsfulla makt: Stockholms homosexuella 1860–1960*, Göran Söderström, ed. (Stockholm: Stockholmia, 1999), 322–326.

93. Dyer, *Now You See It*, 8–15.

94. See, e.g., Chinoise [Siri Thorngren-Olin], *Stockholms Dagblad*, 5 September 1916.

95. See Rydström, *Sinners and Citizens*; Nilsson, *Såna & riktiga karlar*, 38.

96. Dyer, *Now You See It*, 24–27; Kracauer, *From Caligari to Hitler*, 45.

97. Kracauer, *From Caligari to Hitler*, 44. Sullivan, *A Critical Introduction to Queer Theory*, 4–19.

98. Dyer, *Now You See It*, 30–32.

99. Sullivan, *A Critical Introduction to Queer Theory*, 16–18.

100. Dyer, *Now You See It*, 32–36.

101. SBC, Censorship cards 28 634, 29 566 and 29 567.

102. Bertil Wredlund and Rolf Lindfors, *Långfilm i Sverige 1910–1919* (Stockholm: Proprius, 1991) and Bertil Wredlund and Rolf Lindfors, *Långfilm i Sverige 1920–1929* (Stockholm: Proprius, 1987).

103. Göran Söderström, "Privatpersonen Stiller och hans krets," *Sympatiens hemlighetsfulla makt: Stockholms homosexuella 1860–1960*, Göran Söderström, ed. (Stockholm: Stockholmia, 1999), 327–331. Greger Ekman, "Homosexuella i kulturdebatten," *Sympatiens hemlighetsfulla makt: Stockholms homosexuella 1860–1960*, Göran Söderström, ed. (Stockholm: Stockholmia, 1999), 178.

104. "Fäderneslandets svarta lista," *Fäderneslandet*, 15 December 1923.

105. Edenheim, *Begärets lagar*, 183–195; Sullivan, *A Critical Introduction to Queer Theory*, 16–17; Rydström, "Polisen och de perversa," 382.

106. Svarta Handen, "Gösta Ekman byxor," *Fäderneslandet*, 3 January 1925.

107. See, e.g., [Unsigned], "Gösta Ekman hemma hos sig," *Filmjournalen* 4 (1920); [Unsigned], "Gösta Ekman," *Filmjournalen* 1 (1922).

108. Liliequist, "Från niding till sprätt," 73–94; Tjeder, *The Power of Character*, 168–175.

109. [Unsigned], "Svenskt filmfolk på kontinenten: Gösta Ekmans Faust-engagemang kronan på verket i ett omfattande samarbete," *Svensk filmtidning* 16 (1925) and [Unsigned], "Gösta Ekman i fullt arbete med Faust," *Filmnyheter* 36 (1925).

110. Lindberg, *Gösta Ekman*, 57–58.

111. Arthur Nordén, *Stockholms-Tidningen*, 27 December 1927.

112. Jerome [Göran Traung], *Dagens Nyheter*, 27 December 1927.

113. *Social-Demokraten*, 27 December 1927.

114. P J F. [Per Johan Enström], *Nya Dagligt Allehanda*, 27 December 1927.

115. See, e.g., Ax [Axel Andersson], *Folkets Dagblad Politiken*, 27 December 1927.

116. See, e.g., Arthur Nordén, *Stockholms-Tidningen*, 27 December 1927.

117. Lindberg, *Gösta Ekman*, 58–59.

118. Hyltén-Cavallius, *Följa sitt genius*, 285–286.

119. Ragnar Hyltén-Cavallius, "Våra herrar: Gösta Ekman," *Våra nöjen* 34 (1928).

120. Lindberg, *Gösta Ekman*, 300.

Chapter 5

1. Martin Alm, *Americanitis: Amerika som sjuksom och läkemedel: Svenska berättelser om USA åren 1900–1939* (Lund: Historica Lundensia, 2002), 270.

2. *Historisk statistik för Sveriges befolkning: Historical Statistics of Sweden: 1: Befolkning: Population 1720–1950* (Stockholm: Statistiska centralbyrån, 1955), 66–67.

3. See, e.g., Johan Fornäs, *Moderna människor: Folkhemmet och jazzen* (Stockholm: Norstedts, 2004), 194–195.

4. Dahlqvist, "Snow-White," 238.

5. Lars M. Andersson, *En jude är en jude är en jude ... Representationer av "juden" i svensk skämtpress omkring 1900–1930* (Lund: Nordic Academic Press, 2000), 33, 28, 66, 485.

6. Ibid., 29, 49, 485.

7. Qvist, *Folkhemmets bilder*, 441–450.

8. Rochelle Wright, *The Visible Wall: Jews and Other Ethnic Outsiders in Swedish Film* (Carbondale: Southern Illinois University Press, 1998), 212–213.

9. Ibid., xi, 10.

10. Andersson, *En jude är en jude är en jude...*, 485.

11. Furhammar, *Filmen i Sverige*, 8, 124, 146.

12. *Svensk filmografi 2*, 12.

13. See further in Tommy Gustafsson, "Travelers as Threat in Swedish Film in the 1920s," *Swedish Film: An Introduction and a Reader*, Mariah

Larsson and Anders Marklund, eds. (Lund: Nordic Academic Press, 2010), 92–104.

14. Wright, *The Visible Wall*, 388.

15. Ibid., 61. See further in Gunnar Petterson, *Mannen som kom tillbaka från de döda: En bok om skandalförfattaren Gustaf Ericsson* (Stockholm: Ordfront, 2000), 206–216.

16. Andersson, *En jude är en jude är en jude...*, 485.

17. Ibid., 34. Historisk statistik för Sveriges befolkning, 4, 21.

18. Wright, *The Visible Wall*, 6–8. Pelle Snickars, *Svensk film och visuell masskultur 1900* (Stockholm: Aura, 2001).

19. Fornäs, *Moderna människor*, 193–292.

20. Gunnar Broberg, *Statlig rasforskning: En historik över rasbiologiska institutet* (Lund: Ugglan 4, 1995), 7–11; Fornäs, *Moderna människor*, 203.

21. Herman Lundborg, *Svensk raskunskap: Folkupplaga med text, kartor, diagram och planscher* (Uppsala: Almqvist & Wiksell, 1927), plates X–XIV and XVIII–XIX.

22. Broberg, *Statlig rasforskning*, 19–24, 45–52.

23. e.g., *Stockholms Dagblad*, 6 September 1927.

24. [Unsigned], "Litet frenologi, apterad på några filmstjärnor," *Filmnyheter* 10 (1922). See also Fredrik Chalfork, "När 'svartrockar' blev 'vitrockar.' Om Ivar Bromans bidrag i den rasbiologiska och rashygieniska allmänupplysningen under åren 1920–1940," *Scandia* 1 (2006), 72–92.

25. Broberg 1995, *Statlig rasforskning*, 81–86.

26. Ibid., 51.

27. [Unsigned], "Mexikanarna inga bovar. Amerikansk film portförbjuden i Mexiko så länge filmbovarna äro mexikanare," *Biografrevyn* 4 (1922).

28. [Unsigned], "Svensk film som nationell reklam. Hur den svenska filmtrusten tänker erövra världen," *Filmjournalen* 2 (1919).

29. [Unsigned], "De svenska filmerna i utlandet. Utomordentligt gynnsam kritik," *Filmnyheter* 2 (1920).

30. [Unsigned], "Filmens utlandspropaganda för Sverige. En intervju med direktör Magnusson," *Filmbladet* 10 (1920).

31. e.g., [Unsigned], "Victor Sjöström i London. Ett personligt intryck," *Filmbladet* 8 (1921); [Unsogned], "Svensk konst och svensk film," *Filmbladet* 13 (1921); [Unsigned], "Engelska lovord om 'Körkarlen,'" *Filmnyheter* 8 (1921); [Unsigned], "Svenska filmer sedda med utlandets ögon," *Filmnyheter* 35 (1921).

32. [Unsigned], "Svensk film inför fransk publik. "Cinema" har utgivit ett specialnummer ägnat den svenska filmen," *Filmbladet* 25 (1921).

33. [Unsigned], "Ett utlandssvenskt angrepp på svensk film," *Filmnyheter* 16 (1922).

34. [Unsigned], "Börjar vår film förflackas? Ett märkligt 'giv akt' i en schweizisk tidning," *Biografrevyn* 8 (1923).

35. [Unsigned], "Svensk film inför utlandet," *Svensk filmtidning* 12 (1924).

36. Ibid.

37. See, e.g., [Unsigned], "Svensk filmtrio till Amerika. Stiller—Garbo—Einar Hansson lämna oss," *Svensk filmtidning* 5 (1925).

38. See, e.g., [Unsigned], "Hemberg," *Biografägaren* 3 (1927); [Unsigned], "Europeisk film vinner insteg i Amerika," *Biografägaren* 18 (1927); [Unsigned], "'Parisiskor' en—internationell ensemble i hypermodärn film," *Filmjournalen* 2 (1928).

39. Referenced and cited from Karl Lundegård, "Felaktig ursprungsbeteckning," *Filmbladet* 37 (1921).

40. [Unsigned], "Cirkus Bimbini," *Filmjournalen* 17 (1921).

41. XXX [Johannes Lindberg, Vera von Kraemer och Knut Jeurling], *Stockholm-Tidningen*, 24 September 1918.

42. *Aftonbladet*, 24 September 1918.

43. Marfa o comp [Elsa Danielsson and others], *Dagens Nyheter*, 24 September 1918.

44. Mauritz Edström, *Dagens Nyheter*, 2 April 1963.

45. Alm, *Americanitis*, 270–72.

46. Fornäs, *Moderna människor*, 208, 226.

47. Butters Jr., *Black Manhood on the Silent Screen*, xvi, 3–16.

48. Ibid., 22–36.

49. Ibid., 83–86, 91–120, 166–175.

50. Films from the 1920s offer just one example in *Charley's Aunt* and an allusion to blackface in *Boman at the Exhibition*. Films from the 1910s include a few more cases, e.g., in *The Lion Hunt* (*Lejonjakten*, 1908), *Emigrant* (1910) and *Patrik's Adventures* (*Patriks äventyr*, 1915).

51. See, e.g., "Bananbanans ändpunkt är A/B Banankompaniets Stockholm-Göteborg-Malmö," Advertisement, *Våra nöjen* 7 (1926).

52. Furhammar, *Filmen i Sverige*, 70–72.

53. Jernudd, "Educational Cinema and Censorship in Sweden," 152–162; Pelle Snickars, "'Bildrutor i minnets film'—om medieprins Wilhelm och film som käll- och åskådningsmaterial," *Det förflutna som film och vice versa: Om medierade historiebruk*, Pelle Snickars and Cecilia Trenter, eds. (Lund: Studentlitteratur, 2004), 219.

54. Cynthia Chris, *Watching Wildlife* (Minneapolis and London: University of Minnesota Press, 2006), xii–xxii.

55. Ibid., 30, 60, 77.

56. Ibid., 20.

57. [Prince] Wilhelm, *Bland dvärgar och gorillor: Med svenska zoologiska expeditionen till Centralafrika 1921* (Stockholm: P. A. Norstedt & Söner, 1922).

58. See, e.g., Damsel [Siri Thorngren-Olin], *Stockholms-Tidningen*, 27 December 1923.

59. Åsa Jernudd, *Oscar Olsson's African Films: Examples of Touristic Edutainment* (Örebro: Örebro University, 1999), 56–57, 68, 76–77.

60. [Prince] Wilhelm, *Bland dvärgar och gorillor*, 16–18, 58.
61. Ibid., 44–45, 58, 200–205, 236, 260, 273.
62. Ibid., 170–174, 239–246.
63. Furhammar, *Filmen i Sverige*, 72–73.
64. See, e.g., *Stockholms Dagblad*, 29 November 1921.
65. See, e.g., *Nya Dagligt Allehanda*, 13 March 1922.
66. Les deux, *Svenska Dagbladet*, 29 November 1921.
67. See, e.g., *Folkets Dagblad Politiken*, 29 November 1921.
68. –bis, *Stockholms-Tidningen*, 14 March 1922.
69. Marque [Tora Garm], *Stockholms Dagblad*, 14 March 1922.
70. Tommy Gustafsson, "I skarven mellan fakta och fiktion. Konstruktionen av manlighet och etnicitet i svensk filmkultur under 1920-talet," *Historieforskning på nya vägar*, Klas-Göran Karlsson, Eva Helen Ulvros and Ulf Zander, eds. (Lund: Nordic Academic Press, 2006), 107–118.
71. See, e.g., Bengt Berg, "Bengt Berg om sin elefantfilm samt om bildningsfilmen, publiken, staten, operan m.m.," *Tidskrift för svensk skolfilm och bildningsfilm* 4 (1924); O S, "Abu Markúb och hundra elefanter: Bengt Bergs film och föredrag om resan uppför Nilen," *Tidskrift för svensk skolfilm och bildningsfilm* 8 (1925); [Unsigned] "Negerdans på film sprider glädje både på bio och i skolsal," *Filmnyheter* 6 (1927).
72. SBC, Censorship cards 27245, 27264, 27265. "Skeppsbrutna bland kannibaler," Advertisement, *Filmjournalen* 16 (1921).
73. Reay Tannahill, *Flesh & Blood—A History of the Cannibal Complex* (London: Abacus, 1996), 12–22.
74. [Unsigned], "Kapten Groggs liv och leverne: Berättade av hans pappa, artisten Victor Bergdahl," *Filmnyheter* 2 (1921).
75. Marfa & comp [Elsa Danielsson and others], *Dagens Nyheter*, 19 November 1920.
76. Jens Flik [Carl Björnberg], *Nya Dagligt Allehanda*, 9 November 1920.
77. Nick [Nils Horney], *Social-Demokraten*, 9 November 1920.
78. [Unsigned], "Det var en liten prinsessa ... En liten negerprinsessa som spelat film," *Filmnyheter* 25 (1925); [Unsigned], "Svarta skönheter och vita. Smånytt från inspelningsfronten," *Filmjournalen* 15–16 (1925); [Unsigned], "En tvättäkta neger i svensk film," *Filmnyheter* 18 (1925).
79. H-d, Folkets Dagblad Politiken, 27 October 1925.
80. –xon, *Social-Demokraten*, 27 October 1925.
81. Jens Flik [Carl Björnberg], *Nya Dagligt Allehanda*, 27 October 1925.
82. *Svensk filmografi 2*, 120–21. *Dagens Nyheter*, 27 September 1921.
83. Fornäs, *Moderna människor*, 194.
84. Hjalmar Meissner, "Varning för jazz," *Scenen* 13 (1921).
85. Fornäs, *Moderna människor*, 20–21.
86. *Nya Dagligt Allehanda*, 14 March 1922.
87. Björkin, *Amerikanism, bolsjevism och korta kjolar*, 12–13; Furhammar, *Filmen i Sverige*, 106–108.
88. *Svensk filmografi 2*, 297.
89. Bordwell and Thompson, *Film History*, 253–254.
90. Gvs [Herbert Grevenius], *Stockholms Dagblad*, 9 November 1926.
91. [Unsigned], "Ljudfilmens musikaliska 'kulturfara,'" *Biografbladet* 6 (1929).
92. *Svenska filmografi 2*, 104.
93. Gvs [Herbert Grevenius], *Stockholms Dagblad*, 18 January 1927.
94. See, e.g., "Björktvål Prins av Parma," Advertisement, *Filmnyheter* 17 (1928).
95. V v K [Vera von Kraemer], "Svart inslag i svensk film," *Filmnyheter* 25 (1927).
96. Alm, *Americanitis*, 271.
97. [Unsigned], "Darwins teorier," *Biografbladet* 19 (1922).
98. [Unsigned], "Onkel Toms stuga i pånyttfödelse. Inspelning av Harriet Beecher Stowe's bok som blivit miljonaffär," *Filmjournalen* 14 (1927).
99. P-n, "Romanen som skapade historia: Litet litteraturhistoria inför premiären på 'Onkel Toms stuga,'" *Filmjournalen* 3 (1928).
100. "Onkel Toms stuga," Advertisement, *Filmjournalen* 9–10 (1928).
101. David Pierce, "'Carl Laemmel's Outstanding Achivement': Harry Pollard and the Struggle to Film *Uncle Tom's Cabin*," *Film History* 4 (1998).
102. SBC, Censorship card 40885.
103. M W [Magnus Wester], "Världshistoria som vaknar till liv: Den märkliga Universalfilmen 'Onkel Toms stuga' presenteras nu for svensk publik," *Filmjournalen* 15 (1928).
104. B Fr [Borghild Frendin], *Nya Dagligt Allehanda*, 23 September 1928.
105. e.g., Robin Hood [Bengt Idestam-Almqvist], *Stockholms-Tidningen*, 23 September 1928.
106. "Onkel Toms skyddslingar," Advertisement, *Biografägaren* 4 (1929). Butters Jr., *Black Manhood on the Silent Screen*, 174.
107. Alm, *Americanitis*, 64–73.
108. Wright, *The Visible Wall*, 14–24, 67.
109. Andersson, *En jude är en jude är en jude...*, 120–126.
110. Joseph Zitomersky, "Ambiguous Integration: The Historical Position of the Jews in Swedish Society, 1780s–1980s," *Judarna i det svenska samhället: Identitet, integration, etniska relationer*, Kerstin Nyström, ed. (Lund: Lund University Press, 1991), 82–88.

111. [Unsigned], "Henry Ford, judarna och filmen," *Filmbladet* 13 (1921).
112. See further in Andersson, *En jude är en jude är en jude...*, 115–118.
113. *Svensk filmografi 2*, 344–345.
114. Ibid., 217–218.
115. The name Jakobovsky is a play on words, because "bov" also can be understood as "villain" in Swedish.
116. Västerlånggatan is a commerce street in Stockholm.
117. Wright, *The Visible Wall*, 48.
118. Ibid., 67; Andersson, *En jude är en jude är en jude...*, 120–126, 485.
119. *Nya Dagligt Allehanda*, 9 February 1926.
120. Norlander (i bearbetning av Sam Ask), *Anderssonskans Kalle på nya upptåg*, Film manuscript.
121. *Anderssonskans Kalle på nya upptåg*, Program note.
122. *Social-Demokraten*, 28 August 1923.
123. *Folkets Dagblad Politiken*, 28 August 1923.
124. Andersson, *En jude är en jude är en jude...*, 41–42.
125. Anna Besserman, "Den lågkyrkliga väckelsens syn på judar och judendom," *Judarna i det svenska samhället: Identitet, integration, etniska relationer*, Kerstin Nyström, ed. (Lund: Lund University Press, 1991), 68–69.
126. Tjeder, *The Power of Character*, 73–90.
127. *Svensk filmografi 2*, 102–104.
128. Sigfrid Siwertz, *Lata latituder* (Stockholm: Albert Bonniers, 1924), 26–27, 30–31, 117–118, 127, 160–161, 170, 178, 194, 201, 303.
129. Ibid., 79, 89, 92–96, 114–116, 120, 128, 161, 392.
130. *Dagens Nyheter*, 24 March 1925.
131. [Prince] Wilhelm, *Bland dvärgar och gorillor*, 149–150.
132. Lennart Lundmark, "Vetenskap i rasismens tjänst: Så fick skallmätningen av samer vetenskaplig legitimitet," *Tvärsnitt* 2 (2002). See also, Andrea Amft, "Att skapa en 'autentisk' minoritet: om maktrelationen mellan svenskar och samer från slutet av 1800-talet fram till 1970-talet," *Historisk tidskrift* 4 (1998).
133. Rolf Nordenstreng, "Finnar och lappar," *Rasfrågor i modern belysning*, Herman Lundborg, ed. (Stockholm: P. A. Norstedt & Söner, 1919), 45.
134. Wright, *The Visible Wall*, 148–152.
135. See, e.g., H [Nils Horney], *Social-Demokraten*, 2 January 1923.
136. e.g. Crasnij Diavel, *Arbetet*, 2 January 1923.
137. Quelqu'une [Märta Lindqvist], *Svenska Dagbladet*, 2 January 1923.
138. *Stockholms Dagblad*, 4 December 1923.
139. Max, *Folkets Dagblad Politiken*, 25 September 1923.
140. *Svensk filmografi 2*, 187.
141. Josef Almqvist, "Sverige och utlandet," *Våra nöjen* 45 (1927).
142. I G, "Om film och rasskillnad. 'Ben-Hur'-inspelningen avbruten, amerikanarna resa tillbaka till sitt eget land igen," *Filmjournalen* 5 (1925).
143. Richard Dyer, *White* (London and New York: Routledge, 2002), 14–57.
144. Ibid., 52–70.
145. Nordenstreng, "Finnar och lappar," 29–44.
146. Wright, *The Visible Wall*, 168–179.
147. See, e.g., S S-e [Sven Stolpe], "Den ryska filmen. En originell filmkonst växer fram i sovjetriket," *Filmjournalen* 2 (1927).
148. See Erik Hedling, "Kjell Sundvalls *Jägarna*: svenskt 'High Concept,'" *Blågult flimmer: Svenska filmanalyser*, Erik Hedling, ed. (Lund: Studentlitteratur, 1998).
149. Jerome [Göran Traung], *Dagens Nyheter*, 27 December 1929.
150. –lax, *Arbetet*, 1 March 1921.
151. Marfa [Elsa Danielsson], *Dagens Nyheter*, 1 March 1921.
152. Refil [Ragnar Lindqvist], *Aftonbladet*, 18 January 1927.
153. *Göteborgs-Posten*, 18 January 1927.
154. E-m, *Nya Dagligt Allehanda*, 18 January 1927.
155. *Svensk filmografi 2*, 294–295.
156. Moje [Nils Edgren], *Social-Demokraten*, 2 November 1926.
157. Quoted from [Unsigned], "Inspelningen av Johan Ulfstjerna väcker protest på finskt håll. Skådespelets presenterande som historisk film är vilseledande," *Filmbladet* 4 (1923), (italics in the original).
158. –n [Nanna Berglund], *Stockholms Dagblad*, 4 December 1923.
159. N H [Nils Horney], *Social-Demokraten*, 4 December 1923.
160. Resic, *American Warriors in Vietnam*, 8–9.
161. Almqvist, "Sverige och utlandet."
162. Torsten Burgman, *Rysslandsbilden i Sverige: Från Ivan den förskräcklige till Vladimir Putin* (Lund: Historiska Media, 2001), 16–51.
163. Anthoni, *Karl XII:s kurir*, Film manuscript. Burgman, *Rysslandsbilden i Sverige*, 18–26.
164. See further Gustafsson "Nationell ära och manlighet i *Karl XII*."
165. Robin Hood [Bengt Idestam-Almqvist], *Stockholms-Tidningen*, 3 February 1925.
166. "En äkta tsar Peter," *Annandagens filmnyheter* (1924).
167. Bes [Bernhard Bengtsson], *Folkets Dagblad Politiken*, 3 February 1925.
168. Vladimir Semitjoff, "Två hjältar. Filmens kung Karl och tsar Peter genom ryska ögon," *Filmjournalen* 11 (1925).
169. *Svensk filmografi 2*, 125–127. Hyltén-Cavallius, *Följa sitt genius*, 201–203.
170. See, e.g., "'Bolsjevik-svenska' och 'Alle-

handa-svenska.' Ett uddigt replikskifte," *Biografbladet* 4 (1922).

171. See, e.g., *Aftonbladet*, 18 November 1924.

172. Marfa [Elsa Danielsson], *Dagens Nyheter*, 18 November 1924.

173. Jens Flik [Carl Björnberg], *Nya Dagligt Allehanda*, 18 November 1924.

174. Rune Johansson, "Samlande, lättförståeligt och eggande? Kosacker, kultur och kvinnor i valaffischer från 1928," *Mer än tusen ord: Bilden och de historiska vetenskaperna*, Lars M. Andersson, Lars Berggren and Ulf Zander, eds. (Lund: Nordic Academic Press, 2001), 223–243.

175. [Unsigned], "'Ben Hur,' 'Frestelse' och 'Soluppgång' i täten: Resultatet av Filmjournalens omröstning om de tio basta," *Filmjournalen* 5 (1928).

176. Gerda Marcus, "En rysk film gör sensation i Tyskland: 'Pansarkryssaren Potemkin' av Berlinkritiken kallad 'en vändpunkt i filmkonstens historia,'" *Filmjournalen* 9–10 (1926).

177. SBC, Censorship card 37246.

178. Björkin, *Amerikanism, bolsjevism och korta kjolar*, 103–111.

179. See, e.g., *Folkets Dagblad Politiken*, 2 November 1926.

180. B. Carlberg, "Sydamerikanskt biografliv. Den verkliga sensationsfilmen och den verkligt förstående publiken," *Filmjournalen* 1 (1921).

181. Studlar, *This Mad Masquerade*, 158–165.

182. Björkin, *Amerikanism, bolsjevism och korta kjolar*, 177, 180–181, 190.

183. -lin [Vera von Kraemer], "Rodolph Valentino, den nya idolen. Några ord till porträttet på första sidan," *Filmnyheter* 41 (1922).

184. Studlar, *This Mad Masquerade*, 1–9, 150–198.

185. Anna Nordenström-Law, "Varför älskade kvinnorna Valentino?" *Filmjournalen* 1 (1927).

186. [Unsigned], "Argentinaren Enrique Rivero—den nya älskaren i svensk film," *Filmnyheter* 8 (1927).

187. Dyer, *Stars*, 12–13.

188. Nikolas Glover and Carl Marklund, "Arabian Nights in the Midnight Sun? Exploring the Temporal Structure of Sexual Geographies," *Historisk tidskrift* 3 (2009), 487–509.

189. Serge [Sven Stolpe], "De svenska kvinnorna ha funnit nåd inför Enrique Rivero," *Filmnyheter* 21 (1927).

190. [Unsigned], "Sydamerikansk herre i svensk stad," *Våra nöjen* 24–25 (1927).

191. [Unsigned], "Enrique Rivero blir förföljd på Stockholms gator," *Filmnyheter* 39 (1927).

192. Ibid.

193. Kå, *Folkets Dagblad Politiken*, 6 September 1927.

194. Allan [Allan Beer], *Aftonbladet*, 18 October 1927

195. Søland, *Becoming Modern*, 33. See also, "Shingling och undulering utföres av förstklassig, manlig expert," Advertisement, *Våra nöjen* 12 (1926).

196. M-t F, *Nya Dagligt Allehanda*, 18 February 1928.

197. Hake [Harald Hansen], *Svenska Dagbladet*, 14 February 1928.

198. e.g. Jerome [Göran Traung], *Dagens Nyheter*, 14 February 1928.

199. A N, *Stockholms-Tidningen*, 14 February 1928.

Conclusions

1. Mosse, *The Image of Man*, 17–24.

2. There are also examples of the explicit presence of Swedish men incarnating modern ideal masculinity, e.g., Sven Hedin in *Med Sven Hedin i österled* (*In the Orient with Sven Hedin*, 1928). Gustafsson, "I skarven mellan fakta och fiction," 103–120.

3. See, e.g., Trice and Holland, *Heroes, Antiheroes and Dolts*; Soila, *En kvinnas ansikte*; Andrew Spicer, *Typical Men: The Representation of Masculinity in Popular British Film* (London: I. B. Tauris, 2001).

4. Robinson, "'Emotional Constipation,'" 133–147.

5. John Beynon, *Masculinities and Culture* (Buckingham: Open University Press, 2002), 75–79, 95–96.

6. See, e.g., Tasker, *Spectacular Bodies*; Sonya O. Rose, "Temperate Heroes: Concepts of Masculinity in Second World War Britain," *Masculinities in Politics and War: Gendering Modern History*, Stefan Didink, Karen Hageman and John Tosh, eds. (Manchester and New York: Manchester University Press, 2004); Megan Abbott, *The Street Was Mine: White Masculinity and Urban Space in Hardboiled Fiction and Film Noir* (New York: Palgrave Macmillan, 2003); Mark Gallagher, *Action Figures: Men, Action Film, and Contemporary Adventure Narratives* (New York: Palgrave Macmillan, 2006); Soila, *Kvinnors ansikte*; Hansen, *Babel & Babylon*.

7. See, e.g., Kracauer, *From Caligari to Hitler*; Hansen, *Babel & Babylon* and Soila, *Kvinnors ansikte*.

8. See, e.g., Florin, *Den nationella stilen* and Dahlqvist, "Snow-White."

9. See, e.g., Furhammar, *Filmen i Sverige*.

10. Summary according to *Svensk filmografi 1 1897–1919* (Stockholm: Svenska filminstitutet, 1986) and *Svensk filmografi 2*.

11. See, e.g., Hansen, *Babel & Babylon*; Soila, *Kvinnors ansikte*; Mulvey, "Spelfilmen och lusten att se."

12. Studlar, *This Mad Masquerade: Singer, Melodrama and Modernity*. See also, Søland, *Becoming Modern*; Mick LaSalle, *Complicated Women. Sex and Power in Pre-Code Hollywood* (New York: Thomas Dunne Books, 2000); Trice and Holland, Heroes, Antoheroes and Dolts.

13. LaSalle, *Complicated Women*, 189–213.

14. McLaughlin and Parry, *We'll Always Have the Movies*, 247–248.

Bibliography

Abbott, Megan. *The Street Was Mine: White Masculinity and Urban Space in Hardboiled Fiction and Film Noir*. New York: Palgrave Macmillan, 2003.

Abrams, Mark. *The Teenage Consumer*. London: London Press Exchange, 1959.

Addison, Heather. "'Must the Players Keep Young?': Early Hollywood's Cult of Youth." *Cinema Journal* 4 (2006).

Alm, Martin. *Americanitis: Amerika som sjukdom och läkemedel: Svenska berättelser om USA åren 1900–1939*. Lund: Studia Historica Lundensia, 2002.

Althusser, Louis. *Essays on Ideology*. London: Verso, 1984.

Altman, Rick. *Film/Genre*. London: BFI, 2004.

Ambjörnsson, Ronny. *Den skötsamme arbetaren: Idéer och ideal i ett norrländskt sågverkssamhälle 1880–1930*. Stockholm: Carlssons, 1998.

_____. *Mansmyter: en liten guide till manlighetens paradoxer*. Stockholm: Ordfront, 1999.

Amft, Andrea. "Att skapa en 'autentisk' minoritet: om maktrelationen mellan svenskar och samer från slutet av 1800-talet fram till 1970-talet." *Historisk tidskrift* 4 (1998).

Andersson, Lars M. *En jude är en jude är en jude ... Representationer av "juden" i svensk skämtpress omkring 1900–1930*. Lund: Nordic Academic Press, 2000.

Andersson, Therése. *Beauty Box: Filmstjärnor och skönhetskultur i det tidiga 1900-talets Sverige*. Stockholm: Acta Universitatus Stockholmiensis, 2006.

Andræ, Carl Göran. *Revolt eller reform: Sverige inför revolutionerna i Europa 1917–1918*. Stockholm: Carlssons, 1998.

Ang, Ien. *Watching Dallas: Soap Opera and the Melodramatic Imagination*. London: Methuen, 1985.

Bauman, Zygmunt. *Life in Fragments: Essays in Postmodern Morality*. Cambridge: Blackwell, 1995.

Bentzel, Ragnar. *Det privata konsumtionen i Sverige 1931–65*. Stockholm: Almqvist & Wiksell, 1957.

Berggren, Henrik. *Seklets ungdom: Retorik, politik och modernitet 1900–1939*. Stockholm: Tidens förlag, 1995.

Berglund, Tomas. *Det goda faderskapet i svenskt 1800-tal*. Stockholm: Carlssons, 2007.

Besserman, Anna. "Den lågkyrkliga väckelsens syn på judar och judendom." *Judarna i det svenska samhället: Identitet, integration, etniska relationer*. Kerstin Nyström, ed. Lund: Lund University Press, 1991.

Beynon, John. *Masculinities and Culture*. Buckingham: Open University Press, 2002.

Björkin, Mats. *Amerikanism, bolsjevism och korta kjolar: Filmen och dess publik i Sverige under 1920-talet*. Stockholm: Aura, 1997.

Blomberg, Eva. *Vill ni se en stjärna? Kön, kropp och kläder i* Filmjournalen *1919–1953*. Lund: Nordic Academic Press, 2006.

Bly, Robert. *Iron John: A Book About Men*. London: Ebury Press, 2001.
Boëthius, Ulf. "Högt och lågt inom kulturen. Moderniseringsprocessen och de kulturella hierarkierna." *Ungdom och kulturell modernisering*. Johan Fornäs and Ulf Boëthius, eds. Stockholm: Symposion, 1994.
_____. *När Nick Carter drevs på flykten: Kampen mot "smutslitteraturen" i Sverige*. Södertälje: Gidlunds, 1989.
Bolin, Göran. *Filmbytare: videovåld, kulturell produktion & unga män*. Stockholm: Borea, 1998.
Bordwell, David, and Kristin Thompson. *Film Art: An Introduction*. New York: McGraw-Hill, 1997.
_____, and _____. *Film History: An Introduction*. New York. McGraw Hill, 1994.
Brewster, Ben, and Lea Jacobs. *Theatre to Cinema: Stage Pictorialism and the Early Feature Film*. New York: Oxford University Press, 1997.
Broberg, Gunnar. *Statlig rasforskning: En historik över rasbiologiska institutet*. Lund: Ugglan, 1995.
Bruzzi, Stella. *Bringing Up Daddy: Fatherhood and Masculinity in Post-War Hollywood*. London: BFI, 2005.
Burgman, Torsten. *Rysslandsbilden i Sverige: Från Ivan den förskräcklige till Vladimir Putin*. Lund: Historiska media, 2001.
Butler, Judith, *Gender Trouble: Feminism and the Subversions of Identity*. New York: Routledge, 1990.
Butters, Gerald R., Jr. *Black Manhood on the Silent Screen*. Lawrence: University Press of Kansas, 2002.
Chalfork, Fredrik. "När 'svartrockar' blev 'vitrockar': Om Ivar Bromans bidrag i den rasbiologiska och rashygieniska debatten under åren 1920–1940." *Scandia* 1 (2006).
Chanan, Michael. "Economic Conditions of Early Cinema." *Early Cinema: Space, Frame, Narrative*. Thomas Elsasesser, ed. London: BFI, 1997.
Chris, Cynthia. *Watching Wildlife*. Minneapolis and London: University of Minnesota Press, 2006.
Cohen, Stanley. *Folk Devils and Moral Panics: The Creation of Mods and Rockers*. London: Routledge, 2002.
Connell, R. W. *Masculinities*. Cambridge: Polity Press, 1999.
Dahlqvist, Marina. "Snow-White: The Aesthetic and Narrative Use of Snow in Swedish Silent Film." *Nordic Explorations: Film Before 1930*. John Fullerton and Jan Olsson, eds. Sydney: John Libbey, 1999.
Doane, Mary Ann. *Desire to Desire: The Women's Film of the 1940s*. Bloomington: Indiana University Press, 1987.
Dofs Sundin, Monica. *Rödluvan i filmens tidsålder: Sagospår och filmversioner 1901–2001*. Uppsala: Filmförlaget, 2003.
Dudnik, Stefan, Karen Hagemann, and John Tosh, eds. *Masculinities in Politics and War: Gendering Modern History*. Manchester and New York: Manchester University Press, 2004.
Dufwa, Sune G. *Kön, lön och karriär: Sjuksköterskeyrkets omvandling under 1900-talet*. Göteborg: Växjö University Press, 2004.
Dworkin, Andrea. *Intercourse*. London: Secker & Warburg, 1997.
Dyer, Richard. *Now You See It: Studies in Lesbian and Gay Film*. London and New York: Routledge, 2003.
_____. *Stars*. London: BFI, 2004.
_____. *White*. London and New York: Routledge, 2002.
Edenheim, Sara. *Begärets lagar: Moderna statliga utredningar och heteronormativitetens genealogi*. Stockholm: Symposion, 2005.
Eilberg-Schwartz, Howard. "God's Phallus and the Dilemmas of Masculinity." *Redeeming Men: Religion and Masculinities*. Stephen B. Boyd and Mark W. Muesse, eds. Louisville: Westminster John Knox Press, 1996.

Ekenstam, Claes. "En historia om manlig gråt." *Rädd att falla: Studier i manlighet*. Claes Ekenstam et al., eds. Södertälje: Gidlunds, 1998.

_____. "Män, manlighet och omanlighet i historien." *Män i Norden: Manlighet och modernitet 1840–1940*. Jørgen Lorentzen and Claes Ekenstam, eds. Stockholm: Gidlunds, 2006.

Ekman, Gösta. *Den tänkande August*. Stockholm: Albert Bonniers, 1928.

Ekman, Greger. "Homosexuella i kulturdebatten." *Sympatiens hemlighetsfulla makt: Stockholms homosexuella 1860–1960*. Göran Söderström, ed. Stockholm: Stockholmia, 1999.

_____. "1907: Det homosexuella genombrottet." *Sympatiens hemlighetsfulla makt: Stockholms homosexuella 1860–1960*. Göran Söderström, ed. Stockholm: Stockholmia, 1999.

Ekman, Hasse. *Gösta Ekman*. Stockholm: Albert Bonniers, 1938.

Englund, Thomas. "Skolans samhällsbild—elevernas medborgarfostran via folkundervisningens samhällsorientering." *Från folkskola till grundskola: Tio forskare vid Pedagogiska institutionen, Uppsala universitet belyser utvecklingen under 150 år i anslutning till folkskolejubiléet*. Erik Wallin, ed. Uppsala: Uppsala universitet, 1998.

Faludi, Susan. *Ställd: Förräderiet mot mannen*. Stockholm: Ordfront, 2001.

Fiske, John. *Television Culture*. London: Methuen, 1986.

Florin, Bo. *Den nationella stilen: Studier i den svenska filmens guldålder*. Stockholm: Aura, 1997.

Fornäs, Johan. *Moderna människor: Folkhemmet och jazzen*. Stockholm: Norstedts, 2004.

_____. "Senmoderna dimensioner." *Ungdom och kulturell modernisering*. Johan Fornäs and Ulf Boëthius, eds. Stockholm: Symposion, 1994.

Forslund, Bengt. *Från Gösta Ekman till Gösta Ekman: En bok om Hasse, far och son*. Borås: Askild & Kärnekull, 1983.

Foucault, Michel. *The History of Sexuality: Volume 1: An Introduction*. New York: Vintage Books, 1990.

Fowler, David. *The First Teenagers: The Lifestyle of Young Wage-Earners in Interwar Britain*. London: Woburn Press, 1995.

Furhammar, Leif. *Filmen i Sverige: En historia i tio kapitel och en fortsättning*. Stockholm: Dialogos, 2003.

Gagner, Marie Louise. *Barn och biografföreställningar: Ett föredrag av, jämte ett uttalande i samma ämne av professor B. E. Gadelius*. Stockholm: Lars Hökerberg förlag, 1908.

Gallagher, Mark. *Action Figures: Men, Action Film and Contemporary Adventure Narratives*. New York: Palgrave Macmillan, 2006.

Gens, Ingemar. *Från vagga till identitet: Hur flickor blir kvinnor och pojkar blir män: Teorin bakom pedagogiken på förskolorna Björntomten och Tittmyran*. Jönköping: Seminarium, 2003.

Gerhard, Karl. "Den siste historionen." *Gösta Ekman: Människan: Konstnären*. Gösta Tranströmer, ed. Stockholm: Åhlén & Åkerlund, 1938.

Glover, Nikolas, and Carl Marklund. "Arabian Nights in the Midnight Sun? Exploring the Temporal Structure of Sexual Geographies." *Historisk tidskrift* 3 (2009).

Gunning, Tom. "The Cinema of Attractions: Early Film, Its Spectators and the Avant-Garde." *Early Cinema: Space, Frame, Narrative*. Thomas Elsasesser, ed. London: BFI, 1997.

_____. *D. W. Griffith and the Origin of American Narrative Film: The Early Years at Biograph*. Urbana and Chicago: University of Illinois Press, 1994.

Gustafsson, Tommy. "Ett steg på vägen mot en ny jämlikhet? Könsrelationer och stereotyper i ung svensk ungdomsfilm på 2000-talet." *Solskenslandet: Svensk film på 2000-talet*. Erik Hedling and Ann-Kristin Wallengren, eds. Stockholm: Atlantis, 2006.

_____. "Filmen som historisk källa. Historiografi, pluralism och representativitet." *Historisk tidskrift* 3 (2006).

_____. "I skarven mellan fakta och fiktion: Konstruktionen av manlighet och etnicitet i svensk filmkultur under 1920-talet." *Historieforskning på nya vägar*. Klas-Göran Karlsson, Eva Helen Ulvros and Ulf Zander, eds. Lund: Nordic Academic Press, 2006.

_____. "Nationell ära och manlighet i *Karl XII* (1925)—en historisk filmanalys." *Scandia* 1 (2005).

_____. "Travelers as Threat in Swedish Film in the 1920s," *Swedish Film: An Introduction and Reader*. Mariah Larsson and Anders Marklund, eds. Lund: Nordic Academic Press, 2010.

_____, and Mariah Larsson. "Porren inför lagen: Två fallstudier angående den officiella attityden till offentligt visad pornografisk film 1921 och 1971." *Historisk tidskrift* 3 (2009).

Hall, Donald E. *Queer Theories*. New York: Palgrave MacMillan, 2003.

Halvarsson, Bo. "Anteckningar kring det filmiska stjärnsystemets uppkomst." *I offentlighetens ljus: Stumfilmens affischer, kritiker, stjärnor och musik*. Jan Olsson, ed. Stockholm: Symposion, 1990.

Hansen, Miriam. *Babel & Babylon: Spectatorship in the American Silent Film*. Cambridge and London: Harvard University Press, 1991.

_____. "Early Cinema—Whose Public Sphere?" *Early Cinema: Space, Frame, Narrative*. Thomas Elsaesser, ed. London: BFI, 1997.

Harris, Warren G. *Clark Gable: A Biography*. New York: Three Rivers Press, 2002.

Hedling, Erik. "Filmen som historiegraf eller som historisk källa?" *Historisk tidskrift* 1 (2002).

_____. "Kjell Sundvalls *Jägarna*: svensk 'High Concept,'" *Blågult flimmer: Svenska filmanalyser*. Erik Hedling, ed. Lund: Studentlitteratur, 1998.

Hermele, Vanja. ed. *Män, män, män och en och annan kvinna*. Stockholm: Svenska Filminstitutet/Arena, 2002.

Higson, Andrew. "The Concept of National Cinema." *Film and Nationalism*. Alan Williams, ed. New Jersey and London: Rutgers University Press, 2002.

Hilton, Matthew. *Consumerism in 20th-Century Britain: The Search for a Political Movement*. Cambridge: Cambridge University Press, 2003.

Hirdman, Yvonne. "Konstruktion och förändring—genus och vetenskap." *Kvinnovetenskaplig tidskrift* 3–4 (1998).

Historisk statistik för Sveriges befolkning: Historical Statistics of Sweden: 1: Befolkning: Population 1720–1950. Stockholm: Statistiska centralbyrån, 1955.

Hobson, Barbra, and David Morgan. "Introduction." *Making Men into Fathers: Masculinity and the Social Politics of Fatherhood*. Barbra Hobson, ed. Cambridge: Cambridge University Press, 2002.

Holgersson, Ulrika. *Populärkulturen och samhället: Arbete, klass och genus i svensk dampress i början av 1900-talet*. Stockholm: Carlssons, 2005.

Holloway, Gerry. "Writing Women: The Development of Feminist Approaches to Women's History. *Historical Controversies and Historians*. William Lamont, ed. London: UCL Press, 1998.

hooks, bell. *The Will to Change: Men, Masculinity, and Love*. New York: Washington Square Press, 2004.

Horgby, Björn. *Egensinne och skötsamhet: arbetarkulturen i Norrköping 1850–1940*. Stockholm: Carlssons, 1993.

Horne, John. "Masculinities in Politics and War in the Age of Nation-States and World Wars." *Masculinities in Politics and War: Gendering Modern History*. Stefan Dudnik, Karen Hagemann and John Tosh, eds. Manchester and New York: Manchester University Press, 2004.

Hughes, William. "The Evaluation of Film as Evidence." *The Historian and Film*. Paul Smith, ed. Cambridge and New York: Cambridge University Press, 1976.

Husz, Orsi. *Drömmars värde: Varuhus och lotteri i svensk konsumtionskultur 1897–1939*. Stockholm: Gidlunds, 2004.

_____, and Amanda Lagerqvist. "Konsumtionens motsägelser: En inledning." *Förbjudna njutningar—spår från konsumtionskulturens historia i Sverige*. Peder Aléx and Johan Söderberg, eds. Stockholm: Podium, 2001.

Hyltén-Cavallius, Ragnar. *Följa sitt genius*. Stockholm: Hökerbergs, 1960.

Jancovich, Mark, Lucy Faire, and Sarah Stubbings. *The Place of the Audience: Cultural Geographies of Film Consumption*. London: BFI, 2003.

Jernudd, Åsa. "Educational Cinema and Censorship in Sweden 1911–1921." *Nordic Explorations: Film Before 1930*. John Fullerton and Jan Olsson, eds. Sydney: John Libbey, 1999.

_____. *Oscar Olsson's African Films: Examples of Touristic Edutainment*. Örebro: Örebro University, 1999.

Johansson, Rune. "Samlande, lättförståeligt och eggande? Kosacker, kultur och kvinnor i valaffischer från 1928." *Mer än tusen ord: Bilden och de historiska vetenskaperna*. Lars M. Andersson, Lars Berggren and Ulf Zander, eds. Lund: Nordic Academic Press, 2001.

Johansson, Thomas. *Det första könet? Mansforskning som reflexivt projekt*. Lund: Studentlitteratur, 2000.

Johnston, Clarie. "Women's Cinema as Counter-Cinema." *Movies and Methods: An Anthology*. Bill Nichols, ed. Berkeley and London: University of California Press, 1976.

Jònasdóttir, Anna G. *Kärlekskraft, makt och politiska intressen: En teori om patriarkatet i nutida västerländska samhällen*. Göteborg: Diadalos, 2003.

Jönsson, Mats. *Film och historia: Historisk hollywoodfilm 1960–2000*. Lund: Lund University, 2004.

Kellner, Douglas. *Media Culture: Cultural Studies, Identity and Politics Between the Modern och the Postmodern*. London: Routledge, 1995.

Kimmel, Michael. *Manhood in America: A Cultural History*. New York: Free Press, 1996.

Kosofsky Sedgwick, Eve. *Epistemology of the Closet*. New York: Harvester Weathleaf, 1991.

Kracauer, Siegfried. *From Caligari to Hitler: A Psychological History of the German Film*. Princeton and Oxford: Princeton University Press, 2004.

Krogh, Thomas, *Frankfurtskolan: En introduktion*. Göteborg: Daidalos, 1993.

Kulick, Don, "Är måsar lesbiska? Om biologins relevans för mänskligt beteende." *Res Publica* 1–2 (1997).

Lagerwall, Sture. "Hans vänskap svek aldrig." *Gösta Ekman: Människan: Konstnären*. Gösta Tranströmer, ed. Stockholm: Åhlén & Åkerlund, 1938.

Lane, Linda. *Trying to Make a Living: Studies in the Economic Life of Women in Interwar Sweden*. Kungälv: Göteborgs universitet, 2004.

Langman, Larry. *Destination Hollywood: The Influence of Europeans on American Filmmaking*. Jefferson, NC: McFarland, 1999.

LaSalle, Mick. *Complicated Women: Sex and Power in Pre-Code Hollywood*. New York: Thomas Dunne Books, 2000.

Liander, Halfdan G. *Biografen: Ett ord till fackets män samt till föräldrar och lärare*. Lund: Pedagogiska skrifter utgivna av Sveriges allmänna folkskolelärareförenings litteratursällskap, 1922.

Liliequist, Jonas. "Från niding till sprätt: En studie i det svenska omanlighetsbegreppets historia från vikingatid till sent 1700-tal." *Manligt och omanligt i ett historiskt perspektiv*. Anne Marie Berggren, ed. Stockholm: Forskningsrådsnämnden, 1999.

_____. "Sexualiteten." *Män i Norden: Manlighet och modernitet 1840–1940*. Jørgen Lorentzen and Claes Ekenstam, eds. Stockholm: Gidlunds, 2006.

Liljedahl, Elisabeth. *Stumfilmen i Sverige—Kritik och debatt: Hur samtiden värderade den nya konstarten*. Stockholm: Proprius, 1975.

Lindberg, Per. *Gösta Ekman: Skådespelaren och människan*. Stockholm: Natur och Kultur, 1942.

_____. "Samarbete med Gösta." *Gösta Ekman: Människan: Konstnären*. Gösta Tranströmer, ed. Stockholm: Åhlén & Åkerlund, 1938.

Lindell, Ingrid. *Att se och synas: Filmutbud, kön och modernitet*. Göteborg: Makadam, 2004.

Ljunggren, Jens. *Känslornas krig: Det första världskriget och den tyska bildningselitens androgyna manlighet*. Stockholm: Symposion, 2004.

Lodziak, Conrad. *The Myth of Consumerism*. London: Pluto Press, 2002.

Longwood, Merle W. "Changing Views of Fathering and Fatherhood: A Christian Ethical Perspective." *Redeeming Men: Religion and Masculinities*. Stephen B. Boyd and Mark W. Muesse, eds. Louisville: Westminster John Knox Press, 1996.

Lorentzen, Jørgen, ed. *Blikk på mannen gjenom litteratur og film*. Oslo: Spartacus, 2004.

_____, and Claes Ekenstam, eds. "Federne." *Män i Norden: Manlighet och modernitet 1840–1940*. Stockholm: Gidlunds, 2006.

_____, and _____, eds. "Inledning." *Män i Norden: Manlighet och modernitet 1840–1940*. Stockholm: Gidlunds, 2006.

Lundborg, Herman. *Rasfrågor i Modern belysning*. Stockholm: P A Norstedt & Söner, 1919.

_____. *Svensk raskunskap: Folkupplaga med text, kartor, diagram och planscher*. Uppsala: Almqvist & Wiksell, 1927.

Lundmark, Lennart. "Vetenskap i rasismens tjänst: Så fick skallmätningen av samer vetenskaplig legitimitet." *Tvärsnitt* 2 (2002).

Lutz, Tom. "Men's Tears and the Roles of Melodrama." *Boy's Don't Cry? Rethinking Narratives of Masculinity and Emotion in the U.S.* Milette Shamir and Jennifer Travis, eds. New York: Columbia University Press, 2002.

McCrisken, Trevor, and Andrew Pepper. *American History and Contemporary Hollywood Film*. New Brunswick, NJ: Rutgers University Press, 2005.

McLaughlin, Robert L., and Sally E. Perry. *We'll Always Have the Movies: American Film During World War II*. Lexington: University of Kentucky Press, 2006.

Mendel-Enk, Stephan. *Med uppenbar känsla för stil—ett reportage om manlighet*. Stockholm: Atlas, 2004.

Moland, Tallak. "Konstruksjon av mandighet i det nordlige landskapet: Om Fridtjof Nansens polferder ved århundresskiftet." *Manligt och omanligt i ett historiskt perspektiv*. Anne Marie Berggren, ed. Stockholm: Forskningsrådsnämnden, 1999.

Mosse, George L. *The Image of Man: The Creation of Modern Masculinity*. New York: Oxford University Press, 1998.

Mulvey, Laura. "Spelfilmen och lusten att se." *Modern filmteori 2*. Lars Gustaf Andersson and Erik Hedling, eds. Lund: Studentlitteratur, 1995.

Münsterberg, Hugo. *The Film: A Psychological Study*. New York: Dover Publications, 1970.

Nilsson, Arne. *Såna & riktiga karlar: Om manligt homosexualitet i Göteborg decennierna kring andra Världskriget*. Göteborg: Anamma, 1998.

Nilsson, Bo. *Maskulinitet: Representation, ideologi och retorik*. Umeå: Boréa, 1999.

Nodelman, Perry. "Making Boys Appear: The Masculinity of Children's Fiction." *Ways of Being Male: Representing Masculinities in Children's Literature and Film*. John Stephans, ed. London and New York: Routledge, 2002.

Norlander, Emil. *Anderssonskans Kalle: Pojkstreck och kärringsskvaller*. Stockholm: Christofers bokförlag, [1901] 1960.

Ohlander, Ann-Sofie. "Ekonomisk makt och ekonomsikt ansvar—två skilda storheter." *Mot halva makten—elva essäer om kvinnors strategi och mäns motstånd*. Ingrid Hagman, ed. Stockholm: SOU, 1997.

Olsson, Jan, ed. "I offentlighetens ljus—några notiser om filmstoff i dagspressen." *I offentlighetens ljus: Stumfilmens affischer, kritiker, stjärnor och musik*. Stockholm: Symposion, 1990.

Ottosson, Anders. *Sjukgymnasten—var tog* han *vägen? En undersökning av sjukgymnastyrkets maskulinisering och avmaskulinisering 1813–1934*. Göteborg: Göteborgs universitet, 2005.

Penley, Constance, and Sharon Willis, eds. *Male Trouble*. Minneapolis: University of Minnesota Press, 1993.

Petterson, Birgit. "Journalistyrkets långsamma professionalisering." *Sylwan II: Tema: Presshistoria: Den svenska pressens historia*. Karl Erik Gustafsson and Per Rydén, eds. Göteborg: Göteborgs University, 2002.

Pettersson, Gunnar. *Mannen som kom tillbaka från de döda: En bok om skandalförfattaren Gustaf Ericsson*. Stockholm: Ordfront, 2000.

Pierce, David. "'Carl Laemmel's Outstanding Achivement': Harry Pollard and the Struggle to Film *Uncle Tom's Cabin*." *Film History* 4 (1998).

Qvist, Per Olov. *Folkhemmets bilder: Modernisering, motstånd och mentalitet i den svenska 1930-talsfilmen*. Lund: Arkiv, 1995.

Resic, Sanimir. *American Warriors in Vietnam: Warrior Values and the Myth of the War Experience During the Vietnam War 1965–73*. Malmö: Lund University, 1999.

Ring, R. L. *Kallprat om film*. Stockholm: A-B Tullbergs films förlag, 1928.

Robin Hood [Bengt Idestam-Almqvist]. *Den svenska filmens drama: Sjöström och Stiller*. Stockholm: Åhlen & söner, 1939.

Robinson, Sally. "'Emotional Constipation' and the Power of Damned Masculinity: *Deliverance* and the Paradoxes of Male Liberation." *Masculinity: Bodies, Movies, Culture*. Peter Lehman, ed. New York: Routledge, 2001.

_____. "Men's Liberation, Men's Wounds: Emotion, Sexuality and the Reconstruction of Masculinity in the 1970s." *Boy's Don't Cry? Rethinking Narratives of Masculinity and Emotion in the U.S.* Milette Shamir and Jennifer Travis eds. New York: Columbia University Press, 2002.

Rose, Sonya O. "Temperate Heroes: Concepts of Masculinity in Second World War Britain." *Masculinities in Politics and War: Gendering Modern History*. Stefan Dudnik, Karen Hagemann and John Tosh, eds. Manchester and New York: Manchester University Press, 2004.

Rosenberg, Tiina. *Byxbegär*. Göteborg: Anamma, 2000.

Rydström, Jens. "Polisen och de perversa. Klagomål och angivelser rörande homosexualitet 1925–1944," *Sympatiens hemlighetsfulla makt: Stockholms homosexuella 1860–1960*. ed. Göran Söderström, Stockholm: Stockholmia, 1999.

_____. *Sinners and Citizens: Bestiality and Homosexuality in Sweden 1880–1950*. Stockholm: Stockholm University, 2001.

Scott, Joan W. *Gender and the Politics of History*. New York: Columbia University Press, 1999.

Serra Cary, Diana. *Jackie Coogan, the World's Boy King: A Biography of Hollywood's Legendary Child Star*. Lanham and Oxford: Scarecrow Press, 2003.

Shamir, Milette, and Jennifer Travis. "Introduction." *Boy's Don't Cry? Rethinking Narratives of Masculinity and Emotion in the U.S.* Milette Shamir and Jennifer Travis, eds. New York: Columbia University Press, 2002.

Silvén-Garnert, et al., eds. *Storstadsungdom i fyra generationer*. Stockholm: Tiden, Folksam and Stockholms stadsmuseum, 1991.

Silverstolpe, Fredrik. "Mauritz Stiller och den första homosexuella spelfilmen." *Sympatiens hemlighetsfulla makt: Stockholms homosexuella 1860–1960*. Göran Söderström, ed. Stockholm: Stockholmia, 1999.

Singer, Ben. *Melodrama and Modernity: Early Sensational Cinema and Its Contexts*. New York: Columbia University Press, 2001.

Siwertz, Margit. *Lars Hanson*. Stockholm: Norstedts, 1947.

Siwertz, Sigfrid. *Lata latituder*. Stockholm: Albert Bonniers, 1924.

_____. *Mälarpirater*. Stockholm: Lind, [1911] 2002.

Skoglund, Erik. *Filmcensuren*. Stockholm: Pan/Norstedts, 1971.

Smith, Murry. *Engaging Characters: Fiction, Emotion, and the Cinema*. Oxford: Oxford University Press, 1995.

Snickars, Pelle. "'Bildrutor i minnets film'—om mediaprins Wilhelm och film som käll- och åskådningsmaterial." *Det förflutna som film och vice versa: Om mediterade historiebruk*. Pelle Snickars and Cecilia Trenter, eds. Lund: Studentlitteratur, 2004.

_____. *Svensk film och visuell masskultur 1900*. Stockholm: Aura, 2001.

Söderström, Göran. "Ögonvittnen," *Sympatiens henlighetsfulla makt: Stockholms homosexuella 1860–1960*. ed. Göran Söderström. Stockholm: Stockholmia, 1999.

_____. "Privatpersonen Stiller och hans krets," *Sympatiens hemlighetsfulla makt: Stockholms homosexuella 1860–1960*. ed. Göran Söderström. Stockholm: Stockholmia, 1999.
Soila, Tytti. *Kvinnors ansikte: Stereotyper och kvinnlig identitet i trettiotalets svenska filmmelodram*. Stockholm: Stockholm University, 1991.
Søland, Birgitte, *Becoming Modern: Young Women and the Reconstruction of Womenhood in the 20s*. Princeton, NJ: Princeton University Press, 2000.
Solia, Tytti. "Sweden." *National Nordic Cinemas*. Tytti Solia, Astrid Söderbergh Widding and Gunnar Iversen, eds. London and New York, Routledge, 1998.
Sörensen, Thomas. *Det blänkande eländet: En bok om kronprinsens husarer i sekelskiftets Malmo*. Malmö: Lunds University, 1997.
Spicer, Andrew. *Typical Men: The Representation of Masculinity in Popular British Film*. London: I. B. Tauris, 2001.
Staiger, Janet. "Combination and Litigation Structures of U.S. Film Distribution 1896–1917." *Early Film: Space, Frame, Narrative*. Thomas Elsaesser, ed. London: BFI, 1997.
_____. *Interpreting Films: Studies in the Historical Reception of American Cinema*. Princeton, NJ: Princeton University Press, 1992.
Steorn, Patrik. *Nakna män: Maskulinitet och kreativitet i svensk bildkultur 1900–1915*. Stockholm: Norstedts Akademiska, 2006.
Sterns, Peter N. "Stages of Consumerism: Recent Work on the Issues of Periodization." *The Journal of Modern History* 69:1 (1997).
Studlar, Gaylyn. *This Mad Masquerade: Stardom and Masculinity in the Jazz Age*. New York: Columbia University Press, 1996.
Sullivan, Nikki. *A Critical Introduction to Queer Theory*. New York: New York University Press, 2003.
Svensk filmografi 1 1897–1919. Stockholm: Svenska filminstitutet, 1986.
Svensk filmografi 2 1920–1929. Stockholm: Svenska filminstitutet, 1982.
Tannahill, Reay. *Flesh & Blood—A History of the Cannibal Complex*. London: Abacus, 1996.
Tasker, Yvonne. *Spectacular Bodies: Gender, Genre and the Action Cinema*. London and New York: Routledge, 1993.
Tjeder, David. "Borgerlighetens sköra manlighet." *Män i Norden: Manlighet och modernitet 1840–1940*. Jørgen Lorentzen and Claes Ekenstam, eds. Stockholm: Gidlunds, 2006.
_____. "Konsten att blifva herre öfver hvarje lidelse: Den ständigt hotade manligheten." *Manligt och omanligt i ett historiskt perspektiv*. Anne Marie Berggren, ed. Stockholm: Forskningsrådsnämnden, 1999.
_____. "Maskulinum som problem: Genusforskning om män," *Historisk tidskrift* 3 (2002).
_____. *The Power of Character: Middle-Class Masculinities, 1800–1900*. Stockholm: Stockholm University, 2003.
Tosh, John. "Hegemonic Masculinity and the History of Gender," *Masculinities in Politics and War: Gendering Modern History*. Stefan Dudnik, Karin Hagemann and John Tosh, eds. Manchester and New York: Manchester University Press, 2004.
_____. *A Man's Place: Masculinity and the Middle-Class Home in Victorian England*. New Haven: Yale University Press, 2007.
Tranströmer, Gösta, ed. *Gösta Ekman: Människan: Konstnären*. Stockholm: Åhlén & Åkerlund, 1938.
Trice, Ashton D., and Samuel A. Holland. *Heroes, Antiheroes and Dolts: Portrayals of Masculinity in American Popular Films 1921–1999*. Jefferson, NC: McFarland, 2001.
Tsivian, Yuri. *Early Cinema in Russia and Its Cultural Reception*. Chicago and London: University of Chicago Press, 1998.
Ulvros, Eva Helen. *Fruar och mamseller: Kvinnor inom sydsvensk borgerlighet 1790–1870*. Lund: Historiska media, 1996.
Walby, Sylvia. *Theorizing Patriarchy*. Oxford: Blackwell, 1990.
Wallén, Sigurd, *Revydags: Tystnad—tagning—kamera går*. Stockholm: Medéns, 1944.

Wallenberg, Louise. *Upsetting the Male: Feminist Interventions in the New Queer Wave*. Stockholm: Edith Norstedt, 2002.

Wallengren, Ann-Kristin. *En afton på Röda Kvarn: Svensk stumfilm som musikdrama*. Lund: Lund University Press, 1998.

_____. "Kultur och okultur—bilden av landsbygdens folk." *Solskenslandet: svensk film på 000-talet*. Erik Hedling and Ann-Kristin Wallengren, eds. Stockholm: Atlantis, 2006.

Werner, Gösta. *Den svenska filmens historia: En översikt av*. Stockholm: P. A. Norstedt & Söner, 1978.

Wilhelm [Prince]. *Bland dvärgar och gorillor: Med svenska zoologiska expeditionen till Centralafrika*. Stockholm: P. A. Norstedt & Söner, 1922.

Wredlund, Bertil, and Rolf Lindfors. *Långfilm i Sverige 1910–1919*. Stockholm: Proprius, 1991.

_____, and _____. *Långfilm i Sverige 1920–1929*. Stockholm: Proprius, 1987.

Wright, Rochelle. *The Visible Wall: Jews and Other Ethnic Outsiders in Swedish Film*. Carbondale: Southern Illionis University Press, 1998.

Zelizer, Viviana A. *Pricing the Priceless Child: The Changing Social Value of Children*. New York: Basic Books, 1985.

Zitomersky, Joseph. "Ambiguous Integration: The Historical Position of Jews in Swedish Society, 1780s-1980s." *Judarna i det svenska samhället: Identitet, integration, etniska relationer*. Kerstin Nyström, ed. Lund: Lund University Press, 1991.

Index

Numbers in ***bold italics*** indicate pages with photographs.